Interwar Unemployment
in International Perspective

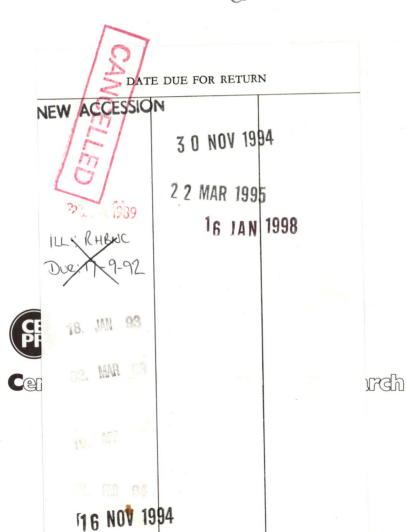

Interwar Unemployment
in International Perspective

edited by

Barry Eichengreen

and

T. J. Hatton

Kluwer Academic Publishers

Dordrecht / Boston / London

Published in cooperation with NATO Scientific Affairs Division and
the Centre for Economic Policy Research

Library of Congress Cataloging in Publication Data

Interwar unemployment in international perspective / edited by Barry
  Eichengreen and T.J. Hatton.
       p.   cm. -- (NATO ASI series. Series D, Behavioural and social
  sciences ; no. 43)
     "Published in cooperation with NATO Scientific Affairs Division
  and the Centre for Economic Policy Research."
     Rev. papers originally presented at a conference held May 7-8,
  1987, at Harvard University.
     Includes index.
     ISBN 902473696X. ISBN 9024736978 (pbk.)
       1. Unemployment--History--20th century. 2. Depressions--1929.
  3. Economic history--1918-1945.   I. Eichengreen, Barry J.
  II. Hatton, T. J. III. North Atlantic Treaty Organization.
  Scientific Affairs Division.   IV. Centre for Economic Policy
  Research (Great Britain) V. Series.
  HD5707.5.I58 1988
  331.13'79'04--dc19   88-3795
                                                            CIP
ISBN 90-247-3696-X
ISBN 90-247-3697-8 (pbk.)

Published by Kluwer Academic Publishers,
P.O. Box 17, 3300 AA Dordrecht, Holland.

Kluwer Academic Publishers incorporates
the publishing programmes of
D. Reidel, Martinus Nijhoff, Dr W. Junk and MTP Press.

Sold and distributed in the U.S.A. and Canada
by Kluwer Academic Publishers,
101 Philip Drive, Norwell, MA 02061, U.S.A.

In all other countries, sold and distributed
by Kluwer Academic Publishers Group,
P.O. Box 322, 3300 AH Dordrecht, Holland.

TABLE OF CONTENTS

LIST OF TABLES

LIST OF FIGURES

Preface

High unemployment has been one of the most disturbing features of the economy of the 1980s. For a precedent, one must look to the interwar period and in particular to the Great Depression of the 1930s. It follows that recent years have been marked by a resurgence of interest amongst academics in interwar unemployment. The debate has been contentious. There is nothing like the analysis of a period which recorded rates of unemployment approaching 25 per cent to highlight the differences between competing schools of thought on the operation of labour markets. Along with historians, economists whose objective is to better understand the causes, character and consequences of contemporary unemployment and sociologists seeking to understand contemporary society's perceptions and responses to joblessness have devoted increasing attention to this historical episode.

Like many issues in economic history, this one can be approached in a variety of ways using different theoretical approaches, tools of analysis and levels of disaggregation. Much of the recent literature on the functioning of labour markets in the Depression has been macroeconomic in nature and has been limited to individual countries. Debates from the period itself have been revived and new questions stimulated by modern research have been opened. Many such studies have been narrowly focused and have failed to take into account the array of historical evidence collected and analysed by contemporaries or reconstructed and re- interpreted by historians. While aggregate data neatly summarise economic trends, there are many questions they cannot definitively resolve and many more which cannot be addressed at all. We believe it is important to study the labour market at both macro and micro levels. In addition there is much to be learned from international comparisons. In the 1930s, there are many common features but also important differences in labour market responses in different countries. The impact of different institutional, social, and economic structures can only be understood in a comparative context.

An ideal study of interwar unemployment would be at the same time international and interdisciplinary, at the same time macroeconomic and disaggregated. A study of this scope would quickly exhaust the resources of any single researcher, however. Hence our idea for a conference bringing together historians, economists and sociologists from a number of different countries. We charged James Symons, Andrew Newell and ourselves with explicitly comparative tasks, to provide internationally comparative overviews of interwar unemployment at the macroeconomic and disaggregated levels, respectively. We charged the other contributors with responsibility for country studies that would, ideally, address a common set of questions: Who was unemployed? How did the incidence of unemployment vary across economic and demographic groups? What can be said about the causes of unemployment when one approaches the question at a disaggregated level? What were the consequences of unemployment for labour force participation, poverty, health and other personal and family circumstances?

One of the first things one discovers upon turning to these questions is how little can be learned from readily available statistics, frequently of poor quality, on unemployment between the wars. Yet the researcher who persists is frequently rewarded with all manner of obscure or neglected data from which a fuller picture of the unemployment experience can be assembled.

A contribution of the articles collected here is their critical scrutiny of standard time-series statistics on interwar unemployment and their attempt to marshall new and heretofore unutilised sources of information. Differences in data influenced the kinds of questions that the authors of the country studies might ask. Hence we have not insisted that the authors of every country study stick rigidly to the same set of questions. Nor have we urged the authors of country studies to engage in explicit international comparisons. The task of synthesis is best left to another conference, now that the groundwork has been laid. Nonetheless, what has emerged is a coherent set of country studies from which the reader can draw a wide range of comparative inferences.

This editorial collaboration between an English and an American economic historian was many years in the making. Our earliest debt is to Nick Crafts, who did much to stimulate the interest of both of us in interwar unemployment, while Tim Hatton was a doctoral candidate at the University of Warwick and Barry Eichengreen was a Fulbright Scholar at Oxford. Our debt to other economists and historians who have worked on interwar unemployment will be clear, whether we agree with them or not! The idea for a conference which moved beyond macroeconomic aspects of interwar unemployment and beyond British and American shores grew out of our independent research projects, each motivated by the quest for new and richer sources of historical data and the desire to analyse the causes and consequences of unemployment at the household and individual levels where its impact was truly felt. Our early researches along these lines were presented to a workshop organised by Tim Hatton under the auspices of the Centre for Economic Policy Research in London in the spring of 1985. Over the course of previous years, the Centre had generously provided office space, computing facilities and other forms of support for Barry Eichengreen's collection of microeconomic data on interwar unemployment from archives in London. The idea of jointly organising a conference was formed while we were visiting the Research School for Social Sciences of the Australian National University in the (Northern Hemispheric) summer of 1985, Barry Eichengreen enjoying the hospitality of N. G. Butlin and the Department of Economic History, Tim Hatton that of Fred Gruen and Robert Gregory of the Department of Economics. ANU generously provided Tim Hatton with a research fellowship for the year in which final preparations for the conference were made.

Running a conference and publishing a volume of proceedings is always a collaborative enterprise, but in this instance even more than most. It would not have been possible without the generous and continual support of the Centre for Economic Policy Research, with which both editors and several of the contributors are associated as Research Fellows. Richard Portes, Director of the Centre, provided encouragement at every stage. Wendy Thompson coordinated our fund-raising efforts. Stephen Yeo provided all manner of logistical support, most importantly as liaison with the publisher and by making arrangements to produce the final volume to high standards. One of the distinguishing features of the Centre as a research institute has been its encouragement of historical analyses of issues of current policy relevance. We hope that this volume can be seen as one small indication that this strategy is a fruitful one.

The conference was hosted by the Center for International Affairs at Harvard University. Samuel Huntington, Director of the Center, provided timely encouragement for the undertaking. Chester Haskell made it possible. Lucinda Merriam oversaw local arrangements and was responsible for the fact that the proceedings themselves went off without a hitch. A NATO grant for scientific collaboration was the principal source of financial support for the conference. The Harvard Center for International

Affairs and Harvard Mellon Center for the Study of Economic History provided supplementary funds. We are grateful to David Landes and Jeffrey Williamson for their generous support through this last channel.

In undertaking revisions of their papers, the editors and contributors benefited greatly from the interchange among conference participants. We are particularly indebted to formal discussants and session chairs. Panels were chaired by Ben Bernanke, Alexander Keyssar, William McNeil, Peter Temin, David Weir and Jeffrey Williamson. Discussants were Martin Baily, N. F. R. Crafts, Charles Feinstein, Stefano Fenoaltea, Robert Gordon, Harold James, Bradford Lee, Charles Maier, Stephen Nickell and John Wallis. Charles Kindleberger regaled us with a stimulating after-dinner talk that we only wish we were able to include here.

We would like to express our appreciation to the Centre for Economic Policy Research which undertook the onerous task of producing the camera-ready copy for this volume. In particular we owe a special debt of gratitude to Paul Compton, who coordinated production of the volume and who with great skill and expertise transformed the original manuscripts into the final proofs. Without his efforts the efficient and speedy production of the volume would not have been possible. We would also like to thank Elizabeth Taylor for excellent copy-editing, Wayne Naughton for producing the graphs, and Geeta Chandra at CEPR for diligent typing.

Barry Eichengreen and Tim Hatton,
Berkeley and Essex, November 1987.

List of Conference Participants

Martin Baily	The Brookings Institution
Ben Bernanke	Princeton University
Michael Bernstein	Princeton University
David Corbett	Harvard University
N F R Crafts	University of Leeds and CEPR
Brad DeLong	Harvard University
Barry Eichengreen	University of California, Berkeley, and CEPR
Charles Feinstein	Nuffield College, Oxford
Stefano Fenoaltea	University of Venice and Swarthmore College
Martine Goossens	Université Catholique de Louvain
Robert Gordon	Northwestern University and CEPR
Alan Green	Queen's University, Ontario
Robert Gregory	Australian National University
Richard Grossman	Harvard University
Bernard Harris	University of Bristol
T J Hatton	University of Essex and CEPR
Harold James	Princeton University
Lars Jonung	University of Lund
Lawrence Katz	Harvard University
Alexander Keyssar	Duke University
Charles Kindleberger	MIT
Lewis Kochin	University of Washington
Bradford Lee	Harvard University
Peter Lindert	University of California, Davis
Mary MacKinnon	Australian National University

William McNeil	Columbia University
Charles Maier	Harvard University
Robert Margo	Colgate University
Andrew Newell	University of Sussex
Stephen Nickell	Institute of Economics and Statistics, Oxford, and CEPR
Stefaan Peeters	Université Catholique de Louvain
Robert Salais	Institut National de la Statistique et des Etudes Economiques, Paris
Stephen Schuker	Brandeis University
Dan Silverman*	Pennsylvania State University
J S V Symons	University College, London
Peter Temin	MIT
Mark Thomas	University of Virginia
Gianni Toniolo	University of Venice
John Wallis	University of Maryland
David Weir	Yale University
Jeffrey Williamson	Harvard University

* Professor Silverman was ill at the time of the Conference. His paper was presented by Professor McNeil.

This volume was produced in camera-ready form at the Centre for Economic Policy Research. The manuscripts which form the basis of the text and tables in this book were prepared by the authors using a variety of word processing systems and submitted to CEPR in electronic form. The pages were composed at CEPR using Xerox Ventura Publisher, version 1.1, running on an IBM AT. The master pages were printed on a Texas Instruments Omnilaser 2115 Postscript page printer. The figures were prepared using MacDraw at the Australian National University, and printed on an Apple Laser Writer.

Chapter 1

Interwar Unemployment in International Perspective: An Overview

Barry Eichengreen and T J Hatton

The outstanding internal economic problem of the interwar period in all countries studied was undoubtedly unemployment. Next to war, unemployment has been the most widespread, most insidious and most corroding malady of our generation, it is the specific disease of western countries in our time. It varied in intensity, and incidence, in the different countries but in nearly every industrial country it held the centre of the social and economic stage in the interwar years. It was a social evil more than an economic evil. Its effects in terms of personal insecurity, maldistribution of income, and the deterioration of health, technical skill and morale were probably graver than the waste of resources and potential wealth involved. At the same time the pressure of the problem on national governments was perhaps the most decisive disrupting factor in international economic relations. (Arndt, 1944, p.250)

1 Introduction

For two decades after the Second World War, many economists and politicians thought that the battle against large-scale unemployment had been won, but since 1970 the armies of full employment have suffered a series of reversals. The US unemployment rate doubled between the late 1960s and 1980 and has shown disturbingly little tendency to decline since. Unemployment in the Common Market countries of Europe also doubled over the decade up to 1980 and, more distressingly, doubled again over the first half of the current decade. For the OECD as a whole, the stand-

1

B. Eichengreen and T. J. Hatton (eds.), Interwar Unemployment in International Perspective, 1–59.
© *1988 by Kluwer Academic Publishers.*

ardised unemployment rate has risen from 5.1 per cent in 1977, when this statistic was first calculated, to 8 per cent in 1985.[1] With increasing frequency, parallels are drawn with the heretofore unprecedented experience of large-scale unemployment during the interwar years.

It is hard to know what to make of the comparison, for the literature on interwar unemployment is circumscribed by two serious limitations. The first limitation is that the recent literature is confined almost exclusively to the experience of two countries: the United States and the United Kingdom. There is little scholarly literature on interwar unemployment in a surprising number of other countries. While the unemployment experience of other countries has been the subject of the occasional study, the specialised approaches taken have not permitted comparisons or generalisations. The second limitation is that the literature on interwar unemployment is heavily macroeconomic and based on highly imperfect macroeconomic indicators. Investigators have remained preoccupied by the behaviour of the aggregate unemployment rate as measured by trade union returns or unemployment insurance statistics. Despite the questions that can be raised about the reliability of those statistics and about their comparability across countries, the standard series continue to serve as the basis for a steady stream of macroeconometric studies. By comparison, little systematic attention has been devoted to the incidence of interwar unemployment (what groups of workers were at risk), the effects of interwar unemployment (particularly implications for poverty, malnutrition and employability), and responses to interwar unemployment by labour force participants and their families.

For observers merely interested in invoking interwar experience as an illustration of how disastrous for an economy and society large-scale unemployment can be, aggregate unemployment rates may suffice, even if limited to the US and the UK and measured with serious error. For the rest, the true dimensions of interwar unemployment experience remain obscure. How, for example, did the characteristics of interwar unemployment vary across countries? How did the characteristics of high unemployment in the 1930s differ from the characteristics of high unemployment in the 1980s? What can we learn about the incidence of unemployment, its effects, and the responses it elicited?

This volume presents a set of specially commissioned studies designed to address these questions. It summarises the proceedings of a conference which brought together an international, interdisciplinary group of scholars concerned with the problem of interwar unemployment. Following a chapter reassessing the macroeconomic evidence are nine country studies focusing on the experiences of the UK, Germany, Italy, Belgium, France, the US, Canada and Australia. While differences in historical circumstances and source materials dictate different approaches to the country studies, each attempts to speak to a common set of issues: the incidence of unemployment, the effects of unemployment, and the response of the unemployed. The all but total absence of a literature on interwar unemployment in a number of these countries means that many authors are venturing out into uncharted terrain. Although as a result they sometimes are unable to provide definitive answers to the central questions - Who was unemployed? What were the effects of unemployment? What was the response of the unemployed? - even the most basic facts about interwar unemployment shed important new light on questions previously shrouded in darkness.

2   The Emergence of the Problem

Though the existence of worklessness had been recognised for centuries, it was not until the 1890s that the term unemployment gained widespread currency. According to Garraty, "Suddenly unemployment had become a burning issue; books and the reports of government investigators began to come out in ever larger numbers" (1978, p. 121). This "discovery" of unemployment can be traced to a combination of factors. First, the growing complexity of the labour market and of its industrial relations drew attention to employment conditions. Second, social surveys linked poverty and moral degradation to low-wage labour and intermittent employment. Third, the depression of the 1890s created growing awareness of the cyclical character of employment opportunities and led ultimately to recognition that unemployment was an economic phenomenon or "problem of industry" rather than one of individual inadequacy.

In Victorian Britain, social commentators referred typically not to unemployment but to pauperism, vagrancy and destitution. According to Harris (1972, p. 1), "For fifty years after the Poor Law Reform of 1834, unemployment as a serious theoretical and practical question was virtually ignored by English economic theorists and social reformers." Not only was the adjective "unemployed" current while the noun "unemployment" was not, but the adjective was used to denote persons not working whatever the reason, including even invalids and women who had ceased to work on marriage. Trade union unemployment rates derived from records of unemployed persons receiving out-of-work donations might themselves include both types of individuals (Garside, 1980, pp. 10-13). Reference to unemployment first became commonplace in the 1880s. Taylor's (1909) bibliography of works on unemployment offers one means of tracing the concept's emergence. Under the categories "unemployment generally" and "causes of unemployment", she lists fewer than three works per decade over the period 1820 to 1880. This rises to sixteen works in the 1880s, seventy-seven in the 1890s, and 160 works from the beginning of 1900 to the middle of 1909. On the basis of this and other evidence it is fair to conclude that only in the final decades of the nineteenth century did unemployment in Britain emerge as a major social issue. Conservative imperialists, Fabian socialists and New Liberals drawn together in the campaign for National Efficiency all saw recurrent short spells of unemployment as the principal cause of working-class poverty and degradation. These concerns, and the agitation they prompted, culminated in 1911 with the adoption of the beginning of Britain's unemployment insurance system.

Widespread recognition of the problem of unemployment emerged simultaneously in the United States.[2] Until the mid-1870s, men and women who had lost their jobs and were seeking employment were described as out of work, idle, involuntarily idle or loafing, but only rarely as unemployed. When the term was used, it referred generally, as in Britain and France, to persons idle or not working whatever the reason. Often individuals who would now be regarded as out of the labour force, including young children and the geriatric, were included under this label. The transition from concern over those with no occupation, "who take no part in the work of life", to concern over those experiencing "forced idleness", and the corresponding tendency to attach the label "unemployed" exclusively to members of the second category, occurred as early, if not earlier, in America as in Britain. Yet as late as 1875, to judge from the Massachusetts State Census of that year, the term "unemployed" had not yet acquired its modern meaning. Of those 350,000 Massachusetts residents classified as unemployed, most were children under the age of 10 living at home. Only in 1878 does a change become discernible. That year Carroll D. Wright, chief of the Massachusetts Bureau of Statistics of Labour (and later first head of the US Bureau of Labour Statistics), attempted to ascertain the number of able-bodied workmen who were unemployed. The instructions issued in conjunction with this survey reflect an evolution in the concept of the unemployed person and in the usage of the term. Police and assessors were instructed to enumerate those experiencing "forced idleness", omitting individuals under 19 years of age and those who did not "really want employment". As the word "unemployed" came to be acknowledged, over the course of the 1880s, as the label for those who were "involuntarily without employment" and its application was increasingly restricted to members of this group, the term began to lose the pejorative connotation it had carried previously. Still, it is revealing that, until the twentieth century, American experts referred not to unemployment but mainly to jobless wage earners, to the involuntarily idle and, as in Britain, to the unemployed. According to Keyssar (1986, p.4), the noun only appeared on the printed page in 1887, in the

Eighteenth Annual Report of the Massachusetts Bureau of Statistics of Labour.

In France, the concept emerged somewhat later. France's rural character and the persistence of small-scale agriculture may have served to disguise the problem. The emergence of unemployment as a category conceptualised with sufficient precision for statistics on its incidence to be gathered has been traced by Salais, Baverez and Reynaud (1986) through the questionnaires used by government agencies. As late as the early 1890s, the French authorities, like their British counterparts, referred not to unemployment but to vagrancy and vagabondism. Social assistance societies distinguished three categories of vagabonds: invalids, the healthy in need of temporary assistance only, and the permanent vagabond who made a profession of seeking assistance. While the last two categories resemble the voluntarily and involuntarily unemployed, revealingly the term unemployment was not used. Similarly, while the 1891 census inquired into each individual's occupation, whether they worked outside the home, and whether they were self-employed or an employee, there was no opportunity to indicate whether a person was out of work. For those without a distinct occupation, the census merely inquired into the occupation of the head of household. In 1896, for the first time, the census included a question for people without a current position, distinguishing three reasons for their lack of work. The census report offered an explicit discussion of people in unemployment ("les personnes qui ont déclaré être en chômage"), suggesting, for example, that persons aged 65 and over should properly be regarded as no longer active and hence not among the unemployed.[3]

By the end of the second decade of the twentieth century, unemployment as a coherent aggregate - on a par with other economic aggregates such as inflation and the trade cycle - was firmly established. The alarming rise in the number of unemployed that occurred in the wake of the First World War in nearly every country reinforced this awareness. Unfortunately, awareness of the problem did not imply that contemporaries were well informed of its magnitude.

3 Aggregate Unemployment Statistics

Aggregate unemployment statistics for the interwar period provide a highly imperfect measure of the phenomenon. It is some comfort that we have available a comprehensive analysis of the sources, characteristics and comparability of the statistics generated by public agencies and private bodies during the interwar years, courtesy of Galenson and Zellner (1957). In addition to reviewing the standard series, Galenson and Zellner attempt to adjust the statistics for some countries to render them com-

Table 1.1   Unemployment Rates in Industry (in percentage points)

Year	Australia	Belgium	Canada	Denmark	France	Germany
1920	5.5	-	4.6	6.1	-	3.8
1921	10.4	9.7	8.9	19.7	5.0	2.8
1922	8.5	3.1	7.1	19.3	2.0	1.5
1923	6.2	1.0	4.9	12.7	2.0	10.2
1924	7.8	1.0	7.1	10.7	3.0	13.1
1925	7.8	1.5	7.0	14.7	3.0	6.8
1926	6.3	1.4	4.7	20.7	3.0	18.0
1927	6.2	1.8	2.9	22.5	11.0	8.8
1928	10.0	0.9	2.6	18.5	4.0	8.6
1929	10.2	1.3	4.2	15.5	1.0	13.3
1930	18.4	3.6	12.9	13.7	2.0	22.7
1931	26.5	10.9	17.4	17.9	6.5	34.3
1932	28.1	19.0	26.0	31.7	15.4	43.8
1933	24.2	16.9	26.6	28.8	14.1	36.2
1934	19.6	18.9	20.6	22.2	13.8	20.5
1935	15.6	17.8	19.1	19.7	14.5	16.2
1936	11.3	13.5	16.7	19.3	10.4	12.0
1937	8.4	11.5	12.5	21.9	7.4	6.9
1938	7.8	14.0	15.1	21.5	7.8	3.2
1939	8.8	15.9	14.1	18.4	8.1	0.9

parable internationally. These series, along with Lebergott's (1964) estimates of unemployment in the US, are presented in Table 1.1.

Trade union reports comprise the principal source of data on unemployment in Australia, Canada, Denmark, the Netherlands, Norway and Sweden. Unions in these and other countries provided benefits when their members fell out of work; it is from the proportion of membership applying for or drawing payments that trade union unemployment rates are obtained. The British data arise from statistics collected in the course of the operation of the unemployment insurance system, under the provisions of which registration at a labour exchange was a condition for receipt of benefit. The Belgian statistics are a by-product of the local unemployment insurance societies established voluntarily between 1918 and 1920 to replace temporary relief measures instituted during the First World War.

The unemployment rate series for France and Germany were estimated by Galenson and Zellner from a variety of sources.[4] For France, the series up to 1930 is Agthe's, calculated as the ratio of the number of unemployed workers (based on a series for unplaced applicants for work) to the number of wage and salary earners enumerated in the 1926 census. After 1930

Table 1.1 (continued)

Year	Netherlands	Norway	Sweden	UK	US
1920	5.8	2.3	5.4	3.2	8.6
1921	9.0	17.7	26.6	17.0	19.5
1922	11.0	17.1	22.9	14.3	11.4
1923	11.2	10.7	12.5	11.7	4.1
1924	8.8	8.5	10.1	10.3	8.3
1925	8.1	13.2	11.0	11.3	5.4
1926	7.3	24.3	12.2	12.5	2.9
1927	7.5	25.4	12.0	9.7	5.4
1928	5.6	19.2	10.6	10.8	6.9
1929	2.9	15.4	10.2	10.4	5.3
1930	7.8	16.6	11.9	16.1	14.2
1931	14.8	22.3	16.8	21.3	25.2
1932	25.3	30.8	22.4	22.1	36.3
1933	26.9	33.4	23.2	19.9	37.6
1934	28.0	30.7	18.0	16.7	32.6
1935	31.7	25.3	15.0	15.5	30.2
1936	32.7	18.8	12.7	13.1	25.4
1937	26.9	20.0	10.8	10.8	21.3
1938	25.0	22.0	10.9	12.9	27.9
1939	19.9	18.3	9.2	10.5	25.2

Note: Australia: trade union reports corrected to eliminate unemployment for reasons other than non-availability of work; Belgium: statistics of voluntary unemployment insurance societies; Canada: trade union reports adjusted from 1921 by the Dominion Bureau of Statistics; Denmark: trade union unemployment insurance fund reports; France, Germany: see text; Netherlands: trade union unemployment insurance fund returns; Norway: trade union reports; Sweden: trade union reports; UK: unemployment insurance system series; US: Lebergott estimates.
Sources: Galenson and Zellner (1957), p. 455, Lebergott (1964), p. 512.

the total number of workers in employment, based on the 1931 census, is extrapolated to other years using the factory inspector's index of employment in industrial establishments of 100 or more workers. The series for Germany uses trade union reports up to 1932, spliced to a series for the subsequent period derived from employment exchange statistics. The overall level is fixed by the 1933 census, which recorded as unemployed 37.3 per cent of workers and employees in manufacturing, construction and mining. Lebergott's estimate for the US is the only measure not based on direct observations of the number of workers unemployed. It is derived instead by applying interpolated participation rates for different demographic groups to the annual movement of population, and subtracting from this estimate of the labour force an estimate of employment constructed from sectoral measures of activity.

These series may be regarded as reasonably reliable indicators of the profile of unemployment among wage earners in the industrial sector. Even here, however, biases arise from the construction of the estimates which may distort both the overall level of unemployment and the volatility of year-to-year fluctuations. Problems of representativeness are particularly glaring in the case of series derived from trade union returns, which are generally weighted by membership rather than by the labour force in each industry or occupation. While trade union unemployment series in most countries are more broadly based for the interwar years than for the period prior to 1914, they still exclude much white-collar employment and most female workers. Undue weight is given to skilled and semi-skilled occupations relative to manual ones, and to old-established industries relative to new and emerging ones. Some union returns such as those for Australia tend to underrepresent the level of unemployment because many unemployed workers, having exhausted their benefits and with little chance of regaining employment in their customary occupation, simply let their union membership lapse.[5]

The unemployment insurance statistics are similarly contaminated by various sources of bias. In the UK where the insurance system was most comprehensive, it still covered only about two-thirds of wage and salary earners (less than half in the case of females), excluding workers in agriculture, domestic service, government, and those with relatively high salaries. In countries where unemployment benefits were funded partly by government and employer contributions there is a natural suspicion that unemployed workers migrated to the covered sector, thereby inflating the unemployment percentages. As Martine Goossens, Stefaan Peeters and Guido Pepermans show in chapter 8, the number of people covered by Belgium's voluntary system of unemployment insurance rose by over 50 per cent between 1930 and 1933 after having remained relatively stable during the 1920s. While in 1930 the percentage of unemployed recorded by the Belgian insurance system was lower than that in the census of 1930, by 1937 the insured percentage was higher than that in the census. In addition to changes in coverage, changing features of the operation of insurance schemes affected measured unemployment. The effect on public outlays of the simultaneous rise in unemployment and in the number insured led to the imposition of stiffer criteria: in Belgium, for example, this involved the exclusion of those who had not been working in trade or industry for at least a year. Similarly, under the Anomalies Regulations introduced in Britain in 1931, new conditions restricting the benefits available to married women and casual workers effectively excluded many from the system. In Germany, with the advent of the Nazi regime,

Table 1.2   Average Unemployment Rates, 1921-29, 1930-38, 1971-79, 1980-85

	Galenson and Zellner		Maddison		OECD	
	1921-9	1930-8	1921-9	1930-8	1971-9	1980-5
Australia	8.1	17.8	-	-	4.1	7.6
Belgium	2.4	14.0	1.5	8.7	5.0	12.2
Canada	5.5	18.5	3.5	13.3	6.8	9.9
Denmark	18.7	21.9	4.5	6.6	-	-
France	3.8	10.2	-	-	3.9	8.3
Germany	9.2	21.8	4.0	8.8	2.4	6.4
Netherlands	8.3	24.3	2.4	8.7	3.9	11.1
Norway	16.8	26.6	-	-	1.7	2.5
Sweden	14.2	16.8	3.4	5.6	2.1	2.8
UK	12.0	15.4	6.8	9.8	4.5	10.9
US	7.7	26.1	4.9	18.2	6.2	7.7

Sources: Galenson and Zellner (1957), pp. 455, 523; Lebergott (1964), p. 512; Maddison (1964), p.220; OECD *Economic Outlook* December 1986, p.167.

administrative change and disruption was even more sweeping, as Dan Silverman shows in chapter 5. This creates considerable uncertainty about the proper interpretation of fluctuations in the level of German unemployment in the critical years of the early 1930s.

While statistics pertaining to industrial employment may be invested with a certain amount of authority, the same cannot be said of other sectors where information on unemployment is more fragmentary. Since the Depression centred on industry, and since wage earners were more susceptible to unemployment than salary earners or the self-employed, series based on the experience of wage earners will tend to overstate unemployment rates among the occupied population as a whole. When the UK unemployment insurance figures are adjusted to a working population basis, the rate for the 1930s falls from 15.4 to 11.7 per cent (Feinstein, 1972, T128, T126). Similarly, according to the 1936 French census unemployment among wage and salary earners as a whole was 7.5 per cent, while for those in industry it was 11.6 per cent. For the US, Lebergott's estimates imply unemployment rates in the non-farm sector for 1930 and 1940 which are 30 per cent higher than the estimates for the aggregate given in Table 1.1

In Table 1.2 average industrial unemployment rates are compared with Maddison's (1964) estimates of economy-wide rates. Maddison estimated his series by adjusting to a labour force basis statistics on the registered unemployed compiled by the International Labour Office. The differences are dramatic: the Danish, German, Dutch and Swedish unemployment percentages are more than halved, while those for other countries are substantially reduced. If these economy-wide estimates are to be believed, then unemployment was significantly less severe in Europe than in North America and in Northern Europe than elsewhere. Comparison with recent OECD statistics is also striking. For Belgium, the Netherlands and the UK, unemployment in 1980-86 appears to have been even more severe than in 1930-38. Maddison's figures for the 1930s are likely to be too low for several reasons, however. The census benchmarks from which Maddison's series were extrapolated typically failed to adequately enumerate underemployment in agriculture and services, particularly of family members (especially women) on farms and in small businesses and of those on temporary lay-off in industry. Younger workers who had never had a job and older workers for whom retirement was a respectable alternative were similarly underenumerated. Hence actual economy-wide rates probably lie somewhere between the industrial rates and the estimates for the aggregate.

The foregoing discussion highlights some of the problems of defining and measuring unemployment in the interwar period. While the shortcomings of these data are evident, it would be a mistake to dismiss them as uninformative. Economic fluctuations in the 1930s were large enough to dominate all but the most dramatic changes in coverage and eligibility. But in countries where industrialisation was a relatively recent phenomenon and where there remained a large "traditional" sector, unemployment was even less well defined and even more poorly measured. In Italy, for example, as Gianni Toniolo and Francesco Piva argue in chapter 6, the economy was characterised by a large underdeveloped rural sector where labour was chronically underemployed. Migration to the cities took the form of a gradual transition, during which a significant portion of the workforce obtained only intermittent employment in industry while maintaining ties with the countryside. As a result of this interconnection of industrial and non-industrial sectors, it is particularly difficult to define the industrial labour force. Different assumptions lead to estimates of the industrial unemployment rate for Italy which for 1932 range from 15.5 per cent to 35.2 per cent. Analogous problems arise for Belgium when one attempts to move from statistics on the percentage of insured unemployed to an estimate of the total number of unemployed, as Goossens, Peeters and Pepermans show in chapter 8.

In France, the severity of unemployment and underemployment varied across rural and urban départements. In chapter 7 Robert Salais shows how the extent of the problem varied with the stage of development of local industry and with the nature of labour contracts. One category of worker, described in the French census as engaged in "isolated work", included the self-employed, those working in their homes and wage earners with irregular jobs. Such individuals typically suffered from underemployment, but did not ascribe themselves as unemployed and were not so enumerated. In small-scale businesses where personal contacts between employer and employed remained close, there was typically an "implicit contract", which in times of slack demand led to job sharing which would not be reflected in measured unemployment. In large firms, in contrast, institutional arrangements for production were more formalised and job separations more common. Hence in large-scale industry the distinction between employment and unemployment was sharply defined.

4   Labour Demand and Supply

Two central questions dominate the literature on the macroeconomics of interwar unemployment. First, why did unemployment reach such unprecedented heights after 1929? Second, why did it remain so high for so long? These questions point inevitably to the issue of how and through what channels aggregate shocks were transmitted to the labour market, and how labour markets adjusted to these disturbances. Central to these issues is the effect of real wages on employment and the effect, in turn, of unemployment on wage adjustment.

The industrial unemployment rates reviewed above are displayed in Figure 1.1. It is immediately apparent that the time series pattern of unemployment differed greatly across countries. Three or four types of profiles can be distinguished. For the US, Canada and Australia, the pattern is one of stable and relatively low unemployment in the 1920s followed by first deep depression and then strong recovery. In Norway and, to a lesser extent, Sweden and the UK, a distinct cyclical pattern is superimposed on an upward trend encompassing the entire two decades. In France, Belgium and the Netherlands, after remaining steady in the 1920s unemployment rises to persistently higher levels after 1930. The pattern of unemployment in Germany is quite distinct by virtue of the sharp peak and dramatic fall in the 1930s.

Though each country's experience is unique, a number of common features of interwar unemployment are evident, notably the brief recession and recovery of the early 1920s and the sharp rise in the 1930s. These features are usually explained with reference to macroeconomic determinants of aggregate demand in all countries involved. The macroeconomic fluctuations of the early 1920s were associated with recovery from war and, in some cases, with economic upheaval attendant on stopping hyperinflation. The reconstruction of international trade and the stabilisation of exchange rates conditioned different rates of monetary growth and ex-

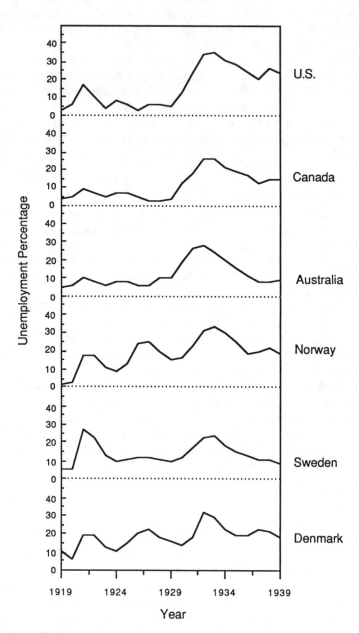

Figure 1.1   Industrial Unemployment Rates, 1919-39

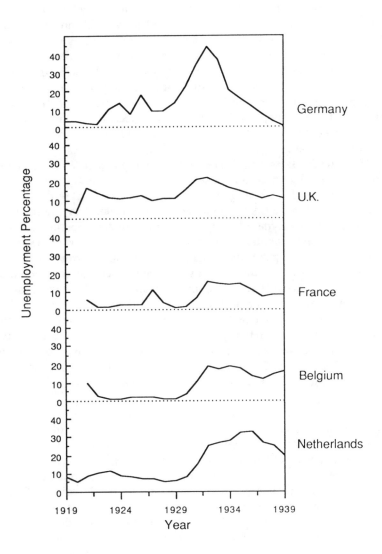

Figure 1.1   Industrial Unemployment Rates, 1919-39 (continued)

pansion of output in the remainder of the 1920s (Eichengreen, 1986a). In the 1930s the story of the origins and international transmission of the Depression is both too familiar and too controversial to warrant retelling here (for useful surveys see Fearon (1979) and Kindleberger (1973)). In the recovery, exchange depreciation and associated monetary policies were principal causes of differences between countries in the extent of recovery (Eichengreen and Sachs, 1985). Domestic policies such as the New Deal in the US are also frequently seen as influencing the course of the upswing. It is not necessary to embrace the importance of one of these macroeconomic factors by dismissing the importance of the others. In Britain, for example, world trade, relative prices, interest rates and tariffs all affected aggregate demand and the pattern of recovery in the 1930s (Hatton, 1986a).

How do such factors find reflection in unemployment? The economist's instinctive reaction is to look to market prices or in this case to labour costs. The neoclassical approach emphasising the causal relationship running from labour costs to the level of employment has a long and chequered history. Keynes (1936), it will be recalled, argued that real wages should fluctuate countercyclically. Positing that wages were less flexible than prices, he argued that a business cycle upturn would put upward pressure on prices, reducing real wages, and by cutting real labour costs facilitate the expansion of employment. Analogously, a business cycle downturn would reduce prices, raise the real wage, increase real labour costs and result in a reduction in employment.[6] This drew the attention of contemporaries, notably Dunlop, Tarshis, Richardson and Ruggles who criticised Keynes's characterisation of British experience, although Tarshis was able to demonstrate a negative relationship between monthly employment data and real hourly wages in the US for the period 1932-38.

The debate over the cyclical behaviour of real wages continues to the present day. Much recent analysis has focused on the case of interwar Britain (see Dimsdale, 1984 and Beenstock and Warburton, 1986). Analysing the cyclical behaviour of real wages for the interwar period raises a multitude of problems, not least those of data. It is important that the price indices used to deflate nominal wages incorporate the price of final output or value-added and not simply input prices. For the interwar years, such measures are less readily available than indices of the cost of living or wholesale prices, which are less appropriate as measures of industrial output prices. Wage rates should properly measure unit labour costs, rather than weekly earnings or other measures which reflect changes in the level of activity. The available series for five countries are displayed in Table 1.3. With the exception of Germany, real product wages in these countries rise more rapidly in the early 1930s than in the late 1920s. In

Table 1.3   **Product Wages (nominal wages relative to manufacturing prices)**

	UK	US	Germany	Japan	Sweden
1924	91.8	95.0	-	-	-
1925	93.5	90.8	-	-	-
1926	95.3	91.2	-	-	-
1927	97.9	96.7	-	-	-
1928	98.4	97.8	-	-	-
1929	100.0	100.0	100.0	100.0	100.0
1930	103.0	106.1	100.4	115.6	116.6
1931	106.4	113.0	102.2	121.6	129.1
1932	108.3	109.6	96.8	102.9	130.0
1933	109.3	107.9	99.3	101.8	127.9
1934	111.4	115.8	103.0	102.3	119.6
1935	111.3	114.3	105.3	101.6	119.2
1936	110.4	115.9	107.7	99.2	116.0
1937	107.8	121.9	106.5	87.1	101.9
1938	108.6	130.0	107.7	86.3	115.1

Source: Manufacturing prices are from Phelps-Brown and Browne (1968), except those for Japan, which are from Butlin (1984).

both Japan and Sweden the initial rise is sharp, although in Japan there is a downward shift in 1931-32. Thereafter real product wages in both countries drift downwards. In the UK and US acceleration in the early 1930s is followed by a sharp rise in the US in 1933-34 which is not paralleled in the UK.

In chapter 2, Andrew Newell and James Symons examine the determinants of employment for fourteen countries for which wage and price proxies are available. An unconventional element of their analysis is the inclusion of the lagged real interest rate. They justify its inclusion as a measure of the cost of variable capital or risk, although an alternative interpretation is that it serves as a proxy for unanticipated fluctuations in aggregate demand. For Europe and Scandinavia but not for the US and UK, they find strong evidence that the real product wage is negatively associated with employment over the cycle. The contrast among countries is ironic, since many of the proponents of the view that real wages fluctuate countercyclically have focused on the US and UK. Toniolo and Piva examine the same issues using monthly data for ten Italian industries for the period 1928-38. They find a negative relationship between own product real wages and employment even though this did not emerge in the aggregate equation for Italy estimated by Newell and Symons. Industry-level estimates for the UK similarly tend to support the hypotheses

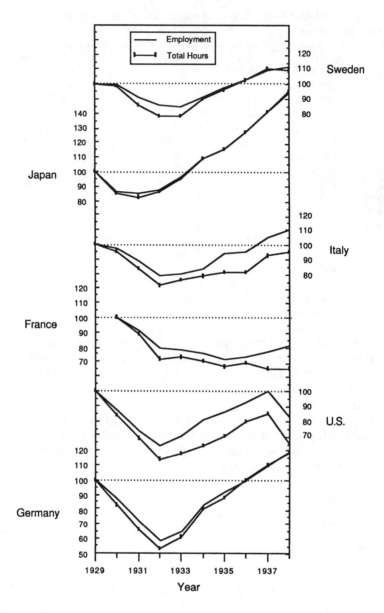

Figure 1.2   Employment and Total Hours in Industry, 1929-38 (1929=100)

of a negative relationship between the product wage and employment (Hatton, 1981).

The fluctuation in industrial employment in the 1930s (as distinct from unemployment) is shown in Figure 1.2. These series, based on contemporary surveys of industrial establishments, reveal a dramatic fall in employment, to less than two-thirds of 1929 levels in Germany and the US and to less than four-fifths of 1929 levels in Italy and France. While those countries which show the most rapid growth of industrial employment during the recovery tend to be those which suffered the greatest employment loss during the slump, there are substantial variations. Germany experienced a much more dramatic recovery in employment than the US, while Japan enjoyed a much more dramatic recovery than the UK or Sweden. It is tempting to associate these variations with differences in the course of real wages, such as those shown in Table 1.3. However, econometric evidence suggests that real wage movements can account for only a portion of international employment variations (Eichengreen and Sachs, 1985).

The correspondence between fluctuations in employment and unemployment depends on the extent to which average hours per employed worker adjusted. Given employers' total labour requirements, a fall in hours could minimise the extent of unemployment. Such adjustments might be regarded as a form of job sharing. In Figure 1.2, the hatched line shows a pattern also evident in recent years, namely a more dramatic decline in total employee hours than in employment. This indicates the existence of job sharing in all countries during the Depression, but for which the rise in industrial unemployment would have been even more severe. It also casts doubt on the long-standing notion that those remaining in employment during the Depression prospered due to the increase in real wages, since the rise in real hourly earnings was offset by the fall in hours worked. While one might expect the change in hours to be a transitory phenomenon which would disappear as soon as the severity of the Depression was apparent, the graphs indicate that typically hours did not begin to recover until total employment began to rise in the second half of the 1930s.

There has been relatively little investigation of the changing mix of employment and hours during the Great Depression. In one study of the issue, Bernanke (1985) attempted to explain interwar hours-employee fluctuations as a function of workers' preference for a positive relationship between hours and employment and firms' desire to minimise labour costs. Since firms find it costly to reduce only hours or only workers, the result is a combination of the two. Monthly data for eight US industries

Table 1.4   Hours of Work in Industry, 1929-38

	Germany (daily)	US (weekly)	France (weekly)	Italy (monthly)	Poland (weekly)	Sweden (weekly)
1929	7.67	48.3	-	182	44.8	-
1930	7.37	43.9	48.0	175	43.9	-
1931	7.08	40.4	46.7	170	43.3	-
1932	6.91	34.8	43.7	168	41.4	-
1933	7.16	36.4	45.3	174	41.5	46.0
1934	7.43	34.7	44.7	172	42.2	47.0
1935	7.41	37.2	44.5	159	42.6	47.4
1936	7.59	39.8	45.7	157	42.7	47.6
1937	7.68	39.2	40.2	163	43.3	47.2
1938	7.75	34.4	38.7	159	43.7	46.3

Source: "Quarterly Statistical Tables", *International Labour Review* 40 (1939), pp. 548-9.

for 1923-39 lend empirical support to Bernanke's interpretation. But the reduction in hours appears to have been much more marked in the US than elsewhere. Still, as Table 1.4 shows, in a number of countries average weekly hours in industry seem to have declined permanently at the beginning of the decade. In Italy and France, hours show a sustained decline, while in Germany average hours actually rose slightly between 1929 and 1938. Clearly, institutions as well as preferences mattered for determining the form of reduction of labour input. In the UK, for example, where hours reductions were small and transitory, the unemployment insurance system imposed a fixed employment cost and provided workers with an alternative income which may have shifted the balance in favour of variations in employment (Harrison and Hart, 1985). In the US, the effect of the codes introduced under the National Recovery Administration (NRA) may have been, *ceteris paribus*, to induce the substitution of employment for hours. In Germany, by contrast, despite pressure for firms to increase employment and despite the introduction of short-time working in 1933-34, hours increased after 1931.

Labour might be hoarded inside or outside the firm. Outside the firm, labour hoarding could take the form of a reduction in weekly hours or temporary lay-offs and job rotation. Inside the firm, it would be reflected in a cyclical decline in labour productivity. The extent of inside labour hoarding can be estimated from variations in output per employee. In chapter 11, Robert Gregory *et al.* compare the output per worker in Australia and the US over the 1930s, finding that while worker productivity in Australian manufacturing increased marginally, indicating little if any labour hoarding or job sharing, labour productivity in the US fell by a full 15 per cent between 1929 and 1933. If labour hoarding in Australia had matched that in the US, Australian unemployment would have peaked at about 12 per cent of the labour force rather than the 19 per cent observed in 1932. Such differences are most readily explained in terms of institutional and historical influences. With a centralised bargaining structure, strong unions and one of the shortest working weeks among industrial countries, there was strong resistance in Australia to proposals for further reductions in weekly hours. In the US, in contrast, the working week had remained at forty-eight hours and, with strong official encouragement under the New Deal, the opportunity was seized to permanently reduce it.

Equally important for understanding the extent as well as the nature of unemployment during the Depression is the behaviour of the labour supply and labour force participation. Fluctuations in the labour force have implications for the construction of unemployment rates as well as for the interpretation of household responses to the Depression. Generally the only available measures of the total labour force come from census benchmarks, which are too far apart to convey much information about cyclical variation. The implication of ignoring these variations is demonstrated in Romer's (1986) revisions of Lebergott's estimates of US unemployment in the 1920s. Instead of assuming a steady secular change in participation rates between censuses, Romer imposes the postwar pattern of procyclical fluctuation in participation on the interwar data, significantly altering Lebergott's estimates of year-to-year variations in unemployment.

Many families responded to the unemployment of the principal breadwinner by sending other family members to work.[7] University students, finding themselves unable to afford continued education, sought full-time work instead. Married women entered the labour force in growing numbers, their share of the American female labour force rising from 29 to 35 per cent between 1930 and 1940. Using data for Boston and Detroit gathered in the winter of 1935-36, Woytinsky (1942) calculated that, for families with two adults in the household, the probability of the second adult participating in the labour market was 25 per cent higher when the head was unemployed than when he was employed. Similarly, the percentage of third adults who participated rose from 47 to 61 per cent in Detroit and from 57 to 66 per cent in Boston as the labour market status of the family head changed from employed to unemployed.

Female participation was widely blamed for male unemployment. As Norman Cousins wrote in 1939,

> There are approximately 1,000,000 people out of work in the United States today ... there are also 1,000,000 or more women, married and single, who are jobholders. Simply fire the women, who shouldn't be working anyway, and hire the men. Presto! No unemployment. No relief rolls. No depression.[8]

The belief that the entry of new workers was adding to the difficulties men experienced in finding employment led to the passage of legislation restricting the employment of married women. The 1932 US Federal Economy Act stipulated that, in the event of personnel reductions, married employees should be fired first when the spouse also held a government job; typically the wife was the one affected. A similar Austrian law stipulated that the wife was the one to be let go (Garraty, 1986, p. 256).

As a result of these conflicting influences, the net effect of the Depression on labour force participation is difficult to discern. For the US, Woytinsky (1942) originally argued that the number of added workers, particularly women, exceeded the number of discouraged workers, thereby exacerbating the unemployment problem of the early 1930s. But subsequent investigations comparing the interwar period with long-run trends in census participation rates suggest that the discouraged worker effect was predominant in the US, the UK and Canada while the added worker effect predominated only in Germany (Long, 1958). All such estimates assume, however, that the secular trend in labour force participation rates between 1910 and 1950 was linear. The only way to relax this assumption is to employ cross-section data. One recent study of female participation across British towns in 1931 finds little evidence that the net discouraged worker effect predominated (Hatton, 1986b). Robert Margo, in his analysis of US experience in chapter 9, similarly concludes in favour of a powerful added worker effect. Using data for individual households from the 1940 census he finds that, where the husband was an experienced worker but unemployed, the wife was 59 per cent more likely to be in the labour force than if the husband held a full-time job. Wives were also likely to work if the husband was out of the labour force or held a part-time job. Though such estimates fail to capture the discouraged worker effect and therefore the net impact of unemployment, the strength of the added worker effect alone suggests it may be a mistake to assume that the discouraged worker effect predominated in the 1930s.

Table 1.5 Nominal Hourly Earnings in Mines, Industries and Transport in Fifteen Countries, 1929-38

	Germany	Austr-alia	Belg-ium	Can-ada	Den-mark	USA	France (Paris)	UK	Italy	Japan	Nor-way	Neth-erlands	Poland	Swe-den	Switz-erland
1929	100	100	100	100	100	100	100	100	100	100	100	100	100	100	100
1930	97	98	108	101	102	100	106	100	99	95	100	102	99	103	101
1931	90	89	101	96	102	96	105	98	93	87	96	100	92	103	102
1932	75	84	92	91	102	84	100	96	91	85	98	93	85	101	98
1933	73	81	90	86	102	83	102	95	89	86	96	89	77	98	97
1934	75	82	86	87	103	98	102	96	86	88	97	86	73	98	94
1935	76	83	82	89	104	102	101	97	85	88	97	83	71	99	92
1936	77	85	88	91	103	104	116	100	90	88	100	81	70	100	90
1937	79	89	99	98	105	117	173	104	101	93	107	82	73	103	89
1938	82	96	105	102	111	121	192	107	108	102	118	86	77	109	93

Note: Hourly earnings except for Canada and Australia (hourly rates), UK (weekly rates), Japan and Norway (daily earnings).

Source: International Labour Review 40 (1939), pp. 552-565.

5   Unemployment and Labour Market Adjustment

The persistence of unemployment in the 1930s raises questions about the strength of self-equilibrating mechanisms in the labour market. Perhaps the most popular question is whether the interwar years were characterised by a high degree of wage rigidity. In Table 1.5 series for nominal hourly earnings in the industrial sector are displayed for fifteen countries. These data suggest that it is wage behaviour not so much in the recession as in the subsequent recovery that is difficult to explain. Whatever the degree of nominal wage rigidity, hourly earnings fell in most countries, and fell very sharply in some. Earnings tended to fall most sharply where the slump was most severe. In the US and Australia they had fallen by nearly 20 per cent by 1933; in Germany they fell by even more. But there are exceptions to this rule. Japanese earnings fell more sharply than those in the UK or Sweden, countries whose recessions were of comparable severity. In France and Denmark, nominal hourly earnings did not fall at all. Turning from slump to recovery, between 1932 and 1935-36 earnings remained fairly constant in almost all countries despite continuing high unemployment. This was then followed, until 1937-38, by sharp increases in wages averaging 10 per cent. This wage inflation persisted despite the fact that unemployment had not yet returned to the lower levels of the 1920s. Overall, the time profile of money wages is "U"-shaped and inversely related to the bulge in unemployment.[9]

Any attempt to explain the behaviour of money wages in the 1920s and 1930s must start with the effect of the First World War. In a number of countries the effect of the war and the postwar inflation was to tie wage rates more closely to the cost of living. The result was an increasing degree of real (consumption) wage rigidity. Yet, despite this fact, data for nominal hourly earnings divided by the cost of living index (Table 1.6) show that in all countries except Germany the real consumer wage rose sharply between 1929 and 1933. The uniformity of the rise is striking. In Australia, where centralised wage setting under the arbitration system linked wage rates directly to the cost of living, because of the lag between wages and prices built into the system, the consumption wage rose during 1929 to 1933 as prices fell. As Gregory *et al.* show in chapter 11, this gave rise to real wage behaviour remarkably similar to that in the US, where no such institutional structure existed.

In the recovery, in contrast, real wage trends among countries were much more diverse, reflecting innovative wage policies pursued by national governments.[10] In the US, the impact of NRA codes is evident in the jump in hourly earnings in 1933-34. It has been estimated that the

Table 1.6   Real Hourly Earnings in Mines, Industries and Transport in Fifteen Countries, 1929-38

	Germany	Austr-alia	Belg-ium	Can-ada	Den-mark	USA	France	UK	Italy	Japan	Nor-way	Neth-erlands	Poland	Swe-den	Switz-erland
1929	100	100	100	100	100	100	100	100	100	100	100	100	100	100	100
1930	101	103	104	101	107	103	101	104	102	110	104	106	108	106	103
1931	102	105	109	108	114	110	103	109	107	116	104	111	112	109	109
1932	96	104	111	111	114	108	106	110	110	113	109	111	114	110	114
1933	95	104	109	111	111	111	109	112	112	108	109	107	115	108	119
1934	95	103	108	113	107	124	110	111	114	107	108	103	118	107	117
1935	95	102	103	113	105	123	116	111	111	105	106	103	119	107	116
1936	96	103	104	118	103	123	127	111	109	100	107	101	122	107	111
1937	99	105	108	121	102	133	155	110	111	97	107	104	119	108	105
1938	100	110	112		105	140	153	113	110	93	114	102	127	112	109

Source: As for Table 1.2.

NRA codes raised nominal wages by 26 per cent and real wages by 14 per cent over the two-year period of their operation (Weinstein, 1981).[11] In France the policies of the Blum government are evident in the sharp rise of 1936-37. In contrast, policies aimed at cutting or holding wages down met with mixed success. In Germany, on the one hand, the minimum wage was held at the nominal rate established in 1933 and voluntary payments above minimum rates were effectively prohibited (Bry, 1960, p. 236). In Australia, on the other hand, the Federal court decision to cut the basic wage by 10 per cent in 1931 was not followed to any significant extent and appears to have had little effect on wages actually paid.

This diversity of experience renders generalisations about interwar wage behaviour rather difficult. In chapter 2, Newell and Symons estimate a real wage equation for fourteen countries covering the period 1923-38. They find movements in the real wage to have been highly persistent. Real wages are negatively related to the cost of living, particularly in Europe, suggesting incomplete indexation of wages to short-run price changes. Surprisingly, however, this nominal inertia appears to have been relatively weak in the UK, the US, and Scandinavia. The tendency of unemployment to depress wage rates appears to have been relatively weak, although with the exception of the UK, unemployment had a small negative effect on real wages with a one-year lag.

Why did wages fail to adjust downward adequately in the face of deflationary nominal shocks? The Keynesian approach emphasises nominal inertia in labour markets. Because of convention, contracts, and the importance workers attach to relative earnings (defined both over time and across individuals), nominal wages are slow to adjust. Thus, the decline in nominal income at the outset of the Depression raised real wages and reduced labour demand, increasing unemployment. *The General Theory* raises questions about whether a reduction in money wages would have been sufficient to reduce unemployment in a closed economy (equivalently, in the world economy as a whole). But there is no question that, in the Keynesian framework, an open economy could increase its competitiveness, raising its output and reducing its unemployment, by lowering its labour costs relative to its trading partners. Interwar evidence makes clear that those countries which succeeded in limiting the rise in real wages after 1929, usually through a combination of currency devaluation and expansionary monetary policy, recovered most quickly from the Great Depression (Eichengreen and Sachs, 1985).

In contrast to the Keynesian model, the classical approach emphasises not inertial money wages but unanticipated nominal shocks. As in Lucas and Rapping (1969), the labour market is, with a single notable exception, assumed to be at the intersection of the labour supply and labour demand curves. That exception is unanticipated shocks which displace workers from their labour supply curves, leaving employment to be demand-determined. In the Great Depression, for example, to some extent deflation took workers by surprise; workers having demanded money wages that turned out to be above market-clearing levels, the economy ended up with high real wages and high unemployment. As soon as they recognised that deflation was under way, workers reduced their wage demands, restoring the labour market to equilibrium. Applying this model to the US experience, Lucas and Rapping find that it nicely tracks the rise in unemployment after 1929. The problem is that it predicts a rapid fall in unemployment as soon as deflation was halted. Thus, the market-clearing-cum-surprises approach fails to provide a full explanation for American unemployment in the 1930s. This has not prevented subsequent investigators from attempting to apply it to other countries.

It was partly the failure of models such as these that led advocates of the market-clearing approach to emphasise the role of relief programmes and unemployment benefits. Darby (1976) argued that those employed on work relief in the US should not be counted as unemployed and that the true unemployment rate in the later 1930s was therefore lower than it appears. Removing relief workers from the numbers unemployed improves the performance of the Lucas-Rapping model but still leaves implausibly long adjustment lags. Furthermore, Darby's central premise has been questioned on the grounds that workers regarded relief as a poor substitute for regular employment (Kesselman and Savin, 1978). In chapter 9, Margo brings microeconomic evidence to bear on this issue, finding some evidence that those on work relief had longer incomplete unemployment spells than other persons out of regular work, thus providing qualified support for the Darby view. At the same time, Margo finds that many of the characteristics associated with low re-employment probabilities were shared by both relief workers and the wholly unemployed, a finding difficult to reconcile with Darby's thesis.

In most other countries, work relief was not nearly as prevalent, but the persistence of unemployment was almost as great. In Canada and Australia, for example, national programmes of sustenance payments were considerably less comprehensive than under the New Deal. But in several countries, most prominently Britain and Belgium, a large proportion of the unemployed were supported by doles or unemployment insurance payments. There has long been a suspicion that by subsidising increased search and leisure, this reduced the competition for jobs and therefore mitigated the downward pressure on wages. Interwar observers as disparate as John Maynard Keynes and Jacques Rueff acknowledged this possibility but differed in the weight they attached to it. The appeal of this notion is to those inclined towards the market-clearing approach in that the wedge between the wage employers can afford to pay and the wage workers demand is nothing but a distortion imposed upon the labour market by government. It thus becomes possible to reconcile the premise that the labour market had a strong tendency to adjust with the observation of persistent unemployment. In a well-known article, Benjamin and Kochin argued that in Britain "the army of the unemployed standing watch at the publication of the *General Theory* was largely a volunteer army" (1979, p.474). Such claims rest on the observation of relatively high rates of benefit relative to wages. However, they are difficult to reconcile with the broad facts of differences across time or between countries. For example, Goossens, Peeters and Pepermans show in chapter 8 that unemployment in the 1930s increased much more rapidly in Belgium than in Britain despite cuts in rates of benefit and increasingly stringent qualification requirements.

The strong inferences drawn from highly aggregated data also fly in the face of qualitative evidence, notably graphic personal accounts of widespread involuntary unemployment. Eighteen annual observations of the economy-wide unemployment rate are far removed from the household level where search and labour force participation decisions were made. But as yet, little progress has been made at getting closer to the decision-making level. Eichengreen (1986b), however, has analysed a sample of several thousand London households in the period 1929-31, concluding that unemployment benefits had no impact on the probability of unemployment among household heads but that it may have had a significant impact among secondary workers. While this finding raises questions about the benefit-induced-unemployment explanation, until more disaggregated studies have been done the jury will remain out.

A striking feature of the 1930s illustrated in a number of studies in this volume is the dramatic rise in long-term unemployment. In a recent study of Britain in the 1930s, Crafts (1986) found that the responsiveness of wages to unemployment is more readily identified when long-term unemployment is entered as a separate term. Crafts's estimates suggest that the long-term unemployed exert little downward pressure on wages, thereby helping to explain the stability of wages in the face of persistent unemployment. The question is why the long-term unemployed were unable to bid down the wage and regain employment. One possibility is duration dependence: that the probability of leaving unemployment fell as the duration of the unemployment spell in progress rose. It is often ar-

gued that long-duration unemployment reduced employability by erod-
ing motivation and skills, engendering fatalistic attitudes and leading to
loss of morale. Furthermore, employers may have viewed a history of
long-term unemployment as a signal of undesirable employee characteristics. Yet such factors lend themselves to exaggeration. With the advent
of the Second World War, virtually all unemployment, including long-
term, quickly melted away. Most workers were clearly employable at
some wage even after a protracted period of unemployment.

Recently attention has turned to the structure of wage bargaining between individual firms or employers' associations and trade unions. The
growth of unionism and the increased scope and formalism of collective
bargaining was a feature of many countries in the period from the turn of
the century to the 1920s. In models of union-firm bargaining the union is
endowed with a set of preferences between wages and employment. The
wage-employment outcome depends on these preferences, the firm's demand for labour and the structure of the bargain between the union and
the firm (McDonald and Solow, 1981). If the union places little weight
on unemployment among its members then adverse shifts in labour demand will have little effect on the wage. In the interwar period union
coverage was far from total, and hence potentially there would be competition from non-unionists. However, unionists and other employed workers may have been insulated against such competition. One recent
suggestion is that there is an important distinction to be made between
"insiders" who are in permanent employment and unemployed "outsiders". Those with long-term attachments could exert pressure on the
firm not to hire outsiders and make it costly to do so and as a result they
would not be hired even at slightly lower wages. The atrophy of skills
among the long-term unemployed may serve to reinforce the distinction
between insiders and outsiders (Blanchard and Summers, 1986). In this
interpretation the impact of large negative shocks to labour demand could
dislodge some proportion of insiders causing them to become outsiders.

The data for union density over the 1930s depicted in Table 1.7 shows
that membership typically followed the course of employment, which is
at least consistent with the insider-outsider explanation. Also consistent
is the limited concern union leaders showed for the unemployed.

> Union officials everywhere claimed to be deeply concerned about the
> fate of the jobless and there is no reason to doubt their sincerity. How-
> ever, the fact remains that their first concern was nearly always for
> their own constituents. Since unemployed members tended to drop
> out of unions - because of a conflict of interest between workers and

Table 1.7   Aggregate Union Density: Six Countries (percentages)

	Australia	Canada	Germany	Sweden	UK	US
1924	39.6	8.4	31.8	27.6	30.6	10.7
1925	42.1	8.6	29.0	28.7	30.1	10.4
1926	44.6	8.6	27.6	29.9	28.3	10.2
1927	46.8	8.9	29.6	30.6	26.4	10.1
1928	46.2	8.9	32.5	32.0	25.6	9.6
1929	45.7	9.3	33.9	33.8	25.7	9.3
1930	43.5	9.2	33.7	36.0	25.4	8.9
1931	38.7	8.8	31.5	37.7	24.0	8.6
1932	36.0	8.1	38.1	-	3.0	7.9
1933	34.9	7.9	-	7.9	2.6	7.3
1934	35.3	7.9	-	38.6	23.5	8.9
1935	36.1	7.8	-	40.7	24.9	9.1
1936	37.1	8.8	-	44.1	26.9	9.8
1937	38.5	10.1	-	48.2	29.6	13.6
1938	38.8	10.1	-	51.0	30.5	14.0

Source: Bain and Price (1980).

the unemployed - this meant unions reflected the attitudes of those with jobs. With only a handful of exceptions unions rejected work sharing as a means of coping with unemployment. (Garraty, 1978, p.191)

Contemporary writers stressed the importance of the institutional framework for wage bargaining. Some, such as Cannan, Clay, Hicks and Pigou, argued that in Britain the bargaining position of unions had been strengthened by the adoption of labour legislation, minimum wage provisions and unemployment insurance benefits, enabling them to resist wage cuts in the mid-1920s and leading to abnormally high unemployment.[12] Recent efforts to capture these arguments econometrically have met with some success, although it has proved difficult to isolate the effects of different variables precisely (Broadberry, 1986; Matthews, 1987; Hatton, 1987). Even more telling, when looking across countries it is difficult to identify which institutional structures were most conducive to wage flexibility. The wage-setting system in Australia was viewed with approbation by many observers, who thought it provided a smooth wage adjustment which more decentralised systems could not deliver (Reddaway, 1938). In cross-country comparisons, it has been argued that centralised wage setting leads to greater responsiveness of the real wage to employment by limiting the power of insiders to set the wage without reference to unemployment (Newell and Symons, 1987). Though evidence for five countries in the postwar period seems broadly consistent with this view, it is less obvious that such distinctions can be sustained for the interwar period.

6 The Incidence of Unemployment

One of the leading features of interwar unemployment is its uneven incidence. Unemployment was much higher in some industries and areas than in others in both the 1920s and 1930s. In most countries, recorded unemployment rates were higher for men than for women and for older workers than for the young. But while unemployment has been frequently noted, its structure has received little systematic study. Many of the contributions to this volume accordingly focus on the questions of who was unemployed and why.

The interwar period in Europe is sometimes seen as a period of readjustment arising from the dislocation caused by the First World War, and from the changing balance of production and trade within and between countries in the 1920s (see Svennilson, 1954). This readjustment was supposedly still incomplete in 1929, and exacerbated the Depression and made recovery all the more difficult.[13] Whatever its relation to the ongoing process of structural change, the effects of the Depression certainly varied widely across industries. As already noted, the Depression was most intense in the industrial sectors of developed countries. In France, where between 1929 and 1933 real GDP fell by just 3 per cent, industrial production fell by nearly 20 per cent. In Germany, an 8 per cent fall in GDP was accompanied by a drop of over 30 per cent in industrial production. In Australia, a small decrease in GDP was associated with a decline of nearly 20 per cent in the volume of manufacturing output. In the US, where real GNP fell by an alarming 25 per cent, manufacturing production declined by a still more alarming 40 per cent.

It has been argued that an increased dispersion of unemployment rates reflects structural dislocation across regions or industries which leads to higher equilibrium levels of unemployment. Such theories of "mismatch" unemployment have been advanced to explain trends and cycles in postwar unemployment (Lilien, 1982). The direction of causation is far from clear, however. In the early 1930s, the rising dispersion of unemployment rates reflects the uneven impact of the Depression on different sectors of the advanced economies. It would be necessary to control for the uneven incidence of the macroeconomic shock before arguing that structural

Table 1.8   Standard Deviation of Industrial Unemployment Rates

	Australia	Belgium	Denmark	Netherlands
1929	3.04	3.80	6.00	5.34
1931	7.05	10.13	6.16	20.99
1933	8.08	8.42	11.66	17.27
1935	6.60	5.38	7.94	15.85
1937	4.64	6.77	9.72	12.37
	Norway	Sweden	UK	US
1929	6.25	7.95	6.11	6.31
1931	13.13	11.46	11.71	12.12
1933	16.67	17.33	11.00	13.87
1935	13.24	11.03	7.87	11.53
1937	11.80	9.03	5.78	11.51

Source: Calculated from ILO *Yearbook of Labour Statistics,* 1948.

factors were an independent cause of the rise in aggregate unemployment. In the later 1930s, it is possible that persistent imbalances impeded recovery. One recent study of Britain in the 1930s (Hatton, 1986c) shows that some industrial and regional unemployment rates were more cyclically sensitive than others. Those which rose most in the Depression also fell most in the recovery, reflecting the uneven incidence of the contraction and expansion.

The reallocation across regions of labour and other factors of production was slow and painful. The mythology of the 1930s depicts the unemployed travelling from state to state or region to region in a desperate and largely fruitless search for work. Such mobility, however evocative, was wholly inadequate to equalise unemployment rates in different areas. Rather, it was largely the recovery itself that regenerated employment opportunities in unemployment black spots. Though the industrial dispersion of unemployment rates rose nearly everywhere (see Table 1.8), the differential impact upon regions was much more marked in some countries than others. A classic example of differing regional impacts is the UK, where the Depression widened the gap between the high unemployment North and the low unemployment South. This was associated with different industrial structures and particularly with the concentration of the ailing staple industries in the North, but this does not wholly account for the observed differences in unemployment rates. Regional unemployment differentials remain even after industry mix is controlled for (Hatton, 1986c). In Germany, in contrast, the regional incidence of unemployment was surprisingly even despite the depth of the Depression. In September 1930, when the national unemployment rate had already reached 18.8 per cent, regional rates ranged only from 15 to 22 per cent (James, 1986, p. 113).

The costs of the Depression in North America are often perceived to have been unevenly borne as a result of regional specialisation. The Depression's uneven regional incidence might be thought to be especially pronounced in Canada, where the composition of economic activity varied so greatly between Montreal and Toronto on the one hand and the Prairies on the other. But, as Alan Green and Mary MacKinnon argue in chapter 10, the increase in dispersion of unemployment rates was not as great as might have been expected from the fall in income across provinces. Green and MacKinnon also show that the ratio of rates in high and low unemployment regions was no greater than in 1951 or 1981. Similarly, as Gregory *et al.* show in chapter 11 for Australian Local Government Areas between 1921 and 1933, while the low unemployment areas show a rise of less than 8 percentage points, and high unemployment areas show an increase of nearly 20 percentage points, the ratio rises only from 2.5 to 3. Such results are quite general, indicating that, in most countries, while the absolute gap in unemployment rates widened (as illustrated in Table 1.8), relative rates diverged to a considerably lesser extent.

Another widespread regularity is that unemployment rates were typically lower among women than men. The UK unemployment insurance statistics consistently show the unemployment rate to have been 50 per cent higher for males than females. While some of this differential may reflect the underreporting of unemployment among women, the more comprehensive measure provided by the 1931 census displays the same relationship (14.7 per cent of male workers unemployed and 9.4 per cent of females). The lower unemployment rates of women largely reflect the different occupational structure of women's employment which was weighted towards low unemployment industries and occupations (Beveridge, 1936). Similar patterns can be found in census data for other countries. In Canada, for example, a large proportion of women worked in clerical, sales and service jobs which were typically characterised by a relatively low incidence of unemployment. In these occupations, unemployment rates were roughly the same for men as for women (Green and MacKinnon, this volume). But as a result of their concentration in such occupations, women suffered less job loss than men. However, one group suffered more than the rest, namely married women. In the UK the rate of unemployment among married women reported in the 1931 census was 17.2 per cent, compared with 6.9 per cent for single women.[14]

The same sources indicate that unemployment was disproportionately borne by the relatively old (those over 55) and relatively young (those in the 21- to 25-year-old age group). This is illustrated in the census data for six countries given in Table 1.9. In Australia, where the census was taken well into the Depression, the "U"-shaped age profile of unemployment rates among men is clearest. Among women, in contrast, there is a tendency for unemployment rates to continue to decline with age, perhaps reflecting the withdrawal of older women from the workforce. In both Canada and the UK there is a well-defined "U"-shaped pattern for both sexes in 1931. In the US, the pattern is just perceptible in 1930 but by 1940 the "U"-shaped age distribution is much more pronounced. This suggests that the persistence of high unemployment tended to accentuate differences among age groups. Woytinsky (1942) attributed this pattern to the inclination of firms to lay off their least productive workers, namely the inexperienced and those whose efficiency had begun to decline with age, and also to the tendency for unemployment to be borne disproportionately by recent entrants to the labour market. Since women entered the labour market at a variety of ages, in contrast to men who uniformly entered when young, the "U"-shaped age distribution was less pronounced for females.

In Belgium the pattern for both sexes is relatively flat up to the 35-39 age group but then shows a sharp rise for both sexes up to age 60-64. The picture in France is rather different. Unemployment rates rise with age for both sexes up to age 55-59 but this hides different patterns in urban and rural areas. According to data summarised by Asselin (1966), while Parisian unemployment displayed the familiar "U"-shaped age distribution, elsewhere unemployment rates fell steadily with age rather than rising among workers in their fifties and sixties. It appears that in advanced industrial areas the usual pattern emerges but elsewhere the economy's rural character better enabled young and old to escape unemployment. This adds a further dimension to the distinctions between industrial and non-industrial regions identified by Salais in chapter 7.

A striking difference between unemployment in the 1930s and the 1980s is the very different relationship between the levels of unemployment among youths and adults. While youth unemployment rates currently exceed unemployment rates for adults throughout the OECD, this was not uniformly the case in the interwar years. In part this difference may be a statistical artefact: since unemployed youths qualified for support under relatively few social programmes and hence had little incentive to make their status known to the authorities, youth unemployment tends to be underreported to an even greater extent than unemployment among

Table 1.9   Unemployment Rates by Age: Six Countries

Age group	Australia (1933) M	F	Belgium (1937) M	F	Canada (1931) M	F	UK (1931) M	F	US (1930) M	F	US (1940) M	F	France (1936) M	F
15-19	20.1	17.0	8.1	3.2	21.6	10.7	9.0	7.2	8.1	6.2	22.6	21.6	5.0	4.3
20-24	25.5	15.2	12.0	3.2	22.6	8.5	15.2	12.0	8.8	4.7	17.8	12.5	4.8	4.2
25-29	21.2	11.7	11.5	2.8	20.7	7.6	13.6	10.4	6.9	4.4	13.1	8.7	4.9	3.5
30-34	17.4	10.5	12.2	2.7			12.6	10.9	6.1	4.3	11.5	8.2	4.7	3.1
35-39	16.3	10.4	12.6	3.2	18.4	7.9	13.0	10.5	6.2	4.4	11.4	9.6	4.8	3.1
40-44	15.8	9.0	13.8	4.5					6.5	4.3			5.0	3.2
45-49	16.8	8.8	16.6	5.9	20.8	8.7	15.9	11.1	6.9	4.3	12.9	10.9	5.1	3.3
50-54	17.8	8.0	21.2	8.5					7.0	4.2			5.7	3.4
55-59	18.7	7.0	29.6	12.8	23.2	9.2	20.1	12.2	7.3	4.2	15.0	12.1	6.4	3.5
60-64	20.8	3.0	40.1	16.1			25.9	13.8	7.3	3.9	15.2	11.7	4.4	2.3
65-69	9.5	1.2	12.1	2.4	27.3	9.7	32.0	11.7	6.5	3.2	10.0	7.0	3.0	1.6
70+	3.1	-			26.2	6.5	25.5	8.6						

Note: For the UK, England and Wales only; for the lowest age group Canada, 14-19, UK 14-20, US (1930) 10-19, US (1940) 14-19; for the next oldest group Britain 21-24; figures for the US (1940) exclude new workers but include unpaid family workers.

Sources: Australia, Canada, Britain: Census Reports; Belgium: Belgium from Goossens, Peeters and Pepermans (this volume), US (1930) from Woytinsky (1942), p. 154; France from Salais (this volume). US (1940), census 5% sample.

adults.[15] Since these programmes were less advanced between the wars, the incentive for youths to register as unemployed may have been even less and the extent of underreporting even greater. Though census reports went some way to eliminating this problem, in some countries such as Canada those who had left school but had never found work were not classified as wage earners at the census. The figures in Table 1.9 suggest that unemployment rates were generally lower for males in the 15- to 19-year-old age group but not for females.

Perhaps most striking in this respect is Britain, where recorded unemployment for juveniles was exceptionally low. Eichengreen (1987) has attempted to decompose the rise in British juvenile unemployment between the 1930s and 1980s. One can dismiss out of hand a number of potentially attractive hypotheses (changes in macroeconomic conditions, demographic effects and changes in the propensity to leave school). The important effects turn out to be a recording effect (confirming that juvenile unemployment was systematically underenumerated), a relatively small shift in the composition of activity from sectors employing a large share of juveniles in their workforces to sectors where the juvenile share is small, and a large, economy-wide shift in the share of juveniles in total employment. The reason for this shift in the age composition of employment does not appear to be any pronounced change in the relative wages of juveniles and adults or in their relative unemployment benefits. Rather, the reason seems to be that youth unemployment has grown increasingly sensitive to macroeconomic fluctuations. Whereas in the 1970s and 1980s youth unemployment has been highly sensitive to business cycle conditions, in the 1920s and 1930s youth unemployment did not exhibit this cyclical sensitivity. Since 1960 the elasticity of youth unemployment with respect to adult unemployment has been considerably in excess of unity; comparable elasticities for the interwar period are unity or even less. The difference points to the possibility that youths experienced exceptionally short unemployment spells and that labour market conventions, such as inverse seniority lay-off rules, played a very different role during the interwar years.

Census and unemployment insurance data indicate that the burden of unemployment was shared unequally in other respects as well. The bulk of unemployment fell on unskilled manual workers. In Canada, for instance, the unskilled accounted in 1930-31 for 56 per cent of male wage and salary earners who lost jobs, 39 per cent of those who were laid off and 51 per cent of total weeks lost (Marsh, 1940, pp. 328, 355). As Green and MacKinnon show in chapter 10, recent immigrants tended to suffer more unemployment than the native-born, a differential particularly marked among those from non-English-speaking backgrounds. For the US, Woytinsky (1942) found that for males the incidence of unemployment was lower among household heads and individuals living alone than for related family members. Unemployment among women differed in that rates were higher among family heads and those living alone, and higher among the married, widowed and divorced than among the single, in these respects resembling female unemployment in Britain.

Unemployment was typically related to a range of variables reflecting individual characteristics, labour market conditions, demographic factors and household status. Among adult males it fell on individuals with low wages and few sources of income beyond their own wages and unemployment benefits, who rented their homes and who had large families. Although interwar analyses presented these regularities as simple tabulations, recent work done by one of the present authors (Eichengreen, 1986c) confirms that they also emerge from multivariate analysis of the correlates of unemployment. In a complementary study of the US, Margo shows in chapter 9 that in 1940 the risk of unemployment was negatively related to years of schooling and positively related to wealth, but essentially unrelated to nativity once other factors are controlled for. However, all three variables as well as marital status affected the probability of obtaining a relief job for individuals not in regular employment. Such findings point to an important conclusion and one which is familiar from the 1980s: that the burden of unemployment fell most heavily on those who were least able to support it.

7 Labour Turnover and Unemployment Duration

Another perspective on the problem is provided by the dynamics of flows into and out of unemployment. While some writers focused on these aspects during the interwar period itself, until recently this has remained a neglected topic.[16] The overall level of unemployment can be decomposed into rates of flow into and out of the unemployed pool and the average duration of spells on the register. As a matter of accounting, unemployment can increase through a rise in the rate at which workers enter and leave the register, or through an increase in average duration of an unemployment spell at constant rates of flow. Thus a given rate of unemployment may be characterised by high turnover and low duration or by precisely the opposite. Such differences may also characterise the experience of different groups of workers at a single point in time.

Attention has been drawn recently to high rates of employment turnover in US manufacturing during the interwar years (Baily, 1983). The

Table 1.10 Labour Turnover in the US and UK

	Employment turnover in the US (average monthly rates)			Annual flows in the UK		
				Vacancies		Labour
				notified	filled	force
	Accessions	Lay-offs	Quits	(millions)	(millions)	turnover
1924	3.3	0.6	2.7	1.37	1.16	-
1925	5.2	0.4	3.1	1.51	1.31	-
1926	4.5	0.5	2.9	1.32	1.16	-
1927	3.3	0.7	2.1	1.46	1.27	-
1928	3.7	0.5	2.2	1.54	1.35	-
1929	5.1	0.4	3.0	1.86	1.63	-
1930	3.8	3.6	1.9	1.97	1.76	-
1931	3.7	3.5	1.1	2.16	1.99	-
1932	4.1	4.2	0.9	2.04	1.88	0.54
1933	6.5	3.2	1.1	2.46	2.22	0.59
1934	5.7	3.7	1.1	2.66	2.33	0.57
1935	5.1	3.0	1.1	2.93	2.53	0.61
1936	5.3	2.4	1.3	3.13	2.65	0.52
1937	4.3	3.5	1.5	3.17	2.65	0.52
1938	4.7	3.9	0.8	3.19	2.74	0.54

Sources: US: Baily (1983), p. 29; UK: *22nd Abstract of Labour Statistics* (and authors' calculations).

first part of Table 1.10 shows that monthly accessions to employment averaged nearly 5 per cent in the 1930s. The Depression of the 1930s does not seem to have been accompanied by a dramatic fall in the rate of flow. Rather, it was characterised by a rise in lay-offs and a fall in voluntary leaving (quits). While quits were the dominant form of separation in the 1920s, in the 1930s lay-offs dominated instead. Although comparable data are not available for other countries, for the UK there is information on vacancies notified to and filled by labour exchanges. The second part of Table 1.10 shows that these grew at a more or less constant rate over the 1920s and 1930s, reinforcing the point that the Depression was not characterised by a decline in the rate of flow into employment. Turnover rates for the insured labour force in 1932-38 indicate that annual flows into employment amount to a strikingly high 50-60 per cent of the labour force. This monthly flow of 4-5 per cent is remarkably similar to employment turnover in the US. Thus, all the evidence points to the conclusion that labour turnover in the interwar years was significantly higher than after the Second World War.[17]

It could be argued that high turnover rates render the search characterisation of the labour market appropriate for the 1920s if not the 1930s. But one recent study estimating a search turnover model of the relationship between unemployment and vacancies for the UK in the 1920s found no support for the model. Shifts in the relationship between unemployment and vacancies do not appear to have responded to wage surprises or the benefit-to-wage ratio. There was a very high ratio of unemployment to vacancies (about 8.5 to 1), even before the 1930s, and no evidence of an inverse UV curve (Hatton, 1985). Instead, there was a strong contemporaneous relationship between the weekly flow of notifications and weekly vacancies filled, which is more consistent with a queuing model than with search theory. It is consistent also with the view of contemporaries such as E. Wight Bakke that

> the behaviour of the unemployed in searching for employment gives no evidence that the possibility of drawing unemployment insurance benefits has retarded the efforts of the unemployed to get back to work. It has removed the cutting edge of the desperation which would otherwise attend that search. (1933, p. 143)

A large proportion of the unemployed remained attached to particular firms or industries in the early 1930s. This proportion declined as the decade wore on, however. In the UK, some 20 per cent of the unemployed were classified as "temporarily.stopped" (laid off with a definite promise of return to work within six weeks). Even among those classified as wholly unemployed, it is estimated that in 1937 some 30 per cent of engagements were returns to the last employer.[18] Similarly in Belgium the number of "partially unemployed" workers exceeded those classified as unemployed in 1930 and 1931, but declined subsequently as a proportion of the total as the Depression took on a more permanent nature. In these two countries, if not elsewhere, the workings of the unemployment insurance system appears to have encouraged temporary lay-offs and continuing attachments of workers to firms. In other countries, there is also evidence that, at least in the early stages of the Depression, a large proportion of unemployed workers retained an attachment to firms. In Germany, for example, nearly as many workers were working short-time as there were wholly unemployed in 1930. In the US, there appears to have been a large proportion on temporary lay-off in 1930. But over the course of the decade, there was a reversal in the proportions temporarily and permanently laid off. By 1940 there were 578,000 male wage and salary earners described as having a job but not at work compared with 3.2 million experienced workers seeking work.

Table 1.11   Distribution of the Unemployed by Duration of Idleness in Philadelphia, 1931-38

Item	1931	1932	1933	1935	1936	1937	1938
I Male							
Enumerated employable							
persons	48,641	48,526	48,320	55,775	54,989	55,848	54,005
Unemployed:							
absolute number	12,839	20,681	22,539	18,332	15,915	13,018	16,834
in per cent	26.4	42.6	46.6	32.9	28.9	23.3	31.2
Duration of idleness			Percentage distribution				
(all duration classes)	100.0	100.0	100.0	100.0	100.0	100.0	100.0
Under 2 months	22.1	15.7	9.7	5.8	13.1	18.7	17.5
3 to 5 months	26.9	16.2	8.4	10.0	10.1	9.6	14.4
6 to 8 months	15.9	10.5	7.9	7.4	7.0	5.8	12.5
9 to 11 months	13.8	18.1	14.4	7.6	7.0	4.2	7.2
Total, under 1 year	78.7	60.5	40.4	30.8	37.2	38.3	51.6
1 but less than 2 years	15.5	28.7	34.0	18.3	16.3	13.7	14.1
2 but less than 3 years	3.0	7.5	17.7	16.0	12.1	10.3	8.6
3 but less than 4 years	1.3	1.8	5.0	14.1	10.6	8.3	6.5
4 but less than 5 years	0.6	0.7	1.7	10.5	9.1	7.8	4.4
5 years and over	0.9	0.8	1.2	10.3	14.7	21.6	14.8

Most disturbing was the extent of long-term unemployment. In the 1930s a key characteristic of unemployment was the rise both in average spell duration and in the proportion of long-term unemployed. For the UK, where in September 1929 78.5 per cent of applicants for benefit or assistance had been out of work for less than three months and only 4.7 per cent for more than a year, by 1936 only 55 per cent had been unemployed for less than three months and fully 25 per cent for more than a year. In Australia long-term unemployment was exceptionally severe. The 1933 census indicated that over 70 per cent of the unemployed had been without work for over a year and 45 per cent for over three years. In the US, where the 1930 census distinguished two categories of unemployed persons - those able to work and looking for jobs and those on temporary lay-off the day preceding the enumerator's visit - more than a third of males and a quarter of females in the first category had been out of work for at least fourteen weeks. Assuming the length of a completed spell to be double the length of a spell in progress, a spell of unemployment lasted at least seven months for members of this sizeable group.[19]

Table 1.11 (continued)

Item	1931	1932	1933	1935	1936	1937	1938
II Female							
Enumerated employable							
persons	16,944	17,953	17,896	22,749	24,833	23,758	21,397
Unemployed:							
absolute number	4,019	7,322	7,904	7,578	8,152	6,439	7,696
in per cent	·23.7	40.8	44.2	33.3	32.8	27.1	36.0
Duration of idleness			Percentage distribution				
(all duration classes)	100.0	100.0	100.0	100.0	100.0	100.0	100.0
Under 2 months	33.0	27.1	17.8	8.2	17.0	27.2	23.2
3 to 5 months	26.8	20.4	12.2	15.1	12.0	12.9	14.2
6 to 8 months	11.5	8.9	11.0	8.1	6.6	6.1	11.8
9 to 11 months	12.3	18.1	17.2	12.3	9.2	5.0	6.9
Total, under 1 year	83.6	74.5	58.2	43.7	44.8	51.2	56.1
1 but less than 2 years	12.4	18.8	26.2	21.5	17.1	13.9	15.3
2 but less than 3 years	2.2	4.5	10.7	15.2	10.8	8.8	9.1
3 but less than 4 years	0.9	1.3	2.9	8.4	7.7	6.5	5.3
4 but less than 5 years	0.3	0.5	1.1	5.4	5.8	5.4	3.9
5 years and over	0.6	0.4	0.9	5.8	13.8	14.2	10.3

Note: Data are for April-May of each year, except 1938 when the survey was made in July-August.
Source: Woytinsky (1942), p. 100.

Table 1.11, drawn by Woytinsky from a survey of Philadelphia, shows the increasing incidence of long-term unemployment as the 1930s progressed. In Philadelphia, the share of unemployed men who had been out of work for less than a year fell from nearly 80 to less than 40 per cent between 1931 and 1937 (from 84 to 44 per cent for women), before rising in the 1938 recession. The proportion of those reporting no work for at least five years rose dramatically from negligible levels to 22 per cent for men and 14 per cent for women. The distribution of unemployment spells by duration displays a bimodal pattern, with a heavy incidence of very short and very long durations. In Philadelphia if not every other city for which data are available, the labour market appears to have been bifurcated into a segment inhabited by workers with rapid turnover and high re-employment probabilities and another comprised of a hard core with little chance of re-employment.

Table 1.12   Percentage of Unemployed by Duration: Four Countries

	Australia 1939 Male	Belgium 1937 Male	Belgium 1937 Female	UK 1938 Male	UK 1938 Female	US 1940 Male	US 1940 Female
0 to 1 month	11.4	6.5	9.3			3.3	4.4
1 to 3 months	23.4	14.6	17.6	{ 45.7	60.0 }	16.5	18.6
3 to 6 months	20.8	17.7	14.0	16.6	22.2	25.0	24.2
6 months to 1 year	18.9	10.7	15.5	12.0	8.6	21.4	21.1
1 year to 2 years	11.9			8.5	4.2	15.1	16.8
2 years to 3 years	3.6	{50.4	43.5}	6.3	2.1	7.5	7.0
3 years and above	9.8			10.9	2.8	11.0	8.0

Sources: Australia: National Register, 1939; Belgium: Goossens, Peeters and Pepermans (chapter 8, this volume); UK: Ministry of Labour *Gazette* 1938 (Great Britain only); US: 1940 census, Labor Force 5% Sample.

After losing their attachment to an employer a growing proportion of workers found themselves almost permanently without work and unable to regain it. In Australia, as Gregory *et al.* show in chapter 11, this could lead to extremely long unemployment spells. In 1933, more males had been unemployed for three to four years than for two to three years, and more had been idle for two to three years than for one to two years. Similar patterns can be observed in urban unemployment in the US. This distribution reflects the volume of separations in the early 1930s and contrasts with the normal pattern observed in interwar and postwar unemployment registers of declining numbers of persons unemployed as duration increases. As Table 1.12 shows, by the late 1930s the normal pattern had reasserted itself. Still there remained a large proportion of long-term unemployed (individuals unemployed for more than a year). Among males, long-term unemployment as a percentage of the unemployed was 25 per cent in Australia (1939), 50 per cent in Belgium (1937), 26 per cent in the UK (1938) and 34 per cent in the US (1940).

The number of unemployed persons in different duration categories can be used to calculate the rates at which the unemployed left the register. In his analysis of British unemployment statistics, Thomas (chapter 3) finds that re-employment probabilities declined very steeply with duration. Twenty per cent of unemployed persons with durations of less than three months subsequently appeared in the three- to six-months category. By contrast, 80 per cent of those unemployed for nine to twelve months were still unemployed after a year, confirming that the probability of regaining employment fell very sharply with duration. It appears that by the mid-1930s those with very long durations had a negligible chance of regaining employment. It remains difficult to say whether the phenomenon reflects duration dependence - as workers suffering from a lengthening spell grew detached from labour market contacts and their skills and motivations atrophied - or whether it simply reflects the sorting of the least employable workers into long-duration categories as their more employable counterparts more readily found work.

It is critically important to acknowledge differences in the experience of different labour market groups with regard to turnover and unemployment spell duration. Younger workers appear to have experienced relatively high rates of turnover but to have endured lower unemployment spell durations. In contrast, older workers, particularly those over 50, typically suffered longer durations, largely accounting for their high unemployment rates. As Beveridge put it,

> Prolonged unemployment falls with crushing weight on the older men, once they have lost their niche in industry. The risk of losing one's job is much the same from 60-64 as it is from 35-44. The risk of being out of a job is half as much again at the later age than at the earlier age; the risk of becoming chronically unemployed, that is to say of being out for more than a year, is two and a half times as great. (1944, p.70)

Broomfield's (1978, p.28) analysis of South Australia reveals that the share of unemployed males re-entering permanent employment in less than a year was much higher for those under 35 years of age than for older men. In their study of displaced workers in Hartford and New Haven, Connecticut, Clague, Couper and Bakke (1934) found that young workers were most successful in obtaining employment in two months or less, while skilled workers were most successful in obtaining a lasting situation.

The effects of differing re-employment probabilities among different groups are most clearly seen in the proportions of long-term unemployed. Of those recorded as seeking work in the US in 1940, 26.1 per cent of males aged 20 to 24 had been unemployed for at least a year, compared to 49 per cent for those aged 55 to 59. For females the respective figures were 28 and 44 per cent. Despite their lower unemployment rates, females who continued to seek work suffered spells of unemployment nearly as long as those of males. This contrasts somewhat with the situation in the UK, where the proportion of long-term unemployed was significantly lower for females than males. The difference may be due to the impact of other personal characteristics and economic circumstances on the risk of long-term unemployment. In chapter 9, Margo finds for the US that, in addition to age, industry, occupation and urban versus rural residence were important determinants of the incidence of long-term unemployment. For the UK the importance of region is clear: long-term unemployment increases dramatically as one moves from low to high unemployment regions. Thus in London in 1937, 7.7 per cent of wholly unemployed workers had been unemployed for over a year while in Wales and the Northern region the figure was close to 40 per cent.

To summarise, evidence from a number of countries points to a characterisation of the labour market in the 1930s as bifurcated into two segments, one inhabited by workers with rapid turnover and high re-employment probabilities, the other comprised of a hard core of long-term unemployed. It is tempting to interpret this division in "insider-outsider" terms: once an outsider, it was extremely difficult for an individual to regain permanent employment, particularly if he or she was a member of the upper age groups. The concentration of unemployment in certain regions and industries may have served to exacerbate this segmentation because of the tendency of long-term unemployment to be most serious where the overall level of unemployment was highest. It also suggests the economic returns to migration were limited, since being an outsider in an unfamiliar locality may have been even less desirable than staying put.

8 The Effects of Unemployment

It is for the effects of unemployment on millions of workers and their families that the 1930s are chiefly remembered. Poverty and privation leading to fatalism, hopelessness and social divisiveness are prominent parts of the story. But the effects were often more pervasive and more subtle than the apocalyptic stories of extreme deprivation allow. High unemployment, by interrupting income streams, disrupting rhythms of daily activity and altering relations within the family and community, affected every aspect of social and economic life. In this section we briefly outline some of these effects and assess their impact.

As we have noted, social investigators became concerned with poverty during the nineteenth century, and this continued with renewed concern as unemployment increased in the 1930s. Nowhere was this more marked than in Britain. Following Seebohm Rowntree, interwar social investigators attempted to implement the concept of a poverty line to measure how many families fell below it. The findings of these surveys are discussed in more detail by Bernard Harris in chapter 4. Overall they indicated that unemployment was the major cause of poverty, in contrast to before the First World War when low wages or intermittent employment were typically regarded as the main causes. Repeating his prewar survey of York, Rowntree (1941) found in 1936 that 73 per cent of unemployed workers lived below the poverty line. The longer the duration of unemployment the more likely the family was to fall below it. Surveys of Merseyside, Southampton, Bristol, London and York, while varying in the share of households in poverty, agreed that about a third of families with insufficient income for their basic needs were in that state due to unemployment.

Several points need to be borne in mind when considering the results of these inquiries. First, the extent of poverty was clearly far lower than thirty years earlier, if comparable standards are applied, even though unemployment was higher in the 1930s than it had been pre-First World War. Second, as Harris argues (chapter 4), many of the poverty lines used represented a spartan dietary standard and left little room for non-food items of expenditure. If different poverty lines had been chosen then the degree to which poverty was attributable to unemployment may also have changed. Third, poverty fell disproportionately on certain groups, particularly children in large families and in families with low wages when breadwinners were in employment and long durations when out of work.

In countries where public assistance or unemployment insurance programmes operated these played an important role in alleviating poverty and destitution. Surveys by the Pilgrim Trust and the UK Ministry of Labour found that family incomes fell with unemployment by 45 to 66 per cent. This suggests that unemployment benefits, which were 30 to 40 per cent of average wages over the period, accounted for the vast majority of income for the unemployed. Similar replacement rates apply to Germany in the period up to 1933 and to Belgium where income loss averaged more than 50 per cent for those becoming unemployed. The operation of insurance schemes posed difficult dilemmas for countries which operated them during the 1930s. One problem was that for low wage workers the insurance benefits often approached or exceeded the level of wages when in work even though with full benefit the family might still be in severe poverty. One survey of Wales in the late 1930s indicated that a third of single men and nearly half of married men received more in unemployment benefits than in their previous job. Another problem was that benefits were often more generous for the short-term unemployed than the long-term unemployed who had exhausted their entitlement. Hence while benefits may have blunted incentives for the short-term unemployed they often failed to provide adequate income maintenance for the chronically unemployed. In Britain and Belgium where household means tests were introduced in the early 1930s the long-term unemployed faced further reductions in income as well as the humiliation of official scrutiny.

In countries where insurance or relief systems were not so well developed, the effects of unemployment were much worse. In Canada and Australia income loss on unemployment was significantly larger than in Britain (Green and MacKinnon, chapter 10, this volume). In the case of Australia, large numbers of families were pressed close to the margins of subsistence. As Gregory *et al.* (chapter 11) show, in Australia in 1933 a third of male breadwinners reported incomes of less than one-third of the basic wage (which was itself set as a minimum living wage), and one-eighth reported no income at all for the whole year. In Australia as elsewhere, where relief was given it involved a means test. To qualify for relief an unemployed person was given a form to be signed by a Justice of the Peace declaring that he was destitute, was visited by his local policeman who would report on his economic circumstances to the relief office, and was required to dispose of all bank savings and saleable assets.

Meagre relief payments or work relief were often allocated in accordance with household needs though in some cases other criteria were applied. In Canada, farmers were often given greater support in order to maintain the viability of the farm, and in the US, work relief depended on the capacity to perform manual labour as well as on need. Where relief payments were related to household means this often meant that if one family member was working even at low wages the whole family would be denied benefit. Furthermore in most countries the relief-giving authorities typically favoured whole families; single men and especially women without dependants were typically given low priority for relief. Within the family the burden was often shared unequally with priority frequently given to maintaining children and the male breadwinner while other family members, especially wives and mothers, went without an adequate diet.

The sharp decline in family income naturally led to changing expenditure patterns as the least essential items were given up. In New Haven, Bakke (1940, p.264) found it was most common to economise on clothes, recreation and food, least common to sacrifice home equity and children's schooling. Within the food budget there was often substitution of cheaper foods. In the small town of Marienthal in Austria where the only major source of employment, the flax mill, had closed, investigators found that between 1928 and 1930, while butter consumption fell by over 60 per cent, margarine consumption doubled, and while coffee consumption fell by over a third that of cocoa rose by 40 per cent (Jahoda, Lazarsfeld and Zeisel,1972, p.31). In many cases meat virtually disappeared from the diet. In Marienthal it was typically eaten only once a week, on Sundays.

Households were sometimes able to supplement relief hand-outs in various ways depending on individual ingenuity and local resources. Where garden space or allotments were available, groceries were often supplemented with the produce from vegetable gardens and from keeping chickens or rabbits. In rural areas there was greater opportunity for obtaining agricultural products and game either through charity, barter or stealth but it was often difficult to obtain other necessities. Among the supplies most frequently bartered or stolen was fuel, either wood or coal.

In some cases subsistence production was adopted on a larger scale, either collectively or individually. The branch of the Subsistence Production Society established in the eastern valley of Monmouthshire set up an elaborate scheme for the production and distribution of meat, vegetables and dairy products, and established a bakery, butchery and brickmaking works as well as boot repairing and tailoring services (Jahoda, 1987). Though these goods and services were obtained at less than half the shop price, fewer than 10 per cent of the unemployed in the area were members. In some countries there were greater opportunities for self-employment such as subsistence farming. In South Australia an unemployed man with savings might buy cows with the intention of retailing milk to his neighbours. In urban Connecticut the venturesome might make a go of small-scale cleaning and repairing businesses. Such enterprises were reflected in Canada by the rise in the proportion of the labour force reported in the census as self-employed. Such activities were often unsuccessful and were the exception rather than the rule. In general, unemployment meant a restriction of expenditures and a narrowing of the scope of activity rather than the expansion of alternative income sources.

One avenue for escaping from limited prospects in Europe, that of emigration, narrowed during the interwar years. Intercontinental migration from Europe was much less in the early 1920s than in the prewar decade due to the 1920-21 depression and then to the legal restriction of immigration into the US, but it revived in the later 1920s. The 1920s also saw internal migration in Europe gaining in importance and clearly reflecting economic conditions, particularly the flows from Italy and Poland to France and the Low Countries. In the 1930s, previous trends were largely reversed. For the first time Europe as a whole experienced a net inward movement: not only did returning migrants increase in number but the outstanding change was the fall in new emigration. Those who did emigrate were increasingly re-uniting with their families. Within Europe return flows also took place, particularly from France, though this only amounted to a small proportion of the previous inward movement. In general restricted economic prospects and increasingly national restrictions on entry and exit reduced the volume of migration. As one observer put it, "the thirties was a decade of sitting tight" (Kirk, 1946, p. 109).

Unemployment and the social programmes developed in response affected patterns of migration within each country. In the US it was estimated that there were some 1.25 million "transients", mainly younger men scouring the cities and countryside for jobs or relief, drifting principally to the West where new arrivals in Los Angeles numbered over a thousand a day (Chandler, 1970, p. 46). The drift away from farms was halted as reverse migration took place. In most countries, however, internal migration slowed down. This was particularly the case where the forms of relief involved a residency requirement. In Canada municipalities were reluctant to provide relief to migrants from rural areas; hence 95 per cent of those registering as unemployed in Toronto had lived there for more than a year (Cassidy, 1933, p.39). In France strict residency requirements were imposed. Where relief was financed locally such as in the US, municipalities often faced insolvency and in a number of countries governments attempted to restrict the drift to cities.

These responses had conflicting effects on household structure. On the one hand unemployment might re-unite families by forcing formerly independent youths or older family members to stay with their relatives, on the other hand it might pull families apart. In the US rates of occupancy of housing fell in the major cities as families doubled up or took in lodgers. Studies of Australia commented on the exceptional number of wives and husbands living separately and explained this by the tendency of married men in urban areas to go to the country in search of work.

A widespread effect of the Depression was a reduction in the rate of family formation. Marriage rates and birth rates per thousand population are given for the eight countries examined in this volume in Table 1.13. Comparisons between countries and across time are influenced by the underlying age and sex distribution of the populations but the short-run variations are clear enough. The reduction in marriages in the early 1930s can be discerned in most countries but is perhaps least evident in the UK. Similarly, there is a distinct rise in the recovery phase though not in Belgium and France where the recovery was delayed. The same pattern can be discerned in birth rates though this should be seen relative to the long-term downward trend which had been evident since the late nineteenth century. Viewed in this light, there is a distinct upturn in birth rates in the later 1930s, excepting once again Belgium and France. While these vari-

Table 1.13   Marriage Rates and Birth Rates for Eight Countries

	Australia	Belgium	Canada	France	Germany	Italy	UK	US
Marriages (per 1,000 population)								
1925	7.9	19.1	6.9	17.4	15.5	15.2	15.2	10.3
1926	7.9	18.4	7.0	16.9	15.4	15.0	14.3	10.2
1927	8.0	18.1	7.2	16.4	17.0	15.2	15.7	10.1
1928	7.7	17.9	7.5	16.5	18.5	14.2	15.4	9.8
1929	7.5	17.8	7.7	16.2	18.4	14.2	15.8	10.1
1930	6.7	17.7	7.0	16.4	17.5	14.8	15.8	9.2
1931	6.0	16.2	6.4	15.6	16.0	13.4	15.6	8.6
1932	6.6	15.1	5.9	15.1	15.7	12.8	15.3	7.9
1933	7.0	15.8	6.0	15.1	19.3	13.8	15.8	8.7
1934	7.7	15.2	6.8	14.2	22.3	14.8	16.9	10.3
1935	8.4	15.2	7.1	13.2	19.5	13.4	17.2	10.4
1936	8.7	15.5	7.4	13.4	18.1	14.8	17.4	10.7
1937	8.7	15.2	7.9	13.1	18.3	17.8	17.5	11.3
1938	9.0	14.7	7.9	13.1	18.8	15.0	17.6	10.3
Births (per 1,000 population)								
1925	22.9	19.6	26.1	19.0	20.8	28.4	18.3	24.1
1926	22.0	18.9	24.7	18.8	19.6	27.7	17.8	23.1
1927	21.7	18.2	24.3	18.2	18.4	27.5	16.6	22.7
1928	21.3	18.2	24.1	18.3	18.6	26.7	16.7	21.5
1929	20.3	18.1	23.5	17.7	18.0	25.6	16.3	20.5
1930	19.9	18.6	23.9	18.0	17.6	26.7	16.3	20.6
1931	18.2	18.1	23.2	17.5	16.0	24.9	15.8	19.5
1932	16.9	17.5	22.5	17.3	15.0	23.8	15.3	18.7
1933	16.8	16.3	21.0	16.2	14.7	23.8	14.4	17.6
1934	16.4	15.9	20.7	16.2	18.0	23.5	14.8	18.1
1935	16.6	15.2	20.5	15.3	18.9	23.4	14.7	17.9
1936	17.1	15.1	20.3	15.0	19.0	22.4	14.8	17.6
1937	17.4	15.0	20.1	14.7	18.8	22.9	14.9	17.9
1938	17.5	15.5	20.7	14.6	19.7	23.8	15.1	18.4

Note: US data are on births for the white population only.
Sources: European countries: Mitchell (1975). Australia, Canada, US: Mitchell (1983).

ations could hardly be described as dramatic, they provide some indication of the restricted scope for family formation faced by the unemployed.

Though the Depression is sometimes seen as resulting in severe deterioration in health and physical well-being, this is not reflected in a dramatic increase in crude death rates. These rates, which are shown for the

Table 1.14   Crude Death Rates and Infant Mortality Rates

	Australia	Belgium	Canada	France	Germany	Italy	UK	US
Death rate (per 1,000 population)								
1925	9.2	12.8	10.7	17.4	11.9	17.9	12.1	11.1
1926	9.4	12.8	11.4	17.4	11.7	17.2	11.6	11.6
1927	9.5	13.0	11.0	16.5	12.0	16.2	12.3	10.8
1928	9.5	12.8	11.2	16.4	11.6	16.1	11.7	11.4
1929	9.6	14.4	11.4	17.9	12.6	16.5	13.4	11.3
1930	8.6	12.8	10.8	15.6	11.0	14.1	11.4	10.8
1931	8.7	12.7	10.2	16.2	11.2	14.8	12.3	10.6
1932	8.6	12.7	10.0	15.8	10.8	14.7	12.0	10.5
1933	8.9	12.7	9.7	15.8	11.2	13.7	12.3	10.3
1934	9.3	11.7	9.5	15.1	10.9	13.3	11.8	10.6
1935	9.5	12.3	9.9	15.7	11.8	14.0	11.7	10.6
1936	9.4	12.2	9.9	15.3	11.8	13.8	12.1	11.1
1937	9.4	12.5	10.4	15.0	11.7	14.3	12.4	10.8
1938	9.6	12.5	9.7	15.4	11.7	14.1	11.6	10.3
Infant mortality (per 1,000 live births)								
1925	53	100	93	85	105	119	75	68
1926	54	104	102	86	102	127	70	70
1927	55	98	95	97	97	120	70	61
1928	53	94	90	84	89	120	65	64
1929	51	110	93	98	97	125	74	63
1930	47	100	91	75	85	106	60	60
1931	42	89	86	75	83	113	66	57
1932	41	94	75	71	79	110	64	53
1933	39	92	74	76	77	100	63	54
1934	44	82	73	73	66	99	59	52
1935	40	85	72	67	99	101	57	52
1936	41	86	68	66	66	100	59	53
1937	38	83	77	69	64	109	58	50
1938	38	81	64	68	60	106	53	47

Note: US data are on births for the white population only.
Sources: European countries: Mitchell (1975). Australia, Canada, US: Mitchell (1983).

same eight countries in Table 1.14, appear if anything to have been slightly below trend in the early to mid-1930s. Clearly there is no simple relationship between premature death and unemployment. In the US, there was a continuing decline in most causes of death but particularly in infectious disease and diseases of the genito-urinary and digestive systems.

The number of suicides rose briefly in 1931-32 but this was offset by a decline in deaths from other violent and accidental causes.

Though the effects do not show up in aggregate death rates it is widely believed that the 1930s saw a general deterioration in health. As one visitor to the US put it in 1934, "people do not starve to death, they just starve."[20] The nature and extent of these effects is still much debated, and the UK context of this discussion is outlined by Harris in chapter 4. Most health statistics are affected by subjective perceptions and by institutional factors, but the British statistics on sickness and disablement claims recently examined by Whiteside (1987) indicate a sharp increase in the 1920s followed by a levelling out in the 1930s. Maternal mortality and infant mortality rates are often thought to be sensitive indicators of community health status. Though these differ widely between prosperous and disadvantaged regions the effects of unemployment on fluctuations over time are hard to distinguish. Infant mortality rates per thousand live births are shown in the lower panel of Table 1.14. In some countries infant mortality in the early 1930s appears to be slightly above trend and in others below trend. An alternative measure examined by Harris in chapter 4 is the heights of children. His results indicate that unemployment had slight retarding effects on growth in some areas but not in others. It appears that to the extent that there were significant health effects they are hidden in the aggregate. A deterioration in the health of the unemployed may have been offset by improvements in the health status of the employed. In addition any underlying deterioration in standards of health may have been offset by improved standards of treatment and care.

Perhaps more marked than the physical deterioration of the unemployed was the decline in morale particularly among the long-term unemployed. There has been growing interest in the psychological effects of unemployment, and serious study of the issue began in the interwar period. Eisenberg and Lazarsfeld (1938) surveyed the findings of over a hundred studies of the effects on personality traits and sociopolitical attitudes from a range of countries. These provided widespread evidence of loss of morale and deterioration in mental attitudes but found that this was manifested in widely differing ways depending on the personality of the individual. One of the most notable studies was that of Marienthal. Here the researchers identified several different psychological states and classified the unemployed accordingly. They found that 16 per cent could be described as "unbroken", 48 per cent as "resigned", 11 per cent as "in despair" and 25 per cent as "apathetic". The most common response, resignation, was characterised as an attitude of drifting along, indifferently and without expectations, accepting a situation that cannot be changed. With it goes a relatively calm general mood, and even, sporadically, moments of serenity and joy. But the future, even in the shape of plans, has no longer any place in the thought or even the dreams of these families. (Jahoda *et al.*, 1972, pp. 52-3)

Those in despair and the apathetic exhibited a complete breakdown either in family life or in personal rationality.

Contemporary studies linked the psychological state with loss of income and the decline in family resources. In Marienthal it was found that those described as "broken" had considerably lower average incomes than the other groups. There was also evidence that families moved through these different psychological states as the duration of unemployment increased and resources dwindled. One study of Scotland concluded that the incidence of "psychoneurotic" diseases among the unemployed rose with the duration of unemployment. Psychological effects such as depression bore particularly on skilled workers, who lost status and authority among family and friends, and on older workers who were less adaptable to the change in circumstances (Pilgrim Trust, 1938). However, one of the most important findings to emerge from contemporary studies was that the increased leisure, which might have been expected to benefit the unemployed, had the opposite effect. Time hung heavily on their hands. The lack of a routine structured around work appeared disruptive and led to a loss of purpose. It was often reported that the unemployed read less and participated less in sporting or community activity than when they were employed. Because of lack of resources and loss of motivation the unemployed often found themselves cut off from their former workmates and increasingly detached from the world of work.

Perhaps these effects help to explain the question which is often raised about why the unemployed were not more politically active in the 1930s. Eisenberg and Lazarsfeld suggested that though the unemployed tended to be more critical of the existing economic order, they were not strongly radicalised by unemployment. In countries where there was the greatest privation due to unemployment the willingness and ability of the unemployed to protest was least. In the US survey evidence for 1939 indicated that the unemployed had generally withdrawn from collective activity. This was explained by a low level of class consciousness which in turn arose from the culture of individualism (Verba and Schlozman, 1977). Here, as in other cultural settings, political attitudes were more strongly related to social or occupational status than to whether the individual was unemployed. In Germany, Hitler's growing popularity is often related to the severity of the Depression but it was not the unemployed who brought the regime to power. Though the Hitler youth movement may owe something to unemployment, many of the unemployed resented the regime in its early years (Kershaw, 1983, p.81). In Australia, where there was little fear of repression, there were sporadic and sometimes violent outbursts but little cohesiveness among the unemployed (see MacKinolty, 1982). The most obvious difference in attitude between employed and unemployed was towards relief and benefits where the unemployed were more radical. In fact it was over these issues that successful collective activity and political protest arose. Prominent among these was the British National Unemployed Workers Movement which gradually gained support in the 1920s and organised hunger marches demanding work or maintenance at trade union rates of pay (see Kingsford, 1982).

In summary, unemployment imposed widespread poverty and privation which systems of relief were only partially able to mitigate. The effects on health and vitality are difficult to identify, but psychological effects combined to reduce the employability of the unemployed. Even though the majority continued to search actively for work, the atrophy of skills, loss of morale and possibly declining health as well as loss of contacts left them at a severe disadvantage.

9 Conclusion

Our overview of interwar unemployment experience has been limited to the relatively advanced economies of Western Europe, North America and Australia. The same is true of the chapters to follow. Extending the discussion to the economies of Eastern Europe, Latin America and other parts of the less developed world would no doubt reveal an even greater variety of experience but is beyond the scope of this volume. But even this limited geographical perspective impresses upon the reader the extent of variations in interwar unemployment. On the aggregate level, wage and employment levels diverged markedly across countries both in the early 1920s and later 1930s. Only in the early 1930s is a common pattern evident. On more disaggregated levels, the incidence of unemployment across economic and social groups also diverged markedly across countries. As far as social effects are concerned, the interwar period presents a picture of contrasting and conflicting trends. Clearly, further light can be shed on the reasons for both international similarities and differences only by considering individual country experiences in more detail.

NOTES

1 See US Council of Economic Advisors (1987), Blanchard and Summers (1986) and OECD, *Main Economic Indicators* (various issues).

2 What follows is drawn from the Preface and Introduction to Keyssar (1986).

3 1896 census, vol. 4, pp. cxxi-cxxii, cited in Salais *et al.* (1986), p. 39.

4 See also the discussion below of work by Maddison. Much of the rest of this section draws on Galenson and Zellner's (1957) study.

5 See, for example, Walker (1936), p. 12 and for a recent discussion Forster (1985).

6

It will be found I think that the change in real wage rates associated with a change in money wage rates, so far from being usually in the same direction, is almost always in the opposite direction. When money wage rates are rising, that is to say it will be found that real wages are falling; and when money wages are falling real wages are rising. This is because in the short period falling money wages and rising real wages are each for independent reasons likely to accompany decreasing employment; labour being readier to accept real wage cuts when employment is falling off, yet real wages inevitably rising under the same circumstances on account of the increasing marginal return to a given capital equipment when output is diminished. (Keynes, 1936, p.10)

7 Some have argued that changing social values as well as changing economic circumstances figured in participation trends; see Bolin (1978).

8 Cited in Kessler-Harris (1982), p. 256.

9 This relationship resembles that found by Gordon (1983) whose long-run time series indicated a strong relationship between the wage *level* and employment.

10 For discussion relating real wage changes to differing labour market structure and policies in a multi-country context see Phelps-Brown and Browne (1968) and Bonnell (1981).

11 The NRA was declared unconstitutional by the Supreme Court in 1935 but Weinstein estimates that nullification of the codes did not fully reverse their original effect (1981, p. 267).

12 Pigou put it as follows:

partly through state action and partly through the added strength given to work people's organisations engaged in wage bargaining by the development of unemployment insurance, wage rates have, over a wide area, been set at a level which is too high ... and the very large percentage of unemployment during the whole of the last six years is due to this new factor in our economic life. (1927, p.355)

13 For recent discussion of structural factors in the 1920s and 1930s in the US and Germany see Bernstein (1986) and James (1986, chapter 4), respectively.

14 The greater stability of female employment and their lower average unemployment than men provide another reason for doubting the dominance of the discouraged worker effect on female participation, particularly in the early 1930s. However the effects on married women are likely to have differed from other demographic groups and may have differed between the early 1930s and later in the decade.

15 Such effects can be seen in the data from the US census of 1940 where those seeking work were divided into "experienced workers" and "new workers". For males the new workers accounted for 11 per cent of those seeking work and for females 23 per cent. The bulk of these are concentrated in the 16- to 19-year-old age group. These were excluded in the unemployment rates for 1940 in Table 1.9 (while those on emergency work were included), but if they had been included the unemployment rates for the 14- to 19-year-old group would have been 31.1 per cent for males and 32.2 per cent for females.

16 For early work on these aspects see Singer (1939) and Woytinsky (1942).

17 Comparisons with postwar rates of flow are discussed by Baily (1983) and Thomas (chapter 3, this volume).

18 Beveridge (1944), pp. 68, 80.

19 Since unemployment was rising, doubling the length of spells in progress will tend to underestimate both the average length of spell durations and the share with long completed spells.

20 The observer (from Britain) was Sir A. Maitland and his comments are reported in Royal Institute of International Affairs (1935), p.14.

REFERENCES

Arndt, H.W. (1944), *Economic Lessons of the Nineteen Thirties*, London: Frank Cass.

Asselin, J.C. (1966), "La semaine de 40 heures, le chômage et l'emploi", *Le Mouvement Social* 54, pp. 183-204.

Baily, M. N. (1983), "The Labor Market in the 1930s", in J. Tobin (ed.), *Macroeconomics, Prices and Quantities*, Washington, DC: Brookings Institution, pp. 21-60.

Bain, G.S. and Price, R. (1980), *Profiles of Union Growth: A Comparative Statistical Portrait of Eight Countries*, Oxford: Blackwell.

Bakke, E. Wight (1933), *The Unemployed Man*, London: Nisbet.

Bakke, E. Wight (1940), *The Unemployed Worker*, New Haven: Yale University Press.

Beenstock, M. and Warburton, P. (1986), "Wages and Unemployment in Interwar Britain", *Explorations in Economic History* 23, pp. 153-76.

Benjamin, D.K. and Kochin, L.A. (1979), "Searching for an Explanation for Unemployment in Interwar Britain", *Journal of Political Economy* 87, pp. 441-78.

Bernanke, B.S. (1985), "Employment, Hours and Earnings in the Depression: An Analysis of Eight Manufacturing Industries", *American Economic Review* 76, pp. 82-109.

Bernstein, M.A. (1986), "The Problem of Economic Recovery in the United States: 1929-39", *Rivista di Storia Economica* 3 (International Issue), pp. 158-72.

Beveridge, W.H. (1936), "An Analysis of Unemployment", *Economica* 4, pp. 357-386.

Beveridge, W.H. (1944), *Full Employment in a Free Society*, London: Allen & Unwin.

Blanchard, O.J. and Summers, L.H. (1986), "Hysteresis and the European Unemployment Problem", in *NBER Macroeconomics Annual*, New York: National Bureau of Economic Research.

Bolin, W. (1978), "The Economics of Middle Income Family Life: Working Women During the Great Depression", *Journal of American History* 65, pp. 60-74.

Bonnell, S. (1981), "Real Wages and Employment in the Great Depression", *Economic Record* 57, pp. 277-81.

Broadberry, S.N. (1986), "Aggregate Supply in Interwar Britain", *Economic Journal* 96, pp. 466-81.

Broomfield, R. (1978), *Unemployed Workers: A Social History of the Great Depression in Adelaide*, St Lucia: University of Queensland Press.

Butlin, N.G. (1984), "Select Comparative Economic Statistics 1900-1940: Australia, Britain, Japan, New Zealand and USA", *Source Papers in Economic History*, Department of Economic History, Canberra: Australian National University.

Bry, G. (1960), *Wages in Germany 1871-1945*, New York: National Bureau of Economic Research.

Cassidy, H.M. (1933), *Unemployment and Relief in Ontario 1929-32*, Toronto: J.M. Dent.

Chandler, L.V. (1970), *America's Greatest Depression*, New York: Harper & Row.

Clague, E., Couper, W.J. and Bakke, E. Wight (1934), *After the Shutdown*, New Haven: Yale University Press.

Crafts, N.F.R. (1986), "Long Term Unemployment, Excess Demand and the Wage Equation in Britain, 1925-1939", Discussion Paper no. 147, London: Centre for Economic Policy Research.

Crafts, N.F.R. (1987), "Long Term Unemployment in Britain in the 1930s", *Economic History Review* 40, pp. 418-32.

Darby, M.R. (1976), "Three and a Half Million Workers Have Been Mislaid: or An Explanation of Unemployment 1934-41", *Journal of Political Economy* 84, pp. 487-93.

Dimsdale, N.H. (1984), "Employment and Real Wages in the Interwar Period", *National Institute Economic Review* 110, pp. 94-102.

Dunlop, J. T. (1938), "The Movement of Real and Money Wage Rates", *Economic Journal* 48, pp. 413-34.

Eichengreen, B.J. (1986a), "Understanding 1921-1927: Inflation and Economic Recovery in the 1920s", *Rivista di Storia Economica* 3 (International Issue), pp. 34-66.

Eichengreen, B.J. (1986b), "Unemployment in Interwar Britain: Dole or Doldrums?", *Oxford Economics Papers* (forthcoming).

Eichengreen, B.J. (1986c), "Unemployment in Interwar Britain: New Evidence from London", *Journal of Interdisciplinary History* 17, pp. 335-58.

Eichengreen, B.J. (1987), "Juvenile Unemployment in 20th Century Britain: The Emergence of a Problem", *Social Research* 54, pp. 273-301.

Eichengreen, B.J. and Sachs, J. (1985), "Exchange Rates and Economic Recovery in the 1930s", *Journal of Economic History* 45, pp. 925-946.

Eisenberg, P. and Lazarsfeld, P.F. (1938), "The Psychological Effects of Unemployment", *Psychological Bulletin* 35, pp. 358-90.

Fearon, P. (1979), *The Origins and Nature of the Great Slump, 1929-32*, London: Macmillan.

Feinstein, C.H. (1972), *National Income, Expenditure and Output of the United Kingdom, 1855-1965*, Cambridge: Cambridge University Press.

Forster, C. (1985), "Unemployment and the Australian Economic Recovery of the 1930s", Working Paper no. 45, Department of Economic History, Canberra: Australian National University.

Galenson, W. and Zellner, A. (1957), "International Comparison of Unemployment Rates", in *The Measurement and Behavior of Unemployment*, National Bureau for Economic Research, pp. 439-580, Princeton: Princeton University Press.

Garraty, J. A. (1978), *Unemployment in History*, New York: Harcourt Brace.

Garraty, J. A. (1986), *The Great Depression*, New York: Harcourt Brace.

Garside, W.R. (1980), *The Measurement of Unemployment*, Oxford: Blackwell.

Gordon, R.J. (1983), "A Century of Evidence on Wage and Price Stickiness in the US, the UK and Japan", in J. Tobin (ed.), *Macroeconomics, Prices and Quantities*, pp. 85-133, Washington, DC: Brookings Institution.

Harris, J. (1972), *Unemployment and Politics*, Oxford: Clarendon Press.

Harrison, A. and Hart, R. (1985), "A Labour Market Model of Unemployment Insurance", Discussion Paper no. 85-08, Hamilton: McMaster University.

Hatton, T.J. (1981), "Employment Functions for UK Industries Between the Wars", Economics Discussion Paper no. 181, Colchester: University of Essex.

Hatton, T.J. (1985), "The British Labor Market in the 1920's: A Test of the Search-Turnover Approach", *Explorations in Economic History* 22, pp. 257-70.

Hatton, T.J. (1986a), "Demand, Supply and Economic Policy During the 1930s", Economics Discussion Paper no. 281, Colchester: University of Essex.

Hatton, T.J. (1986b), "Female Labour Force Participation: The Enigma of the Interwar Period", Working Paper no. 71, Department of Economic History, Canberra: Australian National University.

Hatton, T.J. (1986c), "Structural Aspects of Unemployment in Britain Between the World Wars", *Research in Economic History* 10, pp. 55-92.

Hatton, T.J. (1987), "A Quarterly Model of the Labour Market in Interwar Britain", *Oxford Bulletin of Economics and Statistics* (forthcoming).

International Labour Office (1948), *Employment, Unemployment and Labour Force Statistics*, New Series, no. 7, Geneva: ILO.

Jahoda, M. (1987), "Unemployed Men at Work", in D. Fryer and P. Ullah (eds), *Unemployed People*, Milton Keynes: Open University Press.

Jahoda, M., Lazarsfeld, P.F. and Zeisel, H. (1972), *Marienthal*, London: Tavistock.

James, H. (1986), *The German Slump: Politics and Economics 1924-1936*, Oxford: Clarendon Press.

Kershaw, I. (1983), *Popular Opinion and Political Dissent in the Third Reich*, Oxford: Oxford University Press.

Kesselman, J.R. and Savin, N.E. (1978), "Three and a Half Million Workers Never Were Lost, *"Economic Inquiry* 16, pp. 205-225.

Kessler-Harris, A. (1982), *Out to Work: A History of Wage-Earning Women in the United States*, Oxford: Oxford University Press.

Keynes, J. M. (1936), *The General Theory of Employment, Interest and Money*, London: Macmillan.

Keyssar, A. (1986), *Out of Work: The First Century of Unemployment in Massachusetts*, Cambridge: Cambridge University Press.

Kindleberger, C.P. (1973), *The World in Depression, 1929-39*, London: Allen Lane.

Kingsford, P. (1982), *The Hunger Marches in Britain 1920-1940*, London: Lawrence & Wishart.

Kirk, D. (1946), *Europe's Population in the Interwar Years*, New York: Gordon & Breach.

Lebergott, S. (1964), *Manpower in Economic Growth*, New York: McGraw-Hill.

Lilien, D.M. (1982), "Sectoral Shifts and Cyclical Unemployment", *Journal of Political Economy* 90, pp. 777-93.

Llewellyn Smith, H. (1932), *New Survey of London Life and Labour*, vol. 3, London: P.S. King.

Long, C.D. (1958), *The Labor Force under Changing Conditions of Income and Employment*, Princeton, New Jersey: National Bureau of Economic Research.

Lucas, R.E. and Rapping, L. (1969), "Real Wages, Employment and Inflation", *Journal of Political Economy* 77, pp. 721-54.

McDonald, I. and Solow, R.M. (1981), "Wage Bargaining and Employment", *American Economic Review* 71, pp. 896-908.

MacKinolty, J. (ed.) (1982), *The Wasted Years: Australia's Great Depression*, Sydney: Allen & Unwin.

Maddison, A. (1964), *Economic Growth in the West*, London: Allen & Unwin.

Marsh, L.C. (1940), *Canadians In and Out of Work*, Toronto: Oxford University Press.

Matthews, K.G.P. (1987), "Aggregate Supply in Interwar Britain: A Comment", unpublished manuscript, University of Liverpool.

Mitchell, B.R. (1975), *European Historical Statistics 1750-1970*, London: Macmillan.

Mitchell, B.R. (1983), *International Historical Statistics: The Americas and Australasia*, London: Macmillan.

Newell, A. and Symons, J.S.V. (1987), "Corporatism, Laissez Faire and the Rise in Unemployment", *European Economic Review* 31, pp. 567-614.

Organisation for Economic Cooperation and Development (1986), *Economic Outlook* 40.

Organisation for Economic Cooperation and Development (various years), *Main Economic Indicators*, Paris: OECD, Paris: OECD.

Parrish, John B. (1939), "Changes in the Nation's Labor Supply", *American Economic Review* 29, pp. 328-330.

Phelps-Brown, E.H. and Browne, M. (1968), *A Century of Pay*, London: Macmillan.

Pigou, A.C. (1927), "Wages Policy and Unemployment", *Economic Journal* 38, pp. 355-368.

Pilgrim Trust (1938), *Men Without Work*, Cambridge: Cambridge University Press.

Reddaway, W.B. (1938), "Australian Wage Policy 1929-1937", *International Labour Review* 37, pp. 314-38.

Romer, C. (1986), "Spurious Volatility in Historical Unemployment Data", *Journal of Political Economy* 94, pp. 1-37.

Rowntree, B. Seebohm (1941), *Poverty and Progress*, London: Longmans Green.

Royal Institute of International Affairs (1935), *Unemployment: An International Problem*, London: Oxford University Press.

Ruggles, Richard (1940), "The Relative Movements of Real and Money Wage Rates", *Quarterly Journal of Economics* 55, pp. 130-49.

Salais, R.N., Baverez, N. and Reynaud, B. (1986), *L'invention du chômage*, Paris: Presses Universitaires de France.

Singer, H.W. (1939), "Regional Labour Markets and the Process of Unemployment", *Review of Economic Studies* 7, pp. 42-58.

Svennilson, I. (1954), *Growth and Stagnation in the European Economy*, Geneva: Organisation of European Economic Cooperation.

Tarshis, L. (1939), "Changes in Real and Money Wages", *Economic Journal* 49, pp. 150-4.

Taylor, F. I. (1909), *A Bibliography of Unemployment and the Unemployed*, London: P.S. King.

UK Ministry of Health (1935), *Effects of Existing Economic Circumstances on the Health of the Community in Durham*, Cmd 4886, London: HMSO.

US Council of Economic Advisers (1987), *Economic Report of the President*, Washington, DC: Government Printing Office.

Verba, S. and Schlozman, K.L. (1977), "Unemployment, Class Consciousness and Radical Politics: What Didn't Happen in the Thirties", *Journal of Politics* 39, pp. 291-323.

Walker, E.R. (1936), *Unemployment Policy with Special Reference to Australia*, Sydney: Angus & Robertson.

Weinstein, M. (1981), "Some Macroeconomic Impacts of the National Industrial Recovery Act, 1933-1935", in Karl Brunner (ed.), *The Great Depression Revisited*, Boston: Martinus Nijhoff, pp. 262-81.

Whiteside, N. (1987), "Counting the Cost: Sickness and Disability Among Working People in an Era of Industrial Recession 1920-39", *Economic History Review* 40, pp. 228- 46.

Woytinsky, W.S. (1942), *Three Aspects of Labor Dynamics*, Washington, DC: Social Science Research Council.

Chapter 2

The Macroeconomics of the Interwar Years: International Comparisons

Andrew Newell and J S V Symons

1   Introduction

This paper is a study of the interwar years for fourteen countries, which we shall collectively describe as the world. Our major aim is to give an account of the Great Depression. Neither of us is an economic historian, as may become apparent, and our primary motivation in undertaking this work is to see if models we have developed to explain the last thirty years or so can explain the interwar years.

Many of the historical accounts of the Great Depression locate its epicentre in economic events in the United States. Close to sixty years on it is still difficult to draw out the critical events from such a history (see, *inter alia*, Kindleberger, 1973). Capital flights, stock market crashes, waves of protectionism, banking collapses and devaluations followed one another in a bewildering succession. The time-series evidence does allow some stylised facts to be established. Business activity peaked in the United States in early 1929, and the beginnings of a recession were perceptible from, say, the middle of that year. The New York stock market crash in October sent share prices falling worldwide and seemed to impart a further downward step in US industrial activity. Most historians note a period of brief respite in the early months of 1930, after which the "slide into the abyss" (Kindleberger, 1973, p.128) set in.

The story is different in other countries. Germany and Australia, for instance, were experiencing a steadily deepening depression from at least 1929 onwards, whereas in France the decline in activity started almost a year later.

B. Eichengreen and T. J. Hatton (eds.), Interwar Unemployment in International Perspective, 61–96.

That period of respite in the US has led some authors (notably Hicks, 1974, p.210) to characterise the US experience as a "double dip" - a severe depression superimposed on an already extant normal downturn. If that was the case the natural focus of attention would be the causes of the depression in the United States from mid-1930 onwards. The emphasis to date has largely been on the forces which caused that downturn in aggregate demand. The debate over this is perhaps familiar territory (the conference volume edited by Brunner (1981) provides an excellent introduction). We should state at the outset that we do not doubt that such a fall in aggregate demand happened, or that it was the major cause of the Depression, not only in the US, but worldwide - indeed the latter part of this paper discusses its origins.

Our aim here is to present a coherent supply-side story which we believe to be an essential supplement to the fall in aggregate demand in explaining the path of unemployment over the period. We have surely learned over the last twenty years that we ignore the supply side at our peril.

To focus our argument, consider Table 2.1. This traces the movement of wholesale prices for several countries from mid-1929 to October 1930. Note that from October 1929 onwards all the indices show an abrupt downwards change in trend. From October 1929 to June 1930 all the indices fell around 10 per cent. Generally, prices continued to fall until around 1933. Our major contention is that these price falls, in conjunction with the lack of a similar movement in wages, put a massive squeeze on profitability, in particular the profitability of employing labour.

Output is both demanded and supplied, and if the Great Depression was a fall in demand, it must equally have been a fall in supply. If the labour market clears, so that, in price-output space, the aggregate supply curve is vertical, then any leftwards shift of the aggregate demand curve will produce a fall in prices, but no fall in output or employment: the Great Depression could not have happened without an upwards-sloping supply curve. The primary task of this chapter is to document this supply curve, though we will say something about demand as well.

The model we shall use is more or less that of Newell and Symons (1985). Here labour demand depends on the real wage and the real interest rate. The real wage depends on the unemployment rate and the tax and import wedge. Our analysis is conditioned on the path of the labour force, and hence on the participation decision of individual workers. If some significant part of unemployment in the 1930s was due to increased participation then our analysis will not explain this. For our sample of countries we shall see that the labour demand equation works very well indeed, giving a pleasing consistency between interwar and postwar results, and, indeed, between these results and British and US data prior to the First

Table 2.1   Wholesale Price Indices, June 1929 - October 1930
(October 1929 = 100)

	US	UK	France	Germany
June 1929	97.7	99.6	103.6	98.5
August 1929	101.5	99.8	101.2	100.7
October 1929	100.0	100.0	100.0	100.0
December 1929	97.8	97.4	97.7	97.9
February 1930	95.6	93.9	95.7	94.2
April 1930	94.2	90.9	93.0	92.3
June 1930	90.1	88.7	90.3	90.7
August 1930	87.2	86.6	90.2	90.9
October 1930	85.8	83.0	86.2	87.6

Source: League of Nations *Monthly Bulletin of Statistics.*

World War. The wage equations, however, show an intriguing difference. We find nominal rigidity for the interwar years, i.e. an increase in inflation reduces (would have reduced) the real wage: thus we have our upwards-sloping supply curve. This contrasts with post-Hitler's war wage equations (Newell and Symons, 1986a) which show little or no nominal wage rigidity. In our analysis "nominal wage rigidity" means just that the inflation rate enters the real-wage equation with a negative sign. What is the economic behaviour corresponding to this? It might be that inflation proxies expectational errors; but the different results for pre- and post-Hitler's war then present a problem. Our feeling is that Occam's razor supports Keynes and suggests the explanation that workers will resist, by and large, a fall in the nominal wage. Prewar the price level was falling and equilibrium required wage cuts; postwar the price level was rising and such wage cuts were seldom required.

We do not find nominal rigidity for the US. The transmission mechanism from deflation to the real economy in the US was not the real wage. We find that monetary and demand conditions acted directly on employment in the United States via, effectively, a Lucas supply curve. But in most other countries nominal wage rigidity was crucial.

Since we have inflation in the wage equation, we need to explain the price level, i.e. we need a demand side. This contrasts with the postwar years where we find no nominal rigidity and the only role for demand-side variables is through transient shocks. Our demand-side models are the usual IS-LM-BP apparatus. These enable us to trace the impact of world prices and world trade on open economies, and we find very powerful linkages from them to domestic prices.

Thus it is possible to give an account of the Great Depression in individual open economies if one can explain the behaviour of world prices and world output. To explain these in turn we thus require a world model. The world is an appealing object of study as it is a closed economy. We develop a world IS curve, a world LM curve, and a rudimentary world aggregate supply schedule. The IS curve gives output as a function of world wealth - a weighted sum of labour income, equity prices, and money balances. It is via wealth that the stock market crash of 1929 and the subsequent decline in profitability enter our model. The LM curve is conventional. We find however a large leftwards shift over the 1930s corresponding to a huge increase in liquidity preference. This increase is most naturally associated with the continuing poor performance of equities over this period.

What of the Great Depression? Figure 2.1 plots the world average of the important time series. As we see it, what seems to have happened is this. For open economies, the price and volume of traded goods fell around 1930. This, and diminished wealth due to falling equity prices, led to a fall in domestic prices. In consequence the real interest rate and real wage rose, the latter due to nominal wage rigidity. Thus employment fell through adverse shifts in factor prices as these economies moved down their supply curves.

Why did world prices and world trade fall? For similar reasons. The fall in world stock prices led to a fall in world wealth and to an increase in liquidity preference: both the world IS and the world LM curves shifted left, the latter exacerbated in a minor way by monetary contraction. It seems likely, as Kindleberger (1973, p.125) emphasises, that the first wave of price deflation to hit the world economy was directly attributable to liquidation of stocks of commodities following the crash. With an upwards-sloping world supply curve (nominal rigidity again), world prices and world demand fell in consequence.

This chapter is organised as follows. Section 2 compares unemployment performance in the Depression across countries. We show that the extent of the fall in prices in each country is a good explanation of inter-country differences; that it Granger caused unemployment; and that the inflationary consequence of abandoning fixed exchange rates led to recovery. We argue that the fall in prices flowed through to the real economy by causing changes in relative prices. Section 3 describes our model in detail and uses some comparative statics to elucidate its workings. In Section 4 we give estimation results. We find nominal rigidity in the wage equation, and strong real wage and real interest rate effects in the employment equation. (For previous work on real wage effects on employment between the wars, see the survey by Hatton (1986) for Britain, and Bernanke (1985) for the United States.) We find swift and powerful effects of world

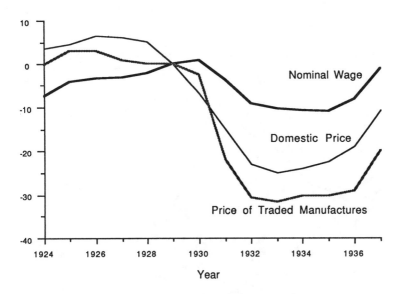

Figure 2.1a **Nominal Wages, Domestic Prices and Price of Traded**
Manufactures (unweighted averages of fourteen countries)

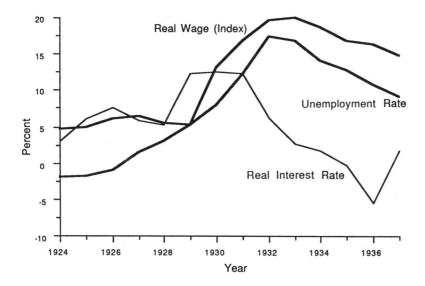

Figure 2.1b **Real Wages, Real Interest Rate and Unemployment**
(unweighted averages of fourteen countries)

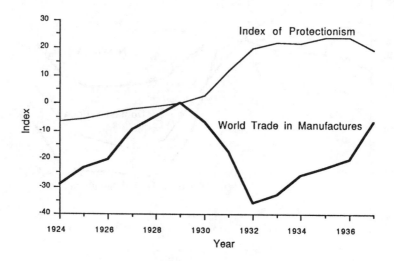

Figure 2.1c **World Trade in Manufactures and Index of Protection (log scale, 1929=0)**

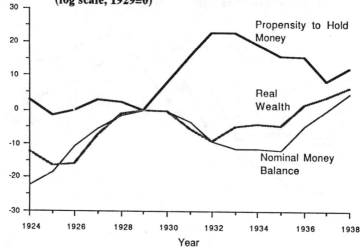

Figure 2.1d **Propensity to Hold Money, Real Wealth and Nominal Money Balances (trade weighted)**

Note: The propensity to hold money is the inverse of velocity. Real wealth is a weighted sum of labour income, equity prices (as a proxy for the valuation of the capital stock), and money balances. See Appendix 2.1 for details.

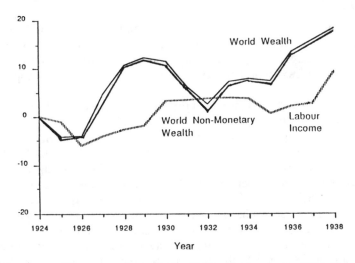

Figure 2.1e   The Components of World Wealth (log scale, 1924=0)

Note: The components of wealth may be recovered from this diagram: labour income plus equity prices equals non-monetary wealth; and non-monetary wealth plus real money balances equals wealth.

prices on domestic prices. Section 5 develops and estimates a world model. Our intention here is to endogenise world prices and output. Section 6 gives a brief concluding discussion.

It seems to us that the proximate cause of the Great Depression was the fall in world stock prices, acting directly on the world IS curve, and indirectly on the LM curve by increasing liquidity preference. Blaming stock prices entails the implicit assumption that they must have had a large exogenous component. We do not attempt to decompose stock prices into an endogenous component influenced by economic activity and an exogenous component corresponding to something like animal spirits.

Where do we stand on the spending versus money debate as set out, for example, in Brunner's volume? We take bits and pieces from both. What got the Depression rolling was price deflation directly due to the Wall Street crash. The crash, and subsequent bearish profit expectations, led to an important deflationary wealth effect; but still more important in propagating the Depression was the shift in liquidity preference due almost certainly to poor performance of equities. This could have been eliminated at any time by a monetary expansion.

2 Relative International Performance in the Great Depression

We have noted in the introduction the outstanding fall in world prices from 1929 to the mid-1930s. Table 2.2 shows fairly unambiguous unidirectional Granger causality flowing from prices to unemployment for the interwar years: of the fourteen countries only the UK gives opposite results. .

We shall see that the magnitude of the price shocks explains most of the inter-country variance in 1930s unemployment performance. To facilitate inter-country comparisons we normalise each unemployment rate (see Appendix 2.1 for details) by its average value between 1921 and 1929. If the 1920s are considered as normal in some sense, the resulting measure is in units of normal unemployment. Where we have more than one measure of unemployment (e.g. Sweden, Germany) this normalisation tends to give similar results. Table 2.3 sets out some unemployment rate statistics for our sample of countries. In particular, column 6 gives our chosen measure of 1930s performance: average normalised unemployment between 1930 and 1938. Note that continental Europe does badly, while Scandinavia and the UK do well. The US is about average.

The model in the first row of Table 2.4 shows that the 1929-32 price shock explains 65 per cent of the variance of inter-country unemployment performance. This is about the same in row 2 if we replace the 1929-32 price change with the total price change from 1929 to each country's price trough. The variance explained rises to 78 per cent if we include the positive price shock from trough to 1938. On the face of it these results show that the balance of inter-country differences can be explained by a negative price shock in the early 1930s - and a subsequent positive price shock. We shall argue below that these shocks caused important changes in relative prices, in particular the real wage and the real interest rate, which acted as the transmission to the real economy. There is some evidence that nominal wage cuts, moderating real wage growth during the first price shock, led to superior performance: see row 4.

The real wage acts over this period to distort simple Okun-type relationships between unemployment and the output gap. Table 2.5 estimates such a relationship including the lagged real product wage as an additional variable. These results show that even if one adopted an extreme Keynesian position where output is exogenous, still one finds that a given increase in aggregate demand drew forth a smaller increase in employment if the real wage rose. Note that the US and UK differ from the other results: we shall say more on this later.

We argue below that the first price shock is derived from a fall in the price of goods in world trade - which itself we shall seek to explain later.

Table 2.2   Granger Causality Between Unemployment and Inflation, 1923-38

(A) Unemployment on lagged inflation

	u_{t-1}	$\dot{p}_{t-1}$	trend	DW
Europe	0.61	-4.51	0.09	1.6
	(3.2)	(-1.7)	(1.0)	
Scandinavia	0.53	-2.69	0.02	1.3
	(2.2)	(-1.2)	(0.6)	
United Kingdom	0.95	4.46	-0.02	1.2
	(4.0)	(1.2)	(-0.9)	
United States	0.51	-9.88	0.08	1.6
	(2.4)	(-2.1)	(1.3)	
World average	0.60	-4.09	0.05	1.5
	(2.9)	(-1.4)	(0.8)	

(B) Inflation on lagged unemployment

	$\dot{p}_{t-1}$	u_{t-1}	trend	DW
Europe	0.37	0.03	0.00	1.8
	(1.5)	(0.4)	(-1.2)	
Scandinavia	0.09	0.00	0.00	1.6
	(0.3)	(-0.1)	(0.8)	
United Kingdom	-0.19	-0.04	0.00	1.5
	(-1.1)	(-4.1)	(4.3)	
United States	0.61	0.02	0.00	1.9
	(2.0)	(1.1)	(-0.6)	
World average	0.25	0.01	0.00	1.8
	(0.9)	(0.4)	(0.02)	

Note: Starting dates vary between countries: see Appendix 2.1.
The country groupings are: Europe - Belgium, Czechoslovakia, France, Germany, Italy and the Netherlands; Scandinavia - Denmark, Finland, Norway and Sweden; World - Europe, Scandinavia, Australia, Canada, UK and US.
t statistics in brackets. For the grouped countries averages of parameters and statistics are reported. If parameter estimates were independent, significance levels for country groupings would be Europe - 0.8, Scandinavia - 1.0, World - 0.5. Since independence is unlikely, some rounding up of these levels is desirable. With complete dependence, the appropriate level would be t=2. Experience with intercountry data has led us to believe that an increase of, say, 50 per cent is required for robust inference. Thus in part (A) of the table we would count the European, US, and World average results as significant with Scandinavia marginal.

Table 2.3   Selected Unemployment and Inflation Data

	Average unemp't rate 1921-29 (1)	Average unemp't rate 1930-38 (2)	Peak unemp't rate (3)	Year of peak (4)	Peak $\bar{U}$ (5)	Average $\bar{U}$ 1930-38 (6)	% change in price level 1929-32 (7)
Belgium	2.4	14.1	19.0	1932	7.9	5.9	-48
Czechoslovakia	2.6	11.9	17.4	1934	6.7	4.6	-28
France	3.8	10.2	15.4	1932	4.1	2.7	-42
Germany	6.5	15.2	30.1	1932	4.6	2.3	-24
Italy	3.3	9.6	11.8	1933	3.6	2.9	-28
Netherlands	2.4	8.7	11.9	1936	5.0	3.6	-20
Denmark	17.1	21.9	31.7	1932	1.9	1.3	-15
Finland	1.6	4.1	6.2	1933	3.9	2.6	-15
Norway	5.8	8.1	10.2	1931	1.8	1.4	-10
Sweden	14.2	15.8	23.3	1933	1.6	1.1	-20
Australia	5.8	13.5	19.1	1932	3.3	2.3	-17
Canada	3.5	13.3	19.3	1933	5.5	3.8	-20
UK	8.3	11.7	15.6	1932	1.9	1.4	-7
US	5.1	14.5	22.9	1932	4.5	2.8	-23
World average				1932	4.0	2.8	-23

Note: $\bar{U}$ is our normalised measure of unemployment, i.e. U / Col.(1). Col.(6) is Col.(2) / Col.(1). Col.(6) we argue is appropriate for inter-country comparison.

Which countries experienced severe price shocks? Half the variance is explained by whether the countries were still on fixed exchange rates by 1932: see Table 2.4, row 5. One might expect that trading countries would fare worse if the price shock was trade-derived. There is some evidence for this in row 6. The relatively low proportion of variance explained in rows 5 and 6 is due to Australia which experienced a large fall in prices due to extremely low prices for her raw material exports. Without Australia, the model in row 6 explains 76 per cent of the inter-country price shocks.

We have seen that countries which had abandoned the gold standard by 1932 experienced less of a price shock. We now investigate in more detail the role of monetary factors in inter-country performance. Table 2.6(A) gives unemployment U_t as a function of a lagged dependent variable, world average U_t, and a version of the real interest rate $(r-\dot{p})_{t-1}$. We think of the real interest rate here as an index of general monetary stance which is, of course, constrained under fixed exchange rates. We have controlled for average U_t to see if an expansionary monetary policy leads to better unemployment performance relative to the world. The results show

Table 2.4   Inter-Country Unemployment Performance, 1930s

Dependent variable: average normalised 1930s unemployment rates

% price change 1929-32	% price change 1929 to price trough	% price change price trough to 1938	% real wage change 1929-32	R^2
-0.13 (4.3)	-	-	-	0.65
-	-0.11 (4.3)	-	-	0.65
-	-0.11 (5.1)	-0.06 (2.3)	-	0.78
-	-0.08 (3.3)	-0.07 (3.1)	0.01 (1.9)	0.85

Dependent variable: percentage price change 1929-32

Dummy if on gold, 1932	Share of exports in GDP, 1929	R^2
-12.0 (4.0)	-	0.47
-11.6 (2.9)	-20.4 (1.1)	0.53

Note: In these regressions each of twelve countries is the unit of observation. Here and elsewhere in this chapter "prices" means the national GDP deflator. As discussed in Appendix 2.1 we do not have GDP deflators for Belgium, Finland and France and in other sections of this chapter we use rough proxies. Since inter-country comparability is paramount here we have discarded Finland and France from our set of countries. Data in Mitchell (1980) give national account statistics for Belgium at enough dates to enable GDP deflators to be reasonably interpolated using WPI data.

Table 2.5   Okun Regressions, 1923-38 (dependent variable unemployment rate)

	$(y-\tilde{y})_t$	$(w-p_v)_{t-1}$	trend	DW	SE
Europe	-0.43 (-4.5)	0.15 (2.3)	0.001 (3.1)	1.6	0.022
Scandinavia	-0.49 (-4.3)	0.25 (3.1)	-0.002 (-0.6)	1.5	0.019
UK	-0.64 (-7.4)	0.04 (0.2)	0.001 (0.6)	1.7	0.013
US	-0.43 (-7.9)	0.04 (0.2)	0.005 (1.3)	0.6	0.019
World average	-0.45 (-4.7)	0.18 (2.1)	0.001 (1.6)	1.4	0.020

Note: t statistics in brackets. Starting dates vary between countries; see Appendix 2.1. For a listing of the country groupings and a brief discussion of the interpretation of average t statistics, see notes to Table 2.1. $(y-\tilde{y})_t$ is the deviation of real GDP from a linear trend.

Table 2.6 Unemployment and Exchange Rate Policy, 1923-38

(A) Dependent variable: unemployment rate, U_t

	U_{t-1}	World average U_t	$(r-\dot{p})_{t-1}$	DW
Europe	0.41	1.17	0.20	1.9
	(4.6)	(6.2)	(1.3)	
Scandinavia	0.29	0.37	0.14	1.3
	(1.2)	(4.0)	(3.0)	
UK	-0.03	0.36	0.14	1.7
	(-0.1)	(3.5)	(3.1)	
US	-0.31	1.60	0.21	1.5
	(-2.2)	(9.4)	(2.5)	
World average	0.26	0.91	0.19	1.6
	(2.2)	(5.4)	(2.1)	

(B) Dependent variable: central bank discount rate, r_t

	r_{t-1}	Gold standard dummy	DW
Europe	0.63	-0.50	1.6
	(3.4)	(-0.7)	
Scandinavia	0.49	-1.10	1.8
	(2.7)	(-2.2)	
UK	0.10	-2.12	1.9
	(0.4)	(-3.7)	
US	0.53	-1.08	1.7
	(2.5)	(-2.3)	
World average	0.52	-0.86	1.7
	(4.3)	(-3.0)	

Note: t statistics in brackets. Starting dates vary between countries: see Appendix 2.1. For a listing of country groupings and a brief discussion of the interpretation of average t statistics, see note to Table 2.2.

quite clearly this was the case. In Table 2.6(*B*) we complete the chain of causation by showing that abandoning the gold standard did indeed release the nominal interest rate. The European countries do not show up well here: by and large they maintained parity until the late 1930s, suffering, in consequence we argue, higher nominal and real interest rates and worse unemployment.

The above analysis has brought out the following points:

(i) The proximate cause of unemployment in the Great Depression as a world phenomenon was a fall in prices.

(ii) This fall in prices was associated with fixed exchange rates.

(iii) Recovery was via a rise in prices associated with leaving the gold standard.

(iv) The fall in prices caused changes in relative prices, in particular the real wage and the real interest rate, which had important effects on the real economy.

The notion that abandoning fixed exchange rates was the source of recovery for many countries has been persuasively argued by Eichengreen and Sachs (1985). Our findings here thus support their conclusions.

3 A Model of the Open Economy, World Prices Given

In this section we shall develop and estimate small structural models to show in more detail the linkages suggested in section 1. First the labour market. We assume a labour demand schedule (here and elsewhere in logs) of the form

$$n^d = n^d (k, w\text{-}p_v, \rho) \qquad (1)$$

where k is capital, w-p_v is the value-added product wage and $\rho = r - \dot{p}_v^e$ is the real interest rate. Sometimes we shall drop the subscript v from p_v. Technical progress should also be included but is omitted in this exposition. Given diminishing returns, we expect a negative sign on the wage, independently of market structure provided only that firms profit maximise and the price elasticity of output demand they face is not violently procyclical. With fixed capital the presence of the real interest rate is nonstandard. This variable, which we have found to be important empirically in virtually all employment time series we have studied (e.g. Newell and Symons, 1987), should be interpreted as measuring the price of capital not included in fixed capital (stocks, firm-specific human capital). There may be other explanations, and for the purposes of our analysis we need only think of it as the direct effect of monetary policy on the hiring decision of firms. It is sometimes convenient to interpret (1) as an output supply equation:

$$y^s = y^s (k, w\text{-}p_v, \rho) \qquad (1')$$

The real wage is assumed to be the outcome of a bargain between workers and firms (Nickell and Andrews, 1983; Newell and Symons, 1987).

$$w\text{-}p_v = h (k\text{-}l, p_c\text{-}p_v, u, \rho) \qquad (2)$$

Here l is the labour force, p_c is the consumption deflator, p_c-p_v is the tax-import wedge, and ρ is the real interest rate. This model is the appropriate generalisation of the competitive wage outcome to a bargaining setting. The capital-labour ratio gives the path of the equilibrium wage; the wedge p_c-p_v is present because firms and workers employ different price deflators; u is specific to the bargaining interpretation and reflects workers' concern for the prospects of displaced workers; and ρ is present because it shifts the labour demand curve. Given w- p_v, employment is determined from (1).

This equation works well for the post-Hitler's war period (Newell and Symons, 1986a). A crucial distinction between the interwar and postwar years is that the latter presumably seldom required a fall in money wages to achieve equilibrium, however defined. Keynes argued about his own period (*General Theory*, chapter 19) that workers would resist a fall in the money wage. In terms of a bargaining approach to wage formation, workers might rationally resist a fall in the nominal wage to maintain employment if this was likely to be misinterpreted as a sign of bargaining weakness bound to cause problems in subsequent negotiations. If, at the micro level, wages move to clear markets with the single restriction that they may not fall in some markets, the economy-wide wage equation will exhibit a form of nominal rigidity:

$$w\text{-}p_v = h \ (k\text{-}l, \ p_c\text{-}p_v, \ u, \ \rho, \ \Delta p_c) \qquad (2')$$

Note that an identical equation could be derived without assuming nominal rigidity from a wage equation containing unanticipated inflation if Δp_c were an appropriate proxy for it. We should also note that the parameter on Δp_c is expected to shift between periods of different average rates of inflation. In fact in previous work we have found no nominal rigidity post-Hitler's war, whereas we shall see below that nominal rigidity is definitely present between the wars. These issues are discussed in more detail in Newell and Symons (1986a).

Conditional on the nominal interest rate, the model could be closed by a reduced form price equation from the demand side of the economy, but we shall develop this in a little more detail as it is useful for descriptive purposes and will be of importance below. Here the model is standard. We assume demand for domestic value-added takes the form:

$$y^d = y^d \ (\rho, \ \theta, \ W^*, \ W^*\text{-}W) \qquad (3)$$

where θ is competitiveness, $\theta = p^*+e\text{-}p$, W^* is world wealth, defined as current plus expected future income, and W is domestic wealth, defined as expected future income. The relative wealth term is required if domestic income is spent in greater proportion on domestic output. If foreigners have different propensities to consume our output out of current and future income we require also current world income in (3). The LM curve takes the form:

$$m = m^d (y, p, r) \tag{4}$$

We have transactions balances in mind here but we leave open the prospect of wealth effects.

Finally, balance of payments equilibrium is given by

$$0 = b (y, \theta, r^*+e^e-r, W^*, W^*-W) \tag{5}$$

Equations (1'), (2'), (3), (4) and (5) give five equations in five unknowns, y, r, p, w, and e or m, depending on the exchange rate regime. We find it helpful to consider the subsystem consisting of (1'), (3), (4) and (5). These equations can be solved to yield quasi-reduced forms for y, m, r and p in terms of the remaining variables. For prices, in particular,

$$p = p (e+p^*, w, \dot{p}^e, r^*+\dot{e}^e, W^*, W^*-W, k) \tag{6}$$

The variable $r^*+\dot{e}^e$ is only present if financial capital is internationally mobile, and for most countries at the time this was much less important than currently. Discarding this, and employing an adaptive scheme for $\dot{p}^e$ so that it becomes embodied in the dynamics of the equation, we have

$$p = p (e+p^*, w, W^*, W^*-W, k) \tag{6'}$$

which is what we shall estimate. Equation (6) is a well-defined relationship irrespective of the exchange rate regime, with the proviso that e will become endogenous for most countries towards the end of the period. One might also consider the possibility that, after floating exchange rates, there might be a shift in (6') due to altered expectation formation. In general this is at the end of the sample for a handful of observations and econometrically is conveniently handled by allowing an intercept shift.

The comparative statics of the open economy on fixed exchange rates are given in Figure 2.2. We assume no relative wealth effects; no real interest rate in y^s; $\dot{p}^e = 0$; no capital mobility; and a severe form of nominal rigidity so that the nominal wage is predetermined. We draw the balance of payments curve (5) and an aggregate demand curve derived from (3) and (4) in p - y space, and also in θ - y space. If we begin at equilibrium at A, a simultaneous fall in the price of goods in trade p* and world wealth W* shifts down both b and AD in p - y space. Equilibrium

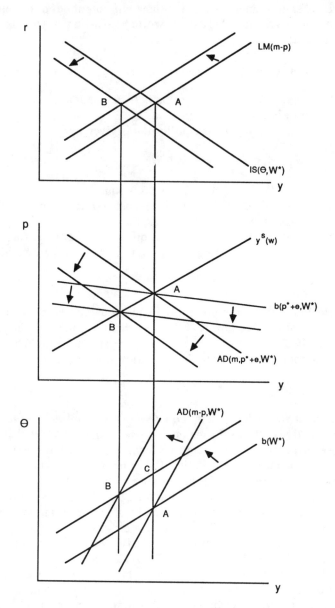

Figure 2.2   The Open Economy

Note: See text for discussion.

is established at B where b meets y^s. If temporarily the economy rests at a y^s = AD equilibrium not at B, monetary changes associated with the balance of payments shift the AD curve until it cuts b at B. On gold, with the world stock of money given, some countries will find themselves temporarily in trade surplus, some in deficit. In θ - y space both schedules shift back with no necessary change in competitiveness. Changes in real money balances, wealth and competitiveness shift both IS and LM curves to a consistent equilibrium at B. For the typical economy there is no change in competitiveness and demand falls because of a fall in world demand for domestically produced goods. Supply falls because prices have fallen and the real wage has risen.

If the economy depicted in Figure 2.2 abandons fixed exchange rates it is able to increase real money balances, so shifting out the AD curve to cut the b curve at C in θ - y space and y^s at A in p - y space. Both competitiveness and prices rise. Aggregate demand rises because of the increased competitiveness. Interest rates may or may not fall because both IS and LM curves shift out. Aggregate supply increases because the real wage falls. If *all* countries pursue this policy, average competitiveness will not change but interest rates will fall because of the increase in real balances. Thus domestic demand will rise and increase further via the current account because of the revival in world activity. With the addition of a few wrinkles this is the story of most countries' experience of the Great Depression.

4 Estimation Results

We discuss first the labour demand equation (1). See Table 2.7. Capital is represented by a trend. We allow for dynamic adjustment by including a lagged dependent variable. We employ the lagged wage and real interest rate to minimise instrumentation. On average (row 5) the results are most pleasing. The average wage elasticity is about -0.7. The wage is wrong-signed in three countries (though insignificantly): Italy and, notably, the US and the UK (rows 3 and 4). We shall study the latter two countries in more detail below. The real interest rate performs even better than the wage: it is wrong-signed only in Belgium (t = 0.1). We wondered whether there was any separate effect from the nominal interest rate. Adding this we found it insignificant in all countries, $\bar{t}$ = 0.005, a comprehensive rejection. Thus tying the nominal interest rate and inflation together in this way is most consistent with the data. We should note that the significance of the wage in this analysis is in no way an artefact of the inclusion of the real interest rate. Without it we find an average t of -2.0, establishing the existence of a raw correlation between employment and the wage over the period, as is obvious anyway from study of

Table 2.7   Labour Demand Equations, 1923-38 (dependent variable employment, n_t)

	n_{t-1}	$(w-p)_{t-1}$	$(r-\overset{\cdot e}{p})_{t-1}$	trend	DW	SE
Europe	0.74	-0.19	-0.54	0.001	1.9	0.03
	(5.3)	(-2.0)	(-2.7)	(0.8)		
Scandinavia	0.44	-0.39	-0.61	0.008	1.5	0.04
	(2.2)	(-2.1)	(-2.2)	(1.8)		
UK	0.74	0.12	-0.08	0.001	1.3	0.02
	(3.0)	(0.3)	(-0.5)	(0.4)		
US	0.61	0.29	-0.53	-0.008	1.8	0.04
	(3.6)	(0.9)	(-2.5)	(-1.4)		
World average	0.59	-0.27	-0.53	0.003	1.7	0.03
	(3.9)	(-2.0)	(-2.7)	(1.4)		

Note: t statistics in brackets. Starting dates vary between countries; see Appendix 2.1. For conventions, see notes to Tables 2.2 and 2.3.

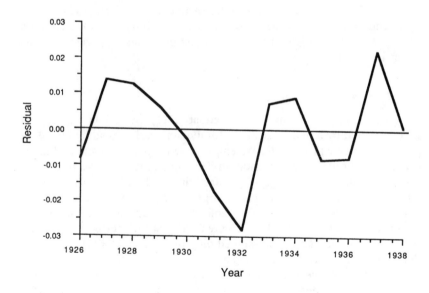

Figure 2.3   Average Residuals from the Labour Demand Equation, 1926-38

the plots in Figure 2.1. All in all, these results are strikingly consistent with what we have found postwar (e.g. Newell and Symons, 1987).

In Figure 2.3 we plot the average residuals from this model for our sample of fourteen countries. Note that only 1931 and 1932 show up with large negative unexplained components: about 2 and 3 per cent respectively. These are small relative to the large falls in employment over the period; and the implication is that the path of relative prices can more or less explain the Great Depression.

For the US and UK it is natural to ask whether the insignificant results for the wage are due simply to chance over a turbulent period or whether they point away from our theoretical framework. For both these countries we have long time series stretching back into the last century and we can estimate the model over longer time periods. See Table 2.8. For both these countries we have measures of capital and technical progress and these have been included. Constant returns to scale have been imposed. We exclude war and war-influenced years from our data, and also the early 1920s from Britain which were characterised by violent but transient changes in relative prices. It will be seen (rows 1 and 4) that the model fits well over the longer period and is consistent with the character of the international interwar results. For the interwar period the wage is wrongsigned in both but, most importantly, it is imprecisely estimated and the Chow test of parameter stability between the two periods is easily accepted. Thus the dependence of employment on relative prices over the interwar years is perfectly consistent with our model.

A generalisation of our model would allow transient demand shocks to influence employment, given relative prices (e.g. as in Newell and Symons, 1986b). If we include shocks (see the notes to Table 2.8 for construction) in the equation over the interwar period (rows 3 and 7) we obtain very similar results to those obtained over the longer period. Plots of these shock variables are given in Figure 2.4. Note the marked negative shocks in the US in 1932 and 1933. We conclude from this analysis that the difficulty of identifying real wage effects on employment for these two countries over this period is wholly due to the amount of noise over a turbulent period.

In summary, we find strong but slow-acting effects of the real wage on employment as well as powerful real interest rate effects. The burden of explanation for the level of employment throughout the Great Depression is thus passed back to explaining these variables.

We turn now to the real wage equations (2'). The real interest rate ρ was very weak in all experiments and typically wrong-signed. Given this, the fact that the real interest rate depresses employment according to the employment equation (1) means that a rise in the real interest rate will increase unemployment because the real wage does not fall to offset the fall

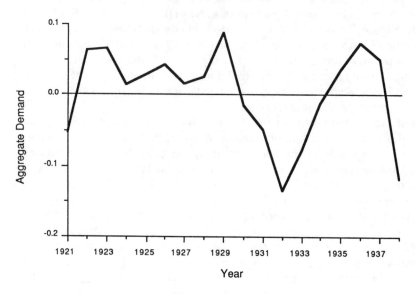

Figure 2.4a **Aggregate Demand Shocks in the United States, 1921-38**

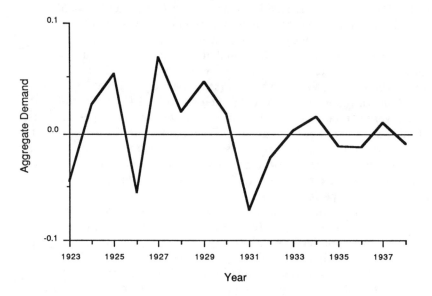

Figure 2.4b **Aggregate Demand Shocks in the United Kingdom, 1923-38**

Table 2.8   **UK and US Labour Demand Equations (dependent variable log employment - capital ratio $(n - k)_t$)**

	$n_{t-1}-k_t$	$(w-p_v)_{t-1}$	$(r-\dot{p}^e)_{t-1}$	λ_t	$(y-y^e)_t$	DW	SE
UK 1872-1913	0.84	-0.11	-0.61	-0.01		1.9	0.02
and 1923-38	(13.9)	(-2.0)	(-4.5)	(-2.5)			
UK	1.00	0.32	-0.75	-0.002		2.4	0.01
1923-38	(6.3)	(0.9)	(-3.0)	(-1.9)			
UK	0.81	-0.14	-0.65	-0.01	0.28	2.2	0.01
1923-38	(2.6)	(-0.2)	(-2.5)	(-0.6)	(1.8)		
US 1892-1916	0.92	-0.22	-0.53	0.14		1.6	0.04
and 1921-38	(9.3)	(-2.3)	(-2.5)	(1.5)			
US	1.15	0.01	-0.79	-0.31		1.8	0.05
1921-38	(6.1)	(0.0)	(-1.4)	(-0.7)			
US	0.81	-0.46	-0.61	0.35	0.69	1.6	0.02
1921-38	(7.1)	(-1.9)	(-2.1)	(1.4)	(5.3)		

Note: t statistics in brackets. The model estimated is (in logs)

$$(n-k)_t = \alpha_0 (n_{t-1} - k_t) - \alpha_2 (w - p_v)_{t-1} - \alpha_3 (r - \dot{p}^e)_{t-1} + \alpha_4 \lambda_t + \alpha_5 (y - y^e)_t$$

where λ_t is the log of an index of labour augmenting technical progress, calculated by the Solow residual method (see Newell and Symons (1985) for details), and $y-y^e$ is unexpected demand, which is represented by the residuals from a regression of y on lagged values of real wages, real interest rates, and real money balances. The real interest rate is its fitted value from a regression on lagged variables. Where appropriate, we take account of the endogenity of $y- y^e$ by using current changes in nominal money balances as an instrument. The equations without unexpected demand pass a Chow test for parameter stability over the two subsamples, the relevant F statistics being 1.65 for the US and 0.9 for the UK, where the 5 per cent significance level is around 4.5 in both cases.

in the demand for labour. It would be paradoxical if a perfectly forecast increase in the real interest rate created unemployment rather than merely reducing the wage. What this seems to mean is that, when the wage bargain is struck, it is assumed that the real interest rate will turn out to be at some normal level. It will be seen, for example, in Figure 2.1 that the real interest rate had returned to normal levels by 1932.

Without the real interest rate, a version of our real wage equation is given in Table 2.9. The capital-labour ratio is represented by a trend. The wedge p_c - p_v is entered in Δ (first difference) form, rather than in levels. This transformation was suggested by our previous work on post-Hitler's war data (Newell and Symons, 1985) and implies that changes in the tax and import wedge are incident only transiently on the product wage and

Table 2.9   Real wage equations 1923-38 (dependent variable real product wage $(w-p_v)_t$)

	$(w-p_v)_{t-1}$	$(\dot{p}_c-\dot{p}_v)$	$\dot{p}_c$	$\dot{p}_v$	U_{t-1}	trend	DW	SE
Europe (i)	0.82	0.85	-0.49		-0.004	0.007	2.2	0.03
	(4.8)	(2.2)	(-2.2)		(-1.0)	(2.6)		
(ii)	0.70			-0.64	-0.009	0.009	2.2	0.03
	(7.1)			(-4.0)	(-1.1)	(3.7)		
Scandinavia (i)	0.71	0.76	-0.81		-0.035	0.008	2.0	0.04
	(3.0)	(1.1)	(-1.0)		(-0.9)	(0.9)		
(ii)	0.66			-0.76	-0.037	0.009	1.7	0.04
	(4.0)			(-2.7)	(-1.2)	(2.2)		
UK (i)	0.16	-0.14	0.21		0.007	0.006	2.6	0.01
	(0.5)	(-0.6)	(1.2)		(0.4)	(1.6)		
(ii)	0.13			0.21	0.006	0.006	2.5	0.01
	(0.4)			(1.3)	(0.4)	(1.8)		
US (i)	0.50	-0.66	0.60		-0.004	0.010	1.8	0.03
	(1.3)	(-0.9)	(3.1)		(-0.4)	(1.1)		
(ii)	0.48			0.60	-0.004	0.010	1.8	0.03
	(1.9)			(3.7)	(-0.5)	(1.7)		
World average (i)	0.68	0.65	-0.43		-0.011	0.007	2.2	0.03
	(3.4)	(1.6)	(-1.2)		(-0.7)	(1.8)		
(ii)	0.58			-0.51	-0.013	0.009	2.0	0.03
	(4.6)			(-2.6)	(-0.8)	(2.8)		

Note: For general notes and conventions, see notes to Table 2.2. Method of estimation: instrumental variables. Current prices or inflation rates were treated as endogenous: instruments were lagged values and lagged world prices and world trade. Here unemployment rates are normalised on their average value 1921-29, so as to make the coefficients internationally comparable.

hence influence employment only transiently. On average (row 9) the model is well supported. The wedge term is fairly strong, indicating that, for our sample of countries, the fall in commodity prices in the late 1920s was benign for employment. Nominal rigidity is significant on average but fairly sporadic. Unemployment is quite weak, indicating that the feedback from unemployment to the wage was weak: this is presumably part of the problem. Inspection of the parameters on $\dot{p}_c$ - $\dot{p}_v$ and $\dot{p}_c$ suggests that these terms could be approximately replaced by $\dot{p}_v$ and this is done in row 10. The estimate is considerably sharpened. Much the same story holds for the European and Scandinavian groups of countries (rows 1 to 4). The results for the UK and the US are contrary. If we estimate this equation for the UK up to 1913 we obtain similar results to the average reported in row 9, though much more sharply estimated. Between the wars our experiments indicate that the UK real wage behaved more or less as a random walk with drift. There is no sign of nominal rigidity, and no indication of unemployment feedback. It should be noted that the UK received only a very minor price shock in 1929. Similarly, for the US we find no nominal rigidity and no unemployment feedback. It would be hard to maintain that nominal wage rigidity was a feature of the US over this period. The nominal wage fell quite sharply in 1931; and Mitchell (1986) shows that wage cuts were common in the US in the 1920s. Our preferred real wage equation for the US is simply:

$$w\text{-}p_v = 0.79 \; (w\text{-}p_v)_{\text{-}1} + 0.21 \; (w\text{-} p_v)^*$$

$$(5.5) \qquad\qquad (\text{imposed})$$

$$DW = 1.9 \qquad SE = 0.037 \qquad 1921\text{-}38,$$

where $(w\text{-}p_v)^*$ is the equilibrium wage defined as that wage which equates the labour force and employment in the long-run version of the model in Table 2.7, row 4. This means that nominal rigidity cannot be part of our account of the US Great Depression: the logic of our analysis suggests that this must be due to slow recovery from massive demand and/or monetary shocks in the early 1930s. This slowness is due to natural inertia in employment evident in all the employment equations in Tables 2.7 and 2.8. Thus the reduced form supply equation in this model is effectively a dynamic Lucas supply curve of the sort discussed by Sargent, (1973, equation 23). The fact that there is little feedback from unemployment to real wages is characteristic also of US data since the last war. We have discussed this elsewhere (Newell and Symons, 1987): the theoretical meaning of this long-standing phenomenon is still unclear.

In accordance with the comparative statics analysis in section 2, nominal wage rigidity correlates fairly well with unemployment performance over the Depression. See Figure 2.5. Denmark is an outlier, but Denmark experienced a very high level of average unemployment during the 1920s suggesting that our performance measure, which normalises on this average, may give a misleading picture in this case.

We estimate a version of our price equation (6') in Table 2.10. We include results for the US for consistency though the open-economy perspective is in this case clearly misleading. Appendix 2.1 gives details of our construction of the wealth terms W and W*. We found relative wealth W - W* to be weak and we shall not discuss it here. World wealth W* is correctly signed on average, though more diffusely estimated across countries than one would wish. Of course W* is the appropriate variable to represent foreigners' demand for domestic output only in a world of perfect capital markets. If this is not the case current and future foreign income will appear with different weights. In the models labelled (ii) we replace W* with the current and lagged levels of world trade. The improvement in fit is marked, and we prefer these models.

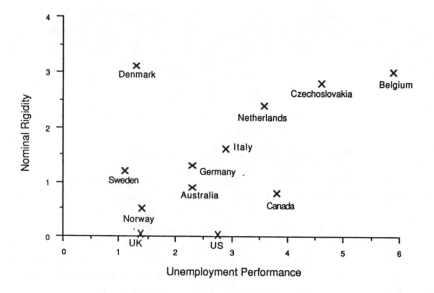

Figure 2.5   Unemployment Performance and Nominal Rigidity

Note: The long-run inflation parameters from the wage equations in Table 2.8 are on the vertical axis (absolute value). On the horizontal axis is the ratio of average 1930s unemployment to average 1920s unemployment.

The effect of world prices on domestic prices is powerful and quite quick-acting: the mean lag is about a third of a year on average. We have sought to include the effect of tariffs on prices by developing an index of the world rate of effective protection τ. This variable is strongly correlated with p*_and world trade, and if entered separately in (6') tends to be very imprecisely estimated. The impact effect of tariffs should be one for one with world prices but decline as domestic resources are moved to the production of the protected good. A simple approximation to this is to enter tariffs as a first difference with the same parameter as p*. This is done in Table 2.10: the implied restriction was always easy to accept. Note that in terms of our model tariffs work by allowing an increase in prices without a deterioration in the balance of trade.

The remaining part of the model is just as one might expect: wages are correctly signed and significant everywhere; and the level of world trade exerts a powerful impact effect on domestic prices. We experimented with dummy variables for the exchange rate regime, but these were always insignificant. This was true also for government expenditure.

Table 2.10   Price Equations, 1923-38 (dependent variable inflation, $p_t - p_{t-1}$)

	$(p^*_t + \dot{\tau} - p_{t-1})$	$(w_t - p_{t-1})$	(world wealth)$_t$	(world trade)$_t$	(world trade)$_{t-1}$	DW	SE
Europe (i)	0.35	0.13	0.32			1.4	0.05
	(3.5)	(2.1)	(0.9)				
(ii)	0.30	0.38		0.56	-0.49	2.2	0.03
	(3.5)	(3.2)		(3.1)	(-3.3)		
Scandinavia (i)	0.46	0.36	0.67			1.9	0.03
	(4.6)	(2.9)	(2.8)				
(ii)	0.46	0.58		0.43	-0.15	1.6	0.03
	(3.4)	(4.6)		(2.7)	(-1.0)		
UK (i)	0.11	0.46	0.04			2.6	0.01
	(3.8)	(5.9)	(0.6)				
(ii)	0.09	0.44		0.05	-0.02	2.3	0.01
	(2.7)	(5.9)		(1.4)	(-0.6)		
US (i)	0.22	0.22	-0.02			1.5	0.02
	(4.7)	(3.7)	(-0.2)				
(ii)	0.15	0.19		0.14	-0.16	1.7	0.02
	(2.4)	(4.0)		(1.2)	(-1.5)		
World average (i)	0.33	0.29	0.32			1.7	0.04
	(3.6)	(2.7)	(1.2)				
(ii)	0.32	0.42		0.45	-0.31	2.0	0.03
	(3.1)	(3.6)		(2.6)	(-2.3)		

Note: For general notes and conventions, see notes to Table 2.2. Method of estimation: instrumental variables. All current variables were treated as endogenous: instruments were lagged values of these variables plus lagged values of the world trade and real money balances variables, as well as a dummy variable for the exchange rate regime. τ_t is a world index of protection. See text for discussion.

We have thus developed a three-equation model for each of our sample of countries: an unemployment equation, a real wage equation, and a price equation. Figure 2.6 gives a flow chart of the implied causation. The models employed are the average version of each of the three preferred specifications. Thus the model used refers to no particular country but is rather an unweighted average of all models. We take as exogenous the price of traded goods, world trade, tariffs and the nominal interest rate. Each cell gives the change in the variable over the indicated period. On each arrow we have written the contribution made by each variable to the change in the variable it influences. These contributions were calculated as follows. We simulated the average model from 1925 to 1937 allowing all independent variables their observed (averaged across all countries) values. The model was then simulated holding each

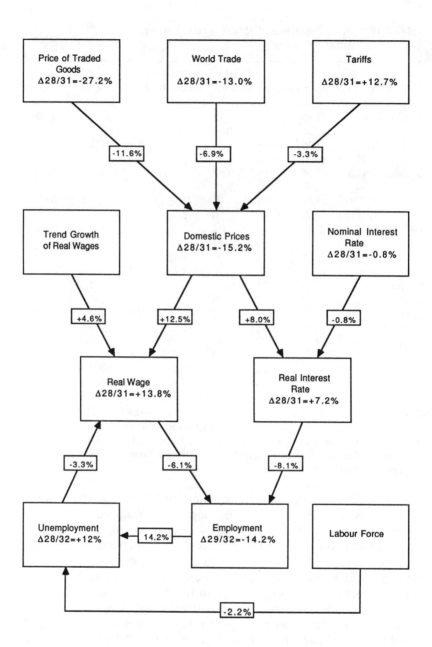

Figure 2.6   Linkages in the Great Depression

independent variable at its 1928 value, once for each independent variable. The change in the simulated dependent variable between each simulation was then attributed to the behaviour of the variable being held constant. For convenience the inflows to each cell, where their total was discrepant with the observed change in the cell, were factored to achieve equality.

Let us now trace the course of the Great Depression. The price of traded goods fell between 1928 and 1931 by 27 per cent, and the level of world trade fell by 13 per cent. In direct consequence domestic prices would have fallen by 18.5 per cent if protectionism had not raised prices by 3.3 per cent. Thus domestic prices fell by 15.2 per cent leading to potential rises of 12.5 per cent and 8.0 per cent in the real wage and real interest rate respectively. Trend growth contributed 4.6 per cent to the wage; but increased unemployment reduced it by 3.3 per cent: the sum of the three effects gives a rise of 13.8 per cent. The nominal interest rate fell by 0.8 per cent so the real interest rate rose by 7.2 per cent. The real interest rate and the real wage contributed 8.1 per cent and 6.1 per cent respectively to the fall in employment. Since the labour force fell by 2.2 per cent, the unemployment rate rose by twelve points, on average. (One feedback is missing in our model: from wages to prices. This was tiny and is omitted.) These numbers should not be taken too seriously: they merely suggest orders of magnitude to the various causalities in our model.

5   The World

So far we have taken world prices and output as given. In this section we apply our model to the world, considered as a single economic entity. The world IS curve takes the form

$$y^* = y^* (\rho^*, W^*)$$

We shall take W^* as a trade-weighted average of industrial country wealth; and ρ^* is a similar average of real interest rates. An estimate of a version of this model is given in Table 2.11. We have imposed the restriction that output is unit-elastic with respect to wealth in the long run, which was almost exactly true in the unrestricted model. Note that a permanent 1 percentage point increase in the real interest rate would produce about a 1 percentage fall in demand, wealth held constant, with a mean lag of about two years. Since W^* fell by about 9 per cent between 1929 and 1932, mainly due to the fall in real stock prices, and ρ^*_{t-1} rose by a similar amount, both are strong variables in accounting for the fall in output.

Table 2.11 The World Model, 1924-38

IS curve: $y^*_t - W^*_t = 0.71 (y^*_{t-1} - W^*_t) - 0.39 \, p^*_{t-1}$	SE = 0.02, DW = 2.3
$\qquad\qquad\quad (4.7) \qquad\qquad\qquad (-3.3)$	

LM curve: $(m - p - y)^*_t = -3.06 \, r^*_t + S$ $\qquad\qquad$ SE = 0.03, DW = 2.7
$\qquad\qquad\qquad\quad (-3.4)$

$$S = 0.04 \, D30 + 0.15 \, D31 + 0.23 \, D32 + 0.20 \, D33 + 0.17 \, D34 + 0.09 \, D35$$
$\quad\;\;(1.1) \qquad\;\; (4.3) \qquad\;\; (6.7) \qquad\;\; (5.6) \qquad\;\; (4.6) \qquad\;\; (2.3)$

Output supply: $y^*_t = 0.94 \, y^*_t + 0.42 \, p_t$ $\qquad\qquad$ SE = 0.02, DW = 2.3
$\qquad\qquad\qquad\quad (14.1) \qquad (4.0)$

Note: Both independent variables in the IS curve are endogenous with instruments: lagged nominal interest rates, labour income, wealth and the change in world trade. In the LM curve, r^*_t is instrumented by its own lagged value and the lagged change in world trade. In the output supply equation p_t is instrumented with lags of wealth, money balances, and nominal interest rates. For simulations p^e in the expression for the real interest rate was replaced by the fitted value from a regression of $\dot{p}$ on its own lagged value and two lags of output.

This analysis implies that the fall in world wealth from 1929 to 1932 was a major deflationary force causing the Great Depression, as was the rise in the real interest rate. We turn now to money.

Money is held for transactions and as an asset. A fall in world wealth will produce a negative income effect on the demand for money as an asset, but a fall in the expected return on equities, as must surely have happened, will produce an opposite substitution effect. A further complication arises from the role of bank collapses which will reduce the demand for deposits and increase the demand for currency. Rather than attempt to unpick these complex interactions we shall simply allow the demand for money function to shift over the 1930s. Thus we estimate:

$$m - p - y = \lambda \, (m-p-y)_{-1} - \alpha \, r + S$$

where S is a set of year dummies for the first half of the 1930s. The results across all countries are summarised in Table 2.12. We especially include Canada as it provides an interesting contrast with the United States.

The dummies reveal a Λ-shaped increase in the demand for money, centred on 1932, which is strikingly consistent across countries. We have cumulated these dummy variables via the lagged dependent variable to give the total shift in the demand for money in Table 2.13. On average there was a fairly modest shift, but in North America the shift was much

Table 2.12   Demand for Money Equations, 1923-38 (dependent variable, m-p-y)

	(m-p-y)$_{t-1}$	(interest rate)$_t$	D30	D31	D32	D33	D34	D35	DW	SE
Europe	0.29	-0.08	0.04	0.03	0.14	0.05	0.04	0.05	2.5	0.09
	(1.6)	(-1.6)	(0.4)	(0.2)	(1.3)	(0.3)	(0.2)	(0.0)		
Scandinavia	0.32	0.00	0.11	0.14	0.10	0.14	0.04	0.00	1.8	0.08
	(1.0)	(0.1)	(1.3)	(1.5)	(1.1)	(1.3)	(0.2)	(0.2)		
UK	-0.54	-0.06	-0.08	0.02	0.07	0.09	0.06	0.01	2.0	0.04
	(0.7)	(-1.6)	(-1.1)	(0.5)	(1.6)	(2.0)	(0.9)	(0.3)		
US	0.51	-0.05	0.06	0.08	0.17	0.08	-0.02	0.05	2.4	0.03
	(2.7)	(-1.8)	(1.3)	(2.1)	(4.2)	(1.3)	(-0.3)	(1.5)		
Canada	0.56	-0.04	-0.03	0.11	0.17	0.17	0.02	0.05	1.9	0.04
	(2.3)	(0.6)	(-0.3)	(0.8)	(2.3)	(1.7)	(0.2)	(0.6)		
World average	0.27	-0.04	0.04	0.07	0.12	0.09	0.04	0.03	2.3	0.08
	(1.2)	(-1.1)	(0.4)	(0.8)	(1.6)	(0.9)	(0.3)	(0.4)		

Note: r$_t$ is instrumented by r$_{t-1}$, r*$_{t-1}$.

Table 2.13   Cumulated Effect of Shift in Demand for Money Functions

	1930	1931	1932	1933	1934	1935
World average	0.04	0.08	0.14	0.13	0.07	0.05
UK	-0.08	0.06	0.04	0.07	0.02	0.00
US	0.06	0.11	0.23	0.20	0.07	0.09
Canada	-0.03	0.09	0.22	0.29	0.18	0.15

stronger: in particular the increase in Canadian demand for money was much greater than in the US. Equities fell much less in Europe and in consequence one would expect a lesser increase in the demand for money. The relative behaviour of Canada and the US, which experienced similar equity behaviour, has been explained by Friedman and Schwartz as due to the absence in Canada of bank failures:

> The bank failures made deposits a much less satisfactory form in which to hold assets than they had been before in the United States or than they remained in Canada ... the demand for the sum of deposits and currency was reduced by the diminished attractiveness of deposits. Of course that effect was not strong enough to offset completely the increased demand for money relative to income as a result of ... the great increase in uncertainty, the decline in

Table 2.14   Simulations, 1930-33

	Change (%) in World GDP	Change (%) in World GDP deflator
Due to decline in wealth	-3.4	-13.8
Due to shift in the demand for money	-4.2	-16.3
Due to monetary contraction	-1.5	-5.7
Simulated	-9.1	-35.9
Actual	-7.0	-22.0

attractiveness of equities and real goods, and so on. (Friedman and Schwartz, 1965, p. 57)

The trade-weighted world version of the LM curve is given in Table 2.11. The Λ-shaped shift is again apparent. It is possible to obtain a similar equation replacing the dummy shifts with changes in world equity prices; but we think our approach is superior in that it allows for changes in wealth, and also for changes in banking risk.

We complete the world model with an aggregate supply equation, giving output as a function of the inflation rate. As discussed above, we think of this as due to nominal wage rigidity, but others may prefer to think of it simply as a Lucas supply equation with $\dot{p}^e = 0$. Alternatively we could replace this supply equation with one giving output as a function of the real wage and the real interest rate lagged: in fact this leads to similar results.

The reduced form of this system gives each of the endogenous variables p^*, y^* and r^* as functions of W^*, S and m. In order to see which of these is the most potent in explaining the Great Depression, we adopted the procedure described at the end of section 4. We simulated the model from 1929 allowing the exogenous variables to take their observed paths, and then held each endogenous variable constant in turn at its 1929 value. The difference between the simulations was, as before, attributed to the behaviour of the variable held constant.

Simulating our model from 1929 we obtain a trough in 1933 rather than 1932. Table 2.14 compares the simulated model at 1933 with observed values and also apportions changes in the endogenous variables to the behaviour of each exogenous variable. We find that the shift in the LM curve is the main culprit: it explains 46 per cent of the simulated fall in output, versus 37 per cent for the fall in wealth. Direct monetary contraction exerted only a minor influence.

6   Concluding Remarks

Let us summarise our argument. We have shown that the world economy was characterised between the wars by significant nominal rigidities on the supply side. These, as a consequence of a collapse in demand in the 1930s, led to increases in the real wage and real interest rates, and hence to the Great Depression. With regard to the fall in demand, we have compared three proximate sources: an observable shift in monetary behaviour, a decline in the money stock, and a fall in world wealth associated principally with a fall in equity prices (see Figure 2.1e). In the preceding section we have shown that the change in monetary behaviour - an increase in liquidity preference - caused a larger fall in demand than the fall in wealth and that the direct contribution of the fall in the money stock was quite slight.

But in a deeper sense this increase in liquidity preference was surely caused in large part by the continued poor performance of the equity market. Can one base an account of the Great Depression on "animal spirits"?

The argument would run like this. The bursting of the Wall Street bubble in 1929, coinciding with a natural downturn, sets in train a rapid deflation derived essentially from a wealth effect on aggregate demand. Pessimistic expectations are transmitted to the rest of the world. Nominal rigidities translate the fall in demand into a fall in real income so that pessimism becomes in part self-fulfilling. A complex of vicious circles is set up, as illustrated in Figure 2.7. The process continues until any lower valuation of the capital stock is implausible. This seems to us a convincing story. What are the problems?

The main problem is that financial panics do not always lead to Great Depressions. In particular Brunner (1981) asks why, if the 1929 crash was the key event in causing the Great Depression, did not the stock market fall in 1974 have catastrophic effects? According to our analysis a num-

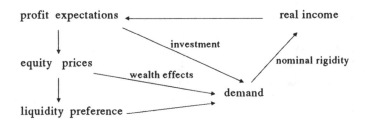

Figure 2.7   Transmission Mechanisms in the Depression

ber of preconditions are required before a collapse in demand can lead to a major depression.

(i) Nominal rigidities. An inwards shift of the aggregate demand schedule can produce enduring effects only if nominal rigidities ensure the aggregate supply schedule is upwards-sloping. We have argued that nominal rigidities become important only at low levels of core inflation. Inflation was very low worldwide in 1929, very high in 1974.

(ii) Governments must be unwilling or unable to take offsetting expansionary monetary action. We have seen how important was the increase in liquidity preference in propagating the Depression. If this increase in the demand for money had been met by an increase in the supply of money, we estimate the unemployment effects of the Depression would have been at least halved. We have shown in the first section that the sooner countries abandoned fixed exchange rates and hence gained control over their stock of money, the better they fared. Presumably only the United States could have acted unilaterally in this regard. We thus accept the central hypothesis of Friedman and Schwartz (1965) that US monetary policy must get the lion's share of the blame.

(iii) International linkages. When the bourses of the world are just a telephone call away, bearishness can rapidly spread from country to country. Kindleberger (1978) quotes Meyer von Rothschild saying in 1875, "The whole world has become a city." A related point is that the development of interest-sensitive international capital flows places greater constraints on short-run domestic monetary policy than those imposed merely by the current account.

Our contention is thus that a low level of core inflation, interlinked capital markets and a regime of fixed exchange rates mean that the world is particularly prone to depressions of the sort experienced after 1929. The most obvious precursor is the depression that followed the financial crash of 1873 ("the first significant international crisis", Kindleberger, 1978, p.132) when for example the British unemployment rate rose steadily until 1879 (Feinstein, 1976, Table 124). Undoubtedly the world was ripe for a depression. Kindleberger points to overinvestment in fixed capital and in particular in stocks of commodities as a consequence of the boom ending in 1929. The liquidation of these commodity stocks after the crash may have been the first deflationary shock to world prices. The readiness to resort to protectionism, though clearly not deflationary, may have exerted a transient influence on employment which helped the Depression on its way.

APPENDIX 2.1   Data

The data for the United States and United Kingdom regressions in Table 2.8 were all taken from *Long-Term Economic Growth in the US* (Department of Commerce, 1964) and Feinstein (1976) respectively.

In all the interwar regressions the starting dates were: 1922 for Australia, Finland, Italy, Norway, the United Kingdom and the United States; 1923 for Belgium, Canada, Denmark, France and the Netherlands; 1924 for Sweden; 1925 for Czechoslovakia; 1926 for Germany.

N   Employment. The employment data used here are discussed in detail in Newell (1986). The intention was to find time series of total civilian employment for every country. This proved impossible in a number of cases, and as a result the series employed vary in quality from official estimates or elaborately reconstructed series (i.e., Australia, Canada, Denmark, Netherlands, Norway, United Kingdom, and United States) to indices calculated employing the few materials available (Finland, France, Sweden).

U   The unemployment rate. There is a detailed discussion of the unemployment rate series in Newell (1985b). The series used here were chosen on two criteria: reliability of source and closeness of definition to the employment series. Series derived from trade union records are used for Australia, Belgium, Czechoslovakia, Denmark and Sweden. For the other countries series are derived in the main from the operation of unemployment insurance schemes.

w   The nominal wage rate. The construction of these data is described in detail in Newell (1986). Our intention was to find series reflecting annual averages of hourly earnings in the widest possible industry grouping. In fact wage rate series are used for Australia, Belgium, Canada, Czechoslovakia, France, Germany, Italy, Netherlands and Norway. Earnings series are used for Denmark, Finland, Sweden, the United Kingdom and the United States.

p_v The GDP deflator. Taken from national historical data sources and from Mitchell (1980, 1983). No series were available for Belgium, Finland and France. The series used for these countries were wholesale price indices adjusted according to the formula:

$$p_v = (1+s)\, p_o - s\, p_m$$

where p_o is the wholesale price index, p_m is an import price index and s is the ratio of imports to GDP.

p_c Consumer price index. Taken from national historical data sources and from Mitchell (1980, 1983).

M A broad monetary aggregate. Taken from national historical data sources and from Mitchell (1980, 1983). The definition used generally is notes and coins in circulation plus all deposits in commercial banks, thus perhaps corresponding to a contemporary definition somewhere between M2 and M3. Sources were the League of Nations *Review of World Trade and Monthly Bulletin of Statistics.*

r The nominal interest rate. The data are central bank discount rates from League of Nations *Monthly Bulletin of Statistics.*

τ Tariffs. The average tariff rate. This variable is the average across the fourteen countries of $\bar{p}-p^*$, where $\bar{p}$ is the log of the wholesale price index and p^* is defined below.

y Real GDP. Taken from national historical data sources and from Mitchell (1980, 1983).

p^* The world price of manufacturing value-added in US dollars. This was constructed using two series, p_m the world price of traded manufactures, and p_o the world price of other goods, according to the formula: $p^* = 1.25\, p_m - 0.25\, p_o$. Both raw series were taken from the UN *Statistical Yearbook 1969.*

World Trade. A quantum index of world trade in manufactures from UN *Statistical Yearbook 1969.*

e Annual average exchange rate as a percentage of gold parity. Sources were: League of Nations *Review of World Trade* and *Monthly Bulletin of Statistics.*

W Wealth. A geometric average of real labour income, real stock prices, and real money balances, with weights 0.7, 0.28, 0.02, respectively. The stock price data were taken from League of Nations, *Monthly Bulletin of Statistics*.

The world variables W*, y*, etc. are trade-weighted averages of the data from the fourteen countries. Trade weights at 1929 from UN *Statistical Yearbook 1969*.

REFERENCES

Bean, C., Layard, P.R.G. and Nickell, S.J. (1986), "The Rise in Unemployment: A Multi-country Study", *Economica*, May.

Bernanke, B.S. (1985), "Employment, Hours, and Earnings in the Depression: An Analysis of Eight Manufacturing Industries", National Bureau of Economic Research, Working Paper no. 1642, June.

Brunner, K. (ed.) (1981), *The Great Depression Revisited*, The Hague: Martinus Nijhoff.

Eichengreen, B. and Sachs, J. (1985), "Exchange Rates and Economic Recovery in the 1930s", *Journal of Economic History* 45, no.4, pp.925-46.

Feinstein, C.H. (1976), *Statistical Tables of National Income, Expenditure and Output of the UK, 1855-1965*, Cambridge: Cambridge University Press.

Friedman, M. and Schwartz, A.J. (1965), *The Great Contraction*, Princeton, New Jersey: Princeton University Press.

Hatton, T.J. (1986), "The Analysis of Unemployment in Interwar Britain: A Survey of Research", in *Economic Perspectives*, London: Harwood.

Hicks, J.R. (1974), "Real and Monetary Factors in Economic Fluctuations", *Scottish Journal of Political Economy*, pp.205-214.

Kindleberger, C.P. (1973), *The World in Depression 1929-1939*, Berkeley: University of California Press.

Kindleberger, C.P. (1978), *Manias, Panics and Crashes*, New York: Basic Books.

Mitchell, B.R. (1962), *Abstract of British Historical Statistics*, Cambridge: Cambridge University Press.

Mitchell, B.R. (1980), *European Historical Statistics*, London: Macmillan, 2nd edn.

Mitchell, B.R. (1983), *Historical Statistics of the Americas, Asia and Australasia*, London: Macmillan.

Mitchell, D.J.B. (1986), "Explanations of Wage Inflexibility: Institutions and Incentives", in W. Beckerman (ed.), *Wage Rigidity and Unemployment*, London: Duckworth.

Newell, A.T. (1985a), "The Revised OECD Data Set", London School of Economics, Centre for Labour Economics, Working Paper no. 781.

Newell, A.T. (1985b), "Historical Unemployment Rate Data", London School of Economics, Centre for Labour Economics, Working Paper no. 804.

Newell, A.T. (1986), "Annual Data for Interwar Employment and Wages", London School of Economics, Centre for Labour Economics, Working Paper no. 841.

Newell, A.T. and Symons, J.S.V. (1985), "Wages and Unemployment in the OECD Countries", London School of Economics, Centre for Labour Economics, Discussion Paper no. 219.

Newell, A.T. and Symons, J.S.V. (1986a), "The Phillips Curve as a Real Wage Equation", London School of Economics, Centre for Labour Economics, Discussion Paper no. 246.

Newell, A.T. and Symons, J.S.V. (1986b), "Showdown for the Labour Demand Curve", London School of Economics, Centre for Labour Economics, Working Paper no. 885.

Newell, A.T. and Symons, J.S.V. (1987), "Corporatism, the Laissez-faire, and the Rise in Unemployment", *European Economic Review* 31, pp. 567-602.

Nickell, S.J. and Andrews, M. (1983), "Unions, Real Wages, and Employment in Britain 1951-1979", *Oxford Economics Papers*, November.

Okun, A.M. (1981), *Prices and Quantities: A Macroeconomic Analysis,* Oxford: Blackwell.

Sargent, T.J. (1973), "Rational Expectations, the Real Rate of Interest, and the National Rate of Unemployment", Brookings Institution, Washington, DC, Brookings Papers on Economic Activity, no. 2.

Symons, J.S.V. (1985), "Relative Prices and the Demand for Labour in British Manufacturing", *Economica* 52, pp. 37-51.

Chapter 3

Labour Market Structure and the Nature of Unemployment in Interwar Britain

Mark Thomas*

1 Introduction

Much of the work that has been undertaken by both historians and economists in examining unemployment in interwar Britain has concentrated on its causes, particularly its macroeconomic origins. A good deal of the analysis of the British condition of the 1930s has been motivated by the search for parallels to the recent past, especially in the light of theoretical controversies which had their beginnings in the literature of the time but which underwent a renaissance during the monetarist-Keynesian debates of the early 1970s and the subsequent birth of the New Classical Macroeconomics.

The central argument of this paper is that it is not possible to draw coherent conclusions from the experience of the 1930s without formal recognition of the structure of the labour market and without appreciation of the circumstances and context of individual unemployment, environment of job loss and job search. An irony of the application of the new labour economics to interwar Britain is that little or no attention has been paid to microeconomic evidence. Unemployment has been transformed from an individual state to an economic process analysed in the aggregate. The purpose of this paper is to provide a preliminary analysis of the incidence and structure of unemployment, without which our understanding of the interwar British malaise is liable to remain partial and inchoate.

B. Eichengreen and T. J. Hatton (eds.), Interwar Unemployment in International Perspective, 97–148.
© 1988 by Kluwer Academic Publishers.

2   Stocks, Flows and Duration of Unemployment

The pattern of unemployment in interwar Britain is well known: a historically high rate of unemployment in the 1920s made worse by the impact of the international recession of 1929-31, followed by a period of steady recovery during the 1930s, interrupted briefly by the downturn of 1937-38 but then accelerated by the march to war. The general contours are shown in Table 3.1. In this table, two estimates of the unemployment rate are shown, for insured workers and all employees respectively. Given the incomplete and changing coverage of the unemployment insurance scheme in the 1930s, Feinstein's (1972) revised figures (column 5) are to be preferred. However, data restrictions limit much of the analysis of this paper to the insured unemployed.

Although data on stocks will be the starting point in any analysis of unemployment, they provide only limited insights into the working of the labour market. In particular, they tell us very little about the character of unemployment. Thus, for example, an unemployment rate of 20 per cent is compatible with states in which all workers are out of work for 20 per cent of the year, 20 per cent of the labour force is out of work for the entire year, or anything between these extremes. These alternative states call for different explanations of the origins of unemployment, imply different welfare costs for those without work, and suggest different strategies for dealing with the problem. Clearly, knowledge of the stock alone without information on the flows into and out of unemployment is likely to leave us relatively uninformed. The use of aggregate stock data is flawed in another direction as well. The incidence of unemployment varies across subpopulations. The individuals on the register are not homogeneous. Neither the risks of becoming unemployed nor the chances of finding a new job are shared equally by everyone in society. Moreover, the characteristics of the unemployed are likely to alter over time, since different demographic groups will vary in their reactions to macroeconomic changes. There may also be divergent secular changes in labour force participation between groups. Clearly, therefore, an understanding of unemployment requires that we go behind the aggregates and analyse its correlates and characteristics. I begin, however, by concentrating on the labour market as a whole in order to introduce the statistical base upon which much of this paper is founded.

The major source of labour market data for Britain in this period is the material produced by the Ministry of Labour relating to the workings of the unemployment insurance scheme. Each month from 1911 onwards, figures on the numbers of insured workers unemployed were published in the *Labour Gazette*. The figures were derived from examination of the insurance books lodged at the local employment exchange.[1] The pub-

Table 3.1   Employment and Unemployment, 1920-38

	Employed workforce	Unemployed		Unemployment rates	
		Insured workers	Total workers	Insured workers	Total unemployed
	1,000s	1,000s	1,000s	%	%
1921	15,879	1,840	2,212	17.0	12.2
1922	15,847	1,588	1,909	14.3	10.8
1923	16,068	1,304	1,567	11.7	8.9
1924	16,332	1,168	1,404	10.3	7.9
1925	16,531	1,297	1,559	11.3	8.6
1926	16,529	1,463	1,759	12.5	9.6
1927	17,060	1,142	1,373	9.7	7.4
1928	17,123	1,278	1,536	10.8	8.2
1929	17,392	1,250	1,503	10.4	8.0
1930	17,016	1,979	2,379	16.1	12.3
1931	16,554	2,705	3,252	21.3	16.4
1932	16,644	2,828	3,400	22.1	17.0
1933	17,018	2,567	3,087	19.9	15.4
1934	17,550	2,170	2,609	16.7	12.9
1935	17,890	2,027	2,437	15.5	12.0
1936	18,513	1,749	2,100	13.1	10.2
1937	19,196	1,482	1,776	10.8	8.5
1938	19,243	1,800	2,164	12.9	10.1

Source: Feinstein (1972), T128.

lished figures represent a consistent snapshot, one month apart, of those unemployed. During most of the 1930s, the data distinguished workers by personal characteristic (sex and age) and by labour market situation (wholly unemployed, temporarily stopped and out-of-work casual workers). The aggregate data were also classified by region (citing eight major divisions, 100 large towns, and, with some circumspection, 673 local labour market areas) and industry (distinguishing 101 sectors).

Each unemployment book recorded one year of a worker's insurance history. Annually, in July, the books were replaced. This exchange enabled the Ministry of Labour to tally up the total number of books issued, and therefore the total number of insured workers. This total was used to generate unemployment rates from the benefits data. The exchange also provided additional data which were analysed in occasional sample surveys of the unemployed. These surveys, although organised primarily for actuarial purposes, do contain some useful material on the characteristics and correlates of unemployment. Unfortunately, only one sample survey of both employed and unemployed workers was undertaken in the interwar period, so that in general it is not possible to use these data to draw strong inferences regarding the incidence of unemployment across demographic groups (Ministry of Labour, 1927).[2]

The unemployment register serves as the basis of the stock estimates shown in Table 3.1. It did not, however, cover all workers. The insurance scheme after 1920 applied to all persons over 16 years of age who were employed under a contract of service or an apprenticeship and, if nonmanual workers, received less than £250 per annum. Those employed in sectors where the risk of unemployment was believed to be low, notably agriculture, forestry, horticulture and domestic service, were excluded from the system.[3] So too were persons in military service, the police, teachers, nurses, most civil servants and many workers employed by local authorities and other public utilities (Garside, 1980, pp. 31-2). Before September 1934, juveniles under 16 years were also excluded. In total, of the 19.5 million identified as gainfully employed within the age limits of the insurance scheme at the 1931 census, only 12.5 million were insured against unemployment. It is the population census, with its more complete coverage, that serves as the fulcrum of Feinstein's revised series, shown in Table 3.1, although the fluctuations around the base year observation are largely modelled on movements in the insured unemployed (Feinstein, 1972).

How should we characterise the stock of unemployment at a point in time? As a stagnant pool of jobless waiting for an improvement in macroeconomic conditions? Or as a stream of workers moving through the register in the search for new opportunities, using benefit payments as a subsidy for locating the position that best accords with their comparative advantage? Did the insurance scheme operate as a safety net to minimise the welfare costs of involuntary unemployment, as a means of maximising social welfare by promoting better job matching, or as a way of redistributing income and welfare from those in work towards those who preferred to use benefits to subsidise leisure activity? In order to differentiate these situations we need to know something about turnover in the labour market. The standard route to such information is to examine flows into and out of unemployment. Unfortunately, there is very little direct information on labour market flows for this period. The Ministry of Labour did not systematically collect such data until the mid-1960s. Nevertheless, it is possible to say a considerable amount about the dynamics of the labour market in interwar Britain, although it is necessary to proceed with some caution.

The basic relationships between stocks and flows in the labour market are most easily derived by assuming a steady-state world. The characteristics of a steady state include a constant inflow into unemployment over time and a stable relation between the duration of a spell of unemployment and the probability of outflow into employment (or retirement). The latter condition is derived from the joint assumption that individual exit probabilities do not depend on the date of entry into unemployment and that the heterogeneity of the inflow cohort, as defined by the relevant (re)-employability characteristics, is constant over time. Under these conditions, there will be a constant pool of unemployment, in terms of both size and structure.

The structure of the steady-state model may be approached as follows. Assume that F persons enter unemployment each week. The inflow cohort will be gradually reduced as persons find employment or withdraw from the labour market. Let the probability of continuing in unemployment for one week be P_1 and the probability of outflow be $(1 - P_1)$. For those still on the register at the start of the second week, the probability of continuing in unemployment for a further week is given by P_2, and so on. The continuation rate, P_i, is therefore defined as the conditional probability of remaining unemployed beyond period i, having been unemployed beyond period i-1. The number of survivors in the cohort F after n weeks is:

$$S_n = F \, P_1, ..., P_n \tag{1}$$

or

$$S_n = F \prod_{i=1}^{n} P_i \tag{2}$$

The survivor function may be denoted as $S = f(S_n)$. The average duration of completed spells (ACD) for the F who entered unemployment during the same week is:

$$ACD = (1 - P_1) + 2P_1 (1 - P_2) + 3P_1P_2 (1 - P_3) + ... \tag{3}$$

or

$$ACD = 1 + P_1 + P_1 P_2 + P_1 P_2 P_3 + ... \tag{4}$$

The stock of unemployed persons (U) in any given week will be composed of the survivors of all those (unexhausted) cohorts from past periods. In a steady-state world, in which F is constant:

$$U = F + F P_1 + F P_1 P_2 + F P_1 P_2 P_3 + ... \tag{5}$$

The terms on the right-hand side show the numbers of those in their first, second, third, fourth, etc. weeks of unemployment. Equation (5), taken in conjunction with (4), yields the well-known steady-state identity that unemployment = inflow x average unemployment duration:

$$U = F . ACD \qquad (6)$$

ACD may also be thought of as the mean expected duration of a completed spell of unemployment of the cohort, F. It can also be shown that the expected completed duration is equal to both the inverse of the outflow probability (measured against the stock of unemployed) and the ratio of the unemployment rate and the inflow probability (measured against the stock of employed). To reiterate, these relationships only apply in the steady-state case of the stationary register.

The nearest equivalent to true inflow data available for interwar Britain is for the early 1930s. In 1930, the Ministry of Labour began to experiment with statistics on the duration of unemployment and produced data on the periods of registered unemployment of wholly unemployed workers for weekly periods within the first month. These figures are available at monthly intervals during 1930 and 1931 for six categories of worker, analysed by age and sex. It is possible to use these figures to generate inflow rates from the first duration interval, by calculating the size of the cohort entering unemployment in the previous week. Only those currently unemployed will, however, be captured by this snapshot of the register. It is therefore necessary to flesh out the entire entering cohort by determining the number who returned to work within their first week of unemployment. Assuming that the cohorts entering unemployment on each day of the same week display the same well-behaved survivor function, it is possible to reconstruct outflows from the register that incorporate the missing workers. I have applied a very simple function to the 1931 data[4] and generated the inflow rates shown in Table 3.2.

These figures certainly underestimate the rate of inflow into permanent unemployment, since they only refer to wholly unemployed workers and exclude those categorised as temporarily stopped. Temporarily stopped workers were defined as those who expect to return to their current job within a six-week period. Since these workers do not contribute to labour turnover properly conceived, their inclusion in any statistics of inflow will be misleading. However, in the slump of 1930-31, a large number of workers entered into unemployment in the expectation that they would return to their former positions within a short period. Indeed, as Beveridge shows, at the onset of both economic downturns in the 1930s, there was a great increase in the proportion of those temporarily stopped: in 1930, 26.7 per cent of all claimants to unemployment benefit were so re-

Table 3.2   Statistics on Turnover, 1926-38

I Inflows and Outflows from the Register

	Weekly Inflow Rate	Expected Duration (weeks)	Weekly Outflow Rate	Expected Duration (weeks)
February 1931:				
wholly unemployed	0.0094	22.46	0.0637	15.70
inc. temporarily stopped	0.0107	19.72	--	--
October 1933:				
all registrations	0.0212	8.89	--	--
exc. temporarily stopped	0.0125	14.48	0.0652	15.35

II Vacancies Filled and Total Outflows

	Vacancies Filled	Placing Rate %	Weekly Outflow Rate	Average Completed Duration (weeks)
1926	1,123,638	18.0	0.1383	7.23
1927	1,251,511	18.9	0.1535	6.52
1928	1,327,306	19.7	0.1488	6.72
1929	1,556,271	20.6	0.1613	6.20
1930	1,732,144	22.2	0.1113	8.98
1931	1,952,057	22.3	0.0843	11.87
1932	1,855,841	21.2	0.0788	12.69
1933	2,224,421	23.6	0.0890	11.24
1934	2,331,993	24.8	0.1025	9.75
1935	2,533,456	26.9	0.1061	9.42
1936	2,624,213	28.9	0.1171	8.54
1937	2,624,978	29.2	0.1346	7.43
1938	2,705,064	28.3	0.1283	7.80

Sources: I See text. *II* Beveridge (1944), p. 81 (placing rates, 1932-8); Ministry of Labour (1933b-1938b) (vacancies); Ministry of Labour (1937c) (wholly unemployed); Chegwidden and Myrddin-Evans (1934), pp. 173-6 (vacancies, 1926-32, and placing rates, 1926, 1932); Hatton (1985) (placing rate, 1930). The placing rates for 1927-31 were linearly interpolated between Chegwidden and Myrddin-Evans's 1926 and 1932 estimates; see text.

corded compared to 21.5 per cent a year previously (Beveridge, 1937a). In a significant proportion of cases, hopes of an early return to former jobs were dashed as the depression bit deeper and workers migrated from the register of temporarily stopped to the status of wholly unemployed. These migrants should be considered wholly unemployed from the onset of their separation. Table 3.2 applies a simple correction for this factor, based on the assumption that the proportion of temporarily stopped to total unemployment would, if properly measured, have remained at its 1929 level during the slump.[5]

These are historically very high rates of inflow, as comparison to more recent evidence makes clear. Inflows in the early 1930s were running at some two to three times the volume of fifty years later (Knight, 1987, p. 33). However, these estimates should not be misinterpreted. At the onset of a depression we might expect an increase in the number of people joining the register as involuntary separations intensify. The 1930 cohort of new insurance claimants were not progressing through the complete process of labour turnover, but were rather entering its first stage, unemployment. We should therefore also look at the final stage in the process - re-entering employment. In a steady-state world, outflows and inflows will be equal. This was manifestly not the case in the early 1930s. However, if we compare the expected durations of unemployment calculated from inflow and outflow rates, it appears that the distortion introduced by applying steady-state assumptions is relatively minor. The outflow rate for February 1931 was approximately 0.0637 per week, equivalent to an expected duration of 15.7 weeks for the entering cohort, which is fairly close to the 22.5 weeks calculated from the inflow probability.

Unfortunately, flow data are not available at this level of detail for the remainder of the 1930s. The sole reference to inflows to be found for the post-1931 period is the following remark pertaining to October 1933: "At the present time the number of insured persons who lodge new claims each week is approximately 220,000 (excluding persons who are working short time on a systematic basis, and, generally speaking, persons whose last spell of unemployment continued for less than three days)" (Ministry of Labour, 1933a, p. 356). This figure is considerably higher than inflows in 1930-31 since it includes many temporarily stopped workers as well as the wholly unemployed. Even after excluding these workers, however, the rate of inflow from the employed labour force (0.0125 per week) is if anything slightly higher than in 1930-31.[6] The outflow rate is, moreover, almost exactly the same (0.0652 per week) with a correspondingly similar expected duration (15.35 weeks) of unemployment. The start of the recovery was not, it appears, marked by any great change in flows through the labour market.[7] The higher unemployment rate must, therefore, be accounted for by a rise in the average duration of joblessness. This conclusion is confirmed by other information.

The best continuous source on the volume of flows off the register in this period is the Ministry of Labour's record of the number of wholly unemployed workers placed in vacancies previously notified to the labour exchanges (Hatton, 1985). These "vacancies filled" represent only a small portion of the total outflow of workers into employment. As a measure of its efficiency as an employment agency, the Ministry of Labour published, between 1932 and 1938, an annual "placing index", measured as the share of total new hires accounted for by vacancies filled. This placing rate can be used to estimate the total outflow from the register into new jobs. For the period before 1932, there are estimates made by the Ministry of Labour to the Royal Commission on Unemployment Insurance relating to the second half of 1930 (Hatton, 1985, p. 262) and by two ministry officials for 1926 (Chegwidden and Myrddin-Evans, 1934, p. 176, n. 2). Following the latter's note of "a slow but steady increase in the gross index", I have interpolated between their estimates for 1926 and 1932 to fill in the missing years. The weekly outflow rates derived from these estimates are presented in the bottom panel of Table 3.2, along with their implied expected durations.[8] Turnover in the 1920s appears to have been rapid and unemployment was marked by short spells, on the average. The onset of depression was marked by a fall-off in the rate of outflow and perhaps a doubling in the expected duration of unemployment. After 1932 the labour market gradually returned to more rapid turnover. These figures reveal that the expected duration of unemployment followed an almost identical path to the unemployment rate across the depression. On this basis, it appears that the labour market response to the economic crisis was shared equally by rising numbers of unemployed and increasing average spells of joblessness.

The data on outflows do not, however, distinguish repeat spells and therefore understate the concentration of unemployment among the working population. Failure to recognise the extent of recurrent unemployment will clearly limit our understanding of the operation of the labour market, as well as distort our appreciation of the welfare costs of unemployment. Thus the standard economic judgment is that rapid turnover is beneficial to society as it promotes the most efficient allocation of workers to jobs. However, if rapid turnover is produced by intermittent spells of unemployment of a casual nature, then the efficiency gains become less apparent. Moreover, the welfare costs to the individual look very different. The Ministry of Labour's surveys of the unemployment register in 1929 and 1931 collected data on the number of spells suffered by the currently unemployed during the previous twelve months (1931a, pp. 6-

Table 3.3a   The Sources of Unemployment, 1929-36

	Rate of Unemp't	Average Period of Unemp't	Proportion of Year Unemp'd	Proportion of Labour Force Unemp'd Within Year
	%	Days	%	%
1923-6	11.3	84.0	26.9	42.0
1928	10.7	84.3	27.0	39 6
1929	10.3	84.9	27.2	37.9
1930	15.8	99.2	31.8	49.7
1931	21.1	126.0	40.4	52.2
1932	21.9	129.8	41.6	52.6
1933	19.8	131.4	42.1	47.0
1934	16.6	117.9	37.8	43.9
1935	15.3	117.0	37.5	40.8
1936	12.9	111.1	35.6	36.2

Sources: Calculated from Ministry of Labour (1937a), p. 9; Gilson (1931), pp. 172-3; Royal Commission on Unemployment Insurance (1931), p. 1176.

Table 3.3b   Actuarial Estimate of Duration, 1931

Rate of Unemp't	Days of Unemp't Per Worker	Proportion Unemp'd Within Year	Duration of Claims
%		%	(Days)
2	6.2	17.5	35.7
4	12.5	26.0	48.0
6	18.7	30.2	62.0
8	25.0	31.8	78.5
10	31.2	33.0	94.5
12	37.4	34.0	110.0

Source: J. G. Kyd and G. H. Maddex, "Some Actuarial Aspects of Unemployment Insurance", *Journal of the Institute of Actuaries,* 60 (1929), p. 135, as quoted in Gilson (1931), p. 181.

8; 1932a, pp. 280-2). Those unemployed on 16 September 1929 had experienced on average 2.3 spells of longer than one week in the previous year, with an average duration of 7.62 weeks. In the year ending January 1931, the average number of spells had risen to 2.7, with an average duration of 8.77 weeks.[9] The prevalence of recurrent spells is understated by these figures. If we include spells of less than one week, the average number per benefit claimant in 1931 rises to 7.3, and the average duration falls to 20.84 days. Clearly, short spells formed a considerable part of the unemployment experience of workers in the early 1930s. Unfortunately, in the absence of direct data on the number of spells for other years, we cannot determine whether this was a constant element in the operation of the labour market in the interwar period or merely the product of the peculiar conditions of 1930-31.

There is, however, indirect evidence on the impact of repeat spells on the concentration of unemployment. In 1937, the Ministry of Labour published data for 1929 to 1936 showing the average number of current benefit claims during the calendar year and the total number of separate individuals making claims in the same period (1937a, p. 9). The ratio of these provides an estimate of the total amount of time spent in unemployment by those out of work during the year. This is not, of course, an estimate of the average spell length within the year, since workers may have recorded multiple periods of unemployment. Nor is it a measure of the average completed spell length, since the maximum period of unemployment is truncated at one year. The estimates derived from this series are presented in Table 3.3.[10] They show a clear rise in the proportion of the year spent out of work for those registered as unemployed after 1929. The rise did not take place immediately.

Some two-thirds of labour market adjustment during the first year of the slump fell on to increased job loss. In 1930-31, however, the burden was picked up by the unemployed experiencing longer spells. By 1933, the average length of the year spent out of work was over 50 per cent higher than in 1929. As the economy began to recover, it is noticeable that the decline in days out of work was slower than the rate of recovery as a whole. By 1936, indeed, the proportion of workers experiencing unemployment had fallen below the 1929 level, while the average number of days out of work had risen by over 30 per cent.[11]

These results are helpful in determining where interwar Britain should be placed on the pure stock-pure flow spectrum of labour markets. However, as the discussion has made clear, they need to be treated with some caution. In the first instance, the statistical base is incomplete and uncertain. The division between temporarily stopped and wholly unemployed workers is one source of frustration. The failure of the Ministry of Labour to apply directly the concept of turnover to the statistics of unemployment is another. Second, the statistics do not and cannot provide precisely the information we need. The relations between inflows and expected durations are constructs derived from a steady-state world. However, as I have already emphasised, Britain in the 1930s was not a steady-state world. Indeed, Cripps and Tarling (1974, p. 306) identify

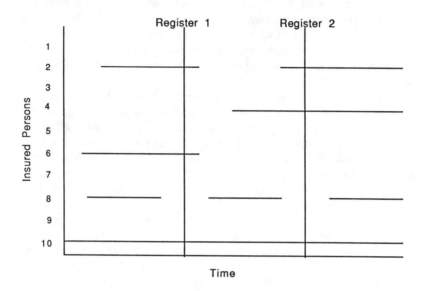

Figure 3.1   Unemployment Spells and Duration

only two quarters in the period between 1932 and 1939 for which "transition proportions and stocks ... look sufficiently steady to justify using them to construct stationary registers". In both cases the actual volume of unemployment is over 12 per cent higher than the appropriate stationary stock[12] (1974, p. 302, n. 1). In principle, the strength of boom and slump between 1929 and 1938, and the resulting imbalance of inflows and outflows, invalidates the application of steady-state assumptions to this period.

Although the extent and direction of bias imposed by assuming steady-state conditions cannot be precisely determined, the general conclusions derived from this approach do stand up to closer scrutiny. That rates of inflow into unemployment were larger in the 1930s than in the postwar world is undeniable. Nor does the observation that turnover rates were cyclically sensitive depend on steady-state assumptions. Finally, the conclusion that the burden of rising unemployment was not shared equally by all in the labour force but tended to be distributed as longer periods of unemployment for those at risk is also a robust result, as the following discussion of non-steady-state duration statistics will make clear.

Monthly statistics of periods of registered unemployment were first made available in rudimentary form by the Ministry of Labour in 1930. From 1932 onwards, the series was redefined and current applicants to benefit or allowance were distinguished according to their length of continuous unemployment. Spells were designated at three-monthly intervals up to one year. At various times between 1935 and 1939, additional information was presented on the duration of spells longer than one year. These data are particularly valuable for interwar Britain because the Ministry of Labour occasionally extended their scope to analyse unemployment by age, sex, region and industry. I shall draw on them in this regard below. We are also fortunate to have two earlier studies, relating to September 1929 and February 1931 respectively, that are compatible with the later series and that can be used to compare the pattern of duration at various stages during depression and recovery.

The various measures of unemployment duration may be approached with the aid of Figure 3.1, derived from Salant (1977) and Main (1981), which follows a sample of the insured population. Two snapshots of the unemployment register are shown. The segment of the insured population covered has ten workers, of whom five suffer unemployment at some time in the period shown. Not all spells of unemployment are, however, captured by the monthly register. Any spells that start after one survey and end before the next are clearly not going to be included in the statistics. The unemployment data are deficient in this respect. Certain workers suffer from long-period unemployment and are included in both surveys. These provide the basis of duration statistics. Other workers are captured by both registers but are identified as separate individuals, having been employed for a period between surveys. The duration statistic that is recorded by the monthly register is the average interrupted spell length, the mean unemployment duration of those currently unemployed. The major drawback of this measure (T) as an indicator of the average spell length of all unemployed persons is that it is length-biased: the probability of being captured by such a measure is directly proportional to the final duration of unemployment. Short spells out of work are underweighted or excluded and longer periods are overrepresented. It is for this reason that most economists consider the mean expected duration spell length (ACD) to be more appropriate. This measure gives equal weight to all spells of unemployment and avoids the length bias of T.

The most straightforward method of calculating the mean expected duration of unemployment from the grouped data of the register uses a nonparametric estimate of the survivor function. In effect, the procedure is to follow the entering cohort through its lifetime on the register and to record the length of each individual spell of unemployment. In the case of grouped data, the aggregate continuation rate is used as an approxima-

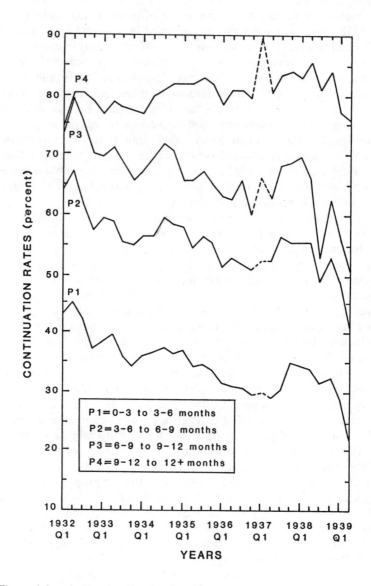

Figure 3.2   Aggregate Continuation Rates, 1932-39

Note: P₁ to P₄ are defined in the text. Continuation rates apply to wholly unemployed only. The broken line indicates a structural break in the series in April 1937, due to a change in the method of counting the unemployed.

tion to the slope of the survivor function within each time period. In a steady state, all survivor functions are assumed identical and the average completed duration can be estimated from a single register. Out of steady state, each register will be composed of survivors from a series of asimilar entering cohorts. Under such circumstances, the average completed duration can be measured by tracing survivors back to their original cohort or by moving forward from the moment of entry on to the register. Bowers and Harkess (1979) apply the former method. Given the coarsely aggregated nature of the register, the latter procedure is more suited to the data of the 1930s. The survivor function in this case may be written as (Baker and Trivedi, 1985):

$$S (S_i) = P_{1,t} P_{2,t} ..... P_{i,t} \qquad\qquad (7)$$

where

$$P_{i,t} = N_{i,t+1} \ / \ N_{i-1,t+i-1} \qquad\qquad (8)$$

denotes the proportion of survivors from a cohort of entrants into unemployment. In the particular case of interwar Britain, grouped data are available for three-monthly intervals as follows: [0,3), [3,6), [6,9), [9,12), [12+). The continuation rates, P_1 to P_4, were calculated as the ratios of the stock of employed in each group at successive quarters. On the basis of this empirical survivor function, the following formula for average completed duration was used:

$$ACD_t = P_{1t} + P_{1t} P_{2t} + P_{1t} P_{2t} P_{3t} + \frac{P_{1t} P_{2t} P_{3t} P_{4t}}{1 - P_{4t}} \qquad (9)$$

Unfortunately, it is not possible to follow particular cohorts through to exhaustion since the register is truncated at one year. The final term is therefore based on the assumption that the continuation rate P_{4t} holds for periods beyond one year. The relative stability of P_{4t} over time (see Figure 3.2) suggests that this may not be an unreasonable assumption. However, to the extent to which the outflow from the register continues to fall as aggregate duration rises, any estimate of ACD calculated from (9) will be biased downwards. There are likely, however, to be additional, albeit compensating, biases at the opposite end of the register unless P_{1t} is the appropriate continuation rate within the first trimester of unemployment. The simplest method of correcting for this bias is to determine the

Table 3.4   Duration Statistics, 1929-38

	ACD II	ACD III	T	Proportion 1 year	Proportion 3 months
	weeks	weeks	weeks	%	%
I All unemployed					
1929	--	--	12.33	4.66	78.49
1932	10.48	8.76	27.46	15.89	57.21
1933	9.84	7.99	35.70	21.38	53.97
1934	10.46	7.89	37.69	22.00	55.48
1935	10.13	8.15	38.20	22.06	54.75
1936	11.55	9.02	41.33	23.32	54.82
1937	12.50	9.32	41.29	22.30	57.73
1938	8.65	7.64	31.23	16.92	62.37
II Wholly unemployed					
1929	--	--	15.44	7.15	43.72
1932	22.23	19.54	34.10	22.00	40.76
1933	18.25	17.86	43.60	28.38	38.88
1934	17.52	16.57	45.77	29.02	41.26
1935	16.59	14.38	45.62	28.49	41.57
1936	15.23	13.90	49.05	29.47	42.91
1937	18.06	14.24	48.68	28.10	46.23
1938	15.39	13.08	38.96	23.23	48.32

Note: Calculated as the average of four quarterly observations (February, May, August, November). No data were available for November 1938. The 1938 figure is the average of the first three months, amended by the average value of November in other quarters for 1932-38.
Sources: 1929: Beveridge (1944), p. 64; 1932-8: Ministry of Labour (1932a-1939a).

total size of the entering cohort by modelling the survivor function. I have used a very simple (semi-logarithmic) functional form for this purpose. The results are reproduced in Table 3.4 and are discussed below.

There has been recent criticism of the use of expected completed durations as a measure of unemployment experience. The argument developed by Clark and Summers (1979), Akerlof and Main (1981) and others is that ACD focuses attention on the spell of employment rather than the individual experiencing unemployment, and therefore produces "quite misleading" welfare implications (Main, 1981, p. 149). A better measure, it is argued, is the average length of spell experienced by those currently unemployed. This is to be preferred because it deals with the experience of the typical unemployed. It is therefore an "experience-weighted" duration statistic, since it gives smaller weight to the short-term unemployed. In a steady state, the experience-weighted spell length (ACDU) is equal to twice the average interrupted spell length (T). However, in periods of falling unemployment, the experience-weighted measure will be less than twice the average interrupted spell and is, moreover, not easy to calculate. Nevertheless, as Layard (1981) suggests, the welfare content of the alternative measure can be derived directly from T, and does not require an estimate of ACDU. Crafts (1987) has recently applied the experience-weighted measure to interwar Britain in his analysis of long-term unemployment.

The continuation rates for 1932-38, upon which the various duration statistics are based, are shown in Figure 3.2. A number of remarks are in order. First, as we would expect, the longer the period of unemployment, the higher are the continuation rates. Second, the relative continuation rates for those unemployed fewer than nine months remained fairly stable throughout the period. This was not, however, the case with the long-term unemployed. There is a distinct divergence between the trend of the short (P_1 to P_3) and long period (P_4) continuation rates. Although P_3 and P_4 take similar values for February 1932, by late 1937, the value of P_4 is over a third higher. In contrast to the experience of periods of unemployment below nine months, the probability of moving from nine months of unemployment to one year remained almost stable throughout the 1930s. Indeed, to the extent that there is a trend in P_4 during the recovery, it is upwards. These figures emphasise the intransigence of long-term unemployment despite the upturn in economic activity after 1932. In contrast, the transitions in the register between three and six months and six and nine months fall consistently throughout the 1930s and at much the same rate. The continuation rate for the short-period (wholly) unemployed falls somewhat faster, suggesting that the speed of outflow from the register was relatively faster for those only recently out of work. Once again, it appears that the burden of labour market adjustment to exogenous shocks fell on to the rate of outflow rather than inflow.

The duration statistics presented in Table 3.4 confirm these general remarks. Duration statistics are calculated for all unemployed (panel I) and for those wholly unemployed (panel II). The expected duration of unemployment, ACD II, calculated from non-steady-state assumptions, is low and stable for the register as a whole throughout much of the 1930s until it speeded up under the pressure of rearmament in 1938. The second expected duration figure, ACD III, estimated by completing the entering cohort, is, as we would expect, somewhat lower than ACD II, but shows a similar pattern over time. In contrast, the average interrupted spell length (T) rises consistently during the period from 1929-36, with a dramatic decline after 1937.[13] The origin of this rising value of T over time is made manifestly clear by the figures on the proportion of the unemployed out of work for a year or longer. This proportion doubles between 1929 and 1933 and rises slowly until 1936. A closer examination of the unemployment register suggests that the volume of short-term unemployed falls throughout the period while the numbers of long-term unemployed decline only slowly. It appears then that the increased difficulties of the "hard-core" unemployed after 1932 were due not only to their own circumstances but also to a falling rate of turnover. The increase in the proportion of the long-term unemployed is not, however, merely a statistical artefact created by movements in the denominator. The average spell length of those unemployed over one year also rises over time: from 90.8 weeks in September 1929 to 99.2 in August 1932, 136.5 in August 1936 and 144.1 weeks in August 1937.[14]

If we exclude the temporarily stopped and casual unemployed from the register to reach a closer approximation to true turnover as well as to the construction of postwar unemployment statistics, the basic pattern does not change. For obvious reasons, the average duration estimates are higher and the proportion of long-term unemployment also rises. There are, however, no major changes in the profile of these indicators over time, save perhaps in 1937-38 when the number of temporary lay-offs rose considerably.

How should we characterise the labour market in interwar Britain on the basis of these figures? The evidence suggests a bifurcated market, in which there is at once rapid turnover and persistent unemployment. This would account for the large discrepancy between completed and interrupted spells of unemployment. The relative stability of the expected duration rate implies that changes in macroeconomic conditions fell on to the rate of outflow rather than inflow and were mirrored in a rise in both T and the proportion of long-term unemployed. How might we explain such a bifurcated market? Hatton has suggested that the rapid turnover of the 1920s labour market is best explained as a queuing process: "Workers were simply queuing at the exchanges and a rise in the unemployment rate merely lengthened the queue - it did not cause vacancies to be taken up any more quickly" (1985, p. 269). This in itself cannot explain the rising prevalence of long-term unemployment in the 1930s: from less than 5 per cent of total unemployment in 1929 to an average of 22 per cent between 1933 and 1937. There needs to be an additional mechanism which lowered some individuals' chances of getting back into employment. There are a number of possibilities: that workers were subsidised into permanent unemployment; that unemployment was effectively a lottery in which some workers were assigned very low probabilities of winning a new job; and that the experience of unemployment itself led to lower re-employment probabilities. In order to address these competing hypotheses, it is necessary to identify the unemployed more carefully.

3 Who Were the Unemployed?

The purpose of this section of the paper is to determine which categories of the population were most at risk of being unemployed. I shall concentrate on three major aspects: unemployment rates, the duration of unemployment and the extent of prolonged unemployment. Subgroups of the population are distinguished by age, sex, marital and family position, skill level and location. Before embarking on a description of the incidence of unemployment across subgroups of the population, a caveat is in order. The sources for most of the following are either the unemployment register or sample surveys of those out of work. This raises two separate problems. First, as already noted, the coverage of the insurance scheme was incomplete. Clearly the identity of those excluded matters in an analysis of the incidence of unemployment. Second, in the majority of cases, analysis of the characteristics of the unemployed was limited to crude single variable tabulation. Consequently, it is not possible to determine the marginal contribution of each characteristic to the overall probability of being unemployed. We cannot address directly the question of the impact of, say, age, holding all other personal factors (health, location, marital status, occupation, etc.) constant. Eichengreen's (1986) recent multivariate analysis of the London unemployed in 1928-32 is the first attempt to tackle this problem directly for interwar Britain. In most cases, his results confirm the picture of (male) unemployment derived from simple analysis of the unemployment register. Finally, we must note that in the absence of detailed inflow statistics, it is not possible to determine the chances of entering unemployment for each demographic group, but only the risks of being unemployed at a particular time.

The main contours of employment and unemployment by gender are depicted in Table 3.5. Women only account for a small proportion of the total volume of unemployment: less than 14 per cent in 1933. This was partly because of the relatively low unemployment rates suffered by women but was largely due to their considerably lower rate of labour force participation (34.2 per cent of those over 14 years old at the 1931 census as opposed to 90.5 per cent for males). There are certain clear features introduced by Table 3.5. Unemployment rates for women were lower than for males; this was largely because of shorter spell lengths. The data also suggest that women were less prone to prolonged unemployment. Beveridge addressed this issue and posited retirement through marriage as the major cause (1937b, p. 176). This is reflected in the very

Table 3.5   Unemployment by Sex

	Unemployment rates		Expected	duration			Average interrupted spell			
			ACD I		ACD II		T		Prolonged	
	M	F	M	F	M	F	M	F	M	F
	%		weeks		weeks		weeks		%	
1927	11.0	6.2	--	--	--	--	--	--	--	--
1928	12.3	7.0	--	--	--	--	--	--	--	--
1929	11.6	7.3	--	--	--	--	14.71	9.62	5.47	1.16
1930	16.5	14.8	--	--	--	--	--	--	--	--
1931 I	22.4	18.4	--	--	--	--	17.03	17.67	5.00	5.09
1931 II	23.1	15.3	--	--	--	--	--	--	--	--
1932	25.2	13.7	15.06	10.73	12.06	4.56	29.23	18.97	17.34	8.87
1933	23.2	11.4	13.49	8.99	10.01	4.60	38.76	17.99	23.71	7.89
1934	19.3	10.0	11.46	7.76	11.52	4.77	41.86	16.80	24.77	6.92
1935	17.7	9.8	11.48	7.60	10.13	4.47	42.46	17.83	25.02	7.69
1936	14.6	8.3	10.21	6.95	8.95	4.71	46.58	19.66	26.52	8.87
1937	12.2	6.7	10.21	6.81	10.58	5.30	46.86	18.35	24.91	8.43
1938	14.7	8.0	--	--	9.01	4.91	36.19	16.18	20.43	6.21

Key:
ACD I: Average completed duration calculated from vacancies data under steady-state assumptions.
ACD II: Average completed duration calculated from non-steady-state assumptions; average of four quarterly estimates.
T: Average interrupted spell length; average of four quarterly estimates.
Prolonged: Proportion of unemployed out of work for more than one year; average of four quarterly estimates.
Note: All data refer to adults (18-64). In recording the unemployment rates, 1931 has been subdivided into January-October (I) and November-December (II). October saw the passage of the Anomalies Act (see note 15). The interrupted spell data for 1929 refer to the results of a special inquiry of the Ministry of Labour for September. The 1931 data refer to February and are derived from a similar sample survey.
Sources: Unemployment rates 1927-35: Beveridge (1936). Unemployment rates 1936-8: Ministry of Labour (1936a-1938a). Duration: Calculated from Ministry of Labour (1932a-1939a).

low participation rates for married women over the age of 25: below 10 per cent, compared to a rate of 66 per cent for single women aged 25-55. A comparison of ACD in steady-state and non-steady-state paradigms suggests a second factor, namely that women after job separation were more likely to leave the register rather than continue to search for employment. The combined effect of these elements was to alter significantly the age structure of female workers compared to males. The relevance of the relative youth of females is made apparent by examination of Table 3.6, which shows that, although women were at all ages less likely to be unemployed than men, the difference at any age is less than in total.[15]

Table 3.6   Unemployment Rates by Age and Sex

	April 1927	February 1931	November 1932	November 1935	February 1938
MALES					
16-17	2.1	--	4.6	4.6	4.1
18-20	} 8.8	15.8	16.3	8.2	8.2
21-24		23.3	23.5	17.8	12.5
25-29	11.0	21.3	22.7 }	15.3	11.1
30-34	9.3	22.0	21.9		11.4
35-39	9.2	22.3	21.4 }	17.1	13.0
40-44	9.5	22.3	22.4		13.5
45-49	10.8	24.4	23.1 }	19.6	15.1
50-54	11.3	27.1	26.5		17.6
55-59	13.0	28.5	26.9	25.2	19.9
60-64	15.1	34.5	32.0	28.2	23.6
18-64	10.2	23.1	22.9	17.3	13.6
FEMALES					
16-17	2.2	--	3.1	4.7	5.5
18-20	} 5.1	13.3	7.9	7.3	8.3
21-24		18.4	9.1	8.5	10.6
25-29	4.3	20.5	9.3 }	8.0	10.7
30-34	4.1	24.1	11.8		11.7
35-39	4.5	27.2	10.9 }	11.5	12.8
40-44	4.3	26.5	9.4		13.8
45-49	4.6	27.8	17.3 }	15.5	15.1
50-54	5.2	30.4	18.3		17.3
55-59	4.8	32.9	20.6	22.2	19.8
60-64	5.5	30.6	16.4	23.8	24.5
18-64	4.8	20.3	10.4	9.3	11.6

Note: All figures are percentages.
Sources: Calculated from Ministry of Labour (1933a), p. 314, (1938a), p. 300-2.

The relationship between age and unemployment is one that attracted considerable attention in the interwar years. The Ministry of Labour regularly instigated sample surveys of the register to determine the age of those out of work. Throughout the 1920s and 1930s, the same fact emerged: a U-shaped relationship for adult males, with the lowest risk of unemployment for 30- to 39-year-olds. For those males under 21, unemployment rates again declined. Those least likely to suffer unemployment were juveniles, whose average rate ran at a third to a quarter that for adults. As the period wore on, the average age of the stock of unemployed rose, while the average age of the insured workforce as a whole declined. These were not, of course, independent elements. As the unemployment rate among older workers rose, an increasing proportion left the register in the fear that work was near impossible to find. Moreover, the institutional response to the elderly unemployed was to siphon off all those over the age of 65 into Old Age Pensions, leaving them ineligible for benefits or transitional payments, although still able to register at the employment office.[16] There are thus two basic issues to address with regard to age. Why were the old so vulnerable to unemployment? And why was juvenile unemployment so low? The first issue was of primary concern to contemporaries. The second question derives, of course, in large part because of the British experience since 1973, during which juvenile unemployment has become a major social hazard.

It has generally been argued that, although the probability of being unemployed was considerably higher after the age of 45, the risks of becoming unemployed were much the same across all age cohorts over 35. Unemployment rates rose with age because of a slower rate of outflow into employment, rather than a faster rate of inflow on to the register. Thus, in Beveridge's words,

> The risk of losing employment is much the same from 60 to 64 as from 35 to 44. The risk of being unemployed is half as great again at the later age than at the earlier. The risk of unemployment prolonged for a year or more is two and a half times as great.... The explanation is obvious - that the older man, once he has lost a job, finds it harder than a younger man to get a new job. The older man has less power of recovery industrially, from loss of employment, as he has less power physically, from sickness or accident. Once he has become unemployed, he is likely to remain unemployed for longer than a young man. (1937a, pp. 15, 13)

The basis of Beveridge's argument, which was shared by other commentators in the 1930s (Gilson, 1931, pp. 187-8; Ministry of Labour, 1927, p. 38), was the record of claims to benefit made by various age groups from 1923 to 1930 and 1924 to 1932. Some of the results of this investigation as they relate to males are shown in Table 3.7. Beveridge's conclusions were based on the proportion of workers in each age group that made no claims for unemployment during the survey periods. This, it can be seen, was reasonably stable for all age cohorts over 35. Indeed, the data imply that it was 25- to 34-year-olds who were most liable to job separation. The high unemployment of this age group was viewed as a particular problem of the labour market throughout the 1920s. The Min-

Table 3.7   **Claimants to Unemployment Benefit, 1923-30**

	16-24	25-34	35-44	45-54	55-64	All Ages
Number claims made (% of sample):						
1923-1930:	52.7	31.2	37.6	39.1	38.3	41.1
1924-1932:	39.3	27.5	33.4	33.3	32.9	33.0
1930-1932:	-13.4	- 3.7	- 4.2	- 5.8	- 5.4	- 8.1
Number claims made (all workers):						
1923-1930:	1.03	2.10	1.97	2.04	2.10	1.72
1924-1932:	1.54	2.66	2.45	2.58	2.80	2.39
1930-1932:	0.66	0.86	0.76	0.83	1.00	0.92
Number claims made (unemployed):						
1923-1930:	2.18	3.05	3.16	3.35	3.40	2.92
1924-1932:	2.54	3.67	3.68	3.87	4.17	3.57
1930-1932:	0.67	1.06	0.96	1.00	1.26	1.07
Annual claim rate (all workers):						
1923-1930:	0.147	0.300	0.281	0.291	0.300	0.246
1924-1932:	0.192	0.332	0.306	0.322	0.350	0.299
1930-1932:	0.330	0.430	0.380	0.415	0.500	0.460
Annual claim rate (unemployed):						
1923-1930:	0.311	0.436	0.451	0.478	0.486	0.417
1924-1932:	0.318	0.459	0.460	0.484	0.521	0.446
1930-1932:	0.335	0.530	0.480	0.500	0.630	0.535

Note and source: Calculated from data reproduced in Beveridge (1937a), pp. 12-13. The calculation assumes that the structure of claims in 1923 was identical with the structure of claims in 1923-30. All changes in the register of claims between the two samples are therefore assumed to take place between 1930 and 1932. The similarity in the male unemployment rate in 1923 and 1924 suggests that this may not be inappropriate. The results for 16- 24-year-olds are not directly comparable with other age groups given the shorter period of employability.

istry of Labour identified the situation as early as 1924, and suggested that it could be accounted for partly by workers being squeezed out of employment when returning soldiers were given preference in hiring, and partly by the many returning ex-servicemen who found it difficult to re-settle after the war (1924; see also Morley, 1922). However, the vulner-ability of this age category was a standing element in the interwar labour market and reflects the higher mobility of single, semi-skilled workers with lower search costs and minimal job attachment, rather than any tem-porary dislocation of the labour market in the wake of war. This conclusion is cemented when it is recognised that the very high proportion of zero claims for 16- to 24-year-old males is a statistical figment created by truncation bias in the construction of Table 3.7. If we include only those who had been insured throughout the period between 1923 and 1930, the proportion making no claims remains much the same for those over 35, falling by about 1 per cent in all cases.[17] For 25- to 34-year-olds it drops to 29.8 per cent, and for those aged 21 to 24 (there are no youths in the revised sample) to 29.2 per cent. The discrete increase after 35 in the proportion never experiencing unemployment remains.

A closer examination of Table 3.7 suggests a further refinement of Beveridge's argument. In particular, if we move to consideration of the number of claims made during the period, it appears that the average number of claims put forward, measured across all workers and for the unemployed alone, rises with age. Although older workers had just as high a probability of never becoming unemployed as those twenty years younger, there was a greater liability to multiple claims for those who did lose their jobs at any time. The point is made clearer if we treat the two sample surveys as snapshots from a longitudinal study. The annual claim rate between 1930 and 1932, which is equivalent to the percentage of claimants within each age group, was considerably higher for older workers (55 to 64) than on average. Comparison of the proportion in each age group making no claims and the average number of claims made by those experiencing unemployment reveals that older male workers were indeed more vulnerable to job separation during the early depression than their younger colleagues.[18]

Nevertheless, it remains true that the much higher unemployment rates for older workers are best explained in terms of longer duration. Thus, in 1938, the average interrupted spell length of unemployment for adult males over 60 was 56.5 weeks compared to 13.1 weeks for 18- to 20-year-olds; over 39 per cent of male claimants over 60 had been unemployed for more than one year and almost 12 per cent had been out of work for over five years. The figures in Table 3.8 show a gradual increase in the average spell length as age rises, for both expected and interrupted durations of unemployment.[19] The same relationship was also found before the onset of depression, as the evidence relating to 1929 makes clear. However, as we would expect, the extent of long-term unemployment, even among elderly workers, was considerably lower than in 1938. The recovery did not return the labour market to the pre-depression position; expected durations and interrupted spells of unemployment were longer throughout, although more so for older workers.[20]

The higher risk of prolonged unemployment with age appears to hold regardless of secondary characteristics. No doubt, as in contemporary Britain, some part of the relation is due to the increased likelihood of the

Table 3.8   **Duration of Unemployment by Age, 1929 and 1938**

	Males				Females			
	ACD I weeks	T weeks	LU %	SU %	ACD I weeks	T weeks	LU %	SU %
I September 1929								
18-24	2.20	10.14	1.79	83.08				
25-34	3.09	13.33	4.28	80.77				
35-44	2.92	14.16	5.18	77.51				
45-54	3.09	15.94	6.70	76.27				
55-59	6.64	19.88	9.08	66.06				
60-64	7.49	24.11	12.55	63.45				
All	3.86	14.58	5.47	77.11				
II February 1938								
18-20	4.24	13.31	3.66	75.41	2.36	9.81	1.52	84.62
21-24	6.04	19.44	8.64	68.26	3.32	11.32	2.45	79.66
25-34	7.60	25.85	14.32	63.09	3.75	12.25	3.26	77.61
35-44	10.15	36.14	20.97	56.17	4.56	14.65	6.05	74.01
45-54	12.26	44.76	25.55	51.46	6.46	21.66	11.17	66.80
55-59	15.76	56.48	31.63	45.20	9.69	31.78	18.14	57.29
60-64	22.22	73.02	39.39	36.91	14.84	45.22	27.20	57.29
All	9.98	35.92	20.58	56.57	4.24	14.72	5.54	75.39

Note: Since there is only one observation of the duration of unemployment, ACD I is calculated applying steady-state assumptions.
Sources: 1929: Ministry of Labour (1930a), p. 8. 1938: Ministry of Labour (1938a), p. 232.

old to fall ill (Nickell, 1980). However, Eichengreen's (1986) multivariate analysis of the London unemployed in 1928-32 suggests that the age-unemployment profile is robust to additional personal factors. Location is the one significant element that Eichengreen cannot control by virtue of his data set. Nevertheless, examination of the age structure of unemployment across administrative divisions in 1938 shows the relation to have been similar across all regions, albeit somewhat intensified in the depressed areas (Crafts, 1987, p. 420).

The answer to the second question, why juvenile unemployment was so low, appears to lie in the structural characteristics of the labour market. Eichengreen (1987a) has subjected the overall change in youth unemployment between 1931 and 1981 to shift-share analysis. The decomposition procedure rejects demographic effects, changes in the school leaving age and macroeconomic explanations of the rise in the juvenile rate. The most important factor is an upward shift in the age structure of employment, a shift that cannot, it seems, be explained in terms of relative wage or relative wage-benefit changes over time. Eichengreen suggests that the considerably lower cyclical sensitivity of youth unemployment exhibited in the 1930s may have been due to short unemployment spells and the application of inverse-seniority lay-off rules.

It is certainly the case that spells of unemployment for juveniles were considerably shorter than for adult workers. The average interrupted spell in May 1932 was 8.9 weeks for boys and 7.98 weeks for girls, compared to 27.89 and 18.53 weeks for adult males and females respectively. Similarly, expected completed spells were lower: 2 weeks for boys and 1.1 for girls, or less than a fifth of the equivalent adult periods. The data suggest, moreover, that ACD fell over time for juveniles. One should be aware that there is a truncation bias in these estimates, since juveniles out of work for long periods are liable to migrate on to the adult register. Nonetheless, the evidence is consistent with the interpretation that juvenile unemployment was dominated by rapid flows through the register, and corroborates Beveridge's claim that age-specific unemployment rates were determined not by the risk of losing a job but by the chances of finding new employment. But why were juveniles so successful at finding new jobs? Eichengreen's results allow only a minor role for the movement to youth and female employment in the growth industries of the 1930s (Heim, 1984). The trend is economy-wide. The issue of why this was so remains unresolved. Contemporaries would have explained it in terms of juveniles finding temporary rather than new jobs. The notion of younger workers being forced into "blind alley" positions by dint of family economic circumstance, coupled with the decline of apprenticeship and the general lack of skilled positions available, was emphasised by both the Pilgrim Trust (1938, p. 198) and the Carnegie UK Trust (1943, p. 39). Indeed, Beveridge saw the imbalance between juvenile and elderly unemployment as originating in this situation: "the perpetual favouring of younger men merely for their youth, in filling jobs within the competence of older men, makes for unemployment" (1937a, p. 17). Not only did the older men suffer, but these jobs also "waste [the] youthful vigour and adaptability" of the juveniles.

One implication of this discussion is that unemployment was likely to be concentrated in the unskilled. Unfortunately, the information available on the skill level of the unemployed is scanty. The sample surveys of 1923 and 1924 contain some material on the proportion of the unemployed with an apprenticeship and training but this is of limited use in the absence of similar evidence relating to the entire population. The best single source of information is the census of 1931, which gives full information on those out of work by occupation. I have aggregated the very detailed oc-

Table 3.9   **Unemployment by Occupational Class, 1931**

		Male			Female	
	Out of work	Total occupied	% unemp'd	Out of work	Total occupied	% unemp'd
Ia. Higher Professional	3280	185076	1.77	286	16662	0.17
Ib. Lower Professional	14310	293559	4.87	9972	363623	2.74
Ic. Semi-professional	15005	103304	14.53	6937	40424	17.16
II. Employers, managers	16948	1225738	1.38	1749	198688	0.88
III. Clerical	42320	753880	5.61	24786	571770	4.33
IV. Foremen, supervisors	15578	305910	5.09	1209	27502	4.40
V. Skilled manual	595789	4938454	12.06	163684	1265961	12.93
VI. Semi-skilled manual	302164	2529994	11.94	90766	934697	9.71
VII. Unskilled manual	494398	2296745	21.53	27855	250169	11.13

Source: Calculated from Census of England and Wales (1931). Occupational structure of classes available on request.

cupational data into nine groups, which accord approximately to the skill content of the job. The aggregation follows the Census Office's allocation of occupations to socioeconomic classes, subject to some minor amendments following Routh (1980).

The results in Table 3.9, which refer to England and Wales only, confirm expectations. In general terms, the risk of unemployment fell as social class rose. Unskilled males were most vulnerable, female higher professionals the least.[21] Unemployment rates were in general lower for females across all social classes; the one exception is in the case of skilled manual workers, perhaps reflecting the collapse of staple sectors after 1929. How far these stock estimates reflect different patterns of in- and outflow cannot be determined in the absence of explicit information. Some fairly obscure data presented by the Unemployment Assistance Board (1938, pp. 73-6) does, however, suggest that the duration of unemployment was lower for unskilled (general) labourers than for skilled workers in engineering or shipbuilding.

The final characteristic that I shall examine here is that of location. Table 3.10 presents evidence on the structure of unemployment by region at three benchmarks between 1932 and 1937. The regions specified are the Ministry of Labour's administrative divisions. These data confirm the traditional view of the British labour market in this period: relatively low unemployment in the south, rising as one moves north and west. This regional pattern of unemployment holds throughout the 1930s, an intransigence that is revealed in the high proportion of long-term unemployed in Outer Britain. The North-west, North, Scotland and Wales divisions

Table 3.10   Unemployment Duration by Region, 1932-37

I June 1932 and June 1936 (males only)

	June 1932					June 1936				
	U %	ACD I weeks	T weeks	LU %	SU %	U %	ACD I weeks	T weeks	LU %	SU %
London	13.5	7.13	14.48	4.43	64.59	6.72	5.70	18.46	8.39	69.53
South-east	14.3	6.42	14.11	3.79	66.93	5.36	6.04	18.72	8.48	68.28
South-west	17.1	7.83	17.86	8.76	62.41	8.20	7.20	23.55	14.07	64.34
Midlands	20.1	8.99	25.46	14.61	59.12	9.75	10.45	39.68	23.11	55.43
North-east	28.5	11.92	32.01	21.04	52.16	20.40	11.46	50.89	28.67	53.14
North-west	25.8	10.27	29.07	18.25	55.87	17.20	13.22	46.05	27.19	49.58
Scotland	27.7	17.32	34.13	27.59	42.88	17.19	19.88	58.34	34.56	39.54
Wales	36.5	10.95	29.56	21.08	54.28	32.99	18.56	64.63	37.68	41.19
Great Britain	28.2	10.47	26.50	17.25	55.38	13.78	12.09	45.22	26.56	51.82

II June 1937 (all workers)

	U %	ACD I weeks	ACD II weeks	T weeks	LU %	SU %
London	4.76	5.32	5.02	17.68	7.68	70.97
South-east	3.85	6.35	5.78	11.60	9.63	67.13
South-west	5.19	5.92	5.00	23.48	12.18	68.89
Midlands	5.78	8.41	7.91	35.94	19.18	60.74
North-east	11.02	6.21	5.37	30.98	16.43	67.61
North-west	11.71	11.79	11.32	45.99	25.24	52.45
North	15.90	22.52	18.14	73.91	40.32	36.60
Scotland	13.13	19.08	16.70	57.73	33.03	40.53
Wales	19.49	23.07	18.33	69.54	39.28	36.04
Great Britain	8.85	11.30	9.97	43.80	24.52	53.49

Note: It is not possible to distinguish temporarily stopped and casuals from the wholly unemployed; the unemployment rate for 1932 refers to all workers, males were not separately reported; administrative divisions were redefined in 1936.
ACD I is the average duration calculated from steady-state assumptions; ACD II is the average duration calculated from non-steady-state assumptions; T is the average interrupted spell length; LU denotes long-term unemployed, SU short-term (less than three months) unemployed.
Sources: 1932, 1936: Unemployment rates from Beveridge (1944), p. 61 (1932) and Beveridge (1937a), p. 8 (1936); duration statistics calculated from Beveridge (1937a), p. 8. 1937: Unemployment rate from Beveridge (1944), p. 67; duration statistics calculated from Ministry of Labour (1939a), p. 123.

together accounted for 57 per cent of the total unemployed in June 1937, but 76 per cent of those unemployed over one year. The average interrupted spell is clearly much higher for these regions than for Inner Britain: twice as high in the North as in the Midlands and more than six times as high as in the prosperous South-east. This pattern was substantially in place by 1932 and was exacerbated by the asymmetrical nature of regional recovery, such that average interrupted spells for the male unemployed more than doubled in Wales between 1932 and 1936 but rose only minimally in London. The regional disparities were not merely the legacy of a dismal past. Even for those entering unemployment in 1937, the pattern of re-employment opportunities remained seriously distorted: expected durations in the North, Scotland and Wales were more than three times as long as in the southern divisions.

This completes the traditional menu of ingredients for a structural interpretation of labour market behaviour. I am tempted to remark that the last few pages demonstrate that we have learned little since Beveridge's pioneering attempt to understand the problem of unemployment by "breaking it up". Within the confines of the materials discussed, this comment is perhaps fair. However, more recently some new thinking has begun to emerge through the development of alternative sources of information on interwar unemployment.

The substance of this new thinking is derived from the recognition that economic decisions are not usually made by independent individuals, but are rather determined within the context of the primary economic unit, the household. This insight in particular applies to the behaviour of secondary workers: the experience of married women's labour force participation during the period of the Anomalies Act and of juvenile employment throughout the interwar period both warrant detailed scrutiny of household decision making. Eichengreen's (1986) use of microeconomic evidence from the New London Survey is a pioneer in this regard. Certain of his results impinge directly on the interests of this paper. Thus, for example, he finds that unemployment of the male household head was likely to push wives into employment, an added worker effect. His results also show that adult male unemployment was directly linked to family circumstance, such that married males had a lower risk of unemployment than their single counterparts. However, although marital status is correlated with lower unemployment *ceteris paribus*, the presence of a large family seems to have increased the probability of being jobless. Eichengreen's results also confirm much of the traditional interpretation of adult male unemployment: the relatively young and old and the unskilled are identified as the groups most at risk.

Although these results provide interesting additions to our stock of knowledge about the microeconomics of unemployment, they are difficult to interpret since they represent correlates rather than causes of joblessness. Thus, the higher risk of unemployment for single males could be because the characteristics that are unattractive to employers are also unappealing to potential mates, rather than because of any strictly economic explanation. Moreover, limitations in the data restrict the generality of the results. In the first place, the survey is a stock sample, with short- and long-term unemployed pooled. Given the dual labour market issues raised by interwar unemployment, the lack of information on duration is a disadvantage. It is also unfortunate that the one study of the correlates of unemployment in this form is for London, hardly representative of the conditions of unemployment at any time in the interwar period. Not only was the unemployment rate for London very low relative to other regions, but there are certain clear differences in the composition of the stock of both the employed and the unemployed. The industrial basis of employment was very much different in London from the British norm: less than 4 per cent of the labour force was attached to the staple sectors in 1931, compared to 25 per cent in Great Britain, while the so-called new industries took a larger share of the workforce in the capital than in the country as a whole. A much higher proportion of London's labour force was attached to the service sector than in the rest of the country. As Eichengreen discusses, industrial structure carries certain implications for the age and sex composition of the labour force. Employment opportunities for women and juveniles were unusually open in London and participation rates were higher in consequence.

Nevertheless, there are certain distinct advantages to this source. For one thing, it includes all unemployed workers and not merely those covered by unemployment insurance. To the extent that there is any systematic difference in the characteristics of the insured unemployed and the body of those out of work as a whole, the use of such a survey will correct biases in our interpretation of the correlates of unemployment. There is some suggestion, for example, that older and younger workers may have been underrepresented in the insurance scheme. Certainly, agricultural and tertiary workers, the self-employed and manual workers of high skill were not covered by insurance. Many of these categories were also, it should be said, excluded from the New London Survey. One can only hope that social survey records as rich as those of London will emerge and that the move towards dealing with the microeconomics of unemployment at the level of individual economic units will continue.

4   Unemployment in the 1930s and the 1980s: Some Comparisons

It was not until the early 1980s that such extensive unemployment was experienced again in Britain. It is tempting to view the 1930s as a control experiment against which to test policy proposals for the current economic crisis. The search for parallels to the recent past should not,

Table 3.11   The Structure of Unemployment: The 1930s and the 1980s

Inflow:		1933			1984	
volume:		c. 220,000 per week			86,630 per week	
probability:		0.0212			0.0041	
ACD I:		8.9 weeks			32.3 weeks	
T:		35.7 weeks			63.2 weeks	
U:		18.1 %			13.1 %	
Duration:	U	ACD I	T	U	ACD I	T
	%	weeks	weeks	%	weeks	weeks
(a) By gender:		1934			1984	
Male:	19.3	11.5	41.9	15.7	34.2	72.4
Female:	10.0	4.8	16.8	9.5	28.2	44.6
(b) By age (males):	February 1938			January 1984		
18-24:	11.1	5.5	17.3	24.9	30.8	55.4
55-59:	19.9	15.8	56.5	16.3	59.7	93.8
(c) By region (males):	June 1936			June 1984		
South-east:	5.4	6.0	19.5	11.1	30.5	61.3
North-west:	17.2	13.2	46.8	18.9	36.4	83.4
Scotland:	17.2	19.9	59.4	17.7	30.2	73.7
Wales:	32.3	18.6	67.7	18.5	33.1	75.3

Note: ACD I: mean completed duration calculated using steady-state assumptions. T for 1936 is calculated using spell lengths of [0,3), [3,6), [6,12), [12+) to conform to the data made available for 1984. ACD I for 1984 by region applies to April-July quarter. T for 1984 by region applies to June.

Sources: 1933-38: see other tables. 1984: Flows: Department of Employment (1985), Tables 2.19 (total, by gender), 2.20 (by age), 2.26 (by region). Unemployment: Department of Employment (1985), Tables 2.1 (total, by gender), 2.7 (by age), 2.3 (by region). Duration (T): Department of Employment (1985), Table 2.8 (total, by gender). Department of Employment (1984), Table 2.6 (by age and region).

however, disguise the fundamental differences in the operation of the labour market between the two periods. The most remarkable difference in the structure of unemployment between the 1930s and the 1980s is the turnover rate. Although the total insured population in 1933 was only half that of fifty years later, the volume of inflows on to the register was almost three times as large. The rapid rate of turnover is reflected in a considerably lower mean duration of completed spells, despite a higher unemployment rate. The lower average interrupted spell length in the

1930s can be attributed to the same factor. A comparison of unemployment registers from the two periods reveals that a higher proportion of those out of work in 1984 were suffering from prolonged unemployment (40 per cent as compared to 22 per cent in 1934).

Table 3.11 reveals that there are also significant differences in the incidence of unemployment between the two periods. Although female unemployment rates were much the same, average spells out of work, both completed and uncompleted, were significantly higher in 1984. This reflects both lower turnover and a greater determination to stay in the labour market after job separation. Indeed, many more women registered for benefit for longer than one year than had been the case in the 1930s. The decline in turnover is also very pronounced among the other major group of secondary workers, juveniles, and provides a major source of their deteriorating employment record in the recent past. If we turn to older workers, we find both lower unemployment rates and declining turnover between 1938 and 1984. It seems that older workers are now both less prone to job separation and less likely to find alternative employment. Finally, regional disparities are less evident in the 1980s than fifty years previously. The variation in unemployment rates is much lower. So too are differences in the duration of joblessness. Indeed, Table 3.11 suggests that the expected duration is much the same across all regions, a very different story from the situation in the 1930s. In all cases, the rate of turnover and the probability of re-employment are lower, reflecting general changes in the structure of the labour market and the nature of unemployment over the past fifty years.

Contemporary investigators of the labour market in the 1930s emphasised the increasing intensity of prolonged and hard-core unemployment, as compared to the previous decade. A more modern perspective on unemployment raises a second question which has too often escaped the notice of the historian: why was the rate of turnover so very high, especially compared to the recent past? A full and proper appreciation of the nature of interwar unemployment requires that we pay attention to both parts of the bifurcated labour market of the 1930s. I begin with long-term unemployment.

5   The Causes of Long-Term Unemployment

I suggested above that there are three major explanations for high long-term unemployment: the impact of benefits and allowances, a dual labour market situation in which certain workers are faced with near-zero re-employment probabilities, and duration dependence. I shall deal with each in turn.

Table 3.12   Replacement Rates, 1937 (%) (continued overleaf)

I Insurance Benefit Claimants (cumulative frequency distribution)

(a) Males	14s.	17s.	20-23s.	26s.	29s.	32s.
≥1.0	3.12	0.37	0.40	0.76	0.60	1.12
≥0.9	4.15	0.46	0.53	2.18	3.23	3.30
≥0.8	6.54	1.01	1.12	4.77	8.18	12.29
≥0.7	9.18	1.30	2.78	10.60	19.74	35.48
≥0.6	15.62	2.97	7.67	33.90	51.96	61.17
≥0.5	29.02	6.88	37.82	66.59	84.73	91.06
≥0.4	47.60	17.61	83.28	94.96	96.00	99.79
≥0.3	77.44	58.60	100.00	99.89	98.86	99.79
≥0.2	97.07	97.15	100.00	99.89	98.86	99.79
≥0.1	99.91	99.89	100.00	99.89	98.86	99.79
not stated	0.09	0.10	0.00	0.11	0.14	0.20
Total	21,470	149,930	15,130	90,890	56,830	39,380

(b) Females	12s.	15s.	18-21s.	24s.+	Total
≥1.0	0.58	1.90	6.58	11.00	2.47
≥0.9	6.22	2.23	10.23	19.00	2.93
≥0.8	8.21	3.86	18.11	- 43.00	4.87
≥0.7	14.96	8.26	37.04	59.00	9.87
≥0.6	23.10	16.07	64.61	86.00	18.20
≥0.5	45.86	45.09	86.00	92.50	46.04
≥0.4	78.76	82.14	97.41	100.00	82.17
≥0.3	95.57	96.51	100.00	100.00	96.49
≥0.2	99.07	99.97	100.00	100.00	99.87
≥0.1	100.00	99.97	100.00	100.00	99.97
not stated	0.00	0.03	0.00	0.00	0.03
Total	15,110	119,680	2,430	1,000	138,220

Official agencies, such as the Unemployment Assistance Board, were aware of the popular perception that many of the unemployed were workshy. However, they found little evidence to support this position and suggested that it could only explain a very small percentage of long-term unemployment (1938, p. 4). A potentially stronger argument was that the reservation criteria of these workers were so high as to make them reject all job offers. As the Pilgrim Trust noted, this situation faced two differ-

Table 3.12   Replacement Rates, 1937 (%) (continued)

II Unemployment Assistance Claimants

(a) Males

Wage less Assessment	20s.	Weekly Wage Rate				60s.	Total
		20s to 29s.11d.	30s. to 39s.11d.	40s. to 49s.11d.	50s. to 59s.11d.		
under 4s.	34.1	6.9	12.7	6.5	1.5	0.3	4.9
4s.-5s.11d.	17.9	11.2	8.7	5.2	2.2	0.1	4.1
6s.-7s.11d.	11.0	9.1	6.1	4.9	2.6	0.2	3.7
8s.-9s.11d.	8.1	15.2	5.8	5.9	3.1	0.2	4.4
10s.-19s.11d.	10.7	48.4	36.2	34.1	26.5	5.8	27.6
20s.-29s.11d.	--	3.2	25.8	27.0	29.8	19.0	25.5
30s.-39s.11d.	--	--	1.7	14.0	26.1	26.2	18.0
≥40s.	--	--	--	1.2	7.9	48.2	10.5
Assessments:							
Below wage rate:	81.8	94.0	97.0	98.8	99.7	100.0	98.7
Equal wage rate:	6.5	1.8	0.6	0.4	0.1	0.0	0.4
Above wage rate:	11.7	4.2	2.4	0.8	0.2	0.0	0.9
Total number:	6,500	14,250	51,000	207,500	165,750	83,000	528,000

(b) Females

Wage less Assessment	20s.	Weekly Wage Rate			50s.	Total
		20s to 29s.11d.	30s. to 39s.11d.	40s. to 49s.11d.		
under 4s.	30.1	7.7	2.2	1.1	--	10.9
4s.-5s.11d.	17.8	11.4	2.2	--	--	10.2
6s.-7s.11d.	17.8	11.9	2.0	1.1	--	10.4
8s.-9s.11d.	11.5	13.2	3.2	1.1	--	10.0
10s.-19s.11d.	11.8	49.8	48.7	13.3	--	38.6
20s.-29s.11d.	--	4.2	37.8	53.3	13.5	12.7
≥30s.	--	--	3.2	30.1	86.5	3.7
Assessments:						
Below wage rate:	89.0	98.2	99.3	100.0	100.0	96.5
Equal wage rate:	4.5	0.6	--	--	--	1.3
Above wage rate:	6.5	1.2	0.7	--	--	2.2
Total number:	9,000	21,700	8,600	1,900	800	42,000

Sources: insurance benefit claimants: Unemployment Insurance Statutory Committee (1937); unemployment assistance claimants: Unemployment Assistance Board (1938).

Table 3.13   Frequency Distribution of Workers According to
              Replacement Rates

| Age | Replacement Rates | | | |
	≥0.7	≥0.8	≥0.9	≥1.0
18-24	31	24	10	0
25-34	33	12	6	3
35-44	38	22	7	2
45-54	12	5	2	0
55-64	3	2	0.4	0

Source: Pilgrim Trust (1938), p. 203.

ent types of workers: "men with large families whose unemployment allowances may approach the normal wage level for the unskilled or semi-skilled worker ... and, secondly, the 'respectable' type of young man who, having once had employment at a good wage, refuses it at rates which seem to him to be unreasonable" (1938, p. 201).

The most useful sources of information on interwar replacement rates (the benefits/earnings ratio) are two official samples of benefit and assistance claimants in 1937 (Unemployment Insurance Statutory Committee, 1938; Unemployment Assistance Board, 1938). The results of these inquiries are shown in Table 3.12. In general they suggest that individuals and households on benefit or relief suffered considerable income reduction. In the case of unemployment benefit claimants, replacement rates of 0.7 or above applied to fewer than 10 per cent of females and no more than 11 per cent of males. The replacement rates for those on assistance were somewhat higher on average. Some 30.6 per cent of males and 30.8 per cent of females had rates above 0.7. These higher figures should not surprise us: assistance claimants were generally workers with only limited attachment to the labour market, and with commensurately lower normal wages.[22] However, not all were long-term unemployed; in December 1937, the month of the UAB survey, over 50 per cent of applicants had been unemployed for less than a year. The long-term unemployed had lower replacement rates than assistance claimants on average. When the Pilgrim Trust examined a sample of case cards of those who had been unemployed for over a year in November 1936, they discovered that only 21 per cent of the total sample had replacement rates above 0.7 (see Table 3.13).[23] Crafts (1987, p. 425) argues that these rates are too low to explain any significant part of the behaviour of the long-term unemployed. Of course, in the absence of direct information regarding individual valuation of added leisure, it is impossible to determine whether on average a replacement rate of 0.7 discourages effort or not.

Nevertheless, the Pilgrim Trust considered that only a small proportion of workers fell into a "danger zone" within which they would be likely to refuse jobs either because of unrealistic reservation wages or because of the "disutility" of the job itself at the going wage. This was perceived to be a problem particularly for younger men, especially those with families and without particular skills. However, the bulk of those out of work beyond one year were older men, very few of whom had replacement rates even as high as 0.7.

The benefits story, of course, has developed into something of a *cause célèbre* in the recent economics literature. No advantage is to be gained from rehearsing the debate in any detail here. However, two recent studies are worth reporting. In a further analysis of the New London Survey material, Eichengreen (1987b) has tested the replacement rate hypothesis with interesting conclusions. Most notably, he finds that the unemployment profile of adult male household heads owed almost nothing to the structure of benefit provisions, after accounting for other personal attributes which are correlated with earnings and risk of unemployment. In contrast, secondary workers did respond to the incentives of the benefit system. Since household heads dominate the London sample, the overall impact of the replacement rate, while non-negligible, is considerably smaller than some have argued. Eichengreen's "best estimate" is that no more than one-fifth of London's unemployment in 1929-32 can be explained by the increased generosity of the benefits scheme after 1920. It should be noted that these results make no distinction between prolonged and short-term unemployment, and that it is therefore difficult to determine the mechanism by which benefits altered labour supply behaviour. Crafts's recent exploration of long-term unemployment in the 1930s has attempted to tackle this issue directly. He extends Benjamin and Kochin's (1979) equation explaining unemployment rates by the benefit to wage ratio and deviations from trend growth in national income, using quarterly data and distinguishing short-term and long-term unemployment. Crafts finds that the increase in long-term unemployment after 1930 cannot be explained by changes in insurance system. Unemployment rates of less than three months' duration are, however, significantly related to the benefit-wage ratio.

The Unemployment Assistance Board put considerably greater emphasis on

> applicants who would probably accept work if it were offered to them but have fallen into such a condition of body and mind that they make no personal effort to attain it. Neither is it likely in view of their lack of skill and loss of industrial efficiency that, in the normal course, an offer of employment would be made to them. These men are usually

victims of their own prolonged unemployment, which has produced a state of indifference and lassitude that tends to become progressively worse. (1939, p. 5)

Other contemporary commentators also believed that long-term unemployment was self-sustaining. In the words of the Pilgrim Trust:

unemployed men are not simply units of employability who can, through the medium of the dole, be put into cold storage and taken out again immediately they are needed. While they are in cold storage, things are likely to happen to them. (1938, p.67)

In particular, psychological impairment and physical deterioration were the lot of the long-term unemployed. As early as 1929, the Ministry of Labour's experiment with industrial transference threatened to collapse because "prolonged unemployment has robbed many men of both the physical fitness and of the attitudes of mind which would enable them to undertake heavy work under ordinary industrial conditions" (Ministry of Labour, 1929b, p. 37). Not only were workers' skills liable to decline as they remained out of shape and practice, but also their very predisposition for work. As the Unemployment Assistance Board argued in 1936,

a man long unemployed is not only in danger of losing his skill and aptitude for work, but he is also likely either to lose heart and feel that he is no longer wanted in the economic and social life of the nation, and then to become embittered, or to accept his state of unemployment and make little effort of his own to change it. (1936, p. 17)[24]

Social commentators were not the only ones who believed that a lengthy period of unemployment was a significant obstacle to re-employment. Employers were reported to discriminate against workers who had been jobless for some time, taking a record of prolonged unemployment as a simple means to screen out the unemployable or unsuitable.[25] On the basis of the contemporary literature, Crafts has concluded that there was "a significant amount of duration dependency in re-employment probabilities in the 1930s" (1987, p. 424).

Unfortunately, it is not possible to determine empirically the extent to which duration dependence was a cause of long-term unemployment. There are no microeconomic data available for the 1930s which would permit the sort of formal testing undertaken by Lancaster (1979), Nickell (1979) and others. The aggregate register does show the continuation rate to rise with the period of unemployment rises, to be sure. However, this is not a sufficient condition for duration dependence. As Carlson and Horrigan (1983) have shown, it is possible to replicate the duration structure of employment registers with relatively simple sorting models that assume zero dependence. The principle of these models is that different individuals have different probabilities of re-entering employment which are established at the time they join the register and remain constant thereafter. As an inflow cohort ages, those with high probabilities find new jobs, leaving the less attractive workers behind. As sorting continues, the average employability of the survivors declines and the tail of the duration distribution fills out. The sorting model does not, of course, preclude positive (or indeed negative) duration dependence.

The very fact of long-period unemployment suggests that re-employment probabilities were very low to begin with. Almost 5 per cent of male claimants in 1938 had been unemployed for five years or longer. Without duration dependence, these workers would have entered unemployment with a weekly continuation rate of 0.996 or more, that is, with virtually no chance of ever getting another job. It might be argued that these very long-term unemployed had high reservation criteria based on unemployment allowances. However, the category of those unemployed over five years was dominated by older workers (69 per cent were over 45), the very age groups identified by the Pilgrim Trust as having low replacement rates. The existence of almost indefinite spells is certainly not compatible with an adaptive search model. Either there is positive duration dependence, in which case workers' reservation criteria fall less slowly than their rapidly declining market value (which is equivalent to saying that the true replacement rate, the one measured against current market opportunities, rises over time), or the problem is to be found in the lack of jobs available. Certainly, the prolonged unemployed were not acting as "indomitable" searchers. Indeed, as the Pilgrim Trust inquiry made clear, many had given up searching for work entirely (1938, pp. 143-9): of 453 "fully employable" men, 66 per cent had either begun to or completely adjusted to unemployment (p. 437).

A full understanding of long-term unemployment in the 1930s needs to confront the issue of why continuation rates for some workers rose so dramatically after 1929. Why was prolonged unemployment a feature of the 1930s when it had not been in the previous decade? The sample surveys of the Ministry of Labour make it clear that there was no dramatic change in the personal attributes of the unemployed. The source of the problem lies rather in the peculiar structural characteristics of the Great Depression of 1929-32. In terms of the queuing model favoured by Hatton and Singer, some workers faced almost infinite queues after 1929. Those workers with very low re-employment probabilities were concentrated in certain regions of the country, regions that were associated with the particular staple trades of Britain's prewar pre-eminence and postwar economic misery. The export staples (coal, iron and steel, engineering, shipbuilding, cotton and woollens) accounted for over 57 per cent of long-term unemployment in 1936 (and 53.5 per cent of unemployment longer than five years in 1935), compared to 18.4 per cent of the insured population. The increase of prolonged unemployment after 1929 can be attributed in large part to a shift in the density function of continuation rates in which structural factors played the dominant role. There was undoubtedly some duration dependence in depressed regions as well. However, its primary effect was to force people further down the unemployment queue, a queue that was extremely long to begin with. The rapidity with which the labour market recovered during the mobilisation to war after 1939 confirms the secondary importance of duration dependence. A commentator from the International Labour Office surveying the transition to war, wisely concluded that,

> "unemployability" has not been an objective concept: its definition has varied with economic circumstances. The absorption of long-term unemployment has depended primarily on the extent and character of available employment openings. In the depth of the depression, the hard core was at its worst. As the economic situation improved, the core became smaller - with some lag of course, *but with far less than might have been expected.* (ILO, 1942, p. 44, italics added)

The structural imbalance of recovery was, in this analysis, a major reason for the slow absorption of the hard core.

6   The Sources of Rapid Turnover

The prevalence of high turnover in the 1930s can be attributed to three major factors: the operation of the insurance system, the prevalence of casual employment, and the extent of low job attachment. The last two elements are, of course, difficult to separate. If we classify casual employment as the demand side of labour market structure, and low job attachment as the supply side, it remains almost impossible to identify each factor.

Underemployment as well as unemployment was a particular feature of interwar Britain. The dominant form that underemployment took in this period was short-time working by employees. In the cotton industry between 1924 and 1929, some 18 per cent of workers were employed for less than a full week. The average shortfall of hours was 14.2, or almost 30 per cent of the normal 48-hour working week (Gilson, 1931, p. 164). Short-time was common in other industries as well, notably coal, shipbuilding and iron and steel. Such work sharing arrangements had been a common element in British industry before 1914. The significant difference between prewar and postwar practice, however, was the status of short-time workers before the insurance scheme. Before the war, restrictions on registration and the duration of benefit discouraged claims, particularly under trade union rules. By 1920, however, short-timers were eligible for benefit. In response, the structure of work sharing altered and grew more prevalent. In 1925, it was stated that,

> There appears ... to be a certain number of employers who systematically resort to organized short time if work is a little slack. They would not do this but for the existence of the benefit ... there is a tendency for benefit to be crudely used as a form of subsidy for industry. (Astor *et al.*, 1923, p. 54; see also Beveridge, 1930, p. 348)

Gilson cites examples of "work pools" in such industries as the shoe and hat trades, as well as coal and cotton (1931, p. 165). Systematic short-time working was sufficiently well known by the mid-1920s to earn the title of the OXO system, so named for the arrangement of days of work (O) and leisure (X). The usual arrangement was for three days in work, and three days out. The workings of the unemployment scheme recognised any three days of unemployment occurring in a period of six as continuous, while any periods of unemployment occurring within ten weeks were considered continuous, thereby requiring no reregistration and no waiting period before payment of benefit. There were restrictions on the availability of benefit under short-time arrangements: if weekly earnings were half or more than the full-time week's wage, payment was denied.

Although systematic short-time working was encouraged by the insurance scheme, there was only limited adherence to it. Entitlement required that employers organise the work week accordingly, something that few were able to do. J. A. Dale of the Ministry of Labour estimated that, out of 650,000 workers on short-time in all, perhaps 150,000 were on systematic schemes (1934, pp. 89-90). The occasionally published official statistics on the loss of hours and earnings due to short-time make the same point. Fewer than twelve hours, less than a quarter of a full working week, were lost on average by those working short-time in British industry in October 1931. Formal work-sharing arrangements account for only a small part of the 15 per cent or so of workers on short time.[26]

Short-timers were recorded as temporarily stopped workers in the unemployment statistics. This category included all workers who expected to return to their former employer within six weeks of registering a claim. Others who had only irregular employment were counted as casual unemployed in the statistics. There were between 60,000 and 120,000 men and women classified as unemployed casuals in the 1930s, or about 4 per cent of the total number on the register. These tended to be untrained and unskilled workers, dominated by building labourers, dock, road and transport workers, and general labourers. In Beveridge's words, the casually unemployed "flow ceaselessly into and out of employment" (1930, p. 391). The unemployment rate among casuals, in the form of rotating underemployment (the phrase is Charles Feinstein's), was upwards of 25 per cent during both depression and recovery.

Because of the structure of the unemployment statistics, it is easily assumed that all those who were intermittently in work are included in the categories of temporarily stopped and casual unemployed. This would be a false inference. The wholly unemployed include many whom logic would dictate should be counted as casual workers, on the basis of low job attachment. As Dale points out,

> There is in [this] group ... a considerable number whose unemployment in a short period is no greater than that of many of the temporarily stopped, the reason why they are not included in [these] figures being that the Employment Exchange does not happen to know that they have a definite expectation of resuming their previous employment. (1934, p. 90)

An upper-bound estimate of the proportion of those who fall into this category in 1936, calculated from the placing indices of the Ministry of Labour, is 35 per cent.[27] There were also, of course, workers who registered as wholly unemployed, not anticipating early re-engagement, but who did return to work after only a short spell. One indication of the intermittent nature of employment in Britain in the Great Depression is provided by figures on the number of spells at work for those on standard and transitional benefit on the first Monday of February 1931 (Ministry of Labour, 1932a, pp. 280-2). On average, men and women on standard benefit experienced 8.62 and 6.59 periods of employment respectively in the previous year. The average length of spells of employment for those on standard benefit was 19.45 days for men and 21.74 days for women. The length of employment for those on transitional benefit was similar: 17.4 days (men) and 22.5 days (women), although the number of spells was much lower for both sexes (1.54 and 1.27). The figures for those on standard benefit include both casual and temporarily stopped workers. Unfortunately, we have no direct evidence on the relative susceptibility of these workers to spells out of work, and so cannot state precisely what the average duration of a spell in work is for those who would be classified as wholly unemployed. However, we can calculate a lower bound of the number of spells, by assuming those on standard benefit who suffered the largest number of spells in the year were casual and temporarily stopped workers. By further assuming that the casual and temporarily stopped account for the shortest spells at work, it is also possible to estimate an

upper bound on the spell length of employment for the wholly unemployed. On this basis, the average number of spells is 2.56 for men and
women combined, with an average duration of 70.7 days. This figure is,
if anything, slightly lower than the estimates of mean completed duration
for the wholly unemployed given in Table 3.4.

These data, although suggestive, do not enable us to determine the true
source of high turnover and low average duration. They do, however,
strongly suggest that the operation of the insurance system, through its
encouragement of organised work-sharing programmes, was not a major
cause. They further suggest that the nature of employment played no
small role in determining susceptibility to unemployment. The short duration of work periods cannot be laid entirely at the feet of casual work,
as classified by the insurance scheme. It seems very probable that the system of short engagements in British industry in the interwar years was
more prevalent than most treatments of the casual labour problem recognise.

Clearly, there may have been other factors that played a role as well,
factors linked to the worker rather than the work. The prevalence of low
job attachment was noted by authorities throughout the 1930s, particularly with regard to juvenile and youth labour. In 1938, the Unemployment Assistance Board condemned the practice of "blind alley"
employment for school leavers:

> On leaving school they obtained employment in which they had no
> opportunity to acquire either skill or aptitude or experience of any
> lasting value, and after the age of 18 found themselves stranded with-
> out any industrial proficiency and having forgotten most of what they
> had learnt at school. Thereafter, if they have had any work at all, it
> has been in short spells and at odd jobs that have never given them
> any proper industrial status. ... The minor unskilled jobs in industry
> are no doubt necessary, but the cumulative result of the casual and
> thoughtless practices which now prevail is at once demoralising to
> the individual and costly to the nation. (1938, pp. 45-6)

How far the short tenure of positions held by juveniles was due to personal decisions, rather than the nature of the job, is difficult to assess.
The Carnegie UK Trust, in its investigation of the employment histories
of young workers between 1937 and 1939, provides some guidance. Out
of 5,314 jobs covered, only 14 per cent ended through voluntary quits.
Although labour supply decisions of secondary workers were in general
more sensitive to the workings of the insurance system, they did not dominate separations in the Carnegie sample. Only 17.6 per cent of separations
were directly linked to the benefit payments (via either quits or being
"paid off due to age" at 18). The dominant reason cited for leaving a job

was that "work had finished" (59 per cent). The implication is strongly that the nature of the work precluded sustained tenure. Moreover, with limited opportunities for apprenticeship and training, the employment histories of many juveniles were little more than a sequence of unskilled, short-duration positions.[28] The extent to which low job attachment accounted for the intermittent employment record of many unemployed adults in the 1930s can only be a matter for speculation in the absence of detailed evidence. The sample surveys of 1931 and 1932 do make clear, however, the importance of short tenure and recurrent spells to the structure of unemployment in the Depression.

7   Conclusion

How might we characterise the nature of interwar unemployment in the light of the evidence on structure and incidence presented in this paper? A recurrent phrase throughout has been that of the bifurcated labour market. The 1930s were marked not only by prolonged unemployment but also by high turnover. However, the seeming duality should not be exaggerated. The low mean durations of unemployment represent averages per spell rather than per individual. The prevalence of recurrent spells of unemployment meant that the average time spent out of work in a given period was much higher than would be imagined by looking at average durations alone. Only 20 per cent of those unemployed in February 1931 had experienced a single spell without work in the previous year; the average number of spells was over eight. This in turn raises questions of labour market structure, particularly regarding the status of job tenure at the time. The average spell of employment for the February 1931 sample of unemployed was twenty-two days. If it is reasonable to infer considerable casual labour from this statistic, it is no longer quite as obvious that high turnover should be identified with market efficiency. Intermittent unemployment suggests an economy with poor job opportunities for many, especially for those entering the labour market. There is a further difficulty: how far do recurrent spells and short duration truly reflect high turnover? This is partially a definitional problem, since casual workers often returned to their previous employer. Unemployment spells of this sort may be a response to surplus labour, but do not contribute to true turnover. There is also a problem of evidence. It is merely an arithmetic truism that workers who experience many employment spells in a given period only suffer from short bouts of unemployment. However, for those who were unemployed for one spell in 1930-31, the time spent out of work was 107 days, while for those having two spells, the average duration was over 50 days (Ministry of Labour, 1932a, p. 281). Nevertheless, the mean duration of unemployment that prevailed in the 1930s was certainly much lower than in the 1980s. The explanation for the difference requires knowledge of how the working of the labour market affected the density of spells and the chances of recurrence in each period. No easy inferences about turnover and market efficiency should be drawn from simple comparisons.

On the other side of this bifurcated market, the statistics understate rather than exaggerate the degree of duality. I have already argued that the true extent of hard-core unemployment was considerably greater than the figures on those out of work for over one year would indicate. This paper argues that structural factors dominated the structure and incidence of hard-core unemployment in the 1930s. The "generosity" of the insurance system played only a small part and was mostly limited to secondary workers and young men with large families and low skills. There is also considerable anecdotal evidence that the unemployed suffered from psychological and physiological impairment that reduced their chances of re-employment. It seems unlikely, however, that duration dependence was a major source of prolonged unemployment in those areas economically decimated by the collapse of the export staples after 1929. It is as well to recognise that this emphasis on structural factors still leaves a wide range of questions unanswered, especially about market wage behaviour, which lies outside the scope of this paper, and the mobility of labour, which does not, and whose low level in the 1930s may be the most significant legacy of duration dependence.

NOTES

* I would like to thank Charles Feinstein for his very helpful comments on the original conference version of this paper.

1

But not all "lodged" books represent unemployed persons. In practice, to obtain the total of unemployed persons, a count is taken only of those lodged books represented by current claims to benefit, by applications for work on the part of insured non-claimants, and by books passing through what is known as the "two months file". (Testimony of John Hilton, Assistant Secretary of the Ministry of Labour, to the Royal Commission on Unemployment Insurance (1931), p. 1160, para. 9)

The "two months file" covered those workers who ceased registration at their employment exchange but who did not declare their employment status. Any person who, after a period of two months, had not returned to the exchange was presumed to have left unemployment. Although there are evident theoretical objections to this procedure, in practice little distortion was introduced. According to Hilton, less than 4 per cent of total books lodged fell into this category in 1931. (ibid., p. 1161, para. 17).

2 The exchange data have also been used to determine the migration of workers by region and industry (Thomas, 1937).

3 Insurance was extended to agricultural and horticultural workers in May 1936 and to private gardeners in February 1937.

4 In the form of a semi-logarithmic function: $S(S_{ti}) = a + b \log (1 + i)$.

5 It might be argued that the true proportion of temporary to permanent lay-offs would be expected to fall during the depression, in which case this procedure will be an undercorrection.

6 I have excluded temporarily stopped workers by assuming that they return to work within four weeks of being laid off.

7 Cripps and Tarling (1974, p. 306), employing the methodology of the stationary register, estimate the total inflow of adult males on to the register at 79,800 per week in April 1933 and 61,800 in April 1937, with implied expected durations of 16.8 and 13.2 weeks respectively.

8 Note that the outflow rates exclude those leaving the register due to retirement or death and that the duration statistics are based on steady-state assumptions.

9 The data for the two surveys are not quite comparable. In 1929,

> this analysis could only be based on the number of complete weeks of continuous unemployment, since in the absence of a record of schedules for each day it was impossible to determine whether the unemployment in any week which contained less than six days of unemployment was continuous with that of an adjacent work week or not. (Ministry of Labour, 1930a, p. 7)

The 1931 data, however, do include all spells of unemployment of a day or longer. I have excluded all spells of six days or less from the 1931 data, in order to make the spell estimates as comparable to 1929 as possible. The total period spent in unemployment in 1930-31 was 23.68 weeks excluding short duration spells, and 25.35 weeks including all spells.

10 The data presented in Table 3.3a, which are based on actuarial estimates of how rising unemployment would be distributed between higher incidence and longer duration, show a similar pattern.

11 Further evidence is provided by a Ministry of Labour survey, undertaken in November 1932, of the unemployment record of certain benefit claimants between 1925 and 1931 (1933a, p. 318). In this case, the incidence of unemployment increased by 75 per cent between 1929 and 1931 while the intensity of unemployment within the year rose by 45 per cent. However, the survey shows a rise in both the extent and the duration of unemployment from as early as 1927. It seems likely that the sample is biased towards the hard-core unemployed and away from those experiencing short spells on the register. This is reflected in the much higher

number of days spent out of work by those covered (123 and 193 days in 1929 and 1931, compared to 85 and 126 days in Table 3.3), which suggests length bias of the sort raised in the discussion of duration measures above.

12 Their choice of April 1937 is particularly peculiar since this month saw an extension of the insurance scheme that added another 78,892 to the unemployment register (Ministry of Labour, 1935a, p. 232).

13 It should be noted that the average interrupted spell length is underestimated by this method. It appears that the continuation rate declines further after one year. The Ministry of Labour published data in 1938 on spell lengths between one and five years: the average value of T for the long-term unemployed from these figures is 194.01 weeks compared to 139.76 weeks using the assumption of a stable continuation rate.

14 The identification of those out of work for over one year with the hard-core unemployed is convenient but inaccurate. As J. A. Dale wrote, "Quite a small amount of work removes a man from that class, though he may be in a desperate plight" (1934, p. 92). The prevalence of recurrent spells among the precariously employed indicates that figures on the long-term unemployed understate the true nature of the problem in the 1930s. For this reason the Ministry of Labour preferred to use statistics of the number of the insured unemployed who had paid less than thirty contributions in the previous two years as a measure of the hard core. The volume of such persons was consistently 30 to 40 per cent higher than the number of those unemployed for over a year. Claimants for transitional payments include these workers as well as those who had been unemployed for more than twenty-six weeks in the previous year and who had not had much work since. Those on transitional benefit totalled 1,087,000 in June 1933 compared to 481,000 out of work for over one year (Dale, 1934, pp. 91-3). I have relied on the figures for prolonged duration because of their consistent availability for the 1930s at levels of detail not present for the other data. There is no evidence of a bias in trends or distribution of the hard core from using the duration statistics.

15 Consideration of both Tables 3.5 and 3.6 shows the female/male ratio of unemployment rates to have been considerably higher in 1930-31 than at any other time during the interwar period. This shows the impact of insurance benefits regulations on labour force behaviour. From 1930 until the passage of the Anomalies Act in October 1931, the condition that those claiming benefit must be "genuinely seeking work" was dropped. This action introduced more women than men to the benefit lines, particularly married women who had "retired" some time before. This accounts for both the steep rise in female unemployment registrations in the first months of the depression as well as the comparatively high level of long-term unemployed in the February survey.

16 I have generated a transition matrix of insured workers for the periods 1927-32 and 1932-37, which is available upon request. The matrix shows that the exit probabilities of all workers over 35 was lower in the first period than in the sec-

ond. It is also noticeable that the continuation rates fell monotonically across age groups (with the exception of 50- to 54-year-old males, who appear to be less prone to leave the register than 45- to 49-year-olds).

17 These figures are calculated from the Minutes of Evidence of the Royal Commission on Unemployment Insurance, Appendix V (1931, p. 261).

18 It should be noted that only one insurance claim needed to be made within a particular year. These statistics therefore represent vulnerability to *at least* one bout of unemployment within the year. Multiple spells are not captured by the claim rate. It is only possible to determine the effect of spell recurrence on the total unemployment suffered by different age categories of worker in 1930-31. The Ministry of Labour survey of male workers claiming standard or transitional benefit on 2 February 1931 shows that on average they had been unemployed in the previous year for the following number of days: 18- to 24-year-olds: 135 days; 25-34: 147; 35-44: 150; 45-54: 161; 55-64: 185. Clearly, recurrent spells among younger workers produced a lower concentration of unemployment by age than examination of the mean duration of individual spells would suggest.

19 If we assume that steady-state conditions held in both 1929 and 1938, it is possible to apply the relationship that the mean expected duration is equal to the ratio of the unemployment rate to the inflow probability to estimate the inflow rate from ACD I. This calculation implies that inflow rates in 1929 were considerably lower (ca. 0.002 per week) for those over 55 than for younger males (ca. 0.0035 per week). The estimates for 1938 show, however, a much more gradual decline in the rate of inflow with age: from 0.002 for those under 24, to 0.0013 for 35- to 59-year-olds, and 0.0011 for those over 60. In 1929, there was a discrete drop in the inflow probability at age 55; in 1938, the rate declined significantly at age 25.

20 The figures for average interrupted spell length given in Table 3.8 are downward biased since they assume the continuation rates are constant for all those unemployed longer than nine months. The data for June 1938 show that continuation rates fell consistently, the longer the interrupted spell. See note 13. This implies that the true extent of increasing duration with age is understated in the text. I have calculated T for February 1938 from data on spell lengths up to five years. The results are as follows: 18-20: 13.6 weeks; 21-24: 21.9; 25-34: 33.4; 35-44: 47.9; 45-54: 61.3; 55-59: 80.4; 60-64: 100.5. The ratio of T between 60- to 64-year-olds and 18- to 20-year-olds rises from 5.5 to 7.4. This correction also affects comparative statistics across the depression. Given the relatively minor amount of long-period unemployment in 1929, the incorporation of spell lengths over one year will raise T by less than at any stage thereafter. The true increase in T between 1929 and 1938 is therefore larger than the estimate in Table 3.8.

21 The high numbers of unemployed for semi-professionals is due to the presence of actors and musicians. If we exclude these, the unemployment rate for class Ic falls to 5.95 (male) and 4.18 (female) per cent.

22 The estimated replacement rates were calculated from Table 3.12 after converting gross wages to net earnings by removing 1s. 7d. for health, old age and unemployment insurance contributions. The higher replacement rates for UAB claimants are largely explained by the lower normal wages earned: fewer than 16 per cent had normal earnings above 60s. a week, compared to 42.5 per cent of benefit recipients. The assistance registers were dominated by persons who did not have the necessary number of insurance contributions to be eligible for benefits: persons whose employment experience in the previous two years did not meet the requirements of thirty weeks in work or thirty days' work in thirty different weeks. These were persons with very low attachment to the labour market. They were poor when in employment and poorer out of work. From materials published by the Unemployment Assistance Board (1939, pp. 71-2) on actual income as against "normal income", if all usually employed members of a household were in work at their regular wage, the average shortfall caused by (multiple) job loss was 24.8 per cent. The highest income losses were borne not by the very poorest households, but by those at the top end of the spectrum, i.e. those with multiple earners in "normal" times, those with secondary earners perhaps on the fringes of the labour market. However, since the clients of the UAB were for the most part to be found in the lower quartile of the wage distribution of the economy as a whole, Eichengreen's conclusion that the tendency was for unemployment to fall most heavily on low-wage workers is certainly well founded, especially for the "hard-core" unemployed (1986, p. 356).

23 These replacement rates are calculated against the "stop" wage, that is, the last normal week's earnings of the unemployed person. It is not therefore a measure of the relation between unemployment allowance and the individual's current reservation wage.

24 See also ILO (1942, p. 57), in which it is further argued that long-unemployed workers also lost confidence in their skill and were afraid to go back to work because of this.

25 Cf. the observation of Bakke's "A":

> Then they say, "How long you been out?" And you don't like to, but you lie. I never thought I'd lie even to get a job. But I know that if I tell them two months they'll say, "What's wrong?" And even if I prove my character is right, I'm started on the wrong foot with him. I don't like it. (Bakke, 1933, p. 66)

26 Figures on the length of unemployment spells in the previous year for those on standard benefit on 2 February 1931 show that, for spells of less than one week, only 21.9 per cent were of three days' duration; 36 per cent of spells lasted only one day (Ministry of Labour, 1932a, pp. 281-2).

27 Beveridge (1944, p. 81) notes that 30 per cent of all engagements in 1937 were re-engagements with the same employer.

28

The subsequent jobs found by the majority of the lads during their first four years were largely a dreary repetition of their first. [For 70 per cent] it was a matter of clinging tenaciously to what they had in the face of an over-supplied labour market, or flitting about from one blind-alley job to another, or from one labouring job to another of a more casual nature. (Carnegie UK Trust, 1943, p. 39)

REFERENCES

Akerlof, George A. and Main, Brian G. M. (1981), "An Experience-weighted Measure of Employment and Unemployment Duration", *American Economic Review* 71, pp.1003-11.

Astor, J. *et al.* (1923), *The Third Winter of Unemployment*, London: P.S. King.

Baker, G.M. and Trivedi, P.K. (1985), "Estimation of Unemployment Duration from Grouped Data: A Comparative Study", *Journal of Labor Economics* 3, pp. 153- 74.

Bakke, E. Wight (1933), *The Unemployed Man*, New Haven: Yale University Press.

Benjamin, Daniel and Kochin, Levis (1979), "Searching for an Explanation for Unemployment in Interwar Britain", *Journal of Political Economy* 87, pp.441-78.

Beveridge, W. H. (1930), *Unemployment: A Problem of Industry*, London: Longmans Green.

Beveridge, Sir William (1936), "An Analysis of Unemployment", *Economica* 3, pp.357-386.

Beveridge, Sir William (1937a), "An Analysis of Unemployment II", *Economica* 4, pp.1-17.

Beveridge, Sir William (1937b), "An Analysis of Unemployment III", *Economica* 4, pp.168-183.

Beveridge, William H. (1944), *Full Employment in a Free Society*, London: Allen & Unwin.

Bowers, J.K. and Harkess, D. (1979), "Duration of Unemployment by Age and Sex", *Economica* 46, pp.239-260.

Burns, E.M. (1941), *British Unemployment Programs, 1920-1938*, Washington, DC: Social Science Research Council.

Carlson, John A. and Horrigan, Michael W. (1983), "Measures of Unemployment Duration as Guides to Research and Policy: Comment", *American Economic Review* 73, pp.1143-1150.

Carnegie UK Trust (1943), *Disinherited Youth*, Edinburgh: A. & T. Constable.

Chegwidden, T.S. and Myrddin-Evans, G. (1934), *The Employment Exchange Service of Great Britain*, New York: Industrial Relations Counselors.

Clark, K.B. and Summers, L.H. (1979), "Labor Market Dynamics and Unemployment: A Reconsideration", *Brookings Papers on Economic Activity* 1, pp.13-72.

Crafts, N.F.R. (1987), "Long Term Unemployment in Britain in the 1930s", *Economic History Review* 40, pp.417- 431.

Cripps, T.F. and Tarling, R.J. (1974), "An Analysis of the Duration of Male Unemployment in Great Britain 1932-73", *Economic Journal* 84, pp.289-316.

Dale, J. A. (1934), "The Interpretation of the Statistics of Unemployment", *Journal of the Royal Statistical Society* 97, pp. 85-101.

Department of Employment (1984-5), *Gazette*, London: HMSO.

Disney, Richard (1979), "Recurrent Spells and the Concentration of Unemployment in Great Britain", *Economic Journal* 89, pp.109-119.

Eichengreen, Barry (1986), "Unemployment in Interwar Britain: New Evidence from London", *Journal of Interdisciplinary History* 17, pp.335-58.

Eichengreen, Barry (1987a), "Juvenile Unemployment in 20th Century Britain: The Emergence of a Problem", *Social Research* 54, pp.273-301.

Eichengreen, Barry (1987b), "Unemployment in Interwar Britain: Dole or Doldrums?", *Oxford Economic Papers* (forthcoming).

Feinstein, C.H. (1972), *National Income, Expenditure and Output of the United Kingdom 1855-1965*, Cambridge: Cambridge University Press.

Fowler, R.F. (1968), *Duration of Unemployment on the Register of Wholly Unemployed*, Studies in Official Statistics Research Studies no. 1, London: HMSO.

Garside, W.R. (1980), *The Measurement of Unemployment*, Oxford: Basil Blackwell.

Gilson, M.B. (1931), *Unemployment Insurance in Great Britain*, Series on Unemployment Insurance, vol. 2, New York: Industrial Relations Counselors.

Hatton, T.J. (1985), "The British Labor Market in the 1920s: A Test of the Search-Turnover Approach", *Explorations in Economic History* 22, pp.257-270.

Heim, C. (1984), "Structural Transformation and the Demand for New Labor in Advanced Economies: Interwar Britain", *Journal of Economic History* 44, pp.585-95.

Hurstfield, J. (1986) , "Women's Unemployment in the 1930s: Some Comparisons with the 1980s", in S. Allen, A. Waton, K. Purcell and S. Wood (eds), *The Experience of Unemployment*, London: Macmillan, pp.29-44.

International Labour Office (1942), "The Impact of War on Long-Term Unemployment in Great Britain", *International Labor Review* 45, pp.44-63.

Knight, K. G. (1987), *Unemployment: An Economic Analysis*, London: Croom Helm.

Lancaster, Tony (1979), "Econometric Methods for the Duration of Unemployment", *Econometrica* 47, pp.939- 956.

Layard, Richard (1981), "Measuring the Duration of Unemployment: A Note", *Scottish Journal of Political Economy* 28, pp.273-277.

McGregor, A. (1978), "Unemployment Duration and Re-employment Probability", *Economic Journal* 88, pp.693-706.

Main, Brian G.M. (1981), "The Length of Employment and Unemployment in Great Britain", *Scottish Journal of Political Economy* 28, pp.146-164.

Ministry of Labour (1921a-1939a), *Gazette*, London: HMSO.

Ministry of Labour (1924), *Report on an Investigation into the Personal Circumstances and Industrial History of 10,000 Claimants to Unemployment Benefit*, London: HMSO.

Ministry of Labour (1925), *Report on an Investigation into the Personal Circumstances and Industrial History of 10,903 Claimants to Unemployment Benefit*, London: HMSO.

Ministry of Labour (1927), *Report on an Investigation into the Employment and Insurance History of a Sample of Persons Insured Against Unemployment in Great Britain*, London: HMSO.

Ministry of Labour (1928), *Report on an Investigation into the Personal Circumstances and Industrial History of 9,748 Claimants to Unemployment Benefit*, London: HMSO.

Ministry of Labour (1929b-1938b), *Reports*, London: HMSO.

Ministry of Labour (1937), *Twenty-Second Abstract of Labour Statistics of the United Kingdom (1922- 1936)*, London: HMSO.

Morley, F. (1922), "The Incidence of Unemployment by Age and Sex", *Economic Journal* 32, pp.477-88.

Nickell, S.J. (1979), "The Effect of Unemployment and Related Benefits on the Duration of Unemployment", *Economic Journal* 89, pp.34-49.

Nickell, S.J. (1980), "A Picture of Male Unemployment in Britain", *Economic Journal* 90, pp.776-94.

Pilgrim Trust (1938), *Men Without Work*, Cambridge: Cambridge University Press.

Routh, Guy (1980), *Occupation and Pay in Great Britain 1906-79*, London: Macmillan.

Royal Commission on Unemployment Insurance (1931), *Minutes of Evidence*, London: HMSO.

Salant, Stephen W. (1977), "Search Theory and Duration Data: A Theory of Sorts", *Quarterly Journal of Economics* 91, pp.39-57.

Singer, H.W. (1939-40), "Regional Labor Markets and the Process of Unemployment", *Review of Economic Studies* 7, pp.42-58.

Thomas, Brinley (1937), "The Influx of Labour into London and the South-East, 1920-36", *Economica* 4, pp.323-36.

Unemployment Assistance Board (1936-1939), *Reports*, London: HMSO.

Unemployment Insurance Statutory Committee (1938), *Report for 1937*, London: HMSO.

Chapter 4

Unemployment, Insurance and Health in Interwar Britain

Bernard Harris*

1   Introduction

In Britain, the years between 1918 and 1939 were characterised by a fall in the birth rate and by increases in the level of real wages and in the participation rates of young married women. As a result of these changes, there was a marked increase in the real income of the average British household, and the effects of this increase were enhanced by a reduction in the number of dependants. This period was also marked by improvements in food supply and housing, and these improvements were reflected in the vital statistics of the period. The standardised death rate in England and Wales fell from 13.8 on the eve of the First World War to 9.3 in 1937, and average life expectancy increased by more than ten years. The decline in the level of infant mortality was equally dramatic. Between 1910 and 1940 the infant mortality rate fell from 110 deaths per thousand live births to 61.0 (Stevenson, 1984, pp.117, 148, 164, 203-4, 221; Lewis, 1984, pp.150-1; Burnett, 1983, pp.298; Mowat, 1968, pp.513-14).

However, despite these advances there were still marked inequalities in the health of the British population on the eve of the Second World War. One of the ways of measuring health inequality is to compare the proportion of all the deaths in a particular area which occur at a certain age. In 1936 Richard Titmuss found that over 10 per cent of all the deaths in Durham and Northumberland occurred between the ages of 0 and 1, but only 5.4 per cent of all the deaths in the most prosperous areas of south-eastern England occurred in this age group.[1] Overall, Titmuss found that the infant mortality rate in Durham and Northumberland was 68 per cent higher than the infant mortality rate in the most prosperous areas, and in

149

B. Eichengreen and T. J. Hatton (eds.), Interwar Unemployment in International Perspective, 149–183.

Wales the infant mortality rate was 38 per cent higher. In 1939 the infant mortality rate in Social Class V of the Registrar-General's classification was 123.4 per cent higher than the infant mortality rate in Social Class I, and the death rate of infants between the ages of 6 and 12 months was 352.2 per cent higher (Titmuss, 1938, pp.60-70; Winter, 1982, p.107).

The existence of such fundamental disparities in the health of different sections of the population, and the clear association between health and social and economic conditions, has led some historians to argue that the increase in unemployment in interwar Britain must have led to a deterioration in the standard of public health. In 1982 Charles Webster argued that

> In view of the impressive body of evidence suggesting that the health problems experienced during the 1930s were rooted in economic disadvantage, it is perverse to argue that the inter- war economic depression was free from adverse repercussions on standards of health. The Depression must be regarded as a significant exacerbating factor, tending to worsen still further prevailing low levels of health, and so contributing towards a crisis of subsistence and health different in kind but similar in gravity to the crises known to students of pre-industrial societies. (Webster, 1982, p.125)

However, in a separate analysis of the statistics of infant and maternal mortality in Britain between 1926 and 1939, Jay Winter argued that "no direct correlation can be made between economic insecurity and the mortality experience of a particularly vulnerable section of the British population". In the case of infant mortality, Winter concluded that "the most important feature of the aggregate data ... is the persistence of the trend towards better ... health ... despite the economic crisis of the early years of the decade" (Winter, 1979, p.443).

This debate raises two important questions which provide the main focus for this chapter. The first question is what effect did unemployment have on the health of the British population; and the second question is how far did the provision of unemployment benefit help to shield the unemployed from the consequences of unemployment? This chapter will argue that unemployment did have an effect on the health of people in some areas, but it had no effect on the health of the population in the most depressed areas. These findings indicate that the level of unemployment benefit was too low to enable unemployed people and their families to satisfy all their physiological needs, but it was able to prevent a deterioration in the health of people in areas where the average level of nutrition was already very low. The chapter itself is divided into four sections. The remaining part of this section gives a brief account of the characteristics of unemployment and unemployment insurance in Britain in the interwar period. The second section examines the most important interwar poverty surveys, and is designed to place the discussion of unemployment in the overall context of interwar poverty. The third section includes a general review of the contemporary evidence regarding the effect of unemployment on the health of unemployed people and their families. Finally, the concluding section of the chapter uses available records of children's height to investigate the impact of unemployment on the average level of public health in eleven British towns.

The principal characteristics of Britain's unemployment problem in the interwar period have been summarised by Mark Thomas in the previous chapter of this volume. The average level of recorded unemployment between 1921 and 1929 was 1.37 million. However, the level of unemployment rose steeply at the beginning of the 1930s, and reached a peak of 2.83 million in 1932. Unemployment fell between 1933 and 1937, but rose again in 1938. Throughout the whole period, the total number of insured workers who were registered as unemployed never fell below 1 million. It is important to remember that these statistics only refer to workers who were covered by the unemployment insurance scheme, and Charles Feinstein has estimated that at any one time the total number of unemployed people was approximately 20 per cent greater than the official figures allow. In 1932, Feinstein's figures suggest that the total number of unemployed people was approximately 3.4 million.

Both Feinstein's figures and the official figures are based on snapshots of the number of people who were unemployed at any one time. They do not reveal how many people experienced a period of unemployment in each calendar year, and they do not reveal the average duration of a period of unemployment. According to Mark Thomas, the main reason for the sharp increase in the level of unemployment after 1930 was not the increase in the number of people who became unemployed, but the increase in the amount of time which elapsed before they were re-employed. By 1933, the average length of a period of unemployment was 50 per cent greater than the average length of a period of unemployment in 1929. It has also been estimated that in September 1929 only 5 per cent of the unemployed workforce had been out of work for more than twelve months, but in 1932 16.4 per cent of claimants were "long unemployed", and by August 1936 this figure had risen still further to 25 per cent. In 1936 63 per cent of the unemployed workers in Rhondda in South Wales had been out of work for more than one year (Thomas, chapter 3, this volume; Constantine, 1980, p.4; Stevenson and Cook, 1976, pp.286-7).

Thomas also examined the incidence of unemployment by age, sex and occupation. He found that men between the ages of 30 and 39 were less likely to be unemployed than men over the age of 40. This was not because younger men were less likely to become unemployed, but simply because they found it easier to find new work. He also found that the level of recorded unemployment among women was much less than unemployment among men, because women who became unemployed remained on the register for shorter periods. Thomas used the 1931 census to investigate the impact of occupation on unemployment. He found that the occupational group with the highest level of unemployment was unskilled males, and that the occupational group with the lowest level of unemployment was female professionals. At the time the census was taken, over 90 per cent of all those who were unemployed were either skilled, semi-skilled or unskilled manual workers (Thomas, chapter 3, this volume).

In order to relieve the distress caused by unemployment, Britain operated a system of unemployment insurance which was extremely comprehensive by international standards. A national system of unemployment insurance was introduced in Britain by the National Insurance Act of 1911. Part II of this Act offered an unemployment benefit of 7 shillings (35 pence) a week for a maximum of fifteen weeks in any fifty-two-week period. These payments were financed by contributions from workers, employers and the state. When it was first introduced, the unemployment insurance scheme was limited to a small number of selected trades, and only 2.25 million workers were covered by it. However, the scheme was extended in 1916 and 1918, and again in 1920. The National Insurance Act which was passed in August 1920 covered approximately 12 million workers, and provided benefits of 15 shillings a week for men and 12 shillings a week for women for a maximum of fifteen weeks. In 1921 dependants' allowances were introduced at the rate of 5 shillings a week for a dependent spouse and 1 shilling a week for each child up to a total of four children (Gilbert, 1970, pp.51-86).

The unemployment insurance scheme was designed to "tide workers over" during short periods of unemployment; it was not designed to cope with the problem of long-term unemployment. This deficiency led to the emergence of a separate form of insurance benefit known as extended benefit. Under this system, workers who had exhausted their entitlement to standard benefit were allowed to apply for extended benefit for a fixed period of eight to ten weeks. In 1924 the first Labour government passed an Act which meant that extended benefit could now be awarded indefinitely. However, in order to secure parliamentary agreement for this measure, the government was obliged to put a two-year limit on the new regulations.

A further change in the system of unemployment insurance was introduced in 1927. The new system imposed the same conditions on all applicants for unemployment benefit, regardless of whether they were applying for standard benefit or extended benefit, and extended benefit now became known as transitional benefit. Applicants for both standard benefit and transitional benefit were required to show that they were "genuinely seeking work but unable to obtain suitable employment". The "genuinely seeking work" clause put the burden of proof on the claimant, but in 1930 this situation was reversed. Under the new regulations, an applicant's claim for benefit could only be turned down if he or she had refused a vacant situation of which they had been notified, or if they had disregarded written instructions about work from the employment exchange. This change meant that insured workers were automatically entitled to unemployment benefit, unless the employment exchange could show that they should not receive it (Gilbert, 1970, pp.86-97).

The question of unemployment insurance played a vital role in the crisis which led to the fall of the second Labour government in 1931. In August 1931 the prime minister, Ramsay MacDonald, asked his cabinet colleagues to resign and formed a new government with Conservative support. One of the first acts of the new government was to pass the National Economy Act, which gave the government the power to impose cuts in the expenditure of specified ministries by issuing Orders in Council. Among the Orders issued under the Act were two which had a special bearing on unemployment insurance. The first of these raised the level of contributions and cut the standard rate of benefit by 10 per cent. The second Order abolished the right to unrestricted transitional benefit, and replaced it with a system of transitional payments, which were subject to a means test administered by the Public Assistance Committees of the Local Authorities.

The changes which were introduced as a result of the National Economy Act were supposed to be temporary, but they remained in force until 1934. The Unemployment Act of 1934 drew a clear distinction between the relief of short- and long-term unemployment. Part I of the Act was designed to deal with unemployed workers who had been out of work for less than six months. It increased the number of workers who were covered by the insurance scheme and restored the 1931 benefit cuts. An Unemployment Insurance Statutory Committee was appointed to administer the scheme, and to ensure that it was financially self-supporting for those who were normally in work.

Part II of the Unemployment Act was designed to deal with those workers who had been unemployed for more than six months, and who had therefore exhausted their entitlement to standard benefit. One of the main aims of this part of the Act was to give the government greater control over the transitional payments scheme by transferring the administration of the scheme from the Public Assistance Committees to a new Unemployment Assistance Board. When this scheme was first introduced, the government had instructed the Public Assistance Committees to make sure that they only made payments to claimants who were already destitute, and also to ensure that the payments which were made did not exceed the standard rate of unemployment insurance. However many Public Assistance Committees ignored the government's instructions, and benefit scales varied widely from area to area. As a result of this, many claimants experienced a significant drop in their income when the new Unemployment Assistance Board scales came into operation, and in South Wales over 300,000 people demonstrated against their imposition. A major political row erupted, and in January 1935 the new regulations were suspended. Under the so-called "Standstill" agreement, claimants were given the right to claim either on the Public Assistance Committee's scale, or on the Unemployment Assistance Board's scale, whichever was the more favourable (Gilbert, 1970, pp.177-92; Fraser, 1973, pp.181-83).

The Standstill obviously made a mockery of the original aims of Part II of the 1934 Unemployment Act. It meant that the Treasury failed to gain control over the amount of money being spent on transitional payments, and that it was unable to impose a uniform scale of benefits on all areas. However, despite this the Standstill remained in force for the next eighteen months, and when the new scales were introduced, the government made every effort to minimise benefit reductions. The apparent generosity of the Unemployment Assistance Board at the end of the 1930s gave rise to accusations that the unemployed were quite happy to live on the income which the Board provided, and in some areas there was very little difference between the Unemployment Assistance Board's benefit scales and local wage rates. Many historians have also stressed the generosity of Britain's unemployment benefit system on the eve of the Second World War, and in 1976 Chris Cook and John Stevenson concluded that although the means test had undoubtedly caused much bitterness and hardship, "the provision of unemployment benefit ... was probably more comprehensive in Britain than in any other country which operated a democratic system" (Deacon, 1987, p.40; Stevenson and Cook, 1976, p.71).

This review of the characteristics of unemployment and unemployment insurance suggests some of the reasons why unemployment may not have affected the health of certain sections of the population as dramatically as some commentators have predicted. Two points in particular stand out. In the first place, it is clear that although the child population may have been the section of the population which was most vulnerable to reductions in income, it was also the case that the biggest increases in unemployment occurred among men over the age of 45 who were unlikely to be solely responsible for the maintenance of young children. Second, it is also clear that unemployed breadwinners who did have dependent children suffered a smaller reduction in their income than breadwinners who had no dependants, because the unemployment benefit system made allowances for dependants whereas wages did not. However, the fact remains that unemployment did increase among the parents of young families, and the vast majority of these families did suffer a loss of income as a result of unemployment. Under these circumstances, one would still expect to find some evidence of the effect of unemployment on the health of the population, if the increase in unemployment also led to an increase in the number of people living below the "poverty line" (Thane, 1982, p.182; Thomas, chapter 3, this volume).

2   The Causes of Poverty

During the interwar period a number of important social surveys were carried out into the standard of living in different British towns. Three of the most famous surveys were designed to compare conditions in the 1920s and 1930s with the results of inquiries carried out before the First World War. In *Has Poverty Diminished?* in 1925 A.L. Bowley and M.H. Hogg repeated an earlier inquiry into conditions in Northampton, Warrington, Reading, Bolton and Stanley. The *New Survey of London Life and Labour* was initiated in 1928 in order to examine the changes which had taken place following the publication of Charles Booth's survey in 1901. Seebohm Rowntree's second survey of conditions in York was published in 1941, forty years after the publication of *Poverty: A Study of Town Life*.

This section also deals with four other studies of the standard of living in interwar Britain. The first of these is the Social Survey of Merseyside, which was organised by David Caradog Jones between 1929 and 1932. The next two surveys were both carried out in the winter of 1931-32. The first was conducted by Percy Ford in Southampton, and the second was organised by A.D.K. Owen for the Social Survey Committee in Sheffield. The final survey was undertaken by Herbert Tout in Bristol in 1937. These surveys provide very little information about conditions in rural Britain, or about conditions in the depressed areas, but despite these limitations they do offer an invaluable guide to the standard of living in most parts of urban Britain between the wars.

One of the main aims of each of these surveys was to estimate the number of people who were living in poverty, and a second aim was to estimate the importance of a number of different factors in the causation of poverty. Those authors who compared present conditions with the results of previous inquiries had no doubt that the amount of poverty in Britain had diminished, and that one of the major causes of poverty was unemployment, even though this factor had been relatively insignificant before the First World War. In 1915 A.L. Bowley observed that "in no town does permanent unemployment or irregularity of work ... rank as an important cause" of poverty, but when he returned to the five towns in 1924 he found that 24.4 per cent of all family poverty was caused by unemployment (Bowley and Burnett-Hurst, 1915, p.41; Bowley and Hogg, 1925, pp.78, 104, 128, 158, 197). In 1932 Hubert Llewellyn Smith attributed nearly half the poverty in London to unemployment, whereas Charles Booth thought that casual work was the major cause of poverty, and made no attempt to place the amount of poverty which was due to total unemployment in a separate category (Smith, 1932, pp.12, 156). In 1901 Seebohm Rowntree felt that only 23.1 per cent of the primary poverty in York was attributable to unemployment, but in 1936 28.6 per cent of all the poverty in the city, and 44.5 per cent of the primary poverty, was attributed to this cause (Rowntree, 1941, pp.41, 110).

It is clear that substantial changes had taken place in the organisation of industry, and that as a result of these changes unemployment featured as a much more significant cause of poverty. It is also clear that the majority of unemployed people received a smaller income under the Unemployment Insurance scheme than they would have received if they had been at work. However it is arguable that these inquiries underestimated the total amount of poverty and that their authors exaggerated the importance of unemployment as a cause of poverty. The corollary of these remarks is that the social investigators of the interwar period failed to give adequate weight to the impact of low wages and bad housing on the lives of the people they were studying.

All the social inquiries of the interwar period adopted the same basic methodology. The authors drew up a list of essential items and compared the cost of these items with the income of each of the families in their survey. Those families whose income exceeded their necessary expenditure were placed above the "poverty line", and those families whose income was below the line were said to be in poverty. It is clear that any attempt to establish an absolute standard of poverty depends upon the accuracy with which the poverty line is defined. In the inquiries carried out by Bowley, Owen, Ford, Llewellyn Smith and Caradog Jones the poverty line was based on the standard used by Seebohm Rowntree in 1901, but during the 1930s this standard was revised to take account of recent developments in nutritional science (Rowntree, 1937, pp.10-11; George, 1937, pp.74-82). If the revised standard had been applied to earlier surveys, the amount of poverty would obviously have been greater. When Rowntree returned to York in 1936 he drew a distinction between the standard of poverty which he applied in 1901 and the standard which he considered appropriate in 1936. He found that only 6.8 per cent of the population was living below the line of primary poverty which had been used in the earlier survey, but that 31.1 per cent of the population was impoverished according to more recent standards (Rowntree, 1941, pp.31, 108). In 1937 Herbert Tout found that 10.7 per cent of the population of

Bristol was living in poverty, but only 6.9 per cent of the population was living below the poverty line used in the *New Survey of London Life and Labour* (Tout, 1938, pp.25, 51).

The interwar surveys may also have underestimated the amount of poverty because they left no room for "inessential" expenditure (Rowntree, 1941, p.29; Tout, 1938, p.26; Owen, 1933, p.21; Inman, 1934, pp.17-18). In his address to the Study Group of the Royal Statistical Society in 1937, R.F. George said that

> It should be emphasised at the very outset that under no circumstances can the "poverty line" be regarded as a desirable level. It seeks to assess the cost of a standard of living so low, that while persons below it are living in extreme poverty, those just above it would generally be regarded as very poor. (George, 1937, p.74)

In an attempt to get round this difficulty Herbert Tout suggested that anyone whose income was less than 50 per cent above the poverty line was living in a state of "insufficiency". Tout discovered that 31.5 per cent of the working-class population of Bristol was either in poverty or else in a state of insufficiency, and that this proportion would not have been substantially reduced even if the whole working population had been fully employed (Tout, 1938, pp.25-6). The continuing importance of low wages as a cause of poverty was also apparent on Merseyside, where the income of the average working-class family was only 43 per cent above the subsistence level used in the survey (D.C. Jones, 1934, p.237).

The methods employed in these surveys also led their authors to underestimate the importance of overcrowding as a manifestation of poverty. Many of the families which were placed above the poverty line owed their apparent prosperity to the presence of a subsidiary wage earner, but these families were also much more likely to be overcrowded. In Sheffield 14.6 per cent of households above the poverty line were overcrowded and three-quarters of all the overcrowded households in the city were above the poverty line (Owen, 1933, p.39). In Liverpool only 1 per cent of the families which contained more than one breadwinner was living in poverty, but 16.6 per cent of these families were overcrowded. On the other hand, over half the families in which there was no earner were living in poverty, and only one in twenty was overcrowded. The authors of this survey found that overcrowding and poverty frequently went hand in hand when the principal wage earner was unemployed, but that overcrowding was more common among families above the poverty line than many people realised (D.C. Jones, 1934, pp.166, 170).[2]

These observations are particularly relevant when one considers the proportion of children who were living in poverty. All the surveys found that the incidence of poverty among children was much greater than the incidence of poverty among families and households. In Bristol Herbert Tout found that 24.9 per cent of all those in poverty were under the age of 15, and that 21 per cent of the children in this age group were living in poverty. This was almost double the percentage of households in poverty (Tout, 1938, p.37). In the Merseyside survey, 16 per cent of families were said to be impoverished, but the proportion of children in poverty was 23 per cent (D.C. Jones, 1934, pp.152-3, 174). In York 52.5 per cent of children under the age of 1, 49.7 per cent of children between the ages of 1 and 5 and 39.1 per cent of children between the ages of 5 and 15 were living in poverty, but in the city as a whole the incidence of poverty was only 31.1 per cent (Rowntree, 1941, pp.32, 156).

These differences are significant because the factors which were responsible for the incidence of poverty in the whole population did not have quite the same effect on child poverty. In York Seebohm Rowntree found that unemployment was responsible for 28.6 per cent of total poverty, and that low wages were responsible for 32.8 per cent. However 33.3 per cent of child poverty could be explained by unemployment, and 45 per cent by low wages (Rowntree, 1941, p.43). The importance of low wages as a cause of child poverty was also illustrated by the Bristol survey. According to Herbert Tout, 17 per cent of the families below the poverty line contained four or more children, and the children in these families accounted for over half the total number of children in poverty. However unemployment was responsible for only 23.5 per cent of the poverty in this group, and in 53 per cent of cases the cause of poverty was low wages (Tout, 1938, p.42). Children were also more likely to be affected by overcrowding. In Liverpool overcrowding affected 24.2 per cent of children under the age of 14, and only 16.8 per cent of the total population, and although only 16.3 per cent of the population of Sheffield was overcrowded, the incidence of overcrowding among children was 38.2 per cent (D.C. Jones, 1934, p.172; Owen, 1933, p.40).

The preceding paragraphs have shown that the social investigators of the interwar period underestimated the amount of poverty in the areas which they studied, and this led them to exaggerate the importance of unemployment as a specific cause of poverty. However, in the areas which were covered by the social surveys, unemployed people and their families were much more likely to be living in poverty, and the poverty which they experienced was much more severe. In Sheffield 42.8 per cent of the families in which the principal breadwinner was unemployed were living in poverty, and in Southampton this figure rose to 58.5 per cent. In both cases unemployed people were two and a half times more likely to be living in poverty than the population as a whole. One of the most important influences on the economic status of an "unemployed family" was the presence or absence of a subsidiary wage earner. In Southampton 70.5

per cent of the unemployed families in which there was a subsidiary wage earner were above the poverty line, but 83.1 per cent of the families in which there was no subsidiary wage earner were below the poverty line (Owen, 1932, p.62; 1933, p.24; Ford, 1934, p.157). In York 86.4 per cent of all the families in which the principal breadwinner was unemployed were living in poverty, and although unemployment accounted for only 28 per cent of all the poverty in the city, 44.5 per cent of the families in primary poverty existed on unemployment benefit (Rowntree, 1941, pp.110, 150).

The greater hardship which was associated with unemployment was reflected in the diets of unemployed people and their families. In 1932 Dr George M'Gonigle carried out a survey of the diets of employed and unemployed families on two estates in the north-eastern town of Stockton-on-Tees. He found that both employed and unemployed groups consumed insufficient quantities of protein, but on both estates the unemployed families consumed less protein, fat and carbohydrate than their employed neighbours (M'Gonigle and Kirby, 1936, p.124) . In York in 1936 Seebohm Rowntree studied the diets of twenty-eight families, of whom thirteen were below the poverty line. These families were then divided into two groups. The first group included seven families whose average income was 35.6 per cent below the minimum, and the average income of the second group was 16.7 per cent below the minimum. Eleven of the thirteen families were seriously underfed, and only one was receiving "almost adequate nourishment", but the diets of the first group were substantially worse than the diets of the second. In each of the seven families in Group A the principal breadwinner was unemployed, and all the families in this group were wholly dependent on unemployment benefit (Rowntree, 1941, pp.182-5). .

Unemployment not only exacerbated the problem of poverty for the individual; it also impoverished the whole community. In a separate inquiry into the incidence of unemployment in Sheffield, A.D.K. Owen suggested that unemployment had seriously affected the trade of the city by reducing the purchasing power of the wage-earning classes of the community, and that the demand for Poor Relief and Public Assistance had imposed an additional burden on the city's ratepayers. In many cases rate increases had been passed on to tenants in the form of higher rents, even though financial circumstances meant that tenants could no longer afford the original rents. This in turn meant that the city's housing problems were being increased at a time when new municipal initiatives were being curtailed. Finally, the social life of the community had also been impoverished, and the hopelessness and desperation of the unemployed had infected the whole city (Owen, 1932, pp.65-6).

It is arguable that one of the most savage effects of the Depression was the way in which it affected the ability of local communities to help themselves. During the interwar period many commentators argued that the worst effects of the Depression had been averted by the provision of school meals and by the operation of the Maternity and Child Welfare Service. However these services were financed out of local rates, and the most impoverished areas were unable to generate enough revenue to maintain an adequate level of provision. The difficulties faced by the depressed areas were illustrated quite graphically by Ellen Wilkinson in her study of Jarrow, "the town that was murdered". She pointed out that the average yield of a penny rate in Jarrow in the 1930s was £400 per annum, but in Holborn the average yield of a penny rate was seventeen times higher (Wilkinson, 1939, p.250; Webster, 1985, p.228; Jewkes and Winterbottom, 1933, pp.14-17).

3   The Results of Unemployment

In Sheffield in 1932 the standard rate of unemployment benefit for a married couple with two children was 27s 3d per week. If the family was being relieved by the Public Assistance Committee it might receive up to 30s a week. These amounts were well below the poverty line calculated by A.D.K. Owen in the winter of 1931-32. He estimated that the minimum expenditure required to sustain a family of this size was between 31s and 31s 11d a week, depending on the age of the children. However, although nearly a quarter of the population was directly affected by unemployment, Owen was unable to find any evidence of a marked decline in the general health of the city. In fact he believed that the standard of public health had increased as a result of improvements in medical and health services and housing conditions (Owen, 1932, pp.60, 63; 1933, p.47).

This verdict was repeated in many of the official publications of the early 1930s, and some of the most optimistic assessments appeared in the Annual Reports of the Chief Medical Officer of the Ministry of Health, Sir George Newman. In his Annual Report for 1932, Newman said there was "no available medical evidence of any general increase in sickness or mortality which can be traced to the effects of economic depression or unemployment" (Newman, 1933b, p.41). Newman repeated this verdict in the Annual Report for 1933. There was no evidence of any general physical deterioration or of any increased physical impairment as a result of economic depression, and the health of the nation compared favourably with previous years (Newman, 1934, p.220).

Newman's account of the health of the British population in the depths of the Depression raises two fundamental questions. The first question is what effect did unemployment have on the health of unemployed people and their families; and the second question is how did fluctuations in the level of unemployment affect the average health of the population generally? These questions form the subject of the next two sections of this paper.

3. 1 The Unemployed Man

In his Annual Reports to the Ministry of Health, George Newman attached particular importance to the effects of unemployment on the health of the insured population. In 1932 and 1933 he asked members of the Regional Medical Staff to say whether the health of insured workers had deteriorated as a result of changing economic conditions. His own analysis of these reports suggested that any changes which had occurred were insignificant and that they had little to do with the effects of the Depression. However, Newman went out of his way to minimise the significance of the Medical Officers' replies, and it is arguable that the conclusions which he drew from them were highly misleading (see McNally, 1935, pp.145-64).

Of the sixty-six Medical Officers who responded to Newman's inquiries in 1933, forty-one said that they were personally aware of a deterioration in the health of the population as a result of unemployment. Over half the sample said that recovery rates had declined, and nineteen of the Medical Officers had noticed a general deterioration in the level of physical fitness. Malnutrition was noted in fifteen of the replies, and seven Medical Officers said that the incidence of anaemia in pregnant women was noticeably greater. It is also worth noting that of the twenty-five Medical Officers who said that they had no personal experience of a decline in health standards, nineteen were stationed in areas of comparatively low unemployment. Newman received thirty-one replies from Medical Officers in Wales and the north of England, and over 80 per cent of these said that the health of the population had been affected by economic conditions (Newman, 1934, pp.216-18; McNally, 1935, pp.145-151).

It is obviously difficult to assess the impact of unemployment on the health of unemployed workers when their previous health status is unknown, and it is also difficult to make straightforward comparisons between the health of employed and unemployed workers. During the interwar period a large number of studies were carried out which showed that unemployed workers were less healthy than those who were in work, but the authors also argued that ill-health was a major cause of unemployment, and that it was an even more important barrier to re-employment (McKinlay and Walker, 1936, p.318; Cathcart, Hughes and Chalmers, 1935, p.25; Whiteside, 1987, p.23; Eisenberg and Lazarsfeld, 1938, pp.361-2). However there is a substantial body of evidence to suggest that unemployment did have a profound effect on the psychological health of unemployed men. In 1935 Dr James Halliday found that unemployed men suffered from a significantly higher incidence of psychoneurotic disease than men who were still employed and that the incidence of psychoneurosis was directly related to the length of unemployment. Psychoneurotic disabilities were observed in 25.7 per cent of men who had been out of work for less than three months, and among 41.5 per cent of men who had been unemployed for between six and twelve months. However men who had been unemployed for more than one year were less likely to have a neurotic disability, and among those who had been unemployed for more than three years the incidence of psychoneurosis was only 36.67 per cent (Halliday, 1935, p.100).

Although it would be difficult to place too much reliance on these findings in themselves, the general impression which they convey is consistent with the impression conveyed by other inquiries of the interwar period, and it is also consistent with the results of more recent inquiries (Beales and Lambert, 1934, pp.25-6; Jahoda, 1982; Fagin and Little, 1984; Kelvin and Jarrett, 1985). Contemporaries were particularly concerned about the psychological health of unemployed people because they feared that prolonged idleness might lead to the destruction of the "work ethic", and also because the psychological effects of unemployment were often much more visible. In South Wales in 1929 Dr James Pearse and Dr Arthur Lowry found that "every thoughtful person with whom we have talked has expressed greater concern at the destructive effect of idleness upon the character and morale of the unemployed than at the hardships involved in the scant supply of the necessaries of life" (Ministry of Health, 1929, p.9). In the winter of 1934-35 Dr Pearse visited the Special Areas of Sunderland and Durham, and although he found little evidence of a deterioration in the physical health of unemployed men, many of his informants reported "an increase in such psychical manifestations as depression, neurasthenia and various neuroses, especially gastric" (Ministry of Health, 1935, p.27).

In a recent study of employment and unemployment across five decades, Marie Jahoda has suggested that the psychological consequences of unemployment can be grouped under four main headings. According to Jahoda, the most important psychological effects of unemployment are the destruction of an established time structure, a sense of purposelessness, social isolation and the loss of status and identity (Jahoda, 1982, pp.22-6; Fagin and Little, 1984, p.28). These effects are clearly visible in the writings of contemporary researchers in interwar Britain. Three studies are of particular interest in the context of this chapter. The first was carried out by Hilda Jennings in the South Wales village of Brynmawr in 1929; the second by E.W. Bakke in Greenwich in south-east London in 1931; and the third by the Pilgrim Trust in six different areas in 1936 and 1937.[3] In this section reference will also be made to the collection of unemployed "memoirs" edited and introduced by H.L. Beales and R.S. Lambert in 1934.

From a psychological point of view, the most important single consequence of unemployment was the destruction of the worker's established time structure. In 1938 the Pilgrim Trust investigators said that "the first and most difficult feature of unemployment is the very obvious one that it leaves the unemployed man with nothing to do", and one of the men interviewed by the Trust commented that time was his "worst enemy". In Greenwich unemployed men tried to "kill time" by going to the cinema or by standing on street corners; in Brynmawr the unemployed resorted to a variety of activities to fill their day, but in almost every individual there was "an abiding sense of waste of life". The monotony of unemployment was brought out very clearly in the *Memoirs of the Unemployed*. One author spoke of time hanging heavily on his hands, while another said that "monotonous and insufficient food and having nothing to do all day after the garden is done kill all a man's interest in life" (Pilgrim Trust, 1938, p.150; Bakke, 1933, pp.178-92; Jennings, 1934, pp.139-40; Beales and Lambert, 1934, pp.105, 127).

Unemployed people also felt a debilitating sense of purposelessness. According to Jahoda, the following phrases can be found in virtually all the interwar surveys: being on the scrap-heap; useless; not needed by anybody (Jahoda, 1982, p.24). One of the men interviewed by the Pilgrim Trust said that "when you're working, you feel like a cog in a machine. When you're out you feel that no-one has any use for you, and to see your wife busy makes you feel ashamed" (Pilgrim Trust, 1938, p.150). In Greenwich E.W. Bakke found that if there was one common satisfaction which ran through the day of every worker, it was the consciousness that he or she was a "producer". The feelings which were engendered by the loss of this "satisfaction" were described to Bakke in the following way:

> Everybody does some work in this world. You can go as far back as Adam, and you'll find that they all work some way, with their brains if not with their hands. That's one thing that makes us human; we don't wait for things to happen to us, we work for them. And if you can't find any work to do, you have the feeling that you're not human. You're out of place. You're so different from all the rest of the people around that you think something is wrong with you. I don't care what your job is, you feel a lot more important when you come home at night than if you had been tramping around the streets all day. The next time you see a lot of fellows standing and watching a gang laying

a pavement or putting up a house, *just ask yourself how much fun it is to stand and watch other men work.* (Bakke, 1933, pp.63-4)

Psychological studies of the interwar period suggest that the health of unemployed people was affected by the destruction of their established time structure and by a sense of purposelessness. Unemployed workers also suffered from feelings of isolation, because they were cut off from the world of work and because the social networks which were formed in employment had been destroyed. The authors of the Pilgrim Trust survey said that the majority of the skilled and semi-skilled workers whom they had interviewed had been deeply absorbed in their work, and that the friendships which they had formed in the course of their work were often the most valuable thing that they had. In Brynmawr unemployed miners were able to maintain some contact by subscribing to the "Unemployed Lodge" of the Miners' Federation, but if they were outside the day-to-day concerns of the mining industry they still found it difficult to maintain close contact with their erstwhile colleagues. In Greenwich E.W. Bakke argued that unemployment insurance ought to be sufficient to enable unemployed workers to participate in the social life of the local community. One unemployed railway worker told him that "what you get at the Labour ain't much, but a lot of us try to save a little out of it to keep on speaking terms with our friends" (Pilgrim Trust, 1938, pp.150-1; Jennings, 1934, p.140; Bakke, 1933, pp.72-3).

Each of the psychological factors associated with unemployment points to the importance of work as a source of status and identity. In 1938 Philip Eisenberg and Paul Lazarsfeld said that it was not surprising that many unemployed people became depressed in a society "where the job one holds is the prime indicator of a man's status and prestige", and this is still the case today (Eisenberg and Lazarsfeld, 1938, p.363; Fagin and Little, 1984, p.28). Work also gave skilled workers the opportunity to compare their own skills with the skills of their fellow workers, and in 1933 E.W. Bakke suggested that the loss of this opportunity was perhaps the most important of all the psychological effects of unemployment. In his view the incentive to work hard, the desire to push ahead and the ambition to perfect one's technique were basic qualities for satisfaction at work, but when a person was out of work these qualities were of little value. He concluded that unemployment insurance may have been sufficient to ease the physical hardship of unemployment, but it was no substitute "for the confidence, self-respect and satisfaction that come from having a place in the ranks of the workers". Although the first half of this statement has yet to be tested, the contemporary evidence does seem to indicate that unemployment exacted a heavy toll on the psychological health of unemployed workers (Bakke, 1933, p.71-4).

3. 2   Women

In the *New Survey of London Life and Labour*, Hubert Llewellyn Smith
said that in the course of his inquiry into unemployment and poverty he
had concentrated on the unemployment of adult men because this was a
much more important factor in the causation of family poverty than the
unemployment of women or children. He pointed out that adult men out-
numbered women in the official employment statistics by a factor of four
to one, and that only a small proportion of families were wholly dependent on female earnings. However the vast majority of women did work
before marriage, and a substantial proportion of women never married.
The proportion of women who continued to work after marriage rose
throughout the interwar period, and in some areas the earnings of married women were just as important as their husbands' earnings (Smith,
1932, pp.181-2; Lewis, 1984, pp.3, 150-1).

These comments highlight the fact that employment played a large part
in the lives of British women in the interwar period, but contemporary
investigators paid very little attention to the effects of unemployment on
the health of women workers. Dr James Halliday argued that unemployment had a negligible effect on the psychological health of unemployed
women because "woman's place is at home", and this view was endorsed
by the Pilgrim Trust. The Trust argued that unlike the unemployed man,
the unemployed woman was not "left stranded" by unemployment because she could always turn to her "domestic duties". However, many of
the unemployed women who were interviewed by the Trust said that they
were desperately anxious to return to work because they missed the social contacts provided by employment. Despite this, the vast majority of
the interwar surveys preferred to concentrate on the effects of unemployment on the health of women as wives and mothers, and not as unemployed workers (Halliday, 1935, p.100; Pilgrim Trust, 1938, pp.232, 238;
Kelvin and Jarrett, 1985, p.2).

The vast majority of contemporary observers believed that the brunt of
the deprivation which was caused by unemployment was borne by the
mothers of young families. The Pilgrim Trust authors stated unanimously
that "in most unemployed families the parents, and particularly the mothers, bore the burden of want, and in many instances were literally starv-
ing themselves in order to feed and clothe the children reasonably well".
The health of women was also affected by the absence of a comprehensive system of medical care. The majority of unemployed men were still
entitled to free medical treatment under the National Health Insurance
scheme, and the health of schoolchildren was partially protected by the
School Medical Service. However the wives of insured workers were not
covered by health insurance, and in many cases they were unable to af-

ford the cost of medical treatment. The effects of this double burden were reflected in a study of the health of mothers and children in eighty unemployed families in Liverpool in 1937. According to the Pilgrim Trust, only twenty-seven of the mothers of these families were definitely healthy, and twenty-six mothers were definitely unhealthy. However, the children were found to be healthy in forty-six families, and only nineteen families contained an unhealthy child (Pilgrim Trust, 1938, pp.111, 127; Balfour and Drury, 1935, pp.8, 10).

These findings merely echoed what many other observers had previously noted. In 1929 Drs Pearse and Lowry said that although there was no evidence of widespread physical deterioration, there could be no question that in some areas the mothers of young children "suffered to an unusual extent from languor and anaemia" (Ministry of Health, 1929, p.6). In 1932 a medical inquiry in Deptford revealed that the following symptoms were unusually common among the maternal population: loss of vitality, mental depression, apathy, anaemia, tooth decay, various skin diseases, chronic colds and a general susceptibility to infectious disease (Hutt, 1933, p.154). In 1937 an investigation into the diets of sixty-nine working-class families in Newcastle showed that 32 per cent of the women whose husbands were unemployed showed signs of anaemia, whereas only 10 per cent of the women whose husbands were employed showed similar signs. The authors of the report believed that the incidence of anaemia was directly related to differences in the diets of employed and unemployed families, and that in comparison with the employed group the diets of the unemployed group were deficient in every respect ("Newcastle Dietary Investigation", 1936-37, p.159; see also Balfour and Drury, 1935, pp.24-26).

This discussion of the effects of unemployment on the health of the female population focuses attention on the question of maternal mortality. In England and Wales, the maternal mortality rate rose from 4.11 deaths per thousand live births in 1919-22 to 4.31 in the period 1930-33, but it fell dramatically during the second half of the 1930s. The decline in the level of maternal mortality is usually attributed to the introduction of powerful sulphonamide drugs which reduced the risks of infection in childbirth, but women's resistance to infection was also affected by defective nutrition. Between 1934 and 1936 the National Birthday Trust Fund conducted an extensive inquiry into the incidence of maternal mortality in the depressed areas of Durham and South Wales. The Trust hoped to show how the level of maternal mortality could be reduced by improvements in medical care, but it soon became apparent that many of the women in these areas were seriously undernourished. The Trust therefore decided to make a number of grants to maternity services, and also to provide free food to expectant mothers in certain areas. They found that improvements in the standard of medical care had little effect on the level of mortality, but in the areas where food was distributed the level of maternal mortality fell very sharply (Balfour and Drury, 1935, p.22; Winter, 1979, p.458; 1982, p.104; Williams, 1936-37a, pp.11-19; 1936-37b, pp.231-3).

These results suggest that the rise in maternal mortality in England and Wales may have been related to a deterioration in the standard of maternal nutrition as a result of unemployment. In 1937 Dr H.W. Singer examined the relationship between unemployment and a range of mortality statistics on behalf of the Pilgrim Trust. He found that unemployment only had a marginal effect on infant mortality and on the rate of mortality from different diseases, but unemployment was related to the level of maternal mortality (Pilgrim Trust, 1938, p.140). Some support for this hypothesis was provided by the Ministry of Health's own inquiry into the causes of maternal mortality in the same year. The ministry found that there was little relationship between the level of unemployment and the level of maternal mortality in individual areas, but when areas with similar levels of unemployment were grouped together, it was found that those areas which experienced high levels of unemployment had above average levels of maternal mortality, and that those areas with low levels of unemployment had below average levels of maternal mortality (Ministry of Health, 1937, p.81). An inquiry by Margaret Balfour and Joan Drury also suggested that unemployment was an important cause of maternal mortality. They compared the increase in maternal mortality in eight depressed areas in Durham and Tyneside with the increase in England and Wales as a whole, and in six of these areas the increase in maternal mortality exceeded the increase in the whole country (Balfour and Drury, 1935, pp. 22-3).

3. 3   Children

From a technical point of view, one of the most serious problems which confronted the Public Health Service in the interwar period was its failure to develop an adequate method of assessing the health and physical condition of schoolchildren. In his Annual Report as Chief Medical Officer of the Board of Education in 1932, Sir George Newman said that "in the country as a whole the general standard of bodily health, nutrition and mental alertness of the schoolchildren" was being well maintained, and that although there had been small variations in the incidence of malnutrition in recent years, these were "of no significance" (Newman, 1933a, pp.127, 134). However, this optimistic assertion was greeted with disbelief by critics who refused to accept that the health of children could be well maintained when so many of their parents were living below the poverty line. The editorial columns of the *Medical Officer* provided an important outlet for these reservations. In July 1933 the editor of the *Medical Officer* wrote:

> It is just possible that our children can live on unemployment diet and that our failure to find ill-nutrition amongst those who have to submit to it is really due to there being no malnutrition to discover. But against this we have such weighty physiological arguments that most of us believe the malnutrition is there, but that we are ignorant of the form it takes and so do not detect it. (p.12, "Unemployment and the Young")

When the School Medical Service was created in 1908, School Medical Officers were asked to submit Annual Reports to the Education Committees of the Local Authority, and these were then forwarded to the Board of Education. These Reports contained a detailed description of the work done by the School Medical Service during the year, together with a statistical account of changes in the health of the children. These statistics were collected during the routine medical examination of every child at the ages of 5, 8 and 12. During the course of the examination, the inspecting Medical Officer was expected to say whether the "nutrition" of the child was good, normal, subnormal or bad. In 1935 the new Chief Medical Officer, Sir Arthur MacNalty, described the criteria on which these judgments were made in the following terms:

> The main issue is to estimate the general well-being of the child. Such general assessment cannot as a rule be based on any single criterion such as any relation of age, sex, height and weight, but should also have regard to other data derived from clinical observation; for example, the general appearance, facies, carriage, posture; the condition of the mucous membranes; the tone and functioning of the muscular system; and the amount of subcutaneous fat. An alert, cheerful child, with bright eyes and a good colour, may usually be accepted as well-nourished without demur. On the other hand, a child who appears dull, listless and tired, who has a muddy complexion or stands slackly, is at once under suspicion, and should be further examined. Too much reliance on a single sign may lead to error. Carious teeth and other local defects should not in themselves be regarded as evidence of faulty nutrition. It is the general impression which decides the issue. (MacNalty, 1935, p.27)

In 1935 the traditional categories were replaced by a slightly different system which divided the children into the following groups: excellent, normal, slightly subnormal and bad. The introduction of new categories was designed to raise the standard by which the nutrition of individual children was assessed, but this attempt was largely unsuccessful. The most obvious criticism of the nutrition statistics was that they were wholly subjective, and that the returns from different areas were often inconsistent (R.H. Jones, 1938; Glover, 1940). However, a more fundamental criticism of all the returns was that the standard by which nutrition was assessed was far too low (e.g. Wilkins, 1937-38, p.298). Towards the end of the 1930s, when a small number of Medical Officers began to apply more rigorous standards, the relationship between nutrition and economic status became much more apparent. This can be illustrated by looking at the results of three different surveys, which do seem to show that the effects of unemployment and poverty were clearly reflected in the health and nutrition of the schoolchild.

In December 1936 Dr W.B. Stott made one of the first serious attempts to use a more sophisticated scale of assessment to measure the nutritional status of schoolchildren. Stott asked 204 families to give a detailed account of their weekly expenditure. He then divided the amount which each family spent on food by the number of people in the family, and compared the results with the nutritional status of the children. The children were divided into six categories, ranging from excellent to subnormal and bad. The results were published in the *Medical Officer* six months later. They showed that 36.8 per cent of the children in families which spent less than 5s per head on food each week showed signs of subnormal nutrition, and that only 24.3 per cent of children whose families spent more than 5s showed similar signs (Stott, 1937, p.259-61).

In 1937 three researchers at the University of Bristol carried out a similar inquiry with the aim of achieving a more rigorous definition of nutritional status. They found that there were no pathogenic signs of malnutrition, but that a well-nourished child was superior to a poorly nourished child in almost every way. They therefore assessed the nutritional status of every child against that of the best nourished child. They then placed the children whose nutrition was excellent or normal in one group, and those whose nutrition was slightly subnormal or bad were placed in a second group. They found that the average size of the families in the second group was larger, that their average income was smaller and that they were more overcrowded. They also found that there was a big difference in the amount of unemployment among the two groups, and that although unemployment was almost unknown in the first group, over 30 per cent of the fathers of the children in the second group were unemployed (Roberts, Stone and Bowler, 1938, pp.209-212, 219-220).

One of the most interesting investigations into the effects of unemployment and poverty on the health of the schoolchild was carried out by Dr John Kershaw, the Medical Officer of Health for Accrington in Lancashire. In 1936 Kershaw obtained details of the average height and weight of children in five local schools. The first two schools were both council schools which were housed in good premises in healthy surroundings. The first school was situated in a mixed middle- and working-class district, and the second school was situated in an area where economic conditions were less satisfactory. The other three schools were voluntary schools funded by local religious bodies, and these were housed in less satisfactory premises with less healthy surroundings. The first of these three schools was situated in a relatively prosperous area in which employment had been consistently good, and the other two schools occupied much poorer areas.

The results of this inquiry showed that the children who attended schools in the more prosperous areas were consistently taller and heavier than children in poorer areas, and that the quality of the school premises had little bearing on these figures. Kershaw then made a special study of the children whose parents had been unemployed for more than one year. He found that they were both smaller and lighter than the children of employed parents. There was no reason to believe that these children were "fundamentally inferior", and they were not confined to one particularly unhealthy part of the town. In Kershaw's view there was no reason to doubt that the deficiencies in the physique of these children were directly attributable to the economic status of their parents (Kershaw, 1938, pp.129-132).

4   Unemployment and Stature

The previous section has shown that unemployment may well have had an effect on the health of unemployed people and their families, even though government officials denied this. There is a substantial amount of evidence which suggests that unemployment had a profound effect on the psychological health of unemployed men, and on the physical health of their wives and children. However, it is difficult to find any evidence of this in the vital statistics of the interwar period, with the possible exception of the maternal mortality statistics. In 1938 Dr E. Lewis-Faning conducted an inquiry into the trend of mortality statistics in urban communities in England and Wales, with special reference to the depressed areas. He agreed that the rate of mortality in these areas was much higher than the average for England and Wales as a whole, but these differences were long-standing, and there was no evidence to support the view "that the health of the population of the Depressed Areas of the North and of Wales has been unfavourably affected by the economic depression" (Lewis-Faning, 1938, p.65). The relationship between unemployment and infant mortality has been studied more recently by the historian Jay Winter. Winter concluded that "unemployment was not the decisive cause of fluctuations in infant mortality rates during this period", and he thought that the pattern of infant mortality ought to be attributed to the nutritional and sanitary improvements of the previous century (Winter, 1983, pp.233-4).

It is possible that mortality rates fail to reveal the impact of unemployment on the health of the British population because they are an inadequate guide to the average level of public health. As Professor Derek Oddy has observed, morbidity and mortality are measures of ill-health, whereas health "is a state of complete physical, mental and social well-being, and not merely the absence of disease or infirmity" (Oddy, 1982, pp.121-2; see also Kosa and Robertson, 1969, p.36). Since the Second World War it has become increasingly apparent that even the most sensitive mortality indicators are unable to give an accurate picture of differences in the health of different communities, and doctors have become increasingly interested in the use of height records to measure the health status of different populations. The main aim of this section is to use these techniques to measure the health of children in interwar Britain. According to Phyllis Eveleth and James Tanner, a child's growth rate is the best available guide to his or her state of health and nutrition, and the average value of children's heights and weights is an accurate reflection of the state of a nation's public health and of the nutritional status of its citizens (Lerner, 1969, pp.91- 4; Eveleth and Tanner, 1976, p.1).

Figures 4.1 and 4.2 depict the average height of British children between the ages of 2 and 18 in 1965. The pattern of growth which is shown here is common to all human populations. Children grow quickly in early childhood, and then more slowly. The rate of growth accelerates again at adolescence, and then slows to a halt. This pattern is most marked in the individual child, but when the heights of a large number of children are plotted the curve is somewhat smoother. This is because different children experience adolescence at different ages. Figures 4.1 and 4.2 also show the range of variations in height in the form of lines representing the 10th and 90th centiles of the 1965 distribution. In an economically homogeneous population the distribution of heights at a given age corresponds closely to the normal or Gaussian distribution, with a standard deviation which reaches a peak during the years of adolescence. In Britain in 1965 the standard deviation in the height of 12-year-old girls was 7.61 centimetres, and the standard deviation in the height of 14-year-old boys was 8.31 centimetres. The standard deviation in the height of late adolescents and adults was 6.4 centimetres or two and a half inches (Floud, 1984, p.6; Sinclair, 1985, pp.23-9; Tanner, Whitehouse and Takaishi, 1966, pp.626-7).

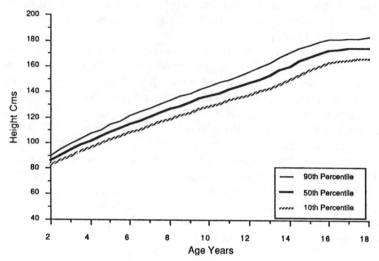

Figure 4.1   Boys' Height Standards, 1965

Source: Tanner, Whitehouse and Takaishi (1966), p. 626, Table 111A.

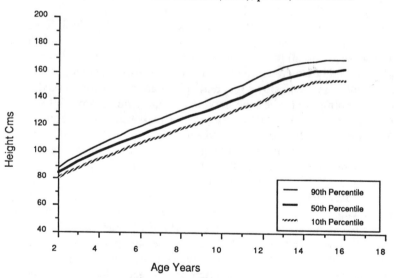

Figure 4.2   Girls' Height Standards, 1965

Source: Tanner, Whitehouse and Takaishi (1966), pp. 626-7, Table 111B.

Variations in the height of individuals are caused by a combination of environmental and genetic factors, but genetic factors have a much smaller effect on the average height of different populations. It is therefore possible to use the height of these populations to infer differences in their nutritional status. In this context, the term "nutritional status" is used to indicate the interaction between a body's resources and the demands which the external environment places on them. The two factors which have the greatest influence on nutritional status are diet and disease. An episode of malnutrition, such as a famine, can lead to a sharp reduction in a child's rate of growth, but if the episode is short-lived normal growth is quickly resumed. On the other hand, children who are consistently undernourished will grow more slowly than children who are well nourished, and their final height will also be lower. The effects of malnutrition can easily be compounded by an outbreak of disease. Poorly nourished children are more susceptible to disease than well nourished children, but infection also leads to a reduction in nutritional intake, and makes greater demands on the body's resources (Floud, 1984, p.7; Sinclair, 1985, pp.158-162; Tanner, 1962, pp.121-130; Eveleth and Tanner, 1976, pp.241-247).

The analysis which follows is based on records of the average height and weight of schoolchildren in a number of British towns between 1923 and 1938. These records have been obtained from the Annual Reports of the School Medical Officers in the areas concerned. The selection of areas was determined by the availability of the records. Although the regulations of the Board of Education stated that every child should be weighed and measured as part of the routine medical examination, School Medical Officers were not required to include tables of average height and weight in their Annual Reports. In fact only a minority of School Medical Officers did include these tables, and it was only possible to discover the names of these officers by examining a large number of reports. Nearly 100 sets of school medical reports were examined, and eleven provided sufficient information for the interwar period to be used in this study.

The towns which have been selected cover a wide geographical area. The largest town in the sample is the Scottish city of Glasgow, which had over 1 million inhabitants at the time of the 1931 census. The sample also includes two towns which are situated in the north-west of England, namely Blackburn and Warrington, and four towns from the West Riding of Yorkshire, namely Leeds, Bradford, Huddersfield and Wakefield. Three towns, Cambridge, Croydon and Reading, are representative of the prosperous south-east, while the urban district of Rhondda has become a symbol of the economic plight of South Wales during the worst years of the Depression. The average height of the children in these areas has been compared with the height of British children in 1965 in the following way.

In 1936 the average height of 5-year-old girls in Bradford was less than the height of 75 per cent of the 5-year-old girls in the 1965 sample, which means that the value of their heights was equivalent to the 25th centile of the 1965 distribution. Figures have been obtained in this way for each of the routine age groups and for both sexes, and the average value of these figures has been used to measure the average height of the children in each area in each of the years for which information was given.[4]

In order to measure the impact of unemployment on the height of children in different areas, it was necessary to calculate local unemployment rates. This was done by examining the monthly unemployment registers kept by each of the local labour exchanges in the areas concerned. The total number of insured workers who were registered as unemployed at the end of March, June, September and December was used to calculate the average for each year. It was not possible to compare these figures with the total number of insured workers in each area, and so an "unemployment rate" has been calculated by dividing the number of unemployed people by the size of the local population. It is well known that female labour-force participation rates varied considerably from area to area, and that the extent of female unemployment was often obscured by administrative practices. It has therefore been decided to restrict this analysis to the total number of unemployed males over the age of 18, in order to ensure that the unemployment rates for each area can be compared more accurately (Garside, 1980, pp.33-40; Lewis, 1984, p.149).

In order to simplify the analysis of these figures, the eleven sample areas have been divided into three groups. The first group includes the three south-eastern towns of Cambridge, Croydon and Reading; the second group includes Blackburn, Bradford, Huddersfield and Warrington; and the third group includes Glasgow, Leeds, Rhondda and Wakefield. The average height of the children in each group of areas is depicted in Figures 4.3 to 4.5. These graphs show that the height of children in each group increased during the course of this period, but the increase in height was greatest in Cambridge, Croydon and Reading, and least in Glasgow, Leeds, Rhondda and Wakefield. The graphs also show the rate of unemployment in each group of areas. The average level of unemployment was lowest in the group of areas in which the increase in height was greatest, and the average level of unemployment was greatest in the group of areas in which the increase in height was lowest.

These results suggest that unemployment was inversely associated with health in the interwar period, but they do not show that unemployment was the cause of ill-health. It is important to ask whether the graph of children's heights would have been any different if the level of unemployment had been lower, and in order to answer this question it is necessary to compare changes in the height of children in each group of areas

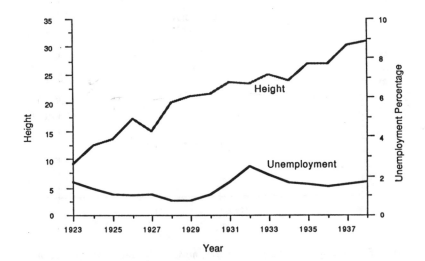

Figure 4.3   **Average Height (in Centiles) and Adult Male Unemployment (as % of Total Population): Cambridge, Croydon and Reading**

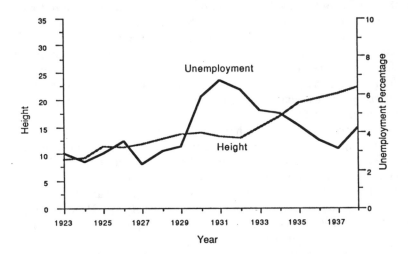

Figure 4.4   **Average Height (in Centiles) and Adult Male Unemployment (as % of Total Population): Blackburn, Bradford, Huddersfield and Warrington**

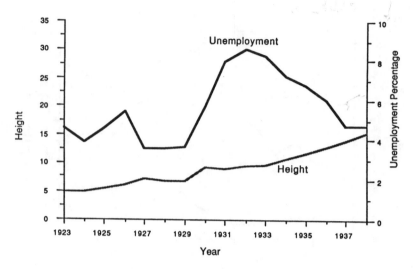

Figure 4.5   Averagé Height (in Centiles) and Adult Male Unemployment
(as % of Total Population): Glasgow, Leeds, Rhondda and
Wakefield

with changes in the level of unemployment. If unemployment did have an effect on the average level of public health, one would expect changes in the height of the school population to be inversely related to changes in the level of unemployment. It is possible to express this relationship in the form of an equation in which $\Delta H = a + b \, \Delta U_{-1}$, where ΔH = change in height since the previous year, and ΔU_{-1} = change in unemployment since the previous year. The results of this equation for each group of areas are given in Table 4.1.

The important question which needs to be asked is, did unemployment lead to a big enough reduction in the income of enough people to have an effect on the average level of child health in each group of areas? It would appear from Table 4.1 that unemployment had very little effect on the average level of child health in the most prosperous areas, and this is probably because unemployment was comparatively low. However, there is a strong and statistically significant relationship ($p < 0.01$) between unemployment and health in the intermediate areas, and it would appear that unemployment benefit was too low to enable the inhabitants of these areas to sustain the standard of living which they had become accustomed to while they remained in work. The paradox is that unemployment had very little effect on the level of child health in those areas where the problem of unemployment was greatest. In areas such as Glasgow and Rhond-

Table 4.1 **Change in Unemployment Since Previous Year, Lagged One Year, 1924-38**

	constant	ΔU_{-1}	R^2
Group A	1.291 (2.359)	-1.245 (-0.717)	-0.036
Group B	0.867 (4.640)	-0.665 (-3.442)	0.455
Group C	0.722 (3.735)	-0.084 (-0.487)	-0.062

Note: *t* statistics in brackets.
Method: Ordinary Least Squares.

da the wages of those who were in work were already very low, and the difference between the level of wages and the level of unemployment benefit was too small to have a significant effect on the health of children whose parents became unemployed. Although unemployment benefit was not sufficient to enable the unemployed to purchase all the constituents of a healthy diet, it was sufficient to prevent any further deterioration in the health of people whose standard of health was already very low.

There are two important statistical factors which may obscure the relationship between unemployment and stature in this inquiry. The first problem is that the data on height do not refer to exactly the same geographical area as the unemployment data, because the height data refer to the area covered by the Local Education Authority and the unemployment data refer to separate Employment Districts. The second problem is that the unemployment data include all males between the ages of 18 and 64, but many of these men will have been too old or too young to have children of school age. Because the incidence of unemployment varied with age, the inclusion of these people is bound to obscure the effects of parental unemployment on the height of the school population. However, it is unlikely that these factors would make a significant difference to the principal conclusions of this paper. It is clear that unemployment benefit was too low to meet all the physiological needs of the growing child, and that the main reason why unemployment failed to have any significant effect on the health of children in the most depressed areas was not the generosity of the benefit system, but the appallingly low standard of health experienced by the children of those in work.

NOTES

* I am grateful to the Economic and Social Research Council, who provided financial support for the research on which this chapter is based. I should also like to thank the following people for their help and advice: Roderick Floud, Barry Eichengreen, Tim Hatton, Nick Crafts, Annabel Gregory, John MacNicol, Doron Lam, Dan Weinbren and Debi Miller.

1 In *Poverty and Population* Titmuss (1938) compared mortality rates in different parts of England and Wales with mortality in the most prosperous areas of southeast England. These prosperous areas were Bedfordshire, Berkshire, Buckinghamshire, Essex, Hertfordshire, Kent, Middlesex, Oxfordshire, Southampton, Surrey, Sussex and the Isle of Wight.

2 Both the Merseyside survey and the Sheffield survey used a similar standard of overcrowding to investigate the housing conditions of families above and below the poverty line. The standard used was more stringent than the one laid down by the Registrar-General, which said that a house was overcrowded if there were more than two people to each room. For a full discussion see D.C. Jones (1934, pp.103-130); Owen (1933, pp.36-8).

3 *Men Without Work* was based on a study of 760 men and 120 women who had been out of work for more than one year on 23 November 1936. The six areas which were visited during the course of the inquiry were Deptford, Leicester, Liverpool, Blackburn, Crook and Rhondda (Pilgrim Trust, 1938, pp.2, 31).

4 A more detailed account of the origin of these figures can be obtained from the author, c/o Department of Economic and Social History, University of Bristol, 13-15 Woodland Road, Bristol BS8 1TB, England. The computer program which was used to convert the raw data into centiles of the 1965 height distribution was written by Dr Annabel Gregory of Birkbeck College, London.

REFERENCES

Astor, J.J. *et al.* (1922), *The Third Winter of Unemployment*, London: P.S. King.

Bakke, E.W. (1933), *The Unemployed Man*, London: Nisbet.

Balfour, Margaret I. and Drury, Joan C. (1935), *Motherhood in the Special Areas of Durham and Tyneside*, London: Council of Action.

Beales, H.L. and Lambert, R.S. (1934), *Memoirs of the Unemployed*, London: Gollancz.

Bowley, A.L. and Burnett-Hurst, A.R. (1915), *Livelihood and Poverty: A Study in the Economic Conditions of Working Class Households*, London: G. Bell.

Bowley, A.L. and Hogg, M.H. (1925), *Has Poverty Diminished?*, London: P.S. King.

Branson, Noreen and Heinemann, Margot (1971), *Britain in the 1930s*, London: Weidenfeld & Nicolson.

Burnett, John (1983), *Plenty and Want: A Social History of Diet in England from 1815 to the Present Day*, London: Methuen, (first published 1966).

Cathcart, E.P., Hughes, D.E.R. and Chalmers, J.G. (1935), *The Physique of Man in Industry*, Industrial Health Research Board, Report no. 71, London: HMSO.

Clark, F. le Gros and Titmuss, R.M. (1939), *Our Food Problem*, Harmondsworth: Penguin.

Constantine, Stephen (1980), *Unemployment in Britain Between the Wars*, London: Longmans.

Deacon, Alan (1987), "Systems of Inter-war Unemployment Relief", in Sean Glynn and Alan Booth (eds), *The Road to Full Employment*, London: Allen & Unwin.

Eisenberg, Philip and Lazarsfeld, Paul F. (1938), "The Psychological Effects of Unemployment", *Psychological Bulletin* 35, pp. 358-90.

Eveleth, Phyllis B. and Tanner, J.M. (1976), Worldwide Variation in Human Growth, Cambridge: Cambridge University Press.

Fagin, Leonard and Little, Martin (1984), *The Forsaken Families: The Effects of Unemployment on Family Life*, Harmondsworth: Penguin.

Floud, Roderick (1984), *The Heights of Europeans Since 1750: A New Source for European Economic History*, NBER Working Papers, no. 1318, Cambridge, Mass.: National Bureau of Economic Research.

Ford, P. (1934), *Work and Wealth in a Modern Port: An Economic Survey of Southampton*, London: Allen & Unwin.

Fraser, D. (1973), *The Evolution of the British Welfare State*, London: Macmillan.

Garside, W.R. (1980), *The Measurement of Unemployment: Methods and Sources in Great Britain, 1850-1979*, Oxford: Blackwell.

George, R.F. (1937), "A New Calculation of the Poverty Line", *Journal of the Royal Statistical Society* 100, part I, pp. 74-95.

Gilbert, Bentley B. (1970), *British Social Policy, 1914-1939*, London: Batsford.

Glover, J.A. (1940), "A Critical Examination of the Nutrition Returns Over a Period of Five Years", PRO ED 50/204 (Kew).

Glynn, Sean (1987), The Scale and Nature of the Problem, in Sean Glynn and Alan Booth (eds), *The Road to Full Employment*, London: Allen & Unwin.

Halliday, James L. (1935) "Psychoneurosis as a Cause of Incapacity Among Insured Persons", *Supplement to the British Medical Journal* 1, pp. 85-8, 99-102.

Hannington, Wal (1937), *The Problem of the Distressed Areas*, London: Gollancz.

Hutt, George Allen (1933), *The Condition of the Working Class in Britain*, London: Martin Lawrence.

Inman, John (1934), *Poverty and Housing Conditions in a Manchester Ward*, Manchester: University of Manchester, Economics Research Section.

Jahoda, Marie (1982), *Employment and Unemployment: A Socio-psychological Analysis*, Cambridge: Cambridge University Press.

Jahoda, Marie, Lazarsfeld, Paul F. and Zeisel, Hans (1972), *Marienthal: The Sociography of an Unemployed Community*, London: Tavistock (first published 1933).

Jennings, H. (1934), *Brynmawr: A Study of a Distressed Area*, London: Allenson & Co.

Jewkes, John and Winterbottom, Allan (1933), *An Industrial Survey of Cumberland and Furness: A Study of the Social Implications of Economic Dislocation*, Manchester: Manchester University Press.

Jones, D. Caradog(1934) (ed.), *The Social Survey of Merseyside*, vol. 1, London: Hodder & Stoughton.

Jones, R.H. (1938), "Physical Indices and Clinical Assessments of the Nutrition of Schoolchildren", *Journal of the Royal Statistical Society* 101, part I, pp. 1-52.

Kelvin, Peter and Jarrett, Joanna E. (1985), *Unemployment: Its Social Psychological Effects*, Cambridge: Cambridge University Press.

Kershaw, John D. (1938), "Physique, Poverty and Nutrition: A Survey of a School Population", *Medical Officer* 59, pp. 129-132.

Kosa, John and Robertson, Leon S. (1969), "The Social Aspects of Health and Illness", in John Kosa, Aaron Antonovsky and Irving Kenneth Zola (eds.), *Poverty and Health: A Sociological Analysis*, Cambridge, Mass.: Harvard University Press.

Kuczynski, Jürgen (1938), *Hunger and Work: Statistical Studies*, London: Lawrence & Wishart.

Lerner, Monroe (1969), "Social Differences in Physical Health", in John Kosa, Aaron Antonovsky and Irving Kenneth Zola (eds.), *Poverty and Health: A Sociological Analysis*, Cambridge, Mass.: Harvard University Press.

Lewis, Jane (1984), *Women in England, 1870- 1950: Sexual Divisions and Social Change*, Brighton: Wheatsheaf.

Lewis-Faning, E. (1938), *A Study of the Trend of Mortality Rates in Urban Communities of England and Wales, with Special Reference to "Depressed Areas"*, Reports on Public Health and Medical Subjects, no. 86, London: HMSO.

M'Gonigle, G.C.M. and Kirby, J. (1936), *Poverty and Public Health*, London: Gollancz.

McKinlay, P.L. and Walker, A.B. (1936), "A Note on the Physique of Young Adult Males During Unemployment", *Glasgow Medical Journal* 8, no. 6.

McNally, C.E. (1935), *Public Ill-Health*, London: Gollancz.

MacNalty, A.S. (1935), *Annual Report of the Chief Medical Officer of the Board of Education for 1934*, London: HMSO.

Ministry of Health (1929), *Report on Investigation in the Coalfields of South Wales and Monmouth*, Cmd. 3272.

Ministry of Health (1935), *Report on the Effects of Existing Economic Circumstances on the Health of the Community in the County Borough of Sunderland and Certain Districts of Durham*, Cmd. 4886, London: HMSO.

Ministry of Health (1937), *Report of an Investigation into Maternal Mortality*, Cmd. 5422, London: HMSO.

Mitchell, Margaret (1984), "The Effects of Unemployment on the Social Conditions of Women and Children in the 1930s", *History Workshop Journal* 19, pp. 105-127.

Mowat, Charles Loch (1968), *Britain between the Wars, 1918-1940*, London: Methuen (first published 1955).

"Newcastle Dietary Investigation, The" (1936-37), *Public Health* 50, pp. 159-160.

Newman, G. (1933a), *Annual Report of the Chief Medical Officer to the Board of Education for 1932*, London: HMSO.

Newman G. (1933b), *Annual Report of the Chief Medical Officer to the Ministry of Health for 1932*, London: HMSO.

Newman, G. (1934), *Annual Report of the Chief Medical Officer to the Ministry of Health for 1933*, London: HMSO.

Oddy, D.J. (1982), "The Health of the People", in Theo Barker and Michael Drake (eds.), *Population and Society in Britain, 1850-1980*, London: Batsford.

Owen, A.D.K. (1932), *A Report on Unemployment in Sheffield*, Sheffield Social Survey Committee.

Owen, A.D.K. (1933), *A Survey of the Standard of Living in Sheffield*, Sheffield: Sheffield Social Survey Committee.

Pilgrim Trust (1938), *Men Without Work*, Cambridge: Cambridge University Press.

Roberts, L., Stone, D.M. and Bowler, V.P. (1938), "An Investigation into the Nutrition of Children of School Age", *Medical Officer* 60, pp. 209-12, 219-20.

Rowntree, B.S. (1937), *The Human Needs of Labour,* London: Longmans, Green (2nd edn).

Rowntree, B.S. (1941), *Poverty and Progress,* London: Longmans, Green.

Sinclair, David (1985), *Human Growth after Birth,* Oxford: Oxford University Press (4th edn).

Smith, H. Llewellyn (1932), *New Survey of London Life and Labour,* vol. 3, London: P.S. King.

Stevenson, John (1984), *British Society 1914- 1945,* Harmondsworth: Penguin.

Stevenson, John and Cook, Chris (1976), *The Slump: Society and Politics during the Depression,* London: Jonathan Cape.

Stott, W.B. (1937), "A Nutrition Survey", *Medical Officer* 57, pp. 259-61.

Tanner, J.M. (1962), *Growth at Adolescence,* Oxford: Blackwell (2nd edn).

Tanner, J.M., Whitehouse, R.H. and Takaishi, M. (1966), "Height, Weight, Height Velocity, Weight Velocity: British Children 1965", *Archives of Disease in Childhood* 41, no. 220, pp. 454-71.

Thane, Pat (1982), *The Foundations of the Welfare State,* London: Longmans.

Titmuss, R.M. (1938), *Poverty and Population: A Factual Study of Contemporary Social Waste,* London: Macmillan.

Tout, H. (1938), *The Standard of Living in Bristol: A Preliminary Report of the University of Bristol Social Survey,* Bristol: Arrowsmith.

"Unemployment and the Young", (1933) *Medical Officer,* 50, p. 12.

Webster, Charles (1982), "Healthy or Hungry Thirties?", *History Workshop Journal* 13, pp. 110-129.

Webster, Charles (1985), "Health, Welfare and Unemployment During the Depression", *Past and Present* 109, pp. 204-30.

Whiteside, Noel (1987), "The Social Consequences of Inter-war Unemployment", in Sean Glynn and Alan Booth (eds.), *The Road to Full Employment,* London: Allen & Unwin.

Wilkins, E.H. (1937-38), "How Do We Assess Nutrition?", *Public Health* 51, pp. 293-8.

Wilkinson, Ellen (1939), *The Town that was Murdered: The Life-story of Jarrow,* London: Gollancz.

Williams, Lady (1936-37a), "Malnutrition as a Cause of Maternal Mortality", *Public Health* 50, pp. 11-19.

Williams, Lady (1936-37b), "Results of Experimental Schemes for Reducing the Maternal Death Rate in the Special Areas of Glamorgan, Monmouthshire and Durham Carried out by the National Birthday Trust Fund during 1934, 1935 and 1936", *Public Health* 50, pp. 231-233.

Winter, J.M. (1979), "Infant Mortality, Maternal Mortality and Public Health in Britain in the 1930s", *Journal of European Economic History* 8, pp. 439-462.

Winter, Jay (1982), "The Decline of Mortality in Britain, 1870-1950", in Theo Barker and Michael Drake (eds), *Population and Society in Britain, 1850-1980*, London: Batsford.

Winter, Jay (1983), "Unemployment, Nutrition and Infant Mortality in Britain, 1920-1950", in Jay Winter (ed.), *The Working Class in Modern British History: Essays in Honour of Henry Pelling*, Cambridge: Cambridge University Press.

Chapter 5

National Socialist Economics: The *Wirtschaftswunder* Reconsidered

Dan P Silverman

1 Introduction

Between January 1933 and July 1935, Hitler's National Socialist government achieved what have been described as "enormous results" in the reduction of unemployment. During his first year in power, Hitler reduced unemployment by over one-third. Within eighteen months, unemployment had been cut by 60 per cent. One is inclined to agree with economist Gerhard Kroll's (1958, p. 473) observation that "a reduction of unemployment by a third in one year borders on the miraculous". Kroll does not describe the process by which the Nazis achieved this incredible result. Economics is not religion; "miracles" have to be explained. Hitler's rapid conquest of German unemployment, a more brilliant feat than any of his *Blitzkrieg* operations on the battlefield, has never been explained satisfactorily in the vast literature on Nazi Germany. How did the National Socialists, who had little respect for traditional economic expertise, manage to bring off this *Wirtschaftswunder?*

In an attempt to answer this question, we shall first trace the development of National Socialist work creation programmes up to the middle of 1935, with a view to discovering an economic theory and body of technique capable of explaining this success in conquering unemployment. Then we shall evaluate the validity of official German labour market statistics during the Nazi era.

A brief overview of the development of the German economy during the interwar period may help to place Hitler's achievement in perspec-

B. Eichengreen and T. J. Hatton (eds.), Interwar Unemployment in International Perspective, 185–220.

Table 5.1   German Economic Trends, 1928-38 (1928 = 100)

	Production[a]	NNP[b]	Hours[c]	Wages[d]	Emp't[e]	Unemp't[f]
1928	100	100	100	100	100	100
1929	102	102	94	104	97	134
1930	89	93	90	105	85	213
1931	71	74	87	106	71	320
1932	61	48	85	100	60	390
1933	70	58	88	99	65	331
1934	87	70	91	99	80	185
1935	102	82	91	99	87	154
1936	115	89	95	99	95	112
1937	128	101	97	101	102	63
1938	141	112	98	104	108	28

Notes:
a Total production of industry and handicrafts.
b Net national product at factor costs, current prices.
c Average hours worked, mining, industry, and handicrafts.
d Real industrial wages.
e Employment in industry and handicrafts.
f Official unemployed reporting to employment office.

Sources: Walther G. Hoffman (1965), pp. 199, 214, 392-95, 508-9; Bry (1960), p. 362; IfK Wochenbericht.

tive. Throughout the era of democracy under the Weimar Republic, instability or the threat of instability plagued the German economy. A major cause of this instability was Germany's responsibility for reparations payments under the terms of the Versailles treaty. It was the government's support of German passive resistance to the Franco-Belgian occupation of the Ruhr in 1923 that produced the hyperinflation of that year. The stabilisation of 1924 and the Dawes Plan for reparations payments inaugurated a period of apparent stability and prosperity between 1925 and 1929. But even this brief spell of "normalcy" ultimately depended upon American loans, which were quickly withdrawn during the contraction of 1929.

From 1929 to 1932, the Depression hit Germany exceptionally hard. Industrial production fell by 40 per cent. Net national product at factor cost declined by 54 per cent. Weekly hours worked dropped by 10 per cent, while real hourly earnings declined by about 4 per cent (nominal hourly earnings fell by 25 per cent). Average annual employment plunged by 37 per cent, and the number of unemployed nearly tripled, with the unemployment rate standing well above 30 per cent when Hitler came to power. These phenomena did not occur in a free market economy. In 1931 the government of Heinrich Brüning decreed substantial wage and price reductions (salaries of public officials were reduced three times during 1931, standard wages as established in collective bargaining contracts were set back to their January 1927 level, house rents were cut by 10 per cent, and interest rates on loans were ordered rolled back in stages to 6 per cent) and imposed foreign exchange controls.

The recovery under Hitler, by 1935, from the low point in 1932 was as spectacular as the collapse. Industrial production had rebounded by 66 per cent by 1935. Net national product at factor cost was up by 71 per cent. Weekly hours worked had risen by 7 per cent, the number of employed had climbed by 46 per cent, and average unemployment in 1935 was 61 per cent lower than in 1932. Only real hourly earnings failed to rise sharply; the 1935 level was less than 1 per cent higher than the 1932 level.

It is tempting to attribute Germany's rapid economic recovery from 1933 to 1935 to a "rearmament boom". Heinrich Stuebel (1951, p. 4136), for example, has asserted that the "German rearmament of the 1930s will go down in economic history as an example of the successful employment of state credit for fighting mass unemployment". Stuebel's connection between rearmament expenditures and the conquest of unemployment appears quite dubious in light of the level of armament expenditures during the early years of the Hitler regime. While there is still some uncertainty about the precise level of Nazi armament expenditures, there is a broad consensus supporting R. J. Overy's (1982, p. 47) contention that "the key years of recovery from 1932 to 1935 were years of relatively low military expenditure". The best estimates of German military expenditures (including both budget and so-called "Mefo-bill" spending) from 1932 to 1935 by Overy and Michael Geyer (1981, p. 253) range between approximately RM 5.5 billion and RM 6 billion, about two-thirds of which was "new" spending above levels already established prior to Hitler's accession to power. There is widespread agreement that military expenditure on this modest scale could not have accounted in any significant way for the apparent recovery of business activity and the dramatic improvement in the labour market prior to mid-1935.[1]

Perhaps the real engine for recovery was the stimulus of National Socialist work creation programmes, particularly in the areas of housing construction and rehabilitation and road building. In fact, expenditures of the Reich government on direct work creation measures from late 1932 to the end of 1935, approximately RM 5.2 billion, more or less matched the level of spending on the military. The impact of these work creation measures on the German recovery from 1933 to 1935 is not clear. It is generally agreed by Marcon (1974), Stelzner (1976), and Wolffsohn (1977) that Hitler took over from his immediate predecessors (Heinrich

Brüning, Franz von Papen and General Kurt von Schleicher) a deflationary fiscal policy and an extremely modest job creation programme. Yet
it has been argued, most forcefully by Marcon (1974, pp. 352-61, 399),
that owing to economic lags, Hitler ultimately reaped the benefits of programmes initiated by Papen and Schleicher. Hitler inherited direct job
creation programmes totalling approximately RM 1,098 million (including RM 269 million in projects undertaken by the Reichsbahn and Reichs-
post). During 1933, Hitler added another RM 100 million to the so-called
Sofortprogramm begun during Schleicher's administration, and sanc-
tioned an additional RM 1.5 billion in job creation measures, the so-called
"Reinhardt programme". Another RM 350 million was authorised for
autobahn construction, though work did not begin until September. Total
expenditure on direct job creation programmes from late 1932 to the end
of 1935 came to approximately RM 5.2 billion, paid out as follows: RM
1.6 billion (1933), RM 2.4 billion (1934), and RM 1.2 billion (1935).
These pay-outs for direct job creation comprised 2.5 per cent of Germany's gross national product at market prices for the three years 1933-
35.

To what extent can the dramatic improvement in the labour market
under Hitler be attributed to direct work creation measures? Overy (1982,
p. 44) and others have observed that "the employment effects of the
policies were in some ways more dramatic and successful than the income
effects". René Erbe (1958, pp. 151-2, 163) has calculated the value of the
multiplier for the period 1932-36 at no more than 1.6, and for 1932-1938
at 1.69. He concludes that if the "secondary effect" from additional public investment reaches only 70 per cent of the original investment, "then
the possibility of full employment is dim." The logic of Erbe's conclusion, deduced from the low value of the multiplier, seems inescapable.
But logic appears to be at odds with the facts. Labour market statistics
improved dramatically during 1933 and 1934, and by the autumn of 1936
the National Socialists claimed full employment. Why did the additional
public investment appear to generate a great deal of employment and relatively little additional income? Part of the answer lies in the conservative
approach reflected in Hitler's early "Battle for Jobs" *(Arbeitsschlacht)*
from 30 January 1933 to the middle of 1935.

2   National Socialist Work Creation Measures, 1933-35

The most striking characteristic of Hitler's "Battle for Jobs" is its lack of
any specifically "National Socialist" imprint. The "Nazi" job-creation
measures of 1933 and 1934 generally conformed to fairly orthodox views
of traditional economic conservatives. Public expenditure for the creation
of "artificial" jobs was never considered as anything but a temporary ex-

pedient until the "organic" recovery of the "natural" economy provided work for all. The government's direct role in the economy was limited by adherence to conservative economic theory and by the constraints of the federal budget and the Reichsbank. Indirect creation of employment through tax incentives was considered preferable to direct creation of jobs through public works programmes. These ideas were held by the business leaders with whom Hitler consulted and by most of the cabinet officers and other government officials (both Nazis and non-Nazis) who participated in the formulation of economic policy during the first thirty months of Hitler's regime.

Hitler's firm committment to the creation of jobs (full employment) as an end in itself has often been questioned. He seems to have been torn between the urgency of putting the German people back to work, and his longer-term plans for rearmament and the rehabilitation of Germany as a respected world power. On 8 February 1933, Hitler told his cabinet, "The next five years in Germany must be devoted to the rearmament of the German people. Every publicly sponsored work creation measure must be considered from the point of view of whether it is necessary in terms of the rearmament of the German people." Later in the same meeting, he "stressed once again that for the next four to five years the guiding principle must be: everything for the Wehrmacht." The cabinet did not unanimously accept the chancellor's priorities; labour minister Franz Seldte "supported" Hitler's statement, "but expressed the opinion that beside the purely military requirements there were also other projects of value to the national economy which ought not be neglected" (BAK, R43I/1459; R43II/536).

On 9 February 1933 Hitler accepted finance minister Schwerin von Krusigk's assumption that for the current 1933 budget year, no more than RM 50 million was available to the army from the *Sofort* programme. He did so only with the stipulation that "in the future when there was a collision between the requirements of the army and demands for other purposes, the interests of the army would under all circumstances have priority."

At this time, Hitler saw no direct conflict between his armament programme and spending on the *Sofort* work creation programme. "The RM 500 million programme", he remarked, "was the largest of its kind and was particularly suited to be made to serve the interests of rearmament. It most quickly permitted the camouflage of work for the improvement of national defence." This exchange of 9 February 1933 between Hitler and his financial and military experts (BAK, R43II/536) illustrates two fundamental points. First, there was in Hitler's mind no clear distinction between expenditures for job creation and defence. He was not prepared to sacrifice one for the other. He told a group of industrialists on 29 May 1933 (BAK, R43II/536) that unemployment was Germany's number one problem, but nevertheless first launched into a short speech on the need to rearm before coming around to a discussion of job creation programmes. Second, neither Hitler nor most of his leading military and financial advisors would disregard the requirements of fiscal responsibility in order to promote either job creation or rearmament during the 1933 budget year. Only when the Nazi regime was politically secure would Hitler feel free to spend recklessly.

If massive public spending programmes for either work creation or rearmament were out of the question for 1933, how was the economy to be cured and prepared for the ultimate task of making Germany ready for war? To rephrase this question for our own purposes, without massive infusions of additional public funds into either job creation programmes or rearmament, how did Hitler's government reduce unemployment by 60 per cent during its first eighteen months in power? At the time, Hitler and economic leaders both within and without the government attributed the miraculous recovery of the labour market to a combination of factors: restoration of "confidence"; direct job creation measures through public works projects; indirect work creation measures generally involving tax incentives; and other measures such as marriage loans and the *Landhilfe* programme. The share of each of these approaches in reducing German unemployment during 1933-34 is no better understood today than it was in 1933-34. For many contemporary observers, the restoration of confidence provided the fundamental impetus to the rapid recovery of Germany's labour market. Wolfram Fischer (1961, p. 23) later stressed the psychological factors of optimism and hope in his history of Nazi economic policy. This recovery of confidence was strictly a *political* phenomenon, and had nothing to do with the public's perception of Hitler's competence as an economic planner. Germany's leading industrialists and businessmen told Hitler on 29 May 1933 that economic recovery required a *stable* government pursuing a fixed, clear policy. Only then could firms make rational long-range plans. German businessmen demanded from Hitler not a "National Socialist" economic policy, but simply *continuity* in economic policy under a stable government.[2]

There were of course those who attributed the recovery of the labour market to the specific type of stability and leadership provided by *Hitler* and the new *National Socialist* state. Such was the view of Fritz Reinhardt, state secretary in the Reich finance ministry, whose name is associated with the RM 1 billion job creation programme of 1 June 1933, the so-called "Reinhardt Plan". The reduction in unemployment, asserted Reinhardt, could be traced back ultimately to "the political events of 30 January and 21-22 March 1933" (Hitler's assumption of the chancellorship and the elections which solidified his power), and to the "replacement of the party-state by the Adolf Hitler-state". "Adolf Hitler",

Reinhardt wrote with adulation, "embodies the political prerequisites for the success of the Plan, and within the limits of his economic possibilities each individual fellow German must do what the politically based general plan of Adolf Hitler prescribes for him" (BAK, R41/4; R43II/308).

To argue that dramatic improvement in the labour market resulted largely from restoration of confidence in the government implies that much if not most of the recovery resulted from an "organic" revival of the private sector. The argument seems to minimise the role of specific government work creation measures. In fact, the Nazi leadership was divided on the efficacy of government direct job creation programmes, and the business community definitely advised Hitler that such measures should be used only as a last resort. Hitler agreed with his advisers and German businessmen that tax incentives for the private sector represented the best way to create jobs.

Of those responsible for designing and implementing Hitler's early economic strategy, Fritz Reinhardt was one of the most enthusiastic proponents of government action to create jobs. The range of such measures, he wrote, should encompass finance policy, taxation policy, and labour market policy (BAK, R41/5). But most public officials and private businessmen sought to limit the magnitude and scope of government measures. Hitler told German industrialists in May 1933 that the conquest of unemployment required action by both the state and the private sector; the state's role was to provide assistance to the private sector mainly through tax incentives. Programmes in housing and highway construction, he said, would provide the key to resolving the entire economic dilemma. But Hitler was willing to commit major public funding (RM 1.2 billion) only for the highway projects; the housing programme could be carried out by means of tax incentives and subsidised mortgages, supplemented by a few million RM from the state. The chancellor also suggested extending the tax exemption on automobiles to all production above existing levels (BAK, R43II/536).

In September 1933, Hitler expressed interest in a demand-side approach to economic recovery. Potential consumers were putting off purchases, he believed, because they feared the social consequences of appearing better off than their less fortunate neighbours National Socialist education and propaganda programmes would soon turn this "anxiety in the presence of one's neighbour" into "lust for life". "That", argued Hitler, "is necessary to psychologically stimulate the economy" (BAK, R43II/321).

Restoring political confidence in the state and combatting anxiety in the presence of one's neighbour were inexpensive means of promoting economic recovery. Hitler saw himself as the *Volkspsychologe*, while other economic policy experts gave substance to his ideas in programmes for debt relief for local governments, assistance for farmers, tax incentives and interest subsidies for home repairs and remodelling, and road construction projects. These projects did cost money, and Hitler, his economic policy makers, and the business and financial community had to decide how much could be financed and how it could be financed. Hitler admitted he did not have all the answers; some measures would work, some would not. But *something* had to be done. "Someone", he said, "must have the courage to make decisions, even when he knows that not everything will turn out right." It was a trial-and-error method, and government officials would make mistakes. He acknowledged that he and his cabinet did not always agree on economic policy, but eventually they came to a decision and from that point on no criticism could be tolerated. To the public, the government must give the appearance of certainty that their policies are absolutely correct (BAK, R43II/321). The historian peeking behind the curtains gets a different impression.

Hitler faced a paradoxical situation. Catastrophic economic conditions seemed to demand innovative initiatives, but public trust could be built up only if the new regime honoured the pledges of the old regime. Looking back on the early days of the Nazi regime from the vantage-point of mid-1935, Württemberg's economics minister Oswald Lehnich illuminated Hitler's dilemma with clarity when he observed that many said the National Socialist government would last only a few weeks. They would have been right, he conceded, had National Socialism continued with the work creation measures of the old regime. Our opponents, he said, never imagined that we would be open to new methods. On the other hand, noted Lehnich, other critics "hoped for dangerous experiments; but these did not take place, either" (BAK, R43II/309a). Hitler's work creation programme had to find an acceptable middle ground between "more of the same" and "dangerous experiments".

Only in late April 1933 did a coherent "National Socialist" work creation programme begin to take shape. Labour minister Franz Seldte, the former Stahlhelm leader who joined the Nazi party only on 26 April, four days earlier sent to the Reich Chancellery the outline for a work creation plan; the full plan followed on 27 April (BAK, R43II/536; R43I/1461). Seldte proposed various measures such as reduction of production costs (wages, taxes, social insurance), removal of women from the labour market and keeping young persons in school for an additional year, shortening the working week to forty hours to spread the work, limiting technical improvement and rationalisation in industry, and compulsory placement of some of the unemployed in private firms. But the heart of Seldte's programme was a RM 1.6 billion work creation programme designed to employ 470,000 to 700,000 jobless persons for one year. Land settlement programmes stood at the top of Seldte's list, but housing construction, repair of public buildings, railway construction and electrification, road building, canal construction, projects for the postal service, agricultural improvements, regulation of rivers, renewal of the merchant marine fleet, and gas, water and electricity projects were to play a prominent role in reducing the level of unemployment.

Seldte's memorandum eventually produced on 31 May 1933 the first high-level discussion of a major work creation programme since Hitler's assumption of power. Prior to that meeting, however, economics minister Hugenberg and Hitler sought to establish their respective positions. Hugenberg had prepared for discussion by concerned ministers and officials a "Memorandum on the Financing of Work Creation" (BAK, R43II/536). Hugenberg expressed fundamental scepticism about the efficacy of previous work creation measures. Germany had to break out of the deflationary trap, but not by employing inflationary means. "A sick economy", asserted Hugenberg, "has never been cured by means of an inflation." The historical accuracy of Hugenberg's claim is beside the point; of greatest interest here is Hugenberg's search for a non-inflationary way out of a vicious circle of deflation. He professed to see inflationary dangers even in the existing depressed economy. Funding new work creation programmes through recourse to the Reichsbank for short-term credits would certainly unleash inflation; and recourse to a long-term government loan would upset the government's plans for conversion and consolidation of its existing debt. Hugenberg's solution was to inflate the economy in what he believed to be a non-inflationary manner through the issue of "Reich treasury notes" (*Reichskassenscheine*) in denominations of 5, 10, 20, 50 and 100 marks. According to Hugenberg, his treasury notes would pose no inflationary danger because they would not serve as forced currency, and they would ultimately return to the government when used by the public to pay taxes. Since the bills would pose no inflationary threat, they could theoretically be issued without limit, though Hugenberg suggested that the initial issue be limited to about RM 1.5 billion - roughly the amount called for in Seldte's work creation programme.

High-level official meetings scheduled for discussion of the economy on 11 and 18 May were postponed owing to Hitler's absence. The chancellor apparently wished to discuss the economic situation with Germany's leading businessmen before committing himself to a programme of action. In his "discussion with industrialists on work creation" on 29 May, Hitler singled out housing and highway construction programmes as the two keys to economic recovery. Many of the businessmen present expressed reservations about any state work creation programmes. Only Carl Bosch, representing the chemical industry, strongly supported the notion of direct state intervention in the economy, and he argued that the house repair and road construction programmes proposed by Hitler would "only partly" eradicate unemployment in Germany. Nothing short of "decisive, compulsory" government measures would put Germany back to work, argued Bosch. Reliance upon the private sector, even with subsidies from the state, was illusory, "for today there are only a few large employers; these alone can hardly take up the millions of unemployed."[3]

The industrialists who were willing to go along with Hitler's work creation projects stressed the need to revive capital markets and find a means of financing both public and private investment. Hitler agreed that "the financial side is for me clearly decisive", but he admitted to having no solution to the problem. On this point Erich Lübbert, the man whom Seldte had suggested as Reichscommissar for Job Creation, took issue with Hugenberg's plan to issue Reich treasury notes. Lübbert proposed to create funds through expansion of credit combined with creation of new money. Whether or not the new money ranked equally with the Reichmark did not concern Lübbert, and he noted that issue of Reich treasury notes was just an indirect way of having the Reichsbank provide the government with funds. Why, he asked, take such a circuitous route to the same end? "Whether we Lombard 100 per cent or whether the Reichsbank gives the money directly to the state, it comes down to the same thing," Lübbert argued (BAK, R43II/536).

Having heard from the industrialists, Hitler was now prepared to deal with the work creation issue in the *Chefsbesprechung über Arbeitsbeschaffung* of 31 May 1933 (BAK, R43II/536). Hitler made it clear that whatever plan was chosen, the budget had to be balanced. Because taxes on business had to be reduced, the budget could be balanced only by reducing expenditures on social programmes. Hitler rejected the idea of increasing government income through taxes, and then supporting increased government expenditures with the proceeds of those taxes, as "too complicated". Seldte observed that tax reform was no less urgent than the reduction of social expenditures. State secretary Reinhardt (finance ministry) assured the group that no tax increase was contemplated; a tax reform measure aiming at tax simplification would be introduced in the spring of 1934. Reinhardt then reported on a work creation proposal drafted by finance minister Schwerin von Krosigk and sent to the Reich Chancellery earlier in the day. This was apparently a modified version of Seldte's proposal; it called for the repair and expansion of public buildings and private dwellings, suburban resettlement, agricultural settlement, regulation of rivers, development of gas, water, and electric resources, and earthworks. An expenditure of RM 1 billion (four years at RM 200-250 million per year) would produce an estimated 700,000 to 800,000 jobs. The finance minister admitted to a certain daring in burdening the budget with the additional expenditure, but it was a necessary gamble. Reichsbank president Hjalmar Schacht supported Schwerin von

Krosigk's proposal insofar as the financing was concerned. He rejected any creation of money or the use of treasury notes as suggested by Hugenberg. But Schacht exacted a price for his support, demanding that he be given control over capital markets (presumably through open market operations by the Reichsbank), and that control of all employment projects and related financial measures be vested in a small committee. Against Hugenberg's lone dissenting voice (he opposed any plan predicated on "artificial" job creation), the cabinet approved Schwerin von Krosigk's plan and it became the so-called "Reinhardt Programme" of 1 June 1933. Precisely how the RM 1 billion would be apportioned among various types of projects was settled at a meeting on 27 June of Schacht, Seldte and Schwerin von Krosigk.[4]

Hitler's "Battle for Jobs" was now well under way. Victory came quickly, if one can believe the archival records. Only a month after the Reinhardt Programme spending priorities had been set, the Reich chancellor's office was deluged with telegrams from various districts proclaiming the total conquest of unemployment. Agricultural districts in East Prussia reported that they no longer had any unemployed persons; so, too, did the industrial city of Nordhorn. A telegram of 16 August to the Reich chancellor from the high president *(Oberpräsident)* of East Prussia proclaimed that within one month they had put all of the province's jobless back to work.[5]

By September 1933 the government could no longer resist demands for significant tax reductions. On 16 September, finance minister Schwerin von Krosigk sent to the Reich Chancellery a proposal to reduce taxes by a total of RM 532 billion per year (BAK, R53/9). Included in the plan were reductions in the house-rent tax (RM 262), the land tax on urban and agricultural landowners (RM 210 million), the agricultural turnover tax (RM 60 million), and tax exemptions for newly constructed small homes and owner-occupied homes.

Schwerin von Krosigk's proposal encountered opposition when it was discussed three days later in the cabinet meeting on 19 September (BAK, R43II/537). Kurt Schmitt, now Reich economics minister, argued that reductions in taxation could relieve the economy only if they were sufficiently large; but the reduction envisioned in Schwerin von Krosigk's proposal seemed quite small. If a comprehensive tax reduction was at the moment out of the question, Schmitt expressed willingness to support for the time being the present proposal just to get the ball rolling. But in the long run, he did not believe tax reductions would revive the economy. Though as a private businessman he had expressed grave doubts about public work creation schemes, as Hitler's economics minister Schmitt now favoured additional sums for repair of housing; in that area, he said, "it was impossible to do too much."

Hitler supported Schmitt. His primary concern was to maintain over the winter of 1933-34 the amazing reduction in unemployment already achieved. "Every measure that might be taken", he declared, "must be viewed primarily from the viewpoint of work creation . . . every measure in the area of taxation policy must in the first instance promote the objective of work creation." As usual, Hitler felt ethical issues were involved in this question. It was important to "re-create the individual's faith in his own initiative". He did not think it expedient to reduce the house-rent tax at that time. Instead, he proposed to give the home owner a subsidy to supplement funds the owner spent on repair and similar purposes during a certain period of time. The state, however, would assume interest payments on funds provided by the home owner, and guarantee the interest out of revenues from the house-rent tax. Hitler found two advantages in his approach: it would create more jobs than a tax cut, and it would go over with the people "psychologically better" than a simple tax reduction. Although Prussian finance minister Johannes Popitz still held out for a reduction in the house-rent tax, Schmitt and state secretary Dr Johannes Krohn (Reich labour ministry) recommended that the entire RM 500 million in proposed tax reductions be applied instead in the manner suggested by Hitler. The "Second Law on the Reduction of Unemployment" of 21 September 1933 embodied Hitler's amendments. The agricultural land tax, the agricultural turnover tax and the land tax on homes completed and occupied between 1924 and 1930 were reduced, and new homes completed for occupancy after 31 March 1934 were to be free of income tax, property taxes, the rural land tax and half of the urban land tax. The house-rent tax was not reduced. Instead, the Reich finance minister was empowered to make available RM 500 million in subsidies for repair, expansion and partitioning of buildings.[6]

The government regarded the tax relief measures and subsidies for house repairs approved in September 1933 as temporary emergency measures designed to maintain current employment levels during the winter of 1933-34. Businessmen supported the government's tax reduction measures, and demanded more, particularly the elimination of employers' contributions to the national insurance programme which added "social costs" to the price of their products. Goossens, Peeters, and Pepermans have argued in chapter 8 of this volume that Belgian employers resolutely opposed the voluntary insurance scheme because it was too closely identified with trade union strength. While the situation in Germany was not identical, it can be acknowledged that the existence of a strong compulsory unemployment insurance fund enhanced the position of German labour as against management. Typical of the employers' position was Vereinigten Stahlwerke AG general director Dr Albert Vögler's statement to the *Generalrat der Wirtschaft* that "the best work creation programme is again and again the lifting of the employers' contribution to national insurance".[7]

While Hitler and his cabinet agreed in principle, they felt the opportune moment for a general reduction of taxes had not arrived. Reich finance minister Schwerin von Krosigk told business leaders and government officials gathered for a meeting of the *Generalrat der Wirtschaft* that the coming winter would provide the critical test for the government's battle for jobs. In view of the need to maintain employment levels throughout the winter months, he said, the government would consider tax reductions only where they would produce the fastest, most direct, and most certain increase in job creation. Once the winter crisis had been negotiated successfully, the government was prepared to consider a "fundamental tax reform".

Apart from tax reduction, the business community seemed most concerned during the autumn of 1933 with the health of the German monetary system and capital market. A perceived capital shortage, disrupted credit markets, and fears that inflationary work creation programmes would once again destroy the German currency threatened to dampen or even derail Germany's economic recovery. Fritz Thyssen maintained that Germany's economic sickness basically resulted from a shortage of liquid capital. The recovery of 1925-28 was financed by RM 10 billion in foreign capital. If Germany expected to recover, it would have to recreate that lost liquid capital.

As president of the Reichsbank, Hjalmar Schacht appeared to hold decisive authority on questions of money, credit and capital. His predecessor at the bank, Hans Luther, had placed strict limits on Reichsbank financing of work creation projects during the Papen and Schleicher presidencies. Without Schacht's cooperation, Hitler's battle for jobs could founder. Schacht professed no interest in theoretical discussions of the nature of capital. "I know in general what capital is," he told the *Generalrat der Wirtschaft*. "Since my third semester, I have not concerned myself with the question." He was certain that Germany suffered from no capital shortage; the market system for efficient allocation had simply broken down. People hoarded capital, people invested in short-term obligations (he estimated about RM 6 billion in short-term obligations floating on the German money market), but the long-term investment market was dead.

For Schacht, the disruption of German capital markets boiled down to a matter of lack of trust. When uncontrolled government expenditures raised fears of deficits, people kept their money in short-term investments. As Germany's central bank, however, the Reichsbank could have influenced German investment patterns by both manipulation of interest rates and control of credit. Schacht was prepared to do both, but to manipulate interest rates he needed a change in regulations governing Reichsbank operations, and before he would expand credit he needed to see signs that the economy needed additional credit. Authority to conduct open market operations was withheld from the Reichsbank under the terms of the Young Plan, but Schacht intended to obtain permission for such operations in talks with the Bank for International Settlements in Basel. In the matter of regulating the volume of credit, Schacht rejected the idea of a massive RM 5 billion expansion of credit by the Reichsbank. He did not object in principle to the amount of RM 5 billion; he in fact promised that he would permit a RM 5 billion credit expansion "if the economy needs it. But first the economy must show that it needs it."

Schacht, of course, was concerned with preserving the value of the German currency. "Holding fast to a stable currency is absolutely decisive in our conduct of the economy," he asserted. Credit expansion to meet the legitimate needs of either the private or the public sector would be non-inflationary. The Reichsbank, he said, stood ready to extend credit for every project that even halfway promised a return on invested capital, no matter whether the project was to be undertaken by a private firm, a bank, or a public institution. He believed the Reichsbank had not even approached the limit of credit it could extend. "I have no anxiety about inflation," he pronounced. "The only danger we see today in an extraordinary expansion of credit", observed Schacht, "lies in higher price levels", which would decrease the purchasing power of the German people. He warned that German firms could not be permitted to raise their prices at the first sign of a credit-induced expansion. In other words, price controls (either formal or informal) would inhibit the inflationary impact of credit expansion.

While Schacht was promising to finance any truly "productive" investment, the government was preparing its strategy for continuing the battle for jobs into 1934. Preliminary discussions among experts from the Reich finance, economics and labour ministries held on 3 November 1933 produced no clear consensus on a programme for the coming year. Some favoured additional work creation measures, but others thought it was time to shift to an "organic" revival of the private sector assisted by further tax reductions (BAK, R43II/537). At a subsequent meeting of ministers and department heads on 6 December, there was a consensus that for 1934 the primary task was to raise purchasing power, not spending on additional work creation programmes. Schwerin von Krosigk ruled out any increase in wages; that left reduction of taxes, reducing contributions to the national insurance programmes, and lowering of interest rates as the only means to raise purchasing power. Although they agreed to place less emphasis on new funding for work creation programmes, some of those present hoped at the least that funds would be forthcoming to com-

plete projects already under way. Publicly financed work creation programmes would be allowed to play themselves out and die a natural death
during 1934.[8] The use of the state's police powers to control the labour
market provided a less expensive substitute for direct work creation programmes.

In their study of Italian unemployment in the Great Depression which
appears as chapter 6 of this volume, Gianni Toniolo and Francesco Piva
argue that Italian-style fascism produced little or no innovative effort in
policies of public works and unemployment insurance. Instead, the
regime sought to gain effective *control* of the Italian labour market.
Through a blend of propaganda and police power, the government enforced wage cuts and a reduction in the number of hours worked, and restricted the workers' mobility.

The same development towards reliance on control of the labour market is evident in Nazi Germany. Efforts to reduce the presence of females
in the labour force had already begun with the work creation programme
of 1 June 1933, which in addition to direct work creation measures provided for government marriage loans to women who agreed to leave the
labour force. By 31 January 1935, the government had issued 379,000
such loans at a total cost of RM 206 million; by the end of 1935, total
loans stood at 523,000 at a cost of RM 300 million. In January 1933,
women comprised 18.76 per cent of the official unemployed; by January
1935, they accounted for only 13.79 per cent of the unemployed. The extent to which marriage loans contributed to this decline is difficult to
judge. It is impossible to estimate the number of marriages that would
have taken place without the loans, and many women normally gave up
their jobs upon marriage in any event.[9]

In chapters 3 and 8 of this volume, Mark Thomas and Martine Goossens, Stefaan Peeters and Guido Pepermans have argued that in Britain
and Belgium, "retirement through marriage" was common, no marriage
loans being offered in these countries. They also hypothesise that women
who became unemployed were more likely to drop out of the labour force
than register as unemployed and search for a new job. The British and
Belgian examples, rather than marriage loans, may explain a large portion
of the declining share of the labour force occupied by women in Germany.

The compulsory aspects of Nazi control of the labour market unfolded
during 1934. Empowered by the 15 May 1934 *Gesetz zur Regelung des
Arbeitseinsatzes*, Reichsanstalt für Arbeitsvermittlung und Arbeitslosenversicherung (Federal Institution for Placement and Unemployment Insurance, hereafter RfAA) president Syrup issued orders barring
immigration of workers into Berlin, Hamburg, and Bremen, cities already
burdened with exceptionally high rates of unemployment. Other orders
prohibited agricultural labourers from accepting employment in mining,

metallurgy, construction, brickworks and railway construction.[10] In August 1934, in a process known as *Arbeitsplatzaustausch*, all factory management was ordered to replace workers under age 25 with older heads of families. In the year October 1934 to October 1935, approximately 130,000 jobs changed hands under this regulation. Young workers thus dismissed supposedly found employment in agriculture or joined the Land Helpers or Labour Service (males), or found household work (females) (Syrup, 1957, pp. 419-20; 1936, pp.107-8). The extent to which this "exchange of workplaces" affected labour market statistics cannot be determined. It is not known how many of the older "new hires" had previously been counted as "unemployed", nor can it be ascertained how many of the displaced younger workers found alternative employment or ended up on the unemployment rolls. Control of the labour market tightened on 26 June 1935, when the government decreed six months of compulsory work in the Labour Service for Germany's young men. State control of the labour market culminated with the introduction of the workbook *(Arbeitsbuch)* for all workers and salaried employees under the law of 26 February 1935. Henceforth, no employment could be secured without presentation of a workbook in proper order, listing vital information such as place of residence, education, skills and previous experience. Now the government could put the right worker in the right job, reduce the pressure in certain overcrowded fields, and halt the flight from the land. It took the RfAA over a year to prepare and issue 22 million workbooks (Syrup, 1957, pp. 436-41).

While the decision in favour of more controls and less new funding for work creation projects rested in part on philosophical considerations, it was also heavily influenced by the military's increasing demands on the Reich budget and the Reichsbank. Schwerin von Krosigk's proposed 1934 budget reflected the burgeoning rearmament programme. The finance minister asked Hitler to convene a meeting of the Reichswehr minister, the Reich minister for air transport, and the Reich chancellor, in order that "the matter of military expenditures, so important for the 1934 budget and the Reichsbank, can be settled definitively". While revenues would decline owing to tax reductions either in place or envisioned for later in the year, military spending was scheduled to rise steadily over the next few years. For work creation, on the other hand, there would still be about RM 1.2 billion from old programmes at the government's disposal after 1 April 1934; adding in funds earmarked for road building and onetime military outlays, observed the finance minister, the means for work creation "will hardly fall below the level of 1933." Even with some cuts in spending requests and possible increases in revenue, the deficit would still come to RM 300 million (RM 900 million if off-budget items were included). The gap could be closed, he observed, by raising estimates of revenue, insofar as no reduction of military expenditure was possible. Overall, Schwerin von Krosigk told Hitler, "I recommend this method of action, even though I am aware that it is in part risky, and in part represents only an illusory balance."[11]

The fiscal year 1934 represents a critical point in Hitler's "Battle for Jobs". Did increased military expenditures compensate for the levelling off and reduction of "pure" work creation expenditures in 1934? The labour market picture for 1934 is anything but clear. Despite the exhortations to maintain momentum through the winter of 1933-34, unemployment increased from a low of 3,714,646 on 30 November 1933 to 4,059,055 on 30 December, but had slipped back to 3,772,792 by 31 January 1934. From February to October 1934 unemployment recorded a steady decline to 2,267,657, but then rose in November and by 31 December, at 2,604,700, had returned to the level of 30 April (2,608,621). Before resuming its downward trend, unemployment peaked at the end of January 1935 at 2,973,544, a level not seen since February 1934.

The cause of the fluctuation in the level of unemployment during 1934 cannot be fixed with certainty, but an educated guess can be made. The RfAA provided significant funding for emergency relief works (*Notstandsarbeiten*). These projects employed 23,665 emergency relief workers on 30 January 1933; one year later the number stood at 416,626, and ultimately peaked at 631,436 on 31 March 1934. Emergency relief workers were paid RM 3 for each day worked. During the fiscal year 1933-34, the RfAA had budgeted RM 140 million for such purposes, and for 1934-35 (1 April to 31 March) planned to spend RM 200 million, providing for an average of 225,000 emergency relief workers. RfAA president Friedrich Syrup estimated the required funding at RM 400 to 500 million, even though the Reich government had rejected any new work creation programmes (BAK, R43II/535).

Instead of substantially raising the RfAA's funding authorisation, the government set the amount at RM 250,000 and reduced the daily pay from RM 3 to RM 2.50 as of 1 March 1934. This reduction of course meant hardship for the emergency relief workers, but the impact on the providers of work, usually state and local governments, was equally devastating. The project management had either to make up the substantial difference between the new reduced level of funding from the RfAA and the total cost of the project, or lay off workers. At either RM 3 or RM 2.50, the wage for emergency relief workers was a poverty-level wage, and many such workers were added to the welfare relief rolls during the first three years of the Nazi regime.[12]

The number of emergency relief workers plunged to 246,116 on 31 October, the low point for 1934, but not without vociferous complaints directly to Hitler from state and local authorities. The high president

(Oberpräsident) of Lower and Upper Silesia, for example, estimated that the reductions had put 55,000 to 60,000 labourers back on the unemployment lines in his province. Projects already begun were being abandoned in mid-stream, and the public purse was now burdened with additional unemployment and welfare payments. The high president, however, was most concerned to point out to Hitler the political significance of the reduction of support for emergency relief work. The dismissed workers would become easy targets for communism, particularly in Silesia, "a province bounded on three sides by Slavonic states, and permeated by communist villages" (BAK, R43II/537).

Official labour market statistics did not appear to substantiate the fears of state and local political leaders; the number of unemployed continued to decline from April to the end of October. As interpreted by Prussian minister-president Hermann Göring (BAK, R43II/537), "the trend of the unemployment statistics indicates that an increase in the capacity of the private sector was by and large able to compensate for the reduction in emergency relief works carried out by the Reich government." Göring was nevertheless not very confident; reports from high presidents and minister-presidents, he noted, spoke more and more of the difficulty in making further progress in the "Battle for Jobs". For the time being, further reductions in unemployment would not be possible. During the coming months, Göring thought, additional stimulation measures from the public hand would be difficult to avoid. Göring's uneasiness was justified; beginning in October 1934, the German labour market was hit by a sharp increase in unemployment and a decrease in employment. The "stimulation measures" required to reverse this dangerous trend now came in the form of rearmament.

As a permanent cure for Germany's unemployment problem, rearmament still had to face the fundamental limitations of the German economy. The year 1934 brought not only increasing demands upon Germany's financial and material resources from the rearmament programme, but it also recorded a raw material import crisis caused by Germany's persistent shortage of foreign exchange. To ensure sufficient foreign exchange to allow for imports of vital foods and raw materials essential to the rearmament programme, Hjalmar Schacht promulgated his New Plan in 1934. While this elaborate system of import and foreign exchange controls represented another step towards German autarchy, it contributed to an increase in unemployment and short-time employment in non-essential consumer goods industries. In theory, government agencies such as the RfAA rejected work sharing (reduction of hours to spread the available work) as a means of dealing with high rates of unemployment. If in normal economic times there were factories which could not be used at full capacity, then, reasoned the RfAA, it was from the viewpoint of the national economy only proper that such excess capacity be closed down rather than be kept operating through subsidies from the RfAA in the form of support for short-time work. By 1932, however, the economic crisis had presumably wrung out the excess capacity built up during the inflation of the 1920s, so that the RfAA could now legitimately furnish support for short-time workers. Between 1928 and 1932, average weekly hours worked in mining, industry, and handicrafts had fallen by 15 per cent, from 49 to 41.5. During the fiscal year 1932, the RfAA provided RM 44 million to support short-time workers. Improvement in the labour market enabled the RfAA to reduce the level of support to RM 22 million (1933) and RM 11 million (1934). But the increase in short-time employment caused by the 1934 raw material shortage forced the RfAA to implement a programme of "enhanced short-time-worker support" (*verstarkte Kurzarbeiterunterstützung*) which cost the RfAA RM 20 million in the fiscal year 1935 (Syrup, 1936, pp. 141-2).

Hitler's "Battle for Jobs" during 1933 and 1934 represented a rather modest effort based upon conservative principles of finance. The only extraordinary measure taken by the Hitler government to assist in the recovery of the labour market was the so-called Reinhardt programme of 1 June 1933. By the beginning of 1934, the government was already scaling down the resources to be allocated to work creation, and by November 1934 the number of unemployed was again on the rise. Through this programme, according to published official labour market statistics, the National Socialist government is supposed to have reduced the unemployment rate from 34 per cent on 30 January 1933 to 12.5 per cent on 31 October 1934. Given the nature of the work creation programmes, a 60 per cent reduction of unemployment over a twenty-month period stretches the limit of credibility.

At the time, officials in the Nazi system credited themselves with an economic miracle without questioning its veracity or probing too deeply into its origins. Historians have by and large followed their lead. The achievements of German work creation programmes are particularly incredible when compared to those in Britain and the United States. Comparing the results of the first two years of Germany's recovery programme with those of England and the United States, Württemberg's economics minister Oswald Lehnich found that while Germany had put over 60 per cent of its unemployed back to work, England had during the same period managed only a reduction of 15 per cent, from 2.7 million to 2.3 million unemployed. As for the United States, Lehnich observed, "unemployment during the past year has fallen from 11.9 million in March 1934 only to 11.7 million in March 1935, despite the strongest expansion of credit and an extraordinarily energetic provision of state funding." To finance its work creation programme, claimed Lehnich,

Germany chose "an expansion of credit prudently directed and limited in time. Germany thus took the path later taken to the greatest extent by the United States of America" (BAK, R43II/309a). It never occurred to Lehnich to ask how such modest, prudently conducted work creation programmes had produced results in Germany unmatched anywhere else in the industrialised world. Perhaps part of the answer lies in analysis of the labour market statistics themselves.

3 National Socialist Labour Market Statistics

Economists and historians have generally accepted at face value the labour market statistics provided by the regime that perfected the propaganda technique of the "Big Lie". In the recent literature on the National Socialist economy, Nazi claims for reducing unemployment have been taken at face value by all but Timothy W. Mason.[13] One must at least consider the possibility that the Nazis manipulated labour market statistics in order to create confidence in the new regime and fulfil Hitler's pledge of February 1933 to wipe out unemployment within four years. Such manipulation might have taken the form of changes in the criteria for classifying the labour force as either employed or unemployed, alterations in the procedures for registering the unemployed and processing labour market statistics, or deliberate alteration of labour market statistics.

The possibility that the Nazis deliberately altered labour market statistics has been considered and rejected by some analysts of the Nazi economy. In chapter 6 of this volume, Toniolo and Piva discuss and reject the possibility that Italy's Fascist government falsified labour market statistics for political reasons. In both cases, the verdict of exoneration flows more from the dictates of logic than the certainty of empirical investigation. C. W. Guillebaud (1939, p. iv), for example, assumed that if the Nazis had wished to hide the truth about unemployment rates, they simply would have ceased publication of the statistics - just as they eventually discontinued publication of the budget in order to maintain the secrecy of military expenditures. Kroll (1958, p. 473), for whom the steep decline in unemployment during 1933 "borders on the miraculous" nevertheless felt "it would be a mistake" to suppose that the Nazis had deliberately altered unemployment statistics. The mass of statistics, he argued, was too large to be falsified in a credible manner, and such altered statistics would have been useless for official internal use.

These purely logical arguments against the possibility of doctored statistics are by no means conclusive. Proof of deliberate alteration of labour market statistics would of course require evidence that any "incorrect" figures resulted from willful activity by the responsible authorities. This author has been unable to uncover archival evidence of deliberate alteration. Although no direct evidence of deliberate alteration of labour market statistics has yet been uncovered, other compelling evidence raises questions concerning the reliability and validity of Nazi labour market statistics. Two possibilities immediately suggest themselves. First, the accuracy and reliability of labour market statistics may have suffered from disorganisation and reduced competence attendant upon the "nazification" of the RfAA.[14] Second, changes made after 30 January 1933 in the method of classifying the "employed" and "unemployed" may have served to "reduce" the "unemployment" rate by artificial means.

The RfAA was established in 1927 as an autonomous, self-governing public body under the supervision of the Reich Labour Ministry. In addition to administering unemployment insurance (made compulsory under the 1927 Act), the RfAA compiled and published labour market statistics, served as a placement office for the unemployed, provided vocational guidance and rehabilitation, and furnished funds for crisis relief and productive unemployment assistance (*wertschaffende Arbeitslosenfürsorge*) in the form of emergency public works (*Notstandsarbeiten*) undertaken to reduce unemployment.

After 30 January 1933, the nazification of the RfAA began with a sweeping purge of the agency's personnel under the terms of the "Law for the Restoration of the Professional Civil Service" (*Gesetz zur Wiederherstellung des Berufsbeamtentums*, or BBG) of 7 April 1933. The number of RfAA civil servants, salaried employees and waged workers dismissed, demoted, transferred, or involuntarily retired during 1933-34 under the terms of the BBG totalled 3,455, of whom 3,037 were dismissed. At least an equal number of salaried employees was fired under the terms of their labour contract in cases where there was no legal basis for dismissal under the BBG. Thus, in 1933-34, at least 6,000 (22 per cent) of the RfAA's staff of 26,606 were dismissed. It has been estimated that during the same year as many as 11,000 new employees were hired, but it is not clear how many of these were replacements for those dismissed. In hiring, firing, and promotion, political reliability and racial desirability were the main criteria for selection.[15]

This massive transformation of personnel compromised the efficiency and competence of the RfAA, particularly since seasoned experts were replaced with inexperienced personnel whose competence was less important than their politics and race. Skills of the thousands of new RfAA employees hired after January 1933 could have been upgraded through a rigorous training programme. Cram courses for salaried employees facing examinations produced meagre results because instruction in Nazi ideology and race theory consumed a disproportionate amount of the curriculum (BAK, R163/28). To make matters worse, quality control procedures within the RfAA broke down completely. With Hitler's assumption of the chancellorship, quality control examination of the employment offices was suspended for at least six or seven months. When resumed in September 1933, the examination of offices was no more than a perfunctory procedure. During the fiscal year 1 April 1933 to 30 March 1934, only forty-two of the 360 local and thirteen district offices were evaluated even on this limited scale ("Sechster Bericht der RfAA", 1933-34, p. 52).

The breakdown of RfAA inspection procedures threatened the reliability of Reich unemployment statistics collected and processed by that agency. In 1932, Friedrich Syrup, president of the RfAA, had ordered unannounced monthly examinations of statistical computations in the local employment offices. As former RfAA official Oscar Weigert (1934, pp. 57, 206) wrote, before Hitler came to power it was considered crucial "that the figures corresponded to the facts". It is not clear whether these special monthly statistical examinations were maintained while regular office evaluations were suspended and emasculated during the early months of the Hitler regime. Much later, in March 1938, Syrup issued revised guidelines which virtually eviscerated procedures for ensuring the accuracy of labour market statistics. Henceforth, unannounced examinations of statistical records were to be made only every second month, and the time allotted was to be sufficient only to "at least scrutinise through random samples the basis of the computations, the recording of statistics, etc. . . . Examinations of less than one hour will not do justice to their objective" (BAK, R163/53).

Personnel purges, the breakdown of discipline, reduced competency levels, and relaxation of examination procedures in the RfAA cast doubt upon the reliability of German labour market statistics after 30 January 1933. The description of Italian labour exchange offices as inefficient, party-controlled, and in some cases corrupt, advanced by Toniolo and Piva in chapter 6 of this volume, would be equally appropriate for Germany's labour exchange and unemployment insurance offices. Into an already chaotic situation the National Socialist government in 1933-34 introduced changes in the statistical classification of Germany's labour force which were both questionable theoretically and extremely confusing to untrained and often unqualified personnel. Cases of erroneous classification of the labour force prior to 30 January 1933 can be found, but uncertainty about the classification regulations intensified after the Nazi takeover. Records of the RfAA abound with clarifications issued by Syrup in efforts to correct recurring classification errors made by personnel in local employment offices. The "Law for the Reduction of Unemployment" (*Gesetz zur Verminderung der Arbeitslosigkeit*) of 1 June 1933 produced certain changes in classification effective in September, and RfAA regulations effective on 1 October further "simplified" statistical reporting of persons on unemployment insurance and emergency relief. These changes in classification and reporting methods required revision of forms used to record and report labour market statistics. Many RfAA employees either did not understand the new classification regulations, or failed to learn how to fill out the new forms properly. The "simplified" statistical reporting methods were in fact quite complex. The fact that jurisdictions of some local employment offices cut across boundaries of *Ländern* created the further possibility that some individuals might be double-counted.[16]

Categories such as emergency relief workers (*Notstandsarbeiter*) and participants in the voluntary Labour Service caused particular classification problems. Regulations implementing the Law for the Reduction of Unemployment of 1 June 1933 stipulated that for purposes of internal RfAA use, emergency relief workers receiving productive unemployment assistance (*wertschaffenden Arbeitslosenfürsorge*) were to be counted in different ways for three specific purposes: (a) in the productive unemployment statistics, as "employed" through the reporting employment office; (b) in the labour market statistics, as "looking for work" through the person's home-town employment office; and (c) in the unemployment insurance or emergency relief statistics, as a primary relief recipient through the home-town employment office (BAK, R163/73). For internal RfAA purposes, emergency relief workers could thus be considered simultaneously as "employed", "looking for work", and "on relief". Published official monthly labour market statistics included no "looking for work" category; beginning with 31 July 1933, emergency relief workers appeared in published official statistics as "employed".[17]

RfAA employees, including the president of the South-west Germany district office, also had difficulty making proper legal distinctions between "first applications", "new applications", and "applications for resumption" of unemployment insurance benefits and emergency relief. Moreover, discrepancies between monthly totals and daily figures could not be ironed out, because statistics were not always entered on the proper forms on a daily basis.[18] Because changes in the number of "unemployed" were calculated from these applications for unemployment support, the reliability of published unemployment statistics seems questionable.

Errors made in recording and computation furnish only one rationale for questioning the reliability of Nazi labour market statistics. The National Socialists made changes in unemployment insurance coverage and eligibility for unemployment compensation which reduced incentives to register at RfAA employment offices and thereby affected the official count of the unemployed. The rules of the game were changed, possibly with the intent of making the labour market picture appear brighter than it actually was.

Persons in the German labour force were classified as either "employed" or "unemployed". For official statistical purposes, the "employed" were those persons currently gainfully employed and covered by compulsory workers' health insurance, and the "unemployed" were those jobless persons who reported to RfAA placement and unemployment insurance offices. It is well documented that persons not covered by unemployment insurance or not eligible for unemployment benefits are less likely to register than those who are covered and eligible; and as the amount of benefit declines, the propensity of eligibles to register also declines. Changes in coverage and eligibility made shortly after the Nazi takeover undoubtedly acted to reduce the number of persons registering at RfAA employment offices. At the end of April 1933, an estimated 2,673,724 persons worked in segments of the labour market that were exempt from (not covered by) unemployment insurance. This meant that neither the workers nor their employers contributed to the compulsory unemployment insurance fund, and that workers in these occupations were not eligible to collect unemployment compensation if they found themselves out of work. By May 1934, owing to Nazi regulations exempting previously covered workers in agriculture, fisheries and forestry, as well as domestic workers, the number of "exempt" workers had increased by 1,384,458, up to an estimated 4,058,582.

The government regarded these new exemptions as "job creation" measures. Relieved of the costly burden of contributions to the unemployment fund, employers of such workers would hire additional personnel. Since agricultural, forestry, fishery and domestic work represent seasonal and casual (irregular, intermittent) employment, a significant portion of these newly exempted persons must have been unemployed at one time or another during 1933 and 1934, and their incentive to report to the placement and unemployment office was now greatly reduced. Thus, as the ranks of the "official" unemployed declined, the number of "invisible" unemployed most likely grew. Estimates of the number of discouraged workers ran as high as 2 million.[19]

The Nazis also changed the classification of those enrolled in various types of government job creation programmes, such as Land Helpers (Landhilfe), Labour Service (Arbeitsdienst), emergency relief workers (Notstandsarbeiter), and public relief workers (Fürsorgearbeiter). Beginning with statistics for 31 July 1933, Land Helpers, emergency relief workers, public relief workers and members of the Labour Service were removed from the "unemployed" category and, with exceptions discussed below, counted as "employed". By the simple stroke of the pen, the Nazis reduced the ranks of the "unemployed" by about 619,000.[20]

Mason (1977, pp. 127-8, 134, 138-9) considered this reclassification of the unemployed as illegitimate "statistical manipulation", a triumph of propaganda designed to give the Nazis credit for an illusory improvement in the labour market.

Mason's scepticism deserves more attention than it has received. During the 1930s, the propriety of National Socialist reclassification schemes was questioned often. So prevalent were such allegations that RfAA president Friedrich Syrup, the trustee of German unemployment statistics, felt compelled to assure key cabinet ministers and their representatives at a meeting on 6 December 1933 (BAK, R43II/537) that, "The amazing decline of the unemployment figures during this year is in no way to be attributed to changes in the statistical methods; rather, it completely corresponds to an actual improvement in the labour market."

The highly respected Institut für Konjunkturforschung (IfK) apparently felt the new scheme for reporting labour market statistics pushed the limits of statistical honesty. Beginning in October 1933, the IfK published, in addition to official *Krankenkassen* employment statistics, its own monthly estimate of German employment. Unlike the government statistics, the IfK's figures provided separate numbers for both "*reguläre*" employment ("real" private sector jobs) and "*zusätzliche*" employment (supplementary or substitute employment of Land Helpers, emergency relief workers, public relief workers, and members of the Labour Service). Table 5.2 provides a comparison of IfK and official employment statistics. In addition to "unofficial" IfK figures, there exist other contemporary official estimates of unemployment and employment which differ significantly from official monthly statistics published in the *Reichsarbeitsblatt*. The German Statistical Office conducted occupational censuses in 1907, 1925, and the middle of June 1933. The 1933 census listed 5,900,000 persons as unemployed, and 14,239,000 as actually working. The occupational census, then, indicated about 800,000 more unemployed than the official RfAA statistics for May/June, and between 900,000 and 1,000,000 more employed than official health insurance statistics.[21]

The precise impact of changes in classification regulations is difficult to establish. There seems to be no rigorous correlation between the number of persons affected by reclassification schemes and monthly changes in employment and unemployment figures. Between the end of June and the end of July 1933, through reclassification, 619,000 persons had been stricken from the list of the unemployed and *presumably* added to the number of "employed". This administrative change was in no obvious way reflected in the labour market statistics set forth in Table 5.3. During the month 30 June-31 July 1933, according to official government figures, unemployment registered a decline of 393,101 while total employment increased by 128,685. One could interpret the June/July decline in unemployment as unusually large, but the June/July increase in total

Table 5.2   Official and IfK Estimates of Employment, 1933-34 (1,000s)

	Official (1)	IfK "substitute" (2)	"Corrected" (1) minus (2) (3)	IfK "regular" (4)	Discrepancy (4) minus (3) (5)
1933					
October	14,062	750	13,312	13,590	278
November	14,020	840	13,180	13,470	290
December	13,287	710	12,577	12,860	283
1934					
January	13,518	830	12,978	12,970	-008
February	13,976	920	13,056	13,330	274
March	14,687	1,050	13,637	13,920	283
April	15,322	1,050	14,242	14,570	328
May	15,560	930	14,630	14,910	280
June	15,530	800	14,730	15,010	280
July	15,533	730	14,803	15,090	287
August	15,559	700	14,859	15,150	291
September	15,621	640	14,981	15,260	279
October	15,636	600	15,036	15,300	264
November	15,476	630	14,846	15,140	294
December	14,873	610	14,263	14,540	277

Sources: Beilage zum Wochenbericht des Instituts für Konjunkturforschung, 30 January, 30 April 1935; *Statistische Beilage zum Reichsarbeitsblatt*, 1934, 1935. Official *Krankenkassen* statistics and IfK estimates include workers and salaried employees (*Arbeiter* and *Angestellten*).

employment was virtually unchanged from the May/June figure. The strikingly sharp break in labour market statistics occurred not so much with the June/July reclassification scheme, but with the February/March development almost immediately after Hitler assumed the chancellorship. This would suggest that labour minister Seldte was correct in attributing a significant portion of the early improvement in the labour market after 30 January 1933 to normal seasonal fluctuations, assisted by particularly favourable weather conditions. By May/June, the "recovery" seemed to be losing momentum. While the reclassification plan may have provided the basis for another significant decline in unemployment, it had no immediately discernible effect on the trend in employment as depicted in Table 5.4.

If one accepts Mason's claim that Land Helpers, emergency relief workers, public relief workers, and members of the Labour Service suddenly "vanished" from the official unemployment statistics on 31 July 1933, one must then indicate where, statistically, these 619,000 people went.

Table 5.3   Development of the German Labour Market, 1933-35

	Unemp'd	Emp'd	Unemp't (%)
1933			
January	6,013,612	11,487,211	34%
February	6,000,958	11,532,788	
March	5,598,855	12,192,696	
April	5,331,252	12,697,620	
May	5,038,640	13,179,941	
June	4,856,942	13,306,896	
July	4,463,841	13,435,581	
August	4,124,288	13,715,795	
September	3,849,222	13,920,977	
October	3,744,860	14,062,337	
November	3,714,646	14,020,204	
December	4,059,055	13,287,238	
1934			
January	3,772,792	13,517,998	22%
February	3,372,611	13,967,253	
March	2,798,324	14,686,865	
April	2,608,621	15,322,237	
May	2,528,960	15,560,487	
June	2,480,826	15,529,683	
July	2,426,014	15,532,793	13.5%
August	2,397,562	15,558,981	
September	2,281,800	15,621,095	
October	2,267,657	15,636,436	12.5%
November	2,352,662	15,476,144	
December	2,604,700	14,873,276	
1935			
January	2,974,000	14,409,075	20%
July	1,754,000	16,640,000	9%

Sources: Reichsarbeitsblatt; Institut für Konjunkturforschung, *Wochenbericht.*
Unemployment percentages calculated by author.

The *presumption* that they were all added to the statistics on "employed"
members of the labour force cannot be sustained. To begin with, the
262,992 enrolled in the Labour Service on 31 July were no longer counted
as "unemployed", but neither were they counted as "employed", even
though, until 30 April 1935, they were counted as insured by the national
workers' health insurance service (Hemmer, 1935, pp. 43, 55-6). Members of the Labour Service were in effect deleted from the German labour
force. Adding these 262,992 Labour Service workers to the June/July recorded increase in "employed" (+128,165) produces a total increase of

Table 5.4   Development of Unemployment and Employment, 1933

End month to end month	Unemployment	Employment
January - February	-12,654	+45,577
February - March	-402,103	+659,908
March - April	-267,603	+504,924
April - May	-292,612	+482,321
May - June	-181,698	+126,955
June - July	-393,101	+128,685
July - August	-339,553	+280,212
August - September	-275,066	+205,182
September - October	-104,362	+141,360
October - November	-30,214	- 42,133
November - December	+344,409	-732,966

Sources: Unemployment calculated from *Statistische Beilage zum Reichsarbeits-blatt*, 1934, no. 7, p. 18; employment calculated from "Siebenter Bericht der RfAA" (1934-35), issued as *Beilage zum Reichsarbeitsblatt*, 1935, no. 35, p. 15.

+391,677, almost precisely the equivalent of the -393,101 decrease in unemployment for that month. While many will find this precise balance aesthetically pleasing, it is most likely completely fortuitous.

Understanding of German labour market statistics for the Nazi era may be enhanced by referring to recent work done by economists on statistics for the United States during the 1930s. Michael R. Darby (1976) has attempted to "correct" American employment and unemployment statistics by adding federal emergency relief workers to the standard BLS/Lebergott employment series for 1929-43 and subtracting emergency relief workers from the standard BLS/Lebergott unemployment series. Darby believes (as did Germany's National Socialist government) such emergency relief workers should have been counted as "employed" rather than "unemployed". In his treatment of interwar unemployment in the United States in chapter 9 of this volume, Robert Margo indicates that for many American emergency relief workers, such "substitute" employment was long-term and stable, if poorly paying. Considering the stability and duration of many emergency relief jobs, Margo argues, it may be appropriate to count some fraction of long-term relief workers among the employed. Aside from questions about the theoretical appropriateness of counting emergency relief workers as employed, it is not at all clear that the "true" count can be established merely by subtracting such persons from one column and adding them to the other. What happens when one applies Darby's technique to German labour market statistics? Assuming it is *not* legitimate to count employees of "federal contracyclical pro-

Table 5.5   Quasi-unemployed, or "Substitute" Employed (end of month, 1,000s)

	Notstands-arbeiter	Fürsorge-arbeiter	Landhelfer	Arbeitsdienst	Total
1933					
January	23	59		175	257
February	37	59		193	289
March	88	64		213	365
April	114	67	16	235	432
May	121	69	77	242	509
June	115	70	123	252	560
July	140	71	150	263	624
August	187	70	160	257	674
September	232	66	165	234	697
October	314	59	164	220	757
November	401	56	163	227	847
December	277	50	160	232	719
1934					
January	471	45	156	225	843
February	507	43	157	241	948
March	631	43	161	240	1075
April	602	46	163	230	1041
May	502	48	153	228	931
June	387	53	140	229	809
July	315	56	129	229	729
August	292	56	117	226	691
September	330	55	104	225	714
October	331	55	91	212	689
November	353	52	76	234	715
December	354	53	66	233	706

Source: Hemmer (1935), p. 189.

grammes" as "employed", one would presumably *reverse* Darby's procedure and *add* 619,000 to the official 31 July 1933 unemployment figure and subtract 356,008 (262,992 Labour Service volunteers have already been "deducted" from the total 619,000) from the official employment total. This procedure would produce the unlikely result that unemployment during July had increased back to the level of 31 May and that employment had decreased back to the level of early May.[22]

There are theoretical as well as practical objections to counting workers on federal emergency relief projects as "employed". Jonathan R. Kesselman and N. E. Savin (1978, pp. 206-7) have pointed out that Darby's "corrected" unemployment series rests on several dubious implied hypotheses. Darby (1976) claims that the "corrected" data revealed the American economy's "true" speed of adjustment from high unemployment rates to the "natural rate". A similar claim would presumably be made for "corrected" German unemployment statistics; "otherwise", as Kesselman and Savin observe with reference to Darby's work, "the corrected figures merely reclassify relief workers from the unemployed to the employed category", and have no theoretical significance.

Kesselman and Savin (1978, pp. 206-7) are not merely arguing that emergency relief workers really were "unemployed"; they are also contesting Darby's inferred hypothesis that the "corrected" data measure how many persons would have been unemployed in the absence of the work creation programmes. (Mason appears to make the same inference for corrected German labour market statistics.) The case for reclassification of emergency relief workers as "employed" (presumably in either Germany or the United States), they argue, requires support from three underlying hypotheses: (1) that the natural rate hypothesis be appropriate for the high unemployment setting of the 1930s; (2) that the natural unemployment rate for the 1930s be close to that of other decades; and (3) that work relief jobs displaced private sector and regular public jobs one-for-one, or, putting it another way, that an equivalent number of private sector or regular public sector jobs would have arisen in the absence of work relief programmes. Without this latter behaviour, the government could have reduced the "unemployment" rate to any desired level simply by expanding work creation programmes. In that case, the "corrected" data would not convey an accurate picture of the economy's *natural* convergence to full employment.

Kesselman and Savin found no theoretical or empirical support for either the natural rate hypothesis or the 100 per cent displacement hypothesis for the US during the 1930s. There was thus no theoretical justification for counting American emergency relief workers as "employed". These hypotheses seem equally inappropriate for German unemployment during the 1930s. Friedrich Baerwald (1934, pp. 618 n.1, 629-30), basically sympathetic towards National Socialist unemployment policy, conceded that "all retrospective and average-figure conceptions of normality have lost their soundness in consequence of certain historical changes". He doubted that Germany would ever return to prosperity in the sense of prewar times or even in the sense of the "illusory" recovery of the 1920s. Nor was he certain that Germany's progress in the struggle against unemployment through work creation programmes could be held and translated into additional private sector jobs. But in the event of an "eventual relapse in the regular business situation", the German government always disposed of "the possibility of expanding again public works when the first signs of decline in business become evident". Surely, it is precisely this type of action to which Kesselman and Savin (1978, p. 207) referred when they observed that without the assumption of a 100 per cent displacement rate "the government could have reduced the unemployment rate . . . to any desired level by expanding work relief programmes". Under such circumstances, the "unemployment rate" becomes meaningless.

In view of theoretically questionable changes in labour market statistics made by the National Socialists, and the confusion resulting from those changes, exacerbated by the RfAA purge of 1933-34 and the influx of untrained personnel, it seems reasonable to suggest that German employment and unemployment statistics after 30 January 1933 should be treated with scepticism. The magnitude of the National Socialist "economic miracle" during the 1933-35 period, before rearmament exerted a significant force in the labour market, needs to be reassessed. How this reassessment is to be achieved is not entirely clear. Ultimately, one might hope that a model of the German economy during the 1930s could serve as a framework for the construction of a credible labour market series. Such a model, however, is not in sight.

NOTES

1 Harold James (1986, pp. 382-3) has argued that although German armament expenditure in the years 1933-36 was "relatively small compared with later sums", it represented more than twice the amount spent on work creation and "represents a major stimulus given to the economy". James arrives at this conclusion by including the 1935-36 armaments expenditures which, at RM 5.487 billion, equals the entire expenditure from 1932-33 to 1934-35 (end of March). The period of German economic recovery which needs to be explained, however, runs from the end of 1932 to the middle of 1935.

2 See for example remarks by Dr Gustav Krupp von Bohlen-Halbach and Dr Kurt Schmitt (the general director of the insurance giant Allianz-Konzern, who served as economics minister from 29 June 1933 to 30 January 1935), in BAK, R43II/536, "Besprechung mit Industriellen über Arbeitsbeschaffung", 29 May 1933. Schmitt expressed this position nicely with the statement, "We have today, thank God, a state in which one need not worry that in six weeks some other policy will be pursued." Shortly after his appointment as economics minister, Schmitt reiterated his belief that the first priority was to create as quickly as possible conditions permitting belief in the "certainty of economic calculations", certainty that the law would not suddenly change. See BAK, R43II/308, Wolff's Telegraphisches Büro account of Kurt Schmitt's speech on 13 July 1933 to "an invited circle of leading personalities from the economy".

3 BAK, R43II/536, "Besprechung mit Industriellen über Arbeitsbeschaffung", 29 May 1933. Fritz Thyssen expressed shock that an industrialist like Bosch could harbour ideas that clearly led to communism, and in fact represented the basis of

the Marxist programme. Bosch responded that, "I believe that all who know me understand that I have no communist tendencies." This exchange illustrates how difficult it was to hold rational discussions of programmes for economic revival in the context of Germany's political climate.

4 For the 1 June 1933 *Gesetz zur Verminderung der Arbeitslosigkeit,* see *Reichsgesetzblatt,* 1933 I, pp. 323- 9.

5 Telegrams in BAK, R43II/536, 534. If such claims found their way into statistics on unemployment collected and reported by local and district offices of the *Reichanstalt für Arbeitsvermittlung und Arbeitslosenversicherung,* there are clear grounds for concern about the validity of Nazi labour market statistics. See below for further discussion of this question.

6 BAK, R43II/537. For the *Zweites Gesetz zur Verminderung der Arbeitslosigkeit* of 21 September 1933, see *Reichsgesetzblatt,* 1933 I, p. 651.

7 BAK, R43II/321. The following several paragraphs present comments made by Schwerin von Krosigk, Fritz Thyssen, Carl Bosch, Friedrich Reinhardt, and Hjalmar Schacht, at the meeting on 20 September 1933 of the *Generalrat der Wirtschaft.*

8 BAK, R43II/537, 6 December 1933, "Chefsbesprechung im Reichsarbeitsministerium", on the subject of combatting unemployment in 1934. Present were the ministers for finance and transportation, and representatives from the ministries for economics, food and agriculture, and labour. Wilhelm Keppler represented Hitler. Reich labour minister Seldte accepted this decision to promote no new work creation initiatives in 1934 most reluctantly. One month later, he told finance minister Schwerin von Krosigk and economics minister Schmitt that although they had reached an understanding that no extraordinary support for construction was to be provided in the new budget year, housing construction was nevertheless a critical component in the government's programme to "heal" the labour market. Government support was particularly essential since no improvement in industrial construction was in sight. Seldte then proposed what he termed a RM 540 million "minimum programme" for various types of construction during the fiscal year 1934. Nothing came of the proposal. See BAK, R53/14, Reich labour minister Seldte to Reich finance and economics ministers, 4 January 1934.

9 Stelzner (1976), pp. 101-2; Syrup (1936), pp. 124-7; Hemmer (1935), pp. 86-7. In 1932, women comprised 28 per cent of the workers and 38 per cent of the salaried employees in firms employing more than five persons; in 1934, the respective figures had fallen to 24 per cent and 36 per cent. Only a portion of this decline can be attributed to marriage loans. Similarly, 121,780 more marriages were recorded in 1933 than in 1932, and in 1934 the number of marriages rose by another 101,592. A large portion of this increase in marriages must have resulted from the improvement in economic conditions. During the last few months of 1933, more than half of all marriages were supported by marriage loans. During the following years, this fraction fell to 30 per cent (1934), 24 per cent (1935), and 28 per cent (1936).

10 For the *Gesetz zur Regelung des Arbeitseinsatzes*, see *Reichsgesetzblatt* 1933 I, p. 381. For Syrup's orders issued under that law, see Syrup (1934).

11 BAK, R43II/758, Reich finance minister to Hitler, 16 February 1934. The budget for the fiscal year 1934 was the last one to be published by the Nazis. See BAK, R43II/758, Reich finance minister to highest Reich authorities, 20 April 1934. Beginning in 1934, the government resorted to financing rearmament through the issue of paper known as "Mefo-bills".

12 Wages of emergency relief workers fell far below the Depression-level earnings prevailing in regular industrial employment. Mason (1975, p. 125) calculates the average wage for a six-day week in sixteen industries in September 1933 at RM 30.27, compared to RM 18 (RM 15 after 1 March 1934) for an emergency relief worker. See also De Witt (1978, pp. 260-66).

13 The most recent argument that Germany's economic recovery resulted from "a dramatic revival in economic activity" rather than from "statistical manipulation", a "statistical conjuring trick", or "jiggery-pokery with numbers" is found in James (1986, p. 371). An exception to the general rule is Mason (1977). While Mason argues that the miraculous recovery of the labour market under Hitler was more appearance than reality, his own treatment of Nazi labour market statistics fails to resolve the problem. Mason's position is discussed below.

14 For a more complete treatment of the nazification of the RfAA, see the author's "Nazification of the German Bureaucracy Reconsidered: A Case Study", *The Journal of Modern History*, September 1988.

15 "Sechster Bericht der Reichsanstalt für Arbeitsvermittlung und Arbeitslosenversicherung für die Zeit vom 1. April 1933 bis zum 31. März 1934" issued as *Beilage zum Reichsarbeitsblatt* (Berlin, 1935, no. 4), p. 39; Weigert (1934), pp. 151-3. For discussion of ongoing attempts to obtain preferential treatment for members of the NSDAP in hiring and promotion, see Silverman, "Nazification of the German Bureaucracy".

16 For the 1 June *Gesetz zur Verminderung der Arbeitslosigkeit* see *Reichsgezetzblatt* 1933, I, p. 323. "Simplified" statistical procedures effective from 1 October 1933 are found in BAK, R163/73, "Statistiken der Arbeitslosenversicherung und der Krisenfürsorge; hier: Neuregelung ab 1 Oktober 1933". These regulations were published in the *Reichs-Arbeitsmarkt-Anzeiger, Beilage*, no. 19, 10 October 1933.

17 Prior to 31 July 1933, emergency relief workers had been counted as "unemployed" if they reported to an RfAA office seeking regular work. Changes in the classification system are discussed below.

18 BAK, R163/53. Given the complexity of the regulations, now being applied in many instances by untrained personnel employed by the RfAA during the purge era, fastidious record keeping should have been a minimal requirement. Yet not until 1 July 1936 did the president of the RfAA order daily statistical entries for the increase in primary support recipients under unemployment insurance and

emergency relief recipients, so as to make possible end-of-month verification of the numbers.

19 For a systematic examination of "invisible unemployment" in Germany during the 1930s, see Hemmer (1935).

20 On 31 July 1933, there were 140,126 emergency relief workers, 144,981 Land Helpers, 262,992 enrolled in the Labour Service, and 71,000 public relief workers, making a total of 619,099 affected by classification changes. When Hitler came to power on 30 January 1933, these groups had numbered approximately 258,321. For statistics, see IfK *Wochenbericht* (Beilage, 25 April, 1934); Hemmer (1935, p. 189).

21 Weigert (1934, pp. 8-9) attributed the discrepancy in unemployment statistics to the unemployment of persons not registered with Reich employment offices ("invisible unemployment"), and "the fact that [in the census] presumably many sick persons incorrectly described themselves as unemployed". The difference in employment statistics, he believed, "reflects the number of persons actually at work who for some reason were not reported to the health insurance authorities." Such persons may have been engaged in either "petty employment" (casual employment) or "concealed employment" (*Schwarzarbeit*).

22 In making any "correction", one must keep in mind an average of 265,000 workers per month who appear in IfK estimates of employment but are not accounted for in official health insurance employment statistics. For "corrections" beginning on or after 31 July 1933, one must add to official statistics on the "employed" the appropriate number from the Labour Service. Monthly discrepancies that need to be accounted for in this manner are given in Table 5.2, column 5. It should also be noted that, beginning on 30 September 1934, emergency relief workers employed on Reich autobahn and waterway projects were no longer counted as either *Notstandsarbeiter* nor as "looking for work". Though they no longer counted as "substitute" employed, they continued to appear in the official *Krankenkassen* employment statistics, which made no distinction between regular and substitute employment. On 30 September 1934, autobahn construction employed 64,250 workers. See Lärmer (1975, p. 54).

REFERENCES

Baerwald, Friedrich (1934), "How Germany Reduced Unemployment", *American Economic Review* 24, pp. 617-30.

Bry, Gerhard (1960), *Wages in Germany, 1871-1945*, Princeton: Princeton University Press.

Bundesarchiv Koblenz (BAK, followed by file number).

Darby, Michael R. (1976), "Three-and-a-half Million US Employees Have Been Mislaid: Or, an Explanation of Unemployment, 1934-1941", *Journal of Political Economy* 84, pp. 1-16.

De Witt, Thomas E.J. (1978), "The Economics and Politics of Welfare in the Third Reich", *Central European History* 11, pp. 256-78.

Erbe, René (1958), *Die nationalsozialistische Wirtschaftspolitik 1933-1939 im Lichte der modernen Theorie*, Zurich: Polygraphischer Verlag.

Fischer, Wolfram (1961), *Die Wirtschaftspolitik des Nationalsozialismus*, Hanover: Gustav Peters.

Geyer, Michael (1981), "Zum Einfluss der nationalsozialistischen Rüstungspolitik auf der Ruhrgebiet", *Rheinische Vierteljahrsblätter* 45, pp. 201-264.

Guillebaud, C. W. (1939), *The Economic Recovery of Germany from 1933 to the Incorporation of Austria in March 1938*, London: Macmillan.

Hemmer, Willi (1935), *Die "unsichtbaren" Arbeitslosen: Statistische Methoden - Soziale Tatsachen*, Zeulenroda: Bernhard Sporn.

Hoffmann, Walther G. (1965), *Das Wachstum der Deutschen Wirtschaft seit der Mitte des 19. Jahrhunderts*, Berlin: Springer-Verlag.

Institut für Konjunkturforschung (1933-35), *Wochenbericht*, Berlin.

James, Harold (1986), *The German Slump: Politics and Economics 1924-1936*, Oxford: Oxford University Press.

Kesselman, Jonathan R. and Savin, N. E. (1978), "Three-and-a-half Million Workers Never Were Lost", *Economic Inquiry* 16, pp. 205-25.

Kroll, Gerhard (1958), *Von der Weltwirtschaftskrise zur Staatskonjunktur*, Berlin: Duncker & Humblot.

Lärmer, Karl (1975), *Autobahnbau in Deutschland 1933 bis 1945: zu den Hintergründen*, East Berlin: Akademie Verlag.

Marcon, Helmut (1974), *Arbeitsbeschaffungspolitik der Regierung Papen und Schleicher: Grundsteinlegung für die Beschäftigungspolitik im Dritten Reich*, Bern, Frankfurt-am-Main: Lang.

Mason, Timothy W. (1975), *Arbeiterklasse und Volksgemeinschaft: Dokumente und Materialien zur deutschen Arbeiterpolitik 1936-1939*, Opladen: Westdeutscher Verlag.

Mason, Timothy W. (1977), *Sozialpolitik im Dritten Reich*, Opladen: Westdeutscher Verlag.

Overy, R. J. (1982), *The Nazi Economic Recovery 1932-1938*, London: Macmillan.

Reichsarbeitsblatt (1933-35), Berlin (official government publication).

Reichsgesetzblatt (1933-35), Berlin (official government publication).

Reichs- und Preussisches Arbeitsministerium, "Sechster Bericht der Reichsanstalt für Arbeitsvermittlung und Arbeitslosenversicherung für die Zeit vom 1. April 1933 bis zum 31. März 1934", *Beilage zum Reichsarbeitsblatt* 1935, 4, Berlin: Reichsdruckerei.

Stelzner, Jürgen (1976), *Arbeitsbeschaffung und Wiederaufrüstung 1933-1936: Nationalsozialistische Beschäftigungspolitik und Aufbau der Wehr- und Rüstungswirtschaft*, Tübingen: Eberhard-Karls-Universität.

Stuebel, Heinrich (1951), "Die Finanzierung der Aufrüstung im Dritten Reich", *Europa-Archiv* 6, pp. 4128-36.

Syrup, Friedrich (1934), *Gesetz zur Regelung des Arbeitseinsatzes und die dazu ergangenen Anordnungen*, Berlin: Otto Elsner Verlagsgesellschaft.

Syrup, Friedrich (1936), *Der Arbeitseinsatz und die Arbeitslosenhilfe in Deutschland*, Berlin: Otto Elsner Verlagsgesellschaft.

Syrup, Friedrich (1957), *Hundert Jahre Staatliche Sozialpolitik 1839-1939*, ed. Otto Neuloh, Stuttgart: Verlag W. Kohlhammer.

Weigert, Oscar (1934), *Administration of Placement and Unemployment Insurance in Germany*, New York: Industrial Relations Counselors.

Wolffsohn, Michael (1977), *Industrie und Handwerke im Konflikt mit Staatlicher Wirtschaft? Studien zur Politik der Arbeitsbeschaffung in Deutschland 1930-1934*, Berlin: Duncker & Humblot.

Chapter 6

Unemployment in the 1930s: The Case of Italy

Gianni Toniolo and Francesco Piva*

1 The Great Depression and Unemployment: An Unexplored Territory

The historiography of the Great Depression is still an infant industry in Italy. The number of books and papers explicitly dealing with it is probably within the single figure range. The reasons for this poverty of research, in an area that in the past decade has become important and fashionable in most other countries, are deeply rooted in the historical culture that sprang from the Resistance and the Reconstruction. For three decades after the end of the Second World War historical research centred on explaining the origins of Fascism, the reasons for its long survival and the causes of its eventual failure. These problems were either studied in broad terms such as the "nature" of Fascism and its "continuity" or "discontinuity" with the previous history of Italian capitalism, or were investigated within the long-standing methodological tradition of local history. Only in the 1970s did the political and, to a lesser extent, the economic life of the country during the 1920s and the 1930s begin to attract standard historical research. This was partly a result of the debate originated by De Felice's monumental and controversial biography of Mussolini. However, the macroeconomics of the Great Depression is still a largely unexplored area, within which the field of employment, unemployment and labour policies has remained almost untouched.

Some work has recently been done on money and banking during the 1930s, but the real sector of the economy remains particularly neglected. The available indices of production in manufacturing (OEEC, 1960 and Fuà, 1969) offer rather different pictures of the severity of the Depression. Between 1929 and 1932, the OEEC's index declines by 24 per cent and Fuà's by only 14 per cent. There is more general agreement about the

B. Eichengreen and T. J. Hatton (eds.), Interwar Unemployment in International Perspective, 221–245.
© 1988 by Kluwer Academic Publishers.

tining of the recovery: most available indicators point to the fact that the level of activity remained low until the early months of 1935 when the government began a programme of substantial deficit spending in preparation for the war in Abyssinia.

For reasons that will be discussed below, employment and unemployment statistics are scarce and have so far received little attention. The lack of detailed inquiries like those made, for instance, in the London area (Eichengreen, 1986) makes qualitative analyses of unemployment in Italy more complex than for other countries. At the same time, the virtual neglect of quantitative aggregate analysis so far makes it appropriate to focus on that side of the problem. This chapter therefore contains a preliminary examination of some quantitative issues in the study of unemployment in Italy during the 1930s.

Section 2 will provide a brief background to the nature of Italian labour markets during the interwar years. Section 3 attempts to measure unemployment in the industrial sector. Section 4 summarises the main features of Fascist labour policies of which section 5 provides a broad quantitative appraisal. Section 6 deals briefly with the issue of wages and unemployment and is followed by some concluding remarks.

2   Italy's Labour Market Between the Wars

The composition and size of Italy's workforce are summarised in Table 6.1. The immediately striking feature is the very large share of the labour force, and its slow decline, in agriculture (59 per cent of the total in 1921 and 52 per cent fifteen years later). The industrial and the so-called tertiary sectors each absorbed about a quarter of the total workforce. Participation rates, while falling, remained extremely high throughout the period. These are the unmistakable signs of the backwardness of a country which by 1935 was playing the imperial powers' game.

Since the pioneering work of Arthur Lewis, the labour market of a backward agrarian country has often been described as one in which the "modern" industrial sector may enjoy the advantages of an unlimited supply of labour coming from a "traditional" agriculture where its marginal productivity is close to zero. This is one of the main features of a "dualistic" economy (Fei and Ranis, 1964), as Italy was described by a generation of economists after the Second World War. Sen (1966) has shown, however, that "the assumption of surplus labour does not conflict with an equilibrium as a positive marginal product of labour, labour being measured in terms of hours of work, rather than in terms of number of persons", in a production function with any degree of substitutability between labour time and other factors.

Table 6.1   Italy's Workforce, 1921-36 (1,000s)

Sector	1921 males	1921 females	1931 males	1931 females	1936 males	1936 females
Agriculture	7,007	4,236	6,527	3,922	6,498	4,004
Industry	3,125	1,160	3,744	1,197	3,854	1,312
Services	2,197	828	2,406	1,006	2,510	1,340
Public Admin.	343	129	487	138	528	161
Total	12,627	6,353	13,164	6,263	13,390	6,817
Participation rate (M+F)	.77		.74		.77	
Annual growth rate (%)			.20		.79	

Note: Participation rate over total population aged 15-65.
Source: Vitali (1970).

Any aggregate approach to Italy's agricultural labour market during the 1920s and 1930s will be dismissed by most historians as unacceptably oversimplified. The variety of agricultural systems was certainly enormous: there are few areas of comparable size where soil conditions, irrigation and climate vary as they do in the Italian peninsula. From the Alps to Sicily, one finds mountain grazing, hills and lakes, the well irrigated and highly developed Po valley, the rough Apennines, the vines and olive trees of Tuscany and Umbria, the intensive vegetable farming of southern Lazio and Campania, the poor pastures of Abruzzo, the rich Tavoliere, and the wheat and citrus fruits of Sicily. And, not long before the period we are discussing here, the quite small but highly diversified area of the kingdom was divided into several independent states each with its own traditions and legislation. It is hardly surprising that labour contracts, which adapted over the centuries both to resource endowments and to institutional arrangements, still varied a great deal during the interwar years even within the space of a few miles. In spite of this, however, one may safely say that labour markets in agriculture were characterised by widespread underemployment.

Measures of labour force underutilisation in agriculture are of course difficult to produce: in the present state of research one has to accept rough quantifications. According to O'Brien and Toniolo (1986), around 1911, Italy's agricultural output could have been produced with 5.7 million fully employed workers instead of the 9.8 million actually employed, without any change in the production function. During the First World War, some 2.6 million male agricultural workers were drafted and therefore entirely lost to productive work without reducing the sector's output. Wartime conditions make it impossible to explain this by the introduction of more capital-intensive techniques; on the contrary there is evidence that the quantity of fertilisers used decreased considerably. It was simply that those who remained on the land worked more days per year, probably without reaching full employment themselves.

Aggregate evidence aside, underemployment in agriculture is documented in a number of inquiries, promoted both by Parliament and private scholars. Shortly before the First World War (*Atti dell' inchiesta,* 1911-13), only a limited number of male *braccianti* (day labourers) in the richest areas of the south were hired for more than 200 days per year. The average for adult females was around 125 to 150 days. In the same period, Serpieri (1910), computing the number of days necessary to farm given plots of land in fertile Lombardy, concluded that most farmers must have been idle for perhaps a third of their time.

The study of a sample of farmers' families undertaken by an official agency in the early 1930s (INEA, 1931-38) shows not only the low consumption patterns of most of them but also that their labour force was, on average, far from fully employed: the persistence of the "extended family" helped to redistribute income among the members so that each of them could receive at least the equivalent of a subsistence wage, irrespective of the total amount of work performed over the year.

Soon after the Second World War, the Italian Parliament undertook an extensive official inquiry into unemployment (Commissione Parlamentare d'inchiesta sulla disoccupazione, 1953-54): the results do not differ very much from those of the previous survey of 1911. Similarly, for the region of Bologna, Medici and Orlando (1952) assumed 230 and 120 days per year for male and female workers respectively as a policy target for full employment of *braccianti;* their inquiry had shown that the average employment was actually much below those figures.

In the simplest versions of Lewis-type models, underemployed agricultural labour tends to migrate to the city whenever the "modern" industrial sector is expanding. Such a process, and its reverse during the Depression, characterises Italy's labour market between the wars in spite of, as we shall see, policies aimed at discouraging workers from leaving the countryside. However, the transfer of labour from low to higher productivity jobs was not a one-stage process. The typical unskilled rural migrant could rarely find a permanent job in the technically advanced manufacturing sectors. The first step, therefore, was a move to factories requiring unskilled work, located within commuting distance (often by bicycle) from the worker's country home. This first move, thus, did not require a change of residence. Furthermore, unlike in many developing countries today, this first step out of agriculture was fully or partly reversible. Partial reversibility derived from the fact that this type of fac-

Table 6.2 **Average Time Spent by Each Worker in Four Large Manufacturing Firms During the Interwar Years (% of the workforce)**

Time	Alfa Romeo	Montecatini	Ilva	Breda
less than 1 month	16.1	35.0	6.5	7.1
1 month to 1 year	40.3	48.1	31.2	39.0
1 to 5 years	33.7	9.9	28.1	31.7
over 5 years	9.9	7.0	35.5	22.2

Sources: Bigazzi (1985); Piva and Tattara (1983).

tory work was not, for the individual, a full-time job: the condition of *braccianti* hired for the day in agriculture was reproduced at the factory gates where a number of workers - not always the same people - were engaged for the day or the week either directly or through an official labour exchange office. One of us has studied this process for the industrial area created at the edge of the Venice Lagoon in the 1920s and 1930s (Piva, 1983) and we believe that case not to have been exceptional.

The core of skilled urban industrial workers, who had irreversibly severed their links with agriculture, was relatively small. Its formation on quite a large scale started in the 1880s but gathered momentum only after the beginning of this century and especially during the First World War. It is worth noting, however, that even for this core of the modern industrial working class permanent employment in the same job seems to have been the exception rather than the rule. Recent studies in the field provide evidence, admittedly still very scanty, of a situation characterised by rapid turnover and long spells of unemployment or of employment in low-paid, less skilled jobs. Table 6.2 shows the average time spent by each worker in the same factory during the 1920s and 1930s. The picture is clearly not one of stability and long-term employment.

On the whole, as far as one can tell from the limited quantitative evidence so far available, it seems that the labour markets both in agriculture and in manufacturing were characterised by the fact that few workers were employed during an entire year or over a long span of years. It seems that income redistribution among workers within Italy's surplus labour economy often took the form of rotation in the same job.

This kind of labour market was far from static. Italian workers had a long tradition of migration both within the country and abroad. Employers were therefore traditionally faced with a fairly flexible and elastic supply of labour. In the interwar years transatlantic emigration was almost halted by the US Immigration Acts of 1921 and 1924 and France, the great remaining hope for so many Poles, Spaniards and Italians, could only absorb a limited fraction of the pre-1913 flow to America. Italian cities and industry were, then, the only outlet for most of the underemployed peasants. Fascist governments tried hard to restrain domestic migration for ideological motives as well as for reasons of public order. During the 1920s prefects and police officers were first instructed to use persuasion and then, in 1928, given legal powers to limit the movement of peasants to towns. Further legislation to the same effect was introduced in 1931 and in 1939. However, as often happens in such cases, police intervention to limit migration was largely ineffective. Treves (1976) has convincingly argued that Fascism was unable to check the movement of Italian workers within the country. She has shown that the domestic migration rates (changes of residence per thousand inhabitants per year) after 1926 were the same order of magnitude (twenty-five to thirty-four per thousand) as those reached in the 1950s when no restriction was imposed on domestic migration and the rate of growth of manufacturing was substantially higher.

Fascism did not freeze Italy's labour market. Confronted with a situation where jobs were few relative to the workforce, people responded with "sharing" arrangements on the one hand and with high mobility on the other. In other words, it seems that legal constraints did not play a significant role in the sectoral allocation of labour. The scarcity of other factors - land, capital and technology - was therefore responsible for the backwardness of the country and, ultimately, for the very low living standard of most of the working class.

3   Measuring Industrial Unemployment

Italy's labour statistics for the interwar years are drawn from four main sources. First, population censuses (taken in 1921, 1931 and 1936) provide estimates of the labour force in the various sectors. Vitali (1970) has carried out the painstaking task of making census classifications comparable. We relied on his work whenever possible. It is worth noting that according to Salvemini, the liberal historian who left Italy under Fascism and taught at Harvard, "in the general census taken on April 21, 1931, people were instructed to report whether they were employed or not" but "the results of the census, as far as unemployment is concerned, have remained to this day wrapped in impenetrable mystery" (Salvemini, 1935).

Second, industrial censuses (taken in 1927 and 1937) provide estimates of actual employment at census dates for industry and for some of the service sectors. Chiaventi (1987) has proposed criteria to make industrial classification comparable for those censuses.

The third important source consists of employment surveys, of which one was made by the government (Ministero delle Corporazioni); League of Nations publications rely on this. Another was made by the Confederation of Italian Industrialists: it provides monthly figures of employment for a sample derived from a survey covering between 15 and 20 per cent of the country's industrial firms. We relied on the latter because of its greater consistency with census data. The same source provides other data: those on the number of hours worked are, as we shall see, particularly useful (ISTAT, 1928-37).

Finally there are unemployment statistics. They are of two kinds. The first report the amount of unemployment benefits paid each month (ISTAT, 1930-34). Such data are accurate but grossly underestimate unemployment since in order to be "on the dole" a person had to have been previously continuously employed for at least forty-eight weeks and payment could not last more than ninety days (120 if previous employment was seventy-two weeks). Unemployment statistics of the second kind are drawn from the records of labour exchange offices and provide figures for the number of people registered as unemployed with those offices (ISTAT, 1928-37). However, the number of "discouraged workers" (those who did not bother to register with labour exchange offices) was certainly large, and increased as the worsening Depression lessened the chances of finding employment. This phenomenon, common to most other countries, was more acute in Italy because workers knew that without the card of a Fascist trade union it was virtually impossible to get a job. It must be added that in July 1933, labour exchange offices were instructed to correct their figures downward taking into account the number of workers who, while registering, "should not be counted as unemployed", according to their own "guesstimates" of those who registered with more than one office and of those who had been unlawfully hired bypassing the offices themselves.

This seems to constitute an indirect invitation to "cook" unemployment statistics. Are we to infer that most labour statistics have been manipulated for political reasons? As we have seen, the methods of collection were such that many of the questions of interest to independent contemporary observers and today's historians were not even asked: this is the major shortcoming of Fascist labour statistics. As for those actually published, both on employment and unemployment, we have to remember that the collection of data was entrusted to a number of fairly independent local bodies, both private and public (Lenti, 1934) who were not likely to have introduced systematic biases into their figures. As for the Central Statistical Office (ISTAT), it would have been difficult for it to manipulate disaggregate figures coming from these bodies without exposing itself to criticism in the scholarly publications which the regime did not bother to or did not want to control. At the time of the Abyssinian war and of the sanctions imposed by the League of Nations, when an outright

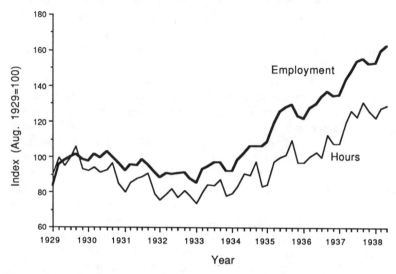

Figure 6.1 **Employment in Industry and Total Number of Hours Worked, 1929-38 (August 1929=100)**

manipulation of information available to foreign observers about the state of the economy was decided upon, the regime simply put an embargo on the publication of employment and unemployment statistics from September 1935 to December 1936.

Before presenting our estimates of unemployment during the 1930s, let us recall some obvious limitations to the analysis deriving from the character of the labour markets outlined in the previous section. The very definition of "unemployed person" is hardly comparable with the standard definitions of today. It is difficult, for instance, to say when a child entered the labour force and when an old person left it. Measuring the female labour force entails other problems of definition well known to those working in the area (e.g. women are included in the labour force when the family works in agriculture and excluded from it when the family migrates to the town). Where underemployment is the rule, its fluctuations over the cycle cannot be measured without *ad hoc* inquiries that were not made at the time (see section 4). Under these conditions, an analysis of unemployment in agriculture seems to be out of the question: it is therefore explicitly excluded from the present essay. Similar considerations seem to apply to some of the service sectors (petty commerce, household service, etc.). Since we were not able to extract these from the

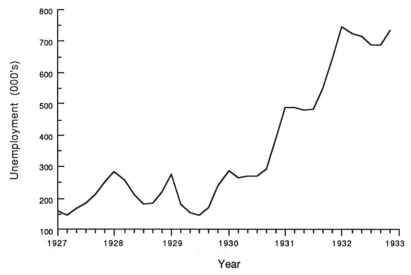

Figure 6.2 **Unemployment, 1927-32 (official statistics)**

aggregate figures (when available), the so-called "tertiary" sector was left out of our analysis as well. We therefore concentrate on industry alone (mining, manufacturing, construction and utilities).

Figure 6.1 shows an index of total employment and of the total number of hours worked by those employed. It is a chain index computed from the monthly surveys mentioned above (ISTAT, 1928-37) and seasonally adjusted. The base (August 1929) is at the pre-Depression cyclical peak. The behaviour of the "employment" and "hours" curves will be discussed in section 5. Here it seems important to draw attention to the fact that at the bottom of the Depression (October 1932) total employment had decreased by only 6.2 per cent from August 1929. Even if the total number of hours worked, a much more precise indicator of the level of activity, had fallen by 23.2 per cent, it appears that Italy entered the international Depression without having overcome its own cyclical downturn induced by the deflationary policies enacted to restore gold convertibility in 1926-27.

Figure 6.2 shows the behaviour of industrial unemployment according to official sources (ISTAT, 1930-34). Data for 1933 and 1934 have not been included for reasons already mentioned.

Our upper- and lower-bound estimates of aggregate unemployment in the industrial sector (Table 6.3) have been estimated as follows. Figures

Table 6.3   Unemployment in the Industrial Sector, 1931-37 (upper- and lower-bound estimates)

	Total industrial labour force (1,000s) (1)	Lower-bound estimates		Upper-bound estimates	
		Total unemp't (1,000s) (2)	Unemp't as % of labour force (3)	Total unemp't (1,000s) (4)	Unemp't as % of labour force (5)
1931	4,594	522	11.4	1,641	35.7
1932	4,616	716	15.5	1,886	40.8
1933	4,637	640	13.8	1,885	40.6
1934	4,659	660	14.2	1,667	35.8
1935	4,681	538 [a]	11.5	1,087	23.2
1936	4,703			825	17.5
1937	4,725			357	7.9

Note: (a) Average for the first 9 months.
Sources: Col. 1: for 1931 and 1936, from Census of Population (see text). Other years: linear interpolation. Col. 2: official unemployment statistics (see text), yearly averages. Col. 4: for 1937, labour force less employment from Industrial Census. For previous years, the 1937 datum is multiplied by our index of total employment (1937 = 1).

for the industrial labour force are available for 1931 and 1936 from population censuses as revised by Vitali (1970). We corrected them slightly downwards to allow for a 95 per cent male participation rate in the 15 to 65 age group. Between these benchmark years, the labour force has been estimated by simple loglinear interpolation. Given the limited number of years involved and the behaviour of the cycle, the procedure seems reliable. However we may have overestimated the industrial labour force for 1932 when it may have shrunk rather than grown. Similarly we have extrapolated forward the 1931-36 rate of growth in order to get the labour force for 1937, the year of the industrial census. Our first estimates of unemployment are simply yearly averages of the official monthly statistics (Figure 6.2). They represent lower-bound estimates since, as already mentioned, all those registered with labour exchange offices were definitely unemployed but it was by no means the case that those who did not register could be defined as employed. It is worth noting that even the lower-bound (official) estimate gives a figure of 15.1 per cent unemployment in the industrial labour force for 1932, a figure that cannot be dismissed as negligible by the international standards of the time. In order to reach an upper-bound estimate we started from the rather reliable figure for employment given by the 1937 industrial census and from our estimate of the industrial labour force. This figure was then extrapolated backward on the basis of our employment index (Figure 6.1). Unemployment data for each year result from labour force less employment figures, and are shown in column 4, Table 6.3. They represent upper-bound estimates since the employment figure from the 1937 industrial census is probably underestimated, because of likely underreporting and less than full coverage.

The figures in Table 6.3 require some comment. The very high unemployment rates for the central years of the Depression appearing in the upper-bound estimates do not mean that 35 to 40 per cent of the industrial workforce was permanently without a job. Given the rapid rotation in jobs briefly described in section 2 and the fact that most workers did not work for all the weeks in a year, that figure can be read to mean that each worker's periods of unemployment were twice as long in 1932 as in 1935-36, at the time of the war-induced industrial "boom". Indirect support for this view comes from the construction industry where unemployment (computed using the same procedure with the aggregate figures) reached 65 per cent of the labour force in 1931 and was still 40 per cent in 1937. Fenoaltea's work for 1911 indicates that census data for this sector are particularly unreliable (Fenoaltea, 1986); however they indicate at least a significantly higher level of unemployment in construction than in manufacturing. Excluding construction, the industrial unemployment rate falls to 35.2 per cent in 1932. The case of construction is telling because the sector typically linked agriculture with industry by providing one of the main sources of employment to those moving for the first time from country to town. The extremely high unemployment in that sector indicates that during the Depression all outlets available to the underemployed peasant were closed and that most construction workers had to go back to the land. On the other hand, it seems reasonable to interpret our lower-bound estimates as representing the "core" of unemployment made up of those workers who registered with labour exchanges and had nothing to do but show up every day to see what the bureaucracy could do for them.

The lower-bound estimates of industrial unemployment in three main regions are shown in Table 6.4, based on the admittedly strong assumption that the ratio of industrial to total unemployment did not vary throughout the period.

A regional analysis of unemployment is beyond the aim of the present preliminary survey of quantitative issues of Italian unemployment between the wars. The unexpected behaviour of the backward southern areas must, therefore, remain unexplained. The nature of our data is such that the relatively low unemployment in the south could be explained simply by poorer organisation of the labour exchange offices. Another possible line of research would focus on the industry mix: sectors

Table 6.4   Unemployment in the Industrial Sector by Region, 1931-36
(lower-bound estimates)

| | Unemployment as percentage of industrial labour force | | |
	North-west	North-east and centre	South
1931	10.9	13.6	9.7
1932	13.0	17.7	13.6
1933	14.4	16.2	9.8
1934	14.2	17.4	12.1
1935	10.3	13.7	10.5

Note: North-west: Piemonte, Valle d'Aosta, Liguria and Lombardia. North-east and centre: Trentino, Veneto, Friuli, Emilia, Marche, Umbria, Toscana and Lazio. South: Campania, Abruzzi, Puglia, Lucania, Calabria, Sicilia and Sardegna. For sources and methods, see text.

enjoying the state's favours (import duties, quotas, subsidies) had a higher relative weight in the south than in the north-eastern and central areas of the country where industrial unemployment seems to have been more severe.

4   Fascism and Unemployment

During the second part of 1929 and the early months of 1930 foreign correspondents for *Il lavoro fascista*, the daily newspaper of the Fascist trade unions, described unemployment in England, Germany and France as the ultimate result of decaying "pluto-democratic" regimes torn to pieces by endless class struggle. But around the summer of 1930 the same newspaper began to discuss - in increasingly alarming tones - the growing unemployment in Italy. Contrary to what happened with the scholarly journals where the characteristics and causes of unemployment were discussed freely (Caffè, 1952), daily newspapers dealt with it in general and ideological terms, describing mass unemployment as the last remnant of the Liberal regime which the Fascist revolution was in the process of liquidating. Cianetti, one of the leading trade unionists, argued that it was precisely mass unemployment that necessitated the end of the free market and the need for a "strong state" that would "represent the interests of the entire population" (Cianetti, 1934). A peculiar feature of this propaganda was the fact that while unemployment as an aggregate phenomenon was acknowledged and discussed, virtually nothing was said of the unemployed worker, of his conditions, his age, his sex, his family, his standard of living. And indeed, in spite of a long-standing Italian tradition of inquiries, no solid statistical survey of those factors was conducted in the 1930s.

According to the official view, the crisis showed that theFascists were right from the beginning. "The way we deal with unemployment", claimed the Fascist trade unions, "indicates that our philosophy is more radical and revolutionary than any socialism or any scientific utopia" (CFLI, 1935a, Unione di Genova). If the old order, or what remained of it after eight years of "revolution", had produced unemployment, the new "corporative economy" (*economia corporativa*) would provide the appropriate remedies.

Fascist labour policies were aimed both at limiting the extent of unemployment and at providing help of some kind to the unemployed. In surveying those to limit unemployment we shall consider only those directly concerned with the labour market: other macroeconomic policies (monetary and fiscal) indirectly connected with the creation of new jobs will not be dealt with here.

Towards the end of the summer of 1931, the government launched a campaign of public works aimed at creating additional jobs during the winter months which were characterised by a seasonal fall in employment, particularly among agricultural *braccianti*. The rationale behind this policy was clearly stated by the daily paper of the Fascist trade unions: a worker living on subsidies "not only loses his interest in and love for work but acquires the evil psychology of the idle and even of the beggar, who assumes that charity is his own right and the duty of others" (*Il lavoro fascista*, 27 August 1931). English policies of unemployment subsidies not connected with previous work and contributions were singled out as a particularly bad example. The ideological background to the Fascist public works policy is not therefore rooted in the views relating unemployment to lack of aggregate demand that were beginning to emerge in England and Sweden and were soon to be reflected in Hitler's recovery programmes. In that respect, Fascist ideology seems to reflect traditional nineteenth-century theories which saw public work as emergency help aimed both at boosting the morale of the needy and at exposing the false poor (Garraty, 1978). It must be added that Mussolini himself imposed the policy of public works against the will and the advice of influential business and party men such as Turati, the party secretary, who favoured direct subsidies to agriculture and industry. The *Duce* preferred to have something tangible to show in response to growing unemployment and to project an image of Italy abroad as a "resounding workshop" (De Felice, 1974). It is difficult to argue that the password "bread and work" marked a radical change from policies enacted by previous Liberal governments during the most critical phases of economic depressions such as the one following the end of the First World War, which saw the creation, in November 1919, of a Public Works Committee precisely in order to fight unemployment.

A second important aspect of direct intervention in the labour market consisted in enacting cuts in nominal wages by decree. Certainly such cuts were motivated by broad macroeconomic considerations as well as by the aim of sustaining employment. The first round of cuts in nominal wages took place, in fact, as part of the policies aimed at stabilising prices and exchange rates after the rapid inflation-devaluation of the spring and summer of 1926 and just before the introduction of the gold exchange standard in December 1927. In these circumstances, the lira appreciated by 30 per cent against the pound in less than a year; in order to restore purchasing power parity, fiscal and monetary policies were supplemented by direct intervention aimed at curbing both prices and wages. Propaganda as well as "stick and castor oil" was used in a large party mobilisation to reach this goal. From a strictly macroeconomic point of view and to the amazement of foreign observers, the policy was remarkably successful (Toniolo, 1980).

In 1930 employers began to argue that the fall in world prices required new cuts in nominal wages; the need to sacrifice purchasing power to maintain employment levels was given as the main reason for their request. Trade unions did not remain silent. In the first place they argued against wage cuts in terms that today would be called aggregate demand arguments; later on, as we shall see, they maintained that actual cuts were much larger than the ones agreed upon thus making living standards of the working class very miserable. In spite of this rather open opposition, the government ordered an initial 12 per cent decrease in wages and salaries for public sector employees (20 November 1930). A few days later (28 November) the so-called Benni-Klinger agreement stipulated similar cuts (from 8 to 10 per cent) for the entire industrial sector. In April 1934, Pirelli and Cianetti signed another agreement for a further 7 per cent decrease in nominal wages across the industrial sector. On this occasion, however, a lower limit was imposed: the daily pay could not fall below 12 lire in towns of more than 200,000 inhabitants and below 8 lire elsewhere. Trade unions claimed that cuts were much more severe than those officially stipulated. At the annual conference of the Milano province in 1932, for instance, it was claimed that workers in the cotton industry had suffered a 40 per cent decline in their wages since 1927 and that most of it depended on arbitrary decisions taken by industrialists. Similarly, Capoferri, the prestigious leader of the Milanese unions, wrote that various cuts had taken place between 1927 and 1930 producing an overall wage reduction of about 30 per cent (Consonni and Tonon, 1981). In March 1934, the annual conference of industrial trade union leaders was unequivocally critical of the new agreement that was in the air on the grounds that industrialists had already secured a reduction in wage bills that was much more substantial than the one agreed upon in November 1930

(CFLI, 1935b). Trade unions pointed out that, cuts aside, there were various ways in which entrepreneurs could reduce their wage bills. A common practice seems to have been the firing of workers only to rehire them with lower official qualifications and therefore lower pay or, whenever possible, to hire workers who would accept a wage below the legal minimum (peasants, women, teenagers). Given the features of the labour market, all this seems highly possible but at the same time it is difficult to believe that such practices were only first introduced during the Depression years.

A third way of fighting unemployment consisted in decreasing the number of hours worked on average by each employee. In the next section we shall show that the practice was widespread well before 11 October 1934, when the Confederation of Fascist Industrialists and the industrial trade unions reached a formal agreement stipulating that: (a) the working week should not exceed forty hours, (b) a bonus should be paid to workers with children out of compulsory contributions from both employees and employers (each being taxed 1 per cent of the wage), (c) overtime should be worked only in exceptional circumstances and should be taxed more heavily, and (d) women, teenagers and retired people should leave their jobs to adult males whenever possible. The agreement was endorsed by the International Labour Office in Geneva but did not go down easily with industrialists. Although Olivetti gave it his full support in Geneva against the opinion of most European industrial leaders and although Agnelli proposed a thirty-six-hour week (with unchanged pay) in an interview to the United Press, the rank and file resented the limitation to their own freedom. As for the trade unions, they fought for a forty-hour week at the existing weekly wage, on the grounds that most industrial sectors were either highly protected or subsidised. But their strategy was aimed mostly at gaining a broader control of the labour market through the labour exchange offices which they claimed could guarantee that "objective" criteria and priorities in providing employment would be respected. In fact, such offices were at best inefficient and party-controlled, if not utterly corrupt.

The expulsion of women from the industrial labour market as part of the 1934 agreement deserves some attention. Here, as in their opposition to migration from agriculture, industrial trade unions found themselves in agreement with the official Fascist ideology stressing the values of motherhood in view of the "defence of the race" and the new "demographic destinies" sought for the country. The ideological screen, however, hid what was perceived as a real phenomenon: the challenge posed by cheaper female labour to the employment of adult males. It was the trade unions' view that such a challenge was grounded in the process of work "rationalisation and dequalification" occurring in tandem with the technical progress resulting partly, but not entirely, from the Depression.

The fourth pillar of Fascist labour policies consisted of unemployment benefits. Up to the First World War only voluntary mutual-assistance (co-operative) forms of insurance against unemployment existed in Italy. A limited form of compulsory insurance against involuntary unemployment was introduced in April 1917 for those working in firms producing military equipment. At the end of the war, unemployment benefits were extended to all workers. They were paid directly by the state out of its ordinary budget and irrespective of whether the recipient had previously made any contribution (decrees of November 1918 and January 1919). The system was abolished a few months later (October 1919) on the grounds that it was too expensive, it lowered incentives to look for a job and it was a source of abuse and corruption. It was not reintroduced until after the Second World War. In 1919 a compulsory insurance was substituted: workers would contribute to a national fund and, if unemployed, would be paid an allowance for a maximum of ninety to 120 days according to the duration of previous continuous work (forty-eight to seventy-two weeks). Such was, with minor changes, the arrangement existing at the time of the Great Depression (see section 3). In 1933 the complex provincial organisation of the system was centralised with the creation of the Istituto Nazionale Fascista per la Previdenza Sociale (INPS) which managed all other compulsory insurances: old age pensions, tuberculosis, maternity, etc.

This brief survey is not the right place for a discussion of "continuity" and "novelty" in Fascist labour policies. It is our opinion that broadly speaking there was little or no innovative effort in the policies of public works and unemployment insurance, in either their qualitative or their quantitative aspects. On the other hand, a peculiarity of Fascism seems to have been its attempt to grant the state active control of the labour market. Propaganda, party mobilisation, bureaucracy and the police were the instruments used to enforce wage cuts and, as we have seen in section 2, to control workers' mobility. The enforcement of such measures required a well-established dictatorship and probably constituted the true "novelty" of labour and economic policies during the late 1920s and the 1930s.

5 An Appraisal of Labour Policies

How successful were the policies outlined in section 4 in containing unemployment and in limiting its effect on the living standards of the population? Or, to phrase it differently, were these policies effective in reaching their much-publicised targets?

Table 6.5   Employment in Public Works, 1928-36

	No. of days (1)	Emp't (2)	Index (3)
1928		116,322	70.7
1930	41,028,000	164,112	100.0
1931	39,272,000	157,088	95.7
1932	42,136,000	168,544	102.7
1933	51,258,000	205,032	124.9
1934	45,238,000	180,952	110.3
1935	38,947,000	155,788	94.9
1936	32,053,000	128,212	78.1

Note: Col.1: number of work days in public works directly or indirectly financed by the state or by provinces and municipalities. Col.2: number of full employment jobs created (col. (1)/250, assuming full employment = 250 days of work per year).
Source: ISTAT, *Annuario Statistico Italiano*, various years.

Table 6.5 summarises our estimates of the number of jobs created by public works. According to our computations, the average yearly number of full- time jobs created by public works between 1931 and 1933 (176,000) corresponds to about 46 per cent of all employment in the construction sector. But not all public works were created as a measure to fight unemployment. When the decision to foster public expenditure in that direction was taken in the summer of 1930, a yearly programme of publicly financed construction was under way for reasons that had nothing to do with unemployment relief. The 1928 figure was taken as a proxy for it. Therefore, the net number of jobs created by public works as a policy directly aimed at reducing unemployment can be estimated, on average, for the years 1931-33, at around 60,000 or 10 per cent of the sector's unemployment and 3 per cent of total unemployment according to our upper-bound estimates (8.8 per cent for lower-bound estimates).

Leaving wage cuts to section 6, the next policy to be discussed is the reduction in the length of the working day. Judging from Figure 6.1, the policy was, in aggregate, successful in so far as its aim was, to use one of today's slogans, "less work, more workers". There seems however to be little correlation between the decision taken in October 1934 and the behaviour of the two curves in Figure 6.1. The more than proportional decline in the number of hours worked relative to total employment began as early as 1929, probably as a result of *de facto* agreements at the factory level that suited employers and for reasons of "social peace" and "consensus". It is interesting to note that the scissor-like movement continued during at least the first part of the rapid recovery of 1935-37 which was, in fact, characterised by a negligible increase of product per man in manufacturing. Given the amount of unemployment that had to be absorbed, this too seems a rational behaviour at least from a social and political point of view.

The success of the campaign for the expulsion of women from factories cannot be assessed on the basis of the existing aggregate figures. Between the population censuses of 1931 and 1936 female participation in the industrial labour force grew more than three times as fast as that of males (a rate of 6 per cent as against 1.8 per cent a year). On the other hand, official statistics seem to show a higher female/male unemployment ratio than the one existing at the time of the 1927 industrial census, at least in the workforce of the food processing, textile and chemical industries (ISTAT, 1930-34). The issue must remain undecided at least as far as the present study is concerned.

Figures for unemployment benefits cover the years 1926-32: over this period they increased ninefold, from 6.3 to 56.3 million days of unemployment payments. No statistics exist on the number of workers being thus subsidised. However, recalling that payments did not last more than ninety to 120 days, the number of people benefiting from them could not have exceeded 625,500 in 1932, or 55 per cent of the official (our lower-bound estimate) number of unemployed (1,147,945 in February 1932, if we include agriculture, not represented in our Table 6.3). Monthly unemployment benefits reached the equivalent of five or six days' pay (Musso, 1981). For a full year, an unemployed worker would receive a sum equivalent, at best, to eighteen to twenty-four days of pay. This is indeed too little for Fascism to claim to have introduced an embryo "welfare state". And it is certainly too little to make today's fashionable hypothesis that the dole is a major cause of unemployment worth investigating in this context.

6   Unemployment and Wages

Direct intervention in the labour market is a specific feature of Fascist economic policies. We have mentioned the attempt to check workers' mobility and its failure. The wage policy does not seem to have enjoyed any greater success, as far as its aim of limiting unemployment was concerned. This statement requires a brief qualification. After the short-lived postwar wage boom, Fascist Italy experienced an almost uninterrupted fall in real wages, unique among industrial countries (Zamagni, 1976). From 1921 to 1937 real wages declined by about 20 per cent. This fall is "explained" by price inflation in 1923-26 and again in 1935-36, and by "wage cuts" imposed from above when the gold exchange standard was introduced in 1927. The only break in the trend took place during the

Figure 6.3   Own-Product Real Wages and Total Hours Worked in Industry, 1929-38 (August 1929=100)

Great Depression. Deflated with an index of consumers' prices, real wages remained stable from 1929 to 1932 and rose by 8 per cent in the following two years (Zamagni, 1976). Fascism was therefore successful in its policy of giving "stick and castor oil" to wages except for the years of the Great Depression when it probably mattered most. In those years its waves of "wage cuts" decrees were somehow frustrated by the pronounced fall in the prices of many goods in the consumer's basket. Within this framework, let us now advance some hypotheses on the issue of wages and unemployment during the 1930s.

Figure 6.3 illustrates the behaviour from 1929 to 1938 of the indeces of own product real wages (i.e. deflated by *factory gate* industrial prices) and of the number of hours worked in the industrial sector.

In order to advance a classical or a Keynesian hypothesis about the relation of wages to employment, the following regression has been estimated:

$$WHj = F\ (C,\ RWj,\ Q,\ d) \tag{1}$$

where C is the constant, WHj is the number of hours worked in sector j, RWj are hourly money wages for sector j deflated by factory gate prices of sector j (own product real wages), Q is the total quantity of raw

Table 6.6   **Regressions for Total Hours Worked in Italian Industries, 1928-38**

Industry	Constant	Own-product real wages	Qty. of imported raw mat'ls	Adjusted R^2	DW	F
Food	0.494	-0.567	-0.032	0.93	2.54	110.69
	(19.19)	(-3.06)	(-0.74)			
Mining	0.023	-0.212	0.017	0.61	1.79	14.34
	(1.51)	(-1.35)	(0.49)			
Construction	0.080	-0.451	0.069	0.93	2.50	106.65
	(3.92)	(-2.05)	(1.50)			
Construction materials	0.036	-0.465	0.059	0.89	1.67	66.62
	(2.58)	(-2.34)	(1.85)			
Metalmaking and engineering	-0.035	-0.463	0.022	0.66	1.96	18.06
	(-2.29)	(-2.41)	(0.80)			
Textiles	-0.065	-0.332	-0.036	0.71	2.16	22.25
	(-3.54)	(-2.18)	(-0.88)			
Chemical	-0.020	-0.345	0.036	0.67	2.13	18.32
	(-1.51)	(-2.21)	(1.43)			
Paper	-0.037	-0.089	0.006	0.68	2.29	19.17
	(-3.23)	(-1.07)	(0.26)			
Wood	-0.017	-0.182	0.036	0.60	2.27	14.08
	(-1.12)	(-1.34)	(1.05)			
Utilities	-0.016	-0.183	0.009	0.67	1.94	18.61
	(1.74)	(-1.62)	(0.43)			
Miscellaneous	-0.068	-0.610	0.032	0.74	2.22	25.42
	(-4.17)	(-3.81)	(0.99)			
Total	0.001	-0.392	0.015	0.74	2.00	25.51
	(0.12)	(-2.68)	(0.65)			

Note: t statistics in parentheses. Number of observations: 64; period: April 1928-August 1938; dependent variable: number of hours worked; seasonal dummies included but not reported.

materials imported into Italy which is used here as the best proxy for industrial activity, in the absence of bimonthly national income or industrial production estimates, and d is a vector of seasonal dummy variables. The results for eleven sectors and for the total are shown in Table 6.6.

From an econometric point of view the regression results tend to favour a classical rather than a Keynesian interpretation of Italy's industrial unemployment during the 1930s. There is little doubt that, as pointed out by Beenstock and Warburton (1986) for the United Kingdom, the issue of own product real wages remains important in the analysis of industrial unemployment, and it needs further attention in the case of Italy too. At the same time, the limitations of the test of a Keynesian hypothesis implicit in the regressions in Table 6.6 are quite obvious. They certainly require a more refined analysis than the one carried out here.

If further research were to strengthen and confirm the own product real wage explanation of unemployment, would that mean that the policy of wage cuts was too mild and that tougher measures could have succeeded? Whatever the merits of a classical explanation of British unemployment during the same years, one has to recall that British real wages (consumer price deflated) rose by 7 per cent between 1929 and 1932 and continued to rise thereafter. During the same period Italian real wages remained stable, after falling by 20 per cent in the previous five years. In this situation, even an established dictatorship in the years of greatest domestic consensus could hardly disregard the implications of further wage cuts. If available data may be believed, the Italian situation was made difficult, in this respect, by the fact that while real wages remained almost constant because of the behaviour of prices of non-traded goods included in the index, own product real wages for the industrial sector showed a substantial growth. A cut in the latter would have entailed a probably unbearable decrease in the already low standard of living of the working class. We must recall that take-home pay was already reduced by the fall in the average number of hours worked by each employed person. To sum up, if it is true, given the standard neoclassical assumptions, that there is always a wage level that clears the labour market, in the case of Italy during the 1930s this level was possibly below subsistence and certainly below what was politically acceptable.

Other avenues were open to Italian governments in order to increase industrial employment during the Depression. They were not pursued mainly because of an irrational obsession with gold parity and with an overvalued currency. But one of us has discussed them elsewhere (Toniolo, 1980) and they need not concern us here.

7   Some Concluding Remarks

At the Geneva International Labour Conference in 1934, the director of the International Labour Office had warm words of praise for Italy where progress had been made "in the construction of the corporative system that breaks away with economic theories based on individualism". According to the director, together with the United States, the Soviet Union and Germany, Italy was at the forefront in the creation of a new economy. To these words, the representative of Italian trade unions replied that such an authoritative acknowledgment was of the greatest value to the Fascists who, during the previous twelve years, had been the heralds of "the new needs of the nation's social and economic evolution" (*Informazioni Sociali*, 1934). This official recognition highlights the changes induced by the Depression in the ideological approach to labour policies at the international level where a sympathetic view of fascism was not uncommon. In the light of what we have seen, the director's statement appears to be more a tribute to the effectiveness of Fascist propaganda than an accurate evaluation of facts. As we have seen, at the time of the Conference, according to *official* statistics, unemployment in industry was two and a half times greater than in 1929, while little improvement had taken place since 1932. Most of the policies were not new and, at any rate, their quantitative relevance was limited and their impact far from crucial.

According to De Felice, the growing consensus in favour of Fascism on an international level was matched by a similar political climate within the country. This is certainly not the place to discuss the issue of "consensus" with its broad social and political implications and with the qualifications that are necessary. But one major question cannot be avoided. Why did unemployment not become an important destabilising factor in Italy? There are, obviously, no definite answers to such a crucial question. In the light of our findings, however, we would not expect to find the reason for social stability and even for a fair degree of "consensus" in the limited number of the unemployed. Their number was high by any international standard. In our opinion a fruitful line of research would focus instead on the character of Italy's labour markets that we have briefly discussed in this chapter. We believe that social "stability" can be better understood in terms of the mechanisms regulating hiring, dismissals and the various forms of rotating underemployment.

By way of preliminary hypotheses one could probably say that the Depression certainly lowered living standards in the countryside but did not introduce dramatic changes in a world that had somehow adjusted, long before October 1922, to the structural situation of excess population on the land. Indifference rather than consensus was probably the prevailing feeling in the countryside. As for industrial workers, most of them were never conquered by Fascist ideology; their growing unemployment, even if tempered by turnover, only strengthened their opposition to the regime whose "social benefits", as we have seen, did not make a major impact on the urban masses. At any rate, they were a minority, kept under watchful police eyes. There is, however, one important aspect of Fascist labour policies that has not been mentioned in this chapter but which seems to have greatly contributed to "consensus", and that is the *increase* in employment in public administration that took place during the Depression. This increase was designed precisely to avoid unemployment in the lower middle class, the mass political backbone of Fascism, thus securing their continuing support.

NOTES

* Financial support from the Italian Ministry of Education is gratefully acknowledged. Thanks are due to Maria Berletti and Christina Giordani for competent research assistance, and to Stefano Fenoaltea and Giuseppe Tattara for helpful comments.

REFERENCES

Arcari, P.M. (1934), *I salari agricoli in Italia del 1905 al 1933*, Rome: Istituto poligrafico dello stato.

Atti dell'inchiesta parlamentare sulle condizioni dei contadini nelle provincie meridionali e nella Sicilia (1911-13), vols 1-8, Rome: Camera dei Deputati.

Beenstock, M. and Warburton, P. (1986), "Wages and Unemployment in Interwar Britain", *Explorations in Economic History* 23, pp. 152-72.

Bigazzi, D. (1985), "Alfa Romeo", unpublished paper presented at the conference on "La mobilità del lavoro operaio in Italia tra Ottocento e prima metà del Novecento", Venice.

Caffè F. (1952), "Considerazioni storico bibliografiche attorno al problema della disoccupazione in Italia", *L'Industria* 15, pp. 236-48.

Caffè F. (1953), "Saggio di bibliografia italiana sulla disoccupazione", in Commissione parlamentare d'inchiesta sulla disooccupazione, *La disoccupazione in Italia, Studi speciali* vol. 4, Rome: Istituto poligrafico dello stato.

CFLI (Confederazione fascista dei lavoratori dell'industria) (1935a), *Caratteri della produzione e attività sindacale dei lavoratori nella provincia di Genova*, Genova: CFLI.

CFLI (Confederazione fascista dei lavoratori dell'industria) (1935b), *Convegno Nazionale dei dirigenti dei sindacati fascisti dell'industria, Roma 17 marzo 1934*, Rome: CFLI.

Chiaventi, P. (1987), "Nota sui censimenti industriali del 1911-1951", *Rivista dil storia economica* 4, pp. 119- 51.

Cianetti, T. (1934), "Prospetto riassuntivo delle deliberazioni della Conferenza", *Informazioni sociali* 13, pp. 809-14.

Commissione parlamentare d'inchiesta sulla disoccupazione (1953-54), *La disoccupazione in Italia*, vols 1-5, Rome: Istituto poligrafico dello stato.

Consonni, G.C. and Tonon, G. (1981), "Milano: classe e metropoli tra due economie di guerra", *Annali della Fondazione G. Feltrinelli* 20, pp. 479-92.

De Felice, R. (1974), *Mussolini il duce: gli anni del consenso*, Turin: Einaudi.

Eichengreen, B. (1986), "Unemployment in Interwar Britain: New Evidence from London", *Journal of Interdisciplinary History* 17, pp. 335-58.

Fei, J.C.H. and Ranis, G. (1964), *Development of the Labor Surplus Economy: Theory and Policy*, Homewood, Ill.: R.D. Irwin.

Fenoaltea, S. (1986), "Public Works Construction in Italy, 1861-1913", *Rivista di storia economica* 3, International Issue, pp. 1-33.

Fuà, G. (ed.) (1969), *Lo sviluppo economico in Italia*, vol. 3, Milan: Angeli.

Garraty, J.A. (1978), *Unemployment in History*, New York: Harper & Row.

INEA (1933), (Istituto nazionale di economia agraria) (1931-38), *Monografie di famiglie agricole*, Rome: INEA.

Informazioni Sociali (1934), "La relazione del direttore alla XVIII Sessione della Conferenza Internazionale del Lavoro", vol. 13, pp. 393-439.

ISTAT (Istituto centrale di statistica) (1928-37), *Bollettino di notizie economiche*, Rome: ISTAT.

ISTAT (Istituto centrale di statistica) (1930-34), *Annuario statistico italiano*, Rome: ISTAT.

Lenti, L. (1934), "Ricerche statistiche sull'occupazione operaia in Italia", *Annali di economia* 13, Cedam, Padua, pp. 293-439.

Medici, G. and Orlando, G. (1952), *Agricoltura e disoccupazione: i braccianti nella bassa padana*, Bologna: Zanichelli.

Molinari, A. (1929), *Contratti di lavoro e salari nelle aziende agricole dell'alto e basso milanese*, Milan: Stucchi-Ceretti.

Musso, S. (1981), "Proletariato industriale e fascismo a Torino: aspetti del territorio operaio", *Annali della Fondazione G. Feltrinelli* 20, pp. 511ff.

O'Brien, P.K. and Toniolo, G. (1986), "Sull'arretratezza del'agricoltura italiana rispetto a quella del Regno Unito attorno al 1910", *Richerche Economiche* 40, pp. 266-85.

OEEC (Organisation of European Economic Cooperation) (1960), *International Industrial Statistics*, Paris: OEEC.

Piva, F. (1983), "Il reclutamento della forza lavoro: paesaggi sociali e politica imprenditoriale", in F. Piva and G. Tattara (eds), *I primi operai di Marghera: mercato, reclutamento, occupazione 1917-1940*, Venice: Marsilio.

Piva, F. and Tattara, G. (eds), *I primi operai di Marghera: mercato, reclutamento, occupazione 1917-1940*, Venice: Marsilio.

Salvemini, G. (1935), "Italian Unemployment Statistics", *Social Research* 2, pp.342-57.

Sen, A. (1966), "Peasants and Dualism With or Without Surplus Labour", *Journal of Political Economy* 74, pp. 425-50.

Serpieri, A. (1910), *Il contratto agrario e le condizioni di vita dei contadini nell'alto milanese*, Milan: Ufficio Agrario.

Toniolo, G. (1980), *L'economia dell'Italia fascista*, Rome/Bari: Laterza.

Treves, A. (1976), *Le migrazioni interne nell'Italia fascista*, Turin: Einaudi.

Vitali, O. (1970), *Aspetti dello sviluppo economico italiano alla luce della ricostruzione della popolazione attiva*, Rome: Ateneo.

Zamagni, V. (1976), "La dinamica dei salari nel settore industriale", in P. Ciocca and G. Toniolo (eds), *L'economia italiana nel periodo fascista*, Bologna: II Mulino, pp. 328-78.

Zamagni, V. (1980), "Distribuzione del reddito e classi sociali nell'Italia fra le due guerre", *Annali della Fondazione G. Feltrinelli* 20, pp. 17-49.

Chapter 7

Why was Unemployment so Low in France During the 1930s?

Robert Salais*

1 Introduction

The aim of this chapter is to understand the reasons for the low rate of unemployment in France in the 1930s. While a satisfactory explanation must take macroeconomic trends into consideration, it must also incorporate a number of additional factors: the effects of the uneven industrial and urban development of the French economy, one implication of which was the late emergence of a modern wage-earning class; the peculiarities of the French system of public assistance and its incentives for individual behaviour; and the rationalisation movement of the 1930s and its implications for the volume of available work. Moreover, a large part of the explanation for the low rate of unemployment in interwar France is definitional and conceptual. It is critical to realise that the institutional preconditions for the existence of a pool of labour conforming to the conventional economic and social definition of "unemployed" workers were not in place in France in the 1930s. The type of employment relationship that would give rise to the category "unemployment" was not yet prevalent outside large towns and rationalised firms. This does not mean that individuals outside large towns and rationalised firms did not lose work and income due to the Great Depression, but that, due to the manner in which their plight was conceived, they were not regarded and tabulated as unemployed in the same manner as in other countries. Neither did they regard themselves as unemployed in the modern sense of the word.

Section 2 of this chapter sums up the main statistical facts and macroeconomic developments affecting unemployment in France during the 1930s. Section 3 describes the procedures used to measure and register

B. Eichengreen and T. J. Hatton (eds.), Interwar Unemployment in International Perspective, 247–288.

unemployment in France during the interwar period. It briefly compares the system of public assistance to the unemployed in France with that of Great Britain.

Section 4 analyses the duration and frequency of unemployment by profession in Paris based on a longitudinal survey of the unemployed receiving benefit between 1930 and 1939. Section 5 then presents a study of regional variations in unemployment, based on population census data. The final section combines these results and develops our arguments for the reasons for the low rate of unemployment in France during the 1930s.

2 Macroeconomic Developments and the Labour Market Statistics

The economic crisis of the 1930s affected the French economy later than other industrial countries. Unlike Germany, where manufacturing production turned down in the summer of 1928, and unlike the US and Britain, where activity began its decline in the summer of 1929, French industrial production continued to increase into 1930. But once the Great Depression arrived in France, its effects were severe. Industrial output fell dramatically, by 32 per cent, from the second half of 1930 to the middle of 1932. A brief recovery, lasting from mid-1932 to mid-1933, then gave way to further recession which lasted until the beginning of 1935. Economic activity recovered slowly, continuing to rise sporadically through the turbulent election of 1936 and the shifts in policy following the accession to power of the Blum government, reaching a peak in 1937. Recovery was not just delayed but insufficiently vigorous to restore output to pre-Depression levels. A sense of the hesitant nature of the French recovery can be gleaned from the fact that between 1931 and 1938, the period of recovery in most of the rest of the world, real GDP in France fell by 1.6 per cent and industrial production expanded by a mere 1.2 per cent. At the beginning of the Second World War industrial production still remained 12 per cent below its 1929 peak.

Table 7.1 shows changes in some of the main economic indicators from 1931 to 1936, the dates of population censuses which provide the benchmarks for aggregate unemployment rates. Industrial production fell by nearly 13 percentage points though a much larger decline occurred between March 1930 and March 1932 when the index fell from 112 to 76. The failure of the industrial sector to recover strongly is linked to the overvaluation of the franc from 1931, and this is reflected in the trade accounts. Imports and exports fell by over 40 per cent in volume and even more in value. At the same time domestic monetary conditions tightened and were reflected in a rise in the long-term interest rate. These developments had a severe impact on employment in industrial plants, which fell

Table 7.1 Some French Macroeconomic Indicators in 1931 and in 1936

	March 1931	March 1936	Percentage change
Industrial production[1] (base 1928=100)	101	88	-12.9
Exports (millions of francs)			
- Value	3,066	1,245	-59.4
- Volume[2]			-45.5
Imports (millions of francs)			
- Value	3,939	1,956	-50.3
- Volume[3]			-40.3
Nominal interest rate[4]	4.55	6.25	+37.4
Labour activity within industrial plants over 100 people[5] (base 1930=100)	90.7	68.1	-24.9
- Employment	94.6	74.6	-21.8
- Weekly working hours	95.9	94.8	- 1.1
Hourly wage rate[5] (base 1930=100)			
- Nominal	101.4	94.6	- 6.7
- Deflated by consumer price index	101.0	124.0	+22.8
Estimated wage bill[6]			
- Value	92.0	64.4	-30.0
- Converted into purchasing power			-7.8

Notes:
1 Seasonally adjusted.
2 Deflated by an index of 45 wholesale prices.
3 Deflated by an index of 16 import prices.
4 Rate on new bonds, net of tax.
5 Extracted from Sauvy (1967), vol. 2, p. 520.
6 Product of the labour activity index (total weekly working hours) and the hourly wage rate.

by nearly 22 per cent, significantly more than production, while average weekly hours for the employed showed only a small decline. The real (consumer) wage increased sharply due to the fall in the price level. As a result, though the total wage bill in nominal terms fell by 30 per cent, the real value of wages paid fell by less than 8 per cent.

In light of the major dimensions of the Great Depression in France, it is surprising to observe that the recorded rate of unemployment remained low throughout the period. Only 4.3 per cent of the active population was counted as out of work *(sans emploi)* in the 1936 population census, when the British unemployment rate remained three times as high, despite that country's relatively rapid recovery from the Depression, and unemployment in the United States remained stuck at an alarming 16.9 per cent

Table 7.2   Effects of Population Growth and Changes in the Age Composition on the Active Population

Demographic Effect	Male	Female	Both
1 On the active French-nationality population (excluding those of foreign origin)	-59,200	-171,900	-231,100
2 On the active foreigner population (including those having acquired French nationality)	-246,200	-12,100	-258,300
3 = 1 + 2 On the active population	-305,400	-184,000	-489,400
4 Actual change in active population	-771,000	-580,000	-1,351,000

Note: Methodology: if P_i is the total population from age group i and t_i its participation rate, we can write, between the dates 0 and 1:

$$\Delta \hat{P} = \Sigma \, t_i \, (P_i^1 - P_i^0)$$

This measures the effect of the composition by age and of the variations of the total population, the participation rates being taken as constant.

Sources: Population censuses of March 1931 and March 1936.

(see chapters 3 and 9 of this volume). This comparison does not hinge upon use of the census: other sources similarly show surprisingly low unemployment rates for France in the 1930s.

How are these low rates of unemployment in interwar France to be understood? Do they cast doubt on the accuracy of the standard indicators of the severity of the macroeconomic crisis of the 1930s? Or do they suggest that somehow the 32 per cent fall in industrial production between 1930 and 1932 and the less dramatic if nonetheless quite considerable fall in gross national product over the same period were somehow accommodated without a dramatic rise in the level of unemployment? Alternatively, do they reveal the extent to which the French authorities underrecorded the incidence of unemployment? Or is the problem subtler: did the ways in which the French economy and society were organised impel not only the authorities but the nation as a whole to conceptualise the problem of unemployment in a different way from what was conventional in other countries?

There is an abundance of existing explanations for the paradox. One popular viewpoint in France emphasises demographic factors (Sauvy, 1967). A lingering effect of the First World War was a fall in the size of the active population, which persisted into the 1930s. The "Malthusian problem" of the French economy was attributed to a combination of the wartime casualties and the subsequent fall in the birth rate. While this ar-

Table 7.3   **Active Population, Distributed by Category in 1931 and 1936 (1,000s of persons)**

	Census of 1931 Both	Male	Female	Census of 1936 Both	Male	Female	Absolute increase or decrease Both	Male	Female
I On one's own account									
Heads of establishment	6,236	3,392	2,844	5,921	3,217	2,704	-315	-175	-140
Isolated small									
independent workers	1,707	1,050	657	1,795	1,128	667	+88	+78	+10
Total	7,943	4,442	3,501	7,716	4,345	3,371	-227	-97	-130
II Wage-earning									
Attached to an establishment:									
white-collar workers	3,025	1,958	1,067	2,978	1,942	1,036	-47	-16	-31
blue-collar workers	9,144	6,492	2,652	7,720	5,496	2,224	-1,424	-996	-428
Without work:	453	308	145	864	625	239	+411	+317	+94
isolated home workers	418	158	260	351	137	214	-67	-21	-46
isolated with irregular jobs	628	353	275	631	395	236	+3	+42	-39
Total	13,668	9,269	4,399	12,544	8,595	3,949	-1,124	-674	-450
Total active population	21,611	13,711	7,900	20,260	12,940	7,320	-1,351	-771	-580

gument has obvious appeal as an explanation for France's low unemployment rate, the reduction in labour supply and consequent tightness of the labour market can more readily explain the low average level of unemployment throughout the interwar period than the failure of recorded unemployment to rise dramatically in response to what was certainly a dramatic fall in the level of production. Moreover, the decline in the active population in the 1930s due to the "Malthusian problem" of the interwar years is too small to explain the stubborn persistence of low unemployment rates. Table 7.2 summarises the results of a calculation designed to quantify its importance. The decline in the active population in the 1930s due to Malthusian factors is estimated to be of the order of 231,000 persons of French nationality. Adding this number of workers to the 1936 census and assuming all of them to have been unemployed (surely a strong assumption), this would have raised the unemployment rate only from 4.3 to 5.5 per cent.

A second popular explanation stresses the extent to which the decline in employment fell on foreign guest workers who, rather than showing up in the French unemployment statistics, were forced to return to their home country. In this view, French unemployment was simply exported. Again, this explanation has obvious appeal. But Table 7.2 shows that the decline in the French labour force due to reductions in immigration and to the return migration of guest workers is of the same order of magnitude as the change in the labour force due to Malthusian factors (258,000). Again, it is too small to dispose of the question of why French unemployment behaved in this unusual fashion.

Table 7.3 shows the change in the active population between 1931 and 1936 broken down into the census categories. There was a significant decline among own-account workers but the fall in the number of employers was partly offset by the increase in the number of independent workers. Among the wage-earning group, blue-collar workers attached to industrial establishments show a decline which substantially exceeds the rise in unemployment. The other categories of wage earners, white-collar workers and the isolated, make only a small contribution to the change in the wage-earning labour force. These changes in the labour force can only be understood by considering the way unemployment was perceived by employers and employees, the way it was conditioned by the system of unemployment relief, and consequently the way it was enumerated at the census and by the relief-giving authorities.

3   The Measurement of French Unemployment

3. 1   Population Censuses

A leading source of information on interwar unemployment is the population census. While the published documents provide little information on the methods by which census officials estimated unemployment, there is information on the instructions provided to persons employed by the French Bureau of Statistics (La Statistique Générale de la France), which processed the census questionnaires.[1] The basis for classifying persons as unemployed was the question concerning occupation. Persons declaring an occupation were subdivided into groups according to the following schema: employees of municipal and local authorities, railway workers and civil servants; domestic servants; and other workers grouped by type of establishment. Those who did not report the name of an establishment to which they were attached were placed in the category *isolé* (isolated), of which the major part was self-employed workers. Those who had given the address of their employer and who reported that they were without work were placed in the category *chômeur* (unemployed). To be classified as unemployed, therefore, a person had to declare an occupation and be attached to an establishment!

Furthermore, an unemployed worker had to satisfy a duration criterion. First, a minimum waiting period of eight days was required: persons who had been without work for fewer than eight days were counted as still at work in their previous establishment. Those who provided no indication of the duration of the current unemployment spell were treated in the same fashion. Similarly, individuals without employment for two years or more were regarded as inactive, or out of the labour force. This instruc-

Table 7.4   Rates of Unemployment by Sex and Age

	Male			Female			Both		
	(1)	(2)	(3)	(1)	(2)	(3)	(1)	(2)	(3)
Less than 15 years	2.1	2.2	2.1	1.7	1.8	1.7	2.0	2.0	2.0
15-19 years	5.0	5.2	5.0	4.3	4.7	4.4	4.7	5.0	4.8
20-24 years	4.8	5.4	5.0	4.2	5.9	5.2	4.5	5.5	5.1
25-29 years	4.9	6.6	5.8	3.5	6.5	5.4	4.4	6.6	5.7
30-34 years	4.7	7.1	6.0	3.1	6.7	5.4	4.2	7.0	5.9
35-39 years	4.8	7.9	6.5	3.1	7.3	5.5	4.2	7.7	6.2
40-44 years	5.0	8.7	7.0	3.2	8.2	5.7	4.3	8.5	6.6
45-49 years	5.1	9.5	7.5	3.3	9.0	6.0	4.4	9.3	7.0
50-54 years	5.7	11.4	8.7	3.4	10.6	6.6	4.8	11.2	8.0
55-59 years	6.4	15.2	10.7	3.5	11.6	6.8	5.3	14.1	9.4
60-64 years	4.4	12.6	8.0	2.3	8.6	4.6	3.6	11.4	6.8
65 and more	3.0	12.2	6.0	1.6	6.8	3.1	2.6	10.4	5.0
Total	4.8	7.7	6.4	3.3	6.8	5.2	4.3	7.5	6.0

Notes:
Column (1) As a proportion of the total active population.
Column (2) As a proportion of the number of blue- and white-collar workers attached to an establishment (unemployed included).
Column (3) As a proportion of the active "wage-earning" population, defined in Appendix 7.2 as the sum of workers and employees with or without work and the "isolated".
Source: 1936 census.

tion reflected a recognition of the distinctiveness of the socioeconomic circumstances of those who had been out of work for extended periods. Whatever the rationale, its effect in practice was to reduce the unemployment rate by eliminating many of those who, in other countries, had been recorded as among the long-term unemployed.

Individuals more than 60 years old were regarded as inactive or out of the labour force if they had been out of work for a minimum of one year, in contrast to two years for younger persons. This instruction reflected an effort on the part of the statisticians to deal with the fact that in interwar France the concept of retirement was still incompletely formed. There was still no conventional retirement age to which the interested parties could refer. This situation had begun to change with the passage of social insurance acts in April 1930, but the adoption of a formal convention regarding retirement awaited the coming of social security in 1945.

The pattern of the incidence of unemployment emerging from the 1936 census is illustrated in Tables 7.4 and 7.5. As Table 7.4. shows, the age profile of unemployment rates is surprisingly flat from the 15-19 age group onwards, though rising slightly for those aged 45-59. However, if unemployment is expressed as a proportion of the number of blue- and white-collar workers, the overall rates are significantly higher and show

Table 7.5   Rates of Unemployment by Industry, Both Sexes

	As a proportion of:			
	the total active pop'n in each industry	the no. of blue- and white-collar workers attached to an establish't (unemp'd incl.)	the active "wage-earning" pop'n	% of "isolated" in the active pop'n
1 Fishing	2.4	7.5	2.9	49.6
2 Agriculture	0.6	2.3	1.6	11.2
3a Mining	1.3	1.3	1.3	0.0
3b Quarrying	2.7	3.1	2.9	5.6
4b Food and drink industries	3.2	4.7	4.4	4.1
4c Chemicals, paints, oils	0.9	0.9	0.9	0.4
4d Rubber, paper	3.2	3.3	3.3	1.3
4e Printing	6.3	7.2	6.9	4.7
4f Textiles	4.9	5.5	5.1	6.5
4g Tailoring, dressmaking	5.2	11.3	5.9	41.4
4i Leather and leather goods	5.4	9.3	6.1	30.5
4j Woodworking	8.2	13.9	9.7	25.6
4k Iron, steel	1.3	1.3	1.3	0.0
4l Metal industries	7.2	8.8	7.9	9.3
4q Building and public works	12.1	16.4	13.7	14.8
4r Brick, tile, pottery works	4.1	4.3	4.3	0.8
5a Handlers, warehousemen, unclassified unskilled workers	41.1	88.2	41.2	53.2
5b Transport	3.0	3.3	3.1	5.1
6a Distributive trades	3.4	7.0	4.8	22.7
6c Banking, insurance	1.3	1.6	1.4	11.3
7 Liberal professions	6.9	10.2	7.5	24.7
8 Personal services	4.5	9.8	6.6	22.1
9 Domestic servants (for household)	5.0	5.2	5.0	3.6
All industries	4.3	7.5	6.1	13.7

Source: 1936 census.

a rising profile, with unemployment rates for those aged 45 and over approximately double those for the younger age groups. If, on the other hand, unemployment is taken relative to the wage-earning population as a whole, there is still a rising profile of unemployment with age but with lower average rates. Thus the intensity of unemployment depends critically on how the population at risk is defined.

Turning to the unemployment rates by industry in Table 7.5, these show surprisingly low unemployment rates in a number of important industries. Among these, however, there are significant variations with relatively high rates in the textile and clothing trades and woodworking, where there was a high proportion of "isolated" workers, as well as in metals, building and the professions. Most striking is the very high proportion of unemployed among handlers, warehouseman and unclassified unskilled workers. This category reflects the high incidence of unemployment among the unskilled and also the fact that by 1936 many workers who had been unemployed for long spells had lost attachment to their former industry or trade.

3. 2   Public Relief

At the onset of the Great Depression, the French system of public relief consisted of a combination of social insurance and public assistance[2]. The French scheme of voluntary unemployment insurance originated in the trade union movement. The first self-financing mutual insurance fund was created in 1892 by the Printers Union. From an early date this and similar insurance schemes were subsidised by municipalities and, from 1905, by the state. In contrast, public assistance was administered not by the unions but either by municipal agencies concerned with unemployment or by public relief agencies (*bureaux de bienfaisance*) concerned with poverty. The first agencies of assistance were created on the initiative of local authorities (*des départements et communes*), and might receive government subsidies if approved by the Ministry of Labour. The public relief agencies supplemented the activities of the municipal unemployment agencies, constituting a last resort for the unemployed before the abolition in June 1932 of the 180-day limit on the receipt of unemployment relief.

In 1914 a National Unemployment Fund was created to rationalise the extension of state subsidies to local unemployment relief schemes. This new National Fund was conceived as temporary. "In constituting the Fund, the government had the intention neither of creating a permanent institution nor of resolving the problem of state intervention in the struggle against unemployment" (circular of 8 December 1914). The immediate aim of the new organisation was to cope with the disruption to the labour market caused by the mobilisation for war. But the National Unemployment Fund, once instituted, was maintained. Subsidies transferred from the National Fund to each local agency were proportional to the activity of the local body as recounted in reports sent each year to the Ministry of Labour. These reports, in turn, constituted the basis for the published statistics generated by the unemployment relief system.

Unemployment insurance in France was limited, covering only 171,000 persons in 1931. In practice, the public relief agencies were forced to aid the vast majority of those rendered unemployed by the macroeconomic crisis. To be entitled to public assistance, a person had to be a resident of a municipality where a relief fund was in existence. The minimum duration of residence was six months. The decree of 28 December 1926 limited state subsidies to funds created in municipalities or groups of municipalities of at least 5,000 inhabitants.[3] In practice, this meant that in order to receive meaningful levels of public assistance, a person had to live in a town and not a rural community.

Besides establishing residence, to receive public assistance an unemployed person had to satisfy seven other conditions.

(1) He had to submit a claim establishing both joblessness and involuntary unemployment due to lack of suitable work. Specifically, he had to furnish proof that he worked for a living, that he had received a regular wage for at least six months, and that he had received a notice of redundancy (*certificat de congediement*) from his last employer.

(2) He had to undergo a waiting period of at least three days before receiving assistance.

(3) He had to demonstrate a desire to work.

(4) He had to be willing to accept any "suitable" employment.

(5) He could not be in receipt of a pension or of any other form of benefit.

(6) His idleness could not be due to an industrial dispute or to temporary or permanent disability.

(7) If a foreigner, he had to satisfy additional conditions laid down by international agreements, generally concerning reciprocal aid agreements between France and the governments of the foreign nationals.

Whether these conditions were satisfied was verified by frequent, sometimes daily, monitoring, achieved by requiring the unemployed person to appear at the bureau or through further independent inquiry.[4]

The basis for the administration of relief was the family, not the individual. Only the head of the household was entitled to receive relief, the level of which was adjusted for the number of dependants, with different supplementary benefits applying to elderly dependants, to children of less than 16 years of age, and to legal spouses. Thus, married women, when unemployed, did not receive public assistance unless the resources of the head of the household were inadequate to elevate household income above the minimum threshold level.[5]

3. 3   Comparison of the British and French Systems of Registration and Relief

It is useful to compare the French system of unemployment relief with the Unemployment Insurance system in Britain to gain a fuller understanding of the incentives to register as unemployed and therefore the chances of being counted as unemployed.

The interwar French system was essentially one of public relief, while in Britain the system was based on compulsory insurance. Claims and payment of benefit were administered through the labour exchanges which had been established shortly before the insurance system itself.[6] While relief grew in importance relative to insurance in France in the interwar period, the reverse took place in Britain. When the British insurance system was extended to cover a majority of the labour force in 1920, it largely supplanted relief administered to the unemployed through the Poor Law. By 1931 it covered about 12.5 million out of a gainfully occupied population of 19.5 million. The occupational groups excluded were agricultural workers, domestic servants, certain municipal and state employees and white-collar workers earning more than £250 per annum.[7] By contrast the French system excluded a greater proportion of the workforce largely through residency requirements and the restriction of relief to urban areas.

The conditions which had to be met to qualify for relief were also more stringent in France since relief was not perceived as a right or earned entitlement like unemployment benefit. This, together with the decentralised nature of relief administration, meant that the onus fell on the individual to prove his status as unemployed and his eligibility for relief by providing the necessary documents such as proof of residence and notice of redundancy. In Britain the administrative instrument used to establish a claim was the insurance book. This was lodged with the employer when the individual was employed and at the labour exchange when unemployed and provided the evidence, through contribution stamps, of entitlements to benefit.[8]

The conditions for receipt of benefit were similar in both countries and included willingness to accept suitable employment, the existence of previous work history and disqualification in the case of an industrial dispute or if unemployment was not the result of lay-off by the employer. Benefit scales in both countries depended on the number and type of dependants but, unlike in France, were not means tested in Britain until 1931. The conditions were generally applied more stringently in France, where a larger proportion of potential claimants was excluded and levels of benefit were typically lower.

In one respect the British and French schemes operated quite differently. In Britain short periods of unemployment occurring within a certain
interval could be linked together as continuous periods of unemployment
for the purposes of benefit without having to serve additional working
days before becoming eligible for payment. Though one of the aims of
the insurance scheme was to eliminate casual labour or intermittent employment such as existed on the docks, it effectively encouraged short-
term lay-offs which were reflected in the unemployment register. This
encouraged firms and workers to rotate employment when there was insufficient work in such a way that claims to benefit could be continuously maintained on lay-off days: the so-called "OXO" system.[9] The French
system did not encourage temporary lay-offs to the same extent: though
the waiting period was shorter it had to be served for every new claim.

Despite the contrasting institutional structures the degree of financial
autonomy of the French and British systems vis-à-vis the state seems to
have been equally limited. In France state intervention took the form of
establishment of maximum relief scales and the yearly voting of the budget for subsidies to local funds. At the outset the British Unemployment
Insurance scheme was intended to be self-financing. Levels of contribution and benefit were set by actuarial calculations based on prewar experience of trade union members. The extension of the scheme and the
raising of benefit levels in 1921 coupled with the rise in unemployment
marked the beginning of increasingly discretionary state intervention.
The granting of extended benefit to those who had exhausted their claims
effectively undermined the self-liquidating nature of the scheme. Successive governments were faced with the dilemma of providing relief to
unprecedented numbers of unemployed while attempting to preserve the
system from financial ruin.[10]

4 Analysis by Occupation and by *Département* of Unemployment in France During the 1930s

4.1 Unemployment Relieved in Paris: The Analysis of Individual Case Histories

A personal file was established for each unemployed person at the unemployment fund where he registered. I was fortunate enough to rediscover
the trace of files completed between 1930 and 1939 by the relief agencies
of the twenty *arrondissements* of Paris. They had been preserved initially
by the public employment bureaux and then by the National Employment
Agency (l'Agence Nationale pour l'Emploi) in order to facilitate the application of regulations concerning the validation of periods of unemploy-

ment in the calculation of social security retirement pensions.[11] These files made possible a detailed analysis of the unemployed receiving relief in Paris, who represented 43 per cent of the total number of unemployed in France in March 1931 and 24 per cent of the total in March 1936.

A random sample of 6,084 individual files was drawn, individual files having been extracted at regular intervals from the files arranged in alphabetical order.[12]

When an individual approached an unemployment fund for the first time in order to seek aid, a file was opened in his name. If he came a second time after having been struck off the register, the same file was taken up anew. If, on the other hand, the individual changed address and went to another agency, the details relating to prior relief were recovered. Thus the files record all the details concerning periods of relief.

The unemployed person was struck off the register not only when he found work, but also when he no longer fulfilled the required conditions. Thus one often encounters "resources greater than scale rate" as a motive for exclusion, particularly for non-heads of households. Such persons could only be aided if the head of household was himself without work or if he had very slim resources.

As tools for the management of the unemployment funds, the files assembled a variety of personal details. On the one hand, the information made it possible to check that the individual really fulfilled the conditions required for receipt of benefit: to be "without work", and to have undergone the waiting period prior to payment of benefits, the dates of hiring and redundancy corresponding to the necessity to be "involuntarily unemployed due to lack of work". The file also showed the individual's address and the date of his taking up residence at this address in order to justify his residence in the municipality granting relief, his nationality, foreigners only being relieved if they came from a country which had established reciprocal arrangements with the French government; and his date of taking up residence in the Seine region (*département*), a prefectorial circular of 1935 having limited the granting of relief to the unemployed resident in this region prior to July 1934.

The files also contained information used in calculating benefits: the position of the unemployed person in the household, his age, profession and wage, together with the same information for all the other people in the household. Rent, payments for the upbringing of children by wet nurses and other resources such as family allowances are also reported.

We are in possession of the case history of every individual registered with a Parisian unemployment fund for every year between 1930 and 1939. It is thus possible to go beyond the study of a single period of unemployment, taking into account the fact that some individuals underwent numerous but short-lived spells of unemployment. In what follows,

we have considered only the first three years following the initial registration. The results are thus limited to the unemployed initially registered
in Paris between 1930 and 1936.

On the basis of these data, a number of questions can be studied. First,
we chose to study the individual's unemployment history: each unemployed person can be traced by a group of variables relating to the cumulative duration of his unemployment and the frequency of registration
with the unemployment funds. Second, we study the characteristics of the
unemployed person himself: his trade, household composition, age and
sex, his living conditions and his former professional life. Both these
groups of variables were analysed using principal components analysis.[13]

The histories are represented by a set of qualitative variables a_{ij}. The
variable a_{ij} relates to the year i following the initial registration (i=1,2,3).
It corresponds to a possible combination of the cumulative duration of
unemployment and the number of entries into unemployment for the year
i. These combinations were chosen as a means to guarantee sufficient representativeness for each case. For year i only one variable is given a value
of 1, the others having zero value. The history of each unemployed person during the three years following his first registration is thus represented by twenty-four dummy variables, three of them taking a value of
1. Appendix 7.1 contains the precise coding of the variables.

This choice preserves rather well the variety of the individual histories,
although the conjunctural aspect is somewhat obscured since it is only to
be found in the "year of initial registration" variable. Moreover, the simultaneous taking into account of "individual time" (the lapse of time from
the moment of registration with a fund) and of "historical time" (the year
in which the events take place) poses theoretical problems familiar to all
econometricians.[14]

Starting from this choice, the analysis of multiple correspondences faci-
litates interconnecting of the major oppositions which emerge from the
types of history with the information we possess on the familial situation,
living conditions and professional history of the unemployed person.[15]

Some explanation may be useful here of how to interpret the results of
a principal components analysis. The purpose of the technique is to construct a new and smaller set of measures out of a series of intercorrelated
variables, the principal components. The principal components are linear
combinations of the original variables that account for most of the original set. In other words, the corresponding axes (the first two being
reported in Figure 7.2) explain the maximum percentages of the total variance, or inertia, in decreasing order. So to interpret each axis in the figure
we have to look for and identify the variables and the observations which
have the strongest absolute coordinates on each axis and which are the
most closely correlated with each of them.

The first axis of analysis captures 11 per cent of the variation.[16] On one side of this axis can be seen a form of unemployment which could be characterised as "heavy": histories in which there is either a belated return to work or no return at all and histories in which, in the long term, there are repeated but short-lived returns to employment. On the other side is "light" unemployment: one short spell in the first year.

The second axis accounts for 7 per cent of the variation. It opposes single-periods of unemployment (the periods ranging from short spells to spells longer than a year) and repeated spells of unemployment (with several registrations often totalling long durations). The second axis cannot really be considered as representing the frequency of spells given that this is also reflected on the first axis. Figure 7.1 indicates that the number of periods cuts across this axis and is linked with the intensity of unemployment as defined by the first axis. This suggests that there was a tendency for multi-period unemployment to be associated with longer total durations. However, this assocation was not uniform. There were frequent cases of single-period unemployment which resulted in either short or long durations. In trades like building where employment was unstable, the duration of individual spells was often relatively short but frequently repeated. This pattern of multi-period unemployment forming long total durations grew in importance during the 1930s. The scale of this phenomenon was demonstrated by the Pouillot Report (Ministère du Travail, 1939) on a qualitative survey of the unemployed in the Paris region undertaken in 1937.

When the supplementary variables are projected on to the figure defined by the first two axes, three configurations or subpopulations appear. Each of these configurations corresponds to a distinct type of unemployment.

4. 1. 1 "Dependent", "Rejected" and "Model" Unemployed. The first subpopulation is made up of unemployed people whose position is subordinate to that of the head of household, such as married women, youngsters living with their parents, and grandparents who were only recognised by the authorities as unemployed people entitled to benefits if the head of household was unemployed. These persons were not aided in their own right; the scale rate for heads of household made no distinction between married women who were unemployed and those who had never worked outside the home.

This subpopulation was subject to short-lived unemployment with fewer spells than of household heads of the same sex. Typically, they experienced brief periods of unemployment benefit which were terminated either after an inquiry had been made (the head of household being in work) or following a change of circumstances (the head of household having started employment). Moreover, institutional effects went beyond the

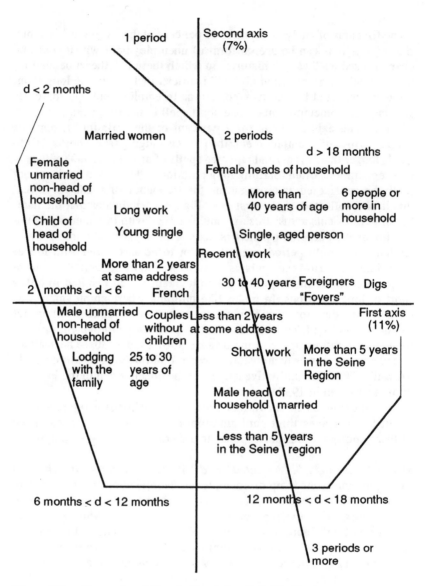

Figure 7.1 Unemployed People Receiving Relief in Paris

Note: Not to scale. d: cumulative duration of unemployment over 3 years. Long work: length of the last period of employment longer than 9 months. Short work: length of the last period of employment of less than 9 months. Recent work: ending 2 months prior to the registration.
Source: Marpsat (1984).

simple application of the regulations governing relief. Once-only registration was particularly noticeable amongst married women. Such behaviour betrayed an internalisation of the regulations which went beyond their strict interpretation. Finally, there was little motivation for these people to declare themselves "unemployed", and perhaps to perceive themselves as such, given that the institutions did not distinguish them from "women who have established their own household".

A second distinct subpopulation is made up of the "rejected": foreigners, the old or single, and people who had been without work for some time, living in furnished accommodation. This population, subject to long periods of unemployment, was accorded minor tasks by the institutions, often involving maintenance or roadwork; such jobs were reserved for the unemployed who, having failed to find work, had been registered with the funds over a long period.

Rejected by the world of work, this population was also marginalised by the institutions dealing with unemployment. The aged and foreigners found themselves on the borderline of the category "unemployed"; registration conditions for foreigners were far more severe than for French citizens and had a tendency to become more severe over time. Yet foreigners were also rejected by the world of work; institutional discrimination by nationality was enshrined in the law of 10 August 1932 which limited the number of foreigners employed in any trade and gave priority to French citizens in the placement services of the employment agencies. The aged were frequently denied relief after the age of 60, in favour of the dependence upon compulsory old age pensions established by the law of 1905. However, examination of individual dossiers suggests that, in practice, the retirement pensions were often supplemented by continued registration with an unemployment fund.

The third subpopulation - the "average" or "model" unemployed - consists of married, middle-aged Frenchmen who were also heads of household. These had priority for job vacancies filled by the funds.

Another characteristic which appears here is stability: the stability of work as measured by the last period of employment, or the stability of residence as indicated by the number of years the claimant was established at the address indicated when the first dossier was opened. Stability is associated with shorter and less frequent spells of unemployment. On the other hand, long-term unemployment is linked with long-standing residence in the Seine region. But this stability was also correlated with professional status, a relationship to which we now turn.

4. 1. 2 Relationship Between Trade and Type of Unemployment. The evidence of a close relationship between professional status and unemployment emerges as one of the most robust findings. We distinguished five

Table 7.6   **Number of Inflows into Unemployment and Cumulative Duration of Unemployment, Within a Period of Three Years since the First Registration, for Five Main Occupational Groups in Paris (%)**

	Labourers, handlers unskilled workers (male)	Building and wood workers (male)	Metal workers (male)	Office workers (female)	Dress makers (female)
Number of spells of unemployment over three years					
One	35	21	36	53	45
Two	24	21	25	19	22
Three or more	41	58	39	28	33
Total	100	100	100	100	100
Cumulative duration of unemployment over three years					
Less than 2 months	18	18	25	20	26
2 to less than 6 months	19	24	28	29	30
6 months to less than a year	20	26	20	21	20
A year to less than 18 months	13	13	9	10	9
18 months and more	30	19	18	20	15
Total	100	100	100	100	100

Source: See text.

main professional groups subdivided by trade in the global analysis, together constituting 42 per cent of the sample. There were three male and two female groups: the male groups consisted of labourers, handlers and unskilled workers; building and woodworkers; and metal workers. The female groups consisted of dressmakers and office workers.

Table 7.6 indicates, for each group, the number of spells of unemployment and the cumulative duration of unemployment within three years after initial registration (limited to unemployed people registered for the first time between 1930 and 1936).

Again, the first axis is associated with "heavy unemployment": the unemployment of male labourers, handlers and unskilled workers rather than that of metal workers, dressmakers and men employed in service.

The second axis is associated with the building and woodworking trades or, more precisely, to the opposition between male woodworkers and construction workers on the one hand and trade or office employees, service workers, labourers and unskilled workers of both sexes on the other.

The building trades can be distinguished by recurrent short spells of unemployment, in contrast with occupations which had longer periods of employment and unemployment. The situation of labourers was one of "heavy" unemployment broken by intermittent spells of work. Office workers experienced a bimodal situation in which long- and short-term unemployment coexisted.

In engineering, where there was a relative shortage of skilled workers due to the expansion of the war industries in the 1930s, periods of unemployment were short and the population of rejected unemployed was underrepresented.

4. 2   Industrialisation, Urbanisation and Unemployment Recorded in the Censuses

In the preceding section, we analysed the heterogeneity of unemployment in Paris from the perspective of individual unemployment histories, covering, on the one hand, the impact of demographic variables and, on the other, the role of occupational status in the functioning of the labour market.

But Paris was a special case. A large and more geographically unified market for wage labour was coming into being. Public relief funding was an established tradition. Paris and its suburbs, together with the Seine & Oise region, contained 40 per cent of the total of unemployed in France, but only 15 per cent of the total population. To what extent can it be said that the effects of the crisis on employment were concentrated in the Paris region? An alternative hypothesis is that the dominant mechanism of adjustment of employment and of labour regulation in Paris took the form of unemployment and that, elsewhere, this form of adjustment competed with other mechanisms.[17]

The correlation coefficient reveals a statistically insignificant relationship between the rise of unemployment and the reduction in employment for the years 1931 to 1936 at the regional level.[18] The increase of unemployment, according to the census, does not seem to be linked directly to the evolution of the employment situation for each region.

How can this paradox be explained? To evaluate the question we again use principal components analysis. This technique is appropriate for analysing the diversity of models of labour regulation and employment relationships existing in the interwar labour market. We argue that a set of complex forces was operating simultaneously on both sides of the labour market and that it is these forces, not supply and demand, which are of analytical interest. Having identified the relevant co-occurrences of variables, we build our interpretation of these relationships on qualitative analysis and case studies of the employment relationship, connecting it to the changing social structures within the enterprise, the occupations of workers, their way of life and the value attached to labour.

We analyse the relationships between variables relating to unemployment (see Appendix 7.3) and variables reflecting the socioeconomic structure of each region (*département*) taken from the population censuses of 1931 and 1936. Demographic characteristics are identified by the age and sex composition of employed workers and the proportion of foreign-born. Types of production relations are represented by the average size of enterprise, industry type, degree of mechanisation, capital intensity, and the proportion of wage earners in the active population. Other socioeconomic characteristics included in the analysis are the proportion of the population living in urban areas, the relative wage level and the degree of geographical mobility. (For further details of these variables see Appendix 7.2.)

The results for men are presented in Figure 7.2. The first factorial axis explains half of the variation. Most of the explanatory variables contribute to it. A close examination shows that the first axis is close to the intersection of two other axes. First is an axis of industrialisation. It distinguishes the regions of small enterprise from those where large-scale industry predominated and where there was a large and consolidated class of workers and employees. In the regions of small enterprise, non-agricultural "isolated" persons were numerous: the census includes, within the category "isolated persons", small independent workers (working on their own account), and people with irregular employment and homeworkers. The use of motive power in order to mechanise work was greatest in those *départements* where heavy industry predominated. It is therefore in these areas that the mechanisation of work was most advanced and this was linked to a large concentration of workers inside large firms. The position of "wage-earning employment" was growing in importance along this industrialisation axis.

The second axis is an "urbanisation" axis which distinguishes urban *départements* from those which were agricultural and rural. In the former, the rate of unemployment was high, whatever the yardstick: those recorded as jobless, those in receipt of unemployment benefit or those registered at labour exchanges. The category "unemployed" was growing in importance along this axis of urbanisation, as is confirmed by the establishment of unemployment funds and labour exchanges. The contrast between low and high wages is also linked to this axis: wages were low in rural areas, high in urban ones.

The two axes are correlated, but not identical, since urbanisation and industrialisation tended to go hand-in-hand. Still, the most heavily indus-

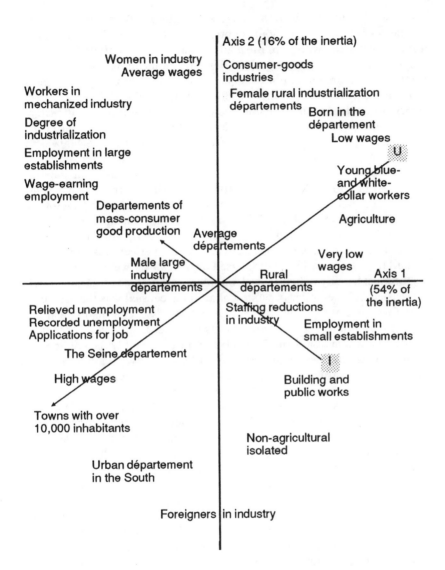

Figure 7.2 Socioeconomic Characteristics and Unemployment in 1936:
The First Two Axes of a Principal Components Analysis

Note: Not to scale. U: urbanisation axis. I: industrialisation axis. Figure 7.3 shows
the classification of the départements according to these criteria.
Source: Salais *et al.* (1986), p. 79.

trialised *départements* were not necessarily those with the greatest concentration of urban population; country boroughs and small towns which had retained a link with rural life could constitute the domicile for a large proportion of workers in large factories. The implications for unemployment could be dramatic. For example, in 1936 Le Nord and Les Vosges (see Figure 7.3) were among the most heavily industrialised *départements*. More than half of the employed worked in manufacturing industry; establishments of over 100 people accounted for nearly three-quarters of all workers. The proportion of wage earners was one of the highest in France, approaching that of the Seine *département*. However, Le Nord was urban while Les Vosges was rural: only 15.5 per cent of the population lived in a town of more than 10,000 inhabitants. In Les Vosges 40 per cent of industrial employees worked in non-mechanised factories, only 11 per cent in Le Nord. There was widespread unemployment in Le Nord (9.3 per cent for men, 4.7 per cent for women), while the average rate in Les Vosges was much lower (2.9 and 2.2 per cent respectively).

Similarly, the most highly urbanised *départements* were not necessarily the most heavily industrialised, nor those in which wage-earning work (classified as blue-collar or white-collar in the census) was the predominant form of employment. It is, of course, necessary to distinguish the large conurbations such as Paris and its suburbs, Lyon and the *département* of Le Rhône, La Seine-Maritime with Rouen and Le Havre or even Saint-Etienne and the *département* of La Loire. These conurbations had prominent and varied industries, a large tertiary sector and a considerable number of wage earners, both male and female.

We observe, particularly in the southern half of France, a style of life and work centred around a slightly industrialised large city and encompassing only a moderate number of wage earners. This is the case of La Haute-Garonne, centred around Toulouse, where almost half of the *département*'s population was grouped and where there was no other city of more than 10,000 inhabitants: 31 per cent of blue- and white-collar employees worked in manufacturing industry, but only 27 per cent of these in establishments of more than 100 employees. The number of wage earners was average, but the proportion of "isolated" employed in non-agricultural work was large: 19 per cent for men and 25 per cent for women. Another example was Les Bouches-du-Rhône, centred around Marseilles where 75 per cent of the population lived. Here there existed an urban lifestyle, little industry, a large tertiary sector and a substantial number of people living off "odd jobs" on the fringe of the wage-earning and skilled population, and falling between regular and irregular employment. The proportion of wage earners in the population was average for men and low for women. In these two *départements*, recorded unemployment was high for both men and women.

**Figure 7.3   A Typology of *Départements* According to Degree of
            Urbanisation and Industrialisation in 1936**

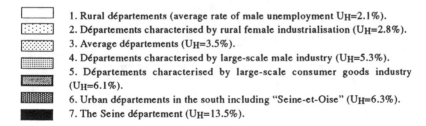

1. Rural départements (average rate of male unemployment U_H=2.1%).
2. Départements characterised by rural female industrialisation (U_H=2.8%).
3. Average départements (U_H=3.5%).
4. Départements characterised by large-scale male industry (U_H=5.3%).
5. Départements characterised by large-scale consumer goods industry (U_H=6.1%).
6. Urban départements in the south including "Seine-et-Oise" (U_H=6.3%).
7. The Seine département (U_H=13.5%).

Note: The rate of unemployment is calculated as a share of the active wage-earning population (see Appendix 7.2). The average for all the *départements* U_H=4.1%.

The second axis of the factorial analysis also has explanatory power. It distinguishes the proportions of women and foreigners in manufacturing industry. It indicates, on the one side, that the south contained a high percentage of "isolated persons" and that its industry was based not on an indigenous labour force but on immigrant workers. It illustrates, on the other side, what could be called industrialised rural regions: industrialisation based on traditional consumer goods, employing a large proportion of women (primarily the textile industry but also shoemaking, leather goods and food). Large establishments were often prominent. Recorded unemployment was generally very low in these "industrialised rural regions".[19]

The second axis thus captures intersectoral variations in unemployment. This is true also of the third axis, which is not represented on the graph, which distinguishes labour-intensive, consumer goods industries from heavy industry.

These conclusions are consistent with the results of hierarchical classifications, based on the same explanatory variables. This analysis reveals seven groups of *départements* (see Figure 7.3). Groups 1 to 5 are classified by increasing degrees of industrialisation and labour concentration. This produces a paradoxical result: rates of employment and unemployment tended to increase together. This tendency of simultaneous increase in wage-earning employment and unemployment reaches its maximum in the Seine *département* (group 7), where the highest values for all but one of the variables (the "isolated") were concentrated: urbanisation, unemployment, geographical mobility, industrialisation, concentration of labour and proportion of waged and salaried jobs. Group 6 is an exception to the rule: in the urban *départements* of the south, the level of unemployment was very high.

5 The Employment Relationship and Unemployment in the 1930s

The study of unemployment in Paris revealed labour market structures whose implications for unemployment were at least as important as sociodemographic criteria for which the unemployment funds were responsible. A regional analysis reveals at least four distinct models. These appear in combinations which vary from one place to another:

(1) The model of unemployment which emphasises the relationship of variations in wage-earning jobs in industry (in cities or their environs) with the incidence of high unemployment.

(2) The contrasting model of "isolated" work (to use the term in the census): homeworkers, those with irregular employment or having several jobs, and the self employed. Regulation of the amount of work is, to

some extent, made by the individual himself. In particular its reduction does not take the form of unemployment.

(3) The model of the small business founded on a kind of "implicit" long-term "contract", based on personalised relationships or common craft values. This permits partial or total unemployment which is self-managed by the trade, all the while maintaining the link with the enterprise. The model of paternalism, where employees' life outside work is also taken care of, is quite similar to this mode.

(4) The model of rural industrialisation which avoids the creation of a wage-earning class and makes use of its rural, agricultural environment to cope with variations in the number of jobs without creating unemployment as such.

This coexistence of these models helps to explain the low level of unemployment in France during the 1930s. The model of unemployment (1 above) is a minority one, or at least not the predominant one. This model, however, underlies most modern empirical approaches inspired by economic theory and, in a more general way, underlies economic policies towards employment.

The employment relationship involves two essential characteristics: the nature of the link between employer and employee, and the concept of time, its subdivision and the resulting compartmentalisation of work and of related social activities. Comparison of the employment relationship between employers and employees in the four models distinguished above allows us to understand why and how big industry defined waged and salaried work between the wars, and how a connection was established with the social position of the "unemployed".

5.1 The Model of "Isolated" Work

First is the model of "isolated" work, the classic example of which is the homeworker. This is a difficult category to enumerate. The population census between the wars used this make-shift category for workers not readily classified as "independent", "blue-collar", "white-collar", or "unemployed blue- or white-collar worker". The category of "isolated" is, therefore, imprecise, both in its content and in its composition. It includes self-employed workers and people working alone, but also includes wage earners with irregular jobs and homeworkers. Population censuses considerably underestimate the number of homeworkers. According to one contemporary study, homeworkers numbered upwards of a million women in 1936. There is no doubt that a large number of homeworkers did not make declarations which would enable the administration to analyse their sources of income. Certain homeworkers also had another occupation, that of small farmer for instance, and they only declared their least remunerative and most easily concealed work, i.e. their secondary occupation. Married women and young women who lived and worked at home generally declared themselves as "jobless" (Paulin, 1938). In 1936 the census counted the number of homeworkers as only 214,000 and the number of wage earners with irregular jobs as 236,000.

Homeworkers' jobs were irregular, both in quantity and rhythm. In the Parisian clothes industry, the "dead season", when there was no work whatsoever, was followed by a rush during which the homeworker worked nights and Sundays (Guilbert and Isambert-Jamati, 1956). Labour shedding in the dead season was generally made at the expense of the homeworkers, no formalities having been asked of them. Homeworking therefore permitted the very flexible management of labour. The regulation of the amount of work was, in certain respects, made by the individual himself and his family. Reductions in the amount of work often took place without the intervention of unemployment.

The dependence of homeworkers on the establishment which offered them work, while considerable, was not mediated by any formal institutional structure. During the dead season, the worker did not know if he or she would be taken back; the employer had no obligation either to do so or even to inform the worker of his decision. But the link with the employer, while implicit and never formalised, was rarely broken. To this extent, it was a stable connection.

Breaking this connection with the employer could not be done without risk to the worker. In order to apply for benefit during the dead season, the worker a notice of redundancy, and in the absence of any agreement between employer and employee this entailed the risk of not being taken on again in the busy season.

In many ways, wage earners in small businesses resembled homeworkers, particularly in the employer/employee relationships. There was often a strong attachment operating through personal relationships, more in the nature of an equal relationship between independent individuals than one resting on authority and hierarchy. Isolation and the fluctuations in the workload were counterbalanced by personal responsibility and the freedom to organise one's own time. The position of these workers was thus similar to that of self-employed workers and contrasted with the hierarchical or bureaucratic organisation which dominated even the smallest details of any job in a large enterprise.

5.2   The Model of the Small Business

The same can be said, but to a lesser degree, of the structure of work in small businesses. In a small business where the employer worked alongside his employees, often together with members of his family, personal relationships continued to be important. As one contemporary observer put it, "the relationships which grow up between employer and employee are today individual; an agreement which has been discussed and possesses all the characteristics of a contract, affects the conditions of work, but is *intuitu personae*" (Laroque, 1938). The distinctions remained fairly blurred since for an individual worker the option of self-employment still existed. The position of the wage earner was not necessarily a permanent one, nor was job loss a problem to be resolved by the application for and acceptance of unemployment benefit.

It could be said that, in many respects, a kind of implicit long-term "contract" was established in this case between an employer and his employees. This implicit contract might include many aspects of activity both at work and outside, and could be of a paternalistic nature. It distributed the roles, rights and duties of the various parties over the organisation of production and the common management of fluctuations in work and in pay. This was still the case at the beginning of the 1950s, as Moscovici (1961) demonstrates for the hat industry in L'Aude (a *département* in the south) where small or average-sized factories, either rural or in small provincial towns, were the principal employers.

The craftsman was in charge of his own tools and sometimes had the right of hiring his own assistants. He organised work according to his own criteria. The responsibility for production time and work rhythm was his own. This was because in any type of manufacturing which was not standardised, there was often no objective way of calculating or forecasting costs incurred outside of and apart from the worker and his team. The freedom given to the skilled worker in his job and working hours, making him liable for the success of the undertaking, was the necessary condition for production of high-quality manufactures. Thus fluctuations in output could be met by variations in work effort or in total hours of labour.

Employers were integrated into the local community as dignitaries. They knew their workers prior to employing them and had close ties with their families outside work. They also had local responsibilities beyond the labour context. This paternal framework shaped the work relationship and, more generally, all social relationships. As Moscovici (1961) says, "Everyone has a position to keep up, he must 'save face' before the others as regards his responsibilities and obligations, and must preserve the individuality he has acquired and which others have recognised in him."

Workers could thus accept periods of partial or total unemployment so long as they were assured of being taken back later. The worker gave his skill and loyalty and expected much more than mere money in return.

Another model, that of rural industry employing a female labour force, can be observed in the *départements* where unemployment was low. In group 2 of our typology (see Figure 7.3), more than half of those employed worked in agriculture, and 71 per cent of the population lived in communities of under 2,000 inhabitants. Small or medium-sized industry was grafted on to this predominantly rural, agricultural base. If this did not create an industrial working class it at least led to its birth. At a union congress in 1933 (the CGTU Congress), one militant, while underlining the difficulties of union action, revealed the existence of 20,000 textile workers, scattered around numerous villages in L'Ardèche. We can presume that sudden interruptions in work were regulated by the rural agricultural world which surrounded these pockets of wage-earning jobs. But in what way? By the family and the small family farm? Did peasant workers have two jobs?

5. 3 Work Relationships in Big Business, and the Establishment of a Model of Unemployment

In big business, the introduction of Taylorism or other similar systems, such as that of Bedaux, led to time management which was accurate, subdivided and ordered. It was a type of management formalised by procedures, rules and calculations. This is particularly true for large urban, mechanised engineering enterprises, notably the car industry. Until 1926 the influence of Taylorism was limited to four large car manufacturers: Berliet, Renault, Citroën and Peugeot. But from 1927 onwards, the desire to cut prices, following on a change in the economic situation and an increase in sales outlets, led to its extension to the whole of the car industry and to certain other manufacturers of consumer goods which were experiencing a boom, notably the food industries. The increase in assembly-line production outside engineering work foreshadowed the mass production of cheap goods which were quickly sold with the help of large-scale advertising campaigns.

Even if this rationalisation remained limited to certain sectors between the wars, it still had a real effect on the job market, and on union and industrial leaders. The writings of Hyacinthe Dubreuil[20] bear this out, as does the creation of various bodies: the French National Committee for Organisation in 1926 which united the followers of F.W. Taylor and H. Fayol; the General Commission for Scientific and Organisational Studies in 1927 which developed from the national employer union, the CGPF (Confederation Générale du Patronat Français); and the French Association for Normalisation in 1928 (see Lequin, 1979 and Moutet, 1983a).[21]

The rise of rationalised big businesses was the major novelty of the interwar period, compared with the end of the nineteenth century.[22] It posed questions for the identity of the people at work, which had to be changed from the identity given to them by craftwork.

As workers began their apprenticeship in rationalised and institution-alised work relationships, they became conscious of new work rhythms. The work/no work frontier became a clear division between two worlds and was lived as such, as a separation between workplace and home. The division of labour tended to split workers into categories and to push them towards work demanding specific qualifications.

Workers were confronted with the need to rebuild or at least partially modify their conception of their work, of its results and of their place in production. The "preindustrial" model had glorified liberal values such as setting up on one's own, something it shared with the professional out-look of skilled workers. The rationalised model emphasised "technical" values: output, speed and production. The spirit of enterprise and worker independence were, for the supporters of the rational model, things to be banished. "The worker is no longer a small entrepreneur who, in deter-mining his wage by bargaining, fixes the fair price by haggling and, at the same time, starts his apprenticeship in the role of future manager of his own small business" (Mottez, 1966, p.138). In the rational model, "the worker stays a worker, all he wants is to earn an honest living."

This model, then, implied (at least for the future) a change in personal identity. The change in the form of payment plays an important role here. As Moscovici put it,

> Piecework - the old pattern - signified a certain independence for the worker in the conduct of his work and in the ordering of its consti-tuent parts, giving him the impression of participating more actively in production whilst reinforcing the link between his manual tech-niques and the object. Hourly payment expressed the uniformity of the technical organisation of work, the dependence of this on central supervision and the identification between skills and periods of time. The worker could no longer visualise the amount to be produced; for the same reason, he derived the impression of a certain regularity in income. (Moscovici, 1961, pp.78-9).

Under these circumstances, the worker could calculate the earnings he would make in relation to the effort put in. This predictability favoured a preference for stable wages. The time perspective was thus considerably transformed for both the individual and collective modes of perception and behaviour. Workers were officially relieved of the need to fix working hours and wages, a responsibility that skilled workers took on board through negotiation. The organisation of work was transferred to manag-ers. Workers were taken from a position of responsibility for production to one of formal subjection, their goal being a stable maximum of earning.

These norms influenced both the volume of work and wage levels. These fluctuations were no longer felt by the workers to be an internal part of work. They could thus become externalised in the form of unemployment. Registration as "unemployed" could henceforth be integrated into the thinking of the workers as a stage in active life. Changes in individual and collective behaviour were congruent with the changes in management procedures in those businesses where rationalisation had been introduced.

To sum up, the rationalisation of management was founded on a technological phase, on mechanisation and on Taylor's principles of the division of labour - the scientific analysis of time and motion. Management ceased to be based on personal relationships, as in the model of small business, and became based on job descriptions. Individual work, in effect, was objectified in the material form of posts, each one defined in terms of tasks and work accomplished. Variations in the volume of work were formalised by regulations relating to hiring and firing. A rationalised business, then, has the ability to measure surplus work in the form of surplus employees. It can also identify these surplus persons by objective criteria, similar to those which define the unemployed. The situation was by no means the same in the models described earlier.

6 Conclusion

The extent and duration of the unemployment brought about by the macroeconomic crisis of the 1930s necessitated state intervention to relieve the unemployed. As a result, the regulations governing the provision of trade union-linked unemployment benefits and public assistance which had traditionally varied by industry and region, were replaced by a set of uniform regulations applying nationwide. The new system of uniform regulations was based on two principles: assistance should be provided to families and not individuals, and the link between the worker and his enterprise of previous employment should be strengthened not weakened.

At one level, the adoption of a uniform set of national regulations governing the provision of public assistance for the unemployed increased the perceived uniformity of the labour market. As unemployed persons grew accustomed to applying for benefits, the national organisation of the unemployment assistance system gave rise to a uniformity in the position of the "unemployed". This uniformity was reinforced by the rationalisation of work in large enterprises. The organisation of work was increasingly based on clearly delimited job descriptions, defined in terms of both time and space. The type of chronic underemployment which had characterised agricultural and artisanal work no longer had a place in French manufacturing. Wage earners were forced to adjust their job search to the increasing uniformity of the jobs offered by rationalised firms on the one hand, and to the increasing uniformity of unemployment benefits offered by the national unemployment system on the other. On another level, waged and salaried employment was increasingly sharply delineated as distinct from unemployment. Unemployment progressively became a distinct category quite separate from sickness or disability.

Yet the transformation of the labour market and the rise of unemployment as a distinct category had only proceeded part way to its conclusion by the end of the 1930s. The sharp distinction between employment and unemployment implanted by the unemployment insurance funds and the large enterprises pervaded only certain sectors of the economy. The distinction was much less clear-cut in rural areas, in the mercantile sector, among skilled artisans and in small companies. The crisis of the 1930s brought about an increase in the number of self-employed (*isolés*) and a decrease in the population of active wage earners, which tended to blur the distinction between the employed and the unemployed.

Although "unemployment" as a social category into which workers might fall began to be used with increasing frequency by both firms and workers, its application remained limited to employees of large, rationalised firms and residents of the towns. The rural character of much of the French economy and the traditional organisation of many firms caused many individuals who suffered some loss of work from the Great Depression not to be counted as unemployed, or even to be conceived as such.

The slowness with which concepts of labour market status changed in France in the 1930s should not be permitted to mask the importance of the conceptual developments of the interwar years. Despite that the treatment of the problem of unemployment remained the domain of social assistance rather than economic policy; the reforms taken after Liberation and in the 1950s took as their point of departure the conceptual models of the labour market that emerged in the 1930s. Ultimately, restoring full employment rather than unemployment insurance became the framework for postwar labour market policy.

APPENDIX 7.1 The Coding of Variables Representing the Histories of the Unemployed Assisted in Paris

Cumulative duration of unemployment	Number of registrations		
First year	1	2	3 or more
Less than 30 days	$a_{1.1}$	$a_{1.2}$	$a_{1.3}$
30-119 days	$a_{1.4}$	$a_{1.5}$	$a_{1.6}$
120-365 days	$a_{1.7}$	$a_{1.8}$	$a_{1.9}$
Over the whole year	$a_{1.10}$		
Second year	0	1	2 or more
0 days	$a_{2.1}$	-	-
1-150 days	$a_{2.2}$	$a_{2.3}$	$a_{2.4}$
More than 150 days	$a_{2.5}$	$a_{2.6}$	$a_{2.7}$
Third year	0	1	2 or more
0 days	$a_{3.1}$	-	-
1-240 days	$a_{3.2}$	$a_{3.3}$	$a_{3.4}$
More than 240 days	$a_{3.5}$	$a_{3.6}$	$a_{3.7}$

Note: Each variable a_{ij} takes the value 1 in the corresponding case and the value 0 in all other cases.

APPENDIX 7.2 Variables Used in the Analysis of Regional Unemployment in the Census of 1936

The choice of variables is limited by the tables made available in the census documents of 1936. Thirteen variables were used for the analysis. Separate analyses were undertaken for men and women. We used a principal components analysis with centred normalised variables. These variables were not weighted; a hierarchical classification was applied in order to produce a regional typology.

A 2.1 Analytical Variables

These are of two types:
1 Employment/Unemployment Characteristics. The rate of unemployment is the proportion of workers and employees without work in what we defined as the active "wage-earning" population (the sum total of workers and employees with or without work and the "isolated").

The proportion of non-agricultural "isolated" is calculated in relation to the active "wage-earning" population as defined above.

The number of employed wage earners in the total population aged 10 years or more was used as an indicator of the rate of wage-earning employment. This procedure tends to overestimate the total active population given that the minimum working age was 13.

The proportion of young workers was based on the number of workers below 25 years of age as a share of workers.

The proportion of individuals born in their *département* of residence was based upon the total population. It is intended as an indicator of mobility, registering low values where immigration from abroad or from another *département* was high. It can be considered as a measure of the preservation of links with the family or with the local community and of the maintenance of roots in a certain locality.

2 *Socioeconomic Characteristics of the Département*. The degree of industrialisation is represented by the percentage of manufacturing workers in white- and blue-collar employment. The definition of the manufacturing labour force includes workers in building and public works but exclude miners, quarrymen, warehousemen and transport workers.

The relative importance of agriculture is calculated as the share of persons in agriculture in the total population.

The share of the population living in towns of more than 10,000 inhabitants is used as an indicator of urbanisation.

The degree of rurality is based on the proportion of the population living in communities of fewer than 2,000 inhabitants.

Industrial structure in manufacturing is characterised by four indicators: the proportion of blue- and white-collar workers employed in establishments of more than 100 people or of less than ten people, and the proportion of women or foreign workers.

A 2.2 Supplementary Variables

The number of unemployed receiving relief from the unemployment funds in each *département* in the first week of March 1936, together with the number of applications for work at the public labour exchanges, were expressed as a share of the active population, as indicated by the census.

The composition of industry was measured by disaggregating into consumer goods industries, building and public works, and engineering.

The reduction in staffing levels for white- and blue-collar workers in industry was calculated from the censuses of 1931 to 1936.

The annual reports on the social insurance law divide insured non-agricultural wage earners into income groups by region. Five categories are distinguished: less than 8 francs a day ("very low wages"), 8 to 15 francs a day ("low wages"), 15 to 20 francs a day ("average wages"), 20 to 32 francs a day, and 32 francs a day or more, the last two categories being "high wages". The importance of the "high wage" category is underestimated because of a ceiling on yearly income imposed on relief applicants.

Following an inquiry into the use of power undertaken in March 1931 by factory and mines inspectors in every industrial establishment (appended to the population census), we have extracted the percentage of manufacturing workers in establishments with power-driven equiment. We can consider this as an indicator of the degree of mechanisation.

APPENDIX 7.3 Rates of Unemployment by *Département*, Classified by Decreasing Rates in Column 1

Départements	In proportion to total pop'n of both sexes	Unemp't in manufacturing industries	In proportion to active "wage-earning" pop'n by sex	
			Male	Female
Seine (Banlieue)	6.4	21.1	17.6	16.3
Seine (Paris)	5.6	15.5	9.9	8.1
Seine-et-Oise	4.0	25.6	12.3	10.1
Haut-Rhin	4.0	16.0	12.8	5.6
Alpes-Maritimes	3.4	25.5	10.1	9.8
Nord	3.1	10.9	9.4	4.8
Seine-Intérieure	3.0	12.5	8.1	6.6
Rhône	2.9	10.7	7.5	6.3
Bas-Rhin	2.5	11.2	8.1	3.7
Bouches-du-Rhône	2.2	12.7	6.8	6.7
Aisne	2.2	12.5	7.6	3.6
Pas-de-Calais	2.1	9.2	7.2	4.7
Somme	2.1	10.8	7.1	3.9
Haute-Vienne	2.1	15.2	5.7	7.4
Gironde	2.0	11.4	5.7	5.3
Seine-et-Marne	2.0	11.2	5.7	4.4
Hérault	1.9	15.2	6.4	5.5
Marne	1.9	10.8	5.7	4.0
Loire-Intérieure	1.8	11.1	6.4	3.3
Oise	1.8	8.9	5.1	4.1
Ardennes	1.7	8.3	5.8	3.1
Haute-Garonne	1.7	11.2	5.1	6.2
Aude	1.7	12.2	6.1	4.1
Calvados	1.6	10.2	5.4	3.1
Aube	1.6	6.5	4.0	4.2
Meurthe-et-Moselle	1.6	6.1	4.3	3.7

Départements	In proportion to total pop'n of both sexes	Unemp't in manufacturing industries	In proportion to active "wage-earning" pop'n by sex	
			Male	Female
Belfort	1.4	5.4	3.5	3.6
Basses-Pyrénées	1.4	13.4	4.7	4.0
Loire	1.4	5.6	4.0	3.5
Pyrénées Orientales	1.4	12.1	5.0	4.1
Eure	1.3	6.7	3.8	3.0
Moselle	1.3	5.7	3.9	2.7
Isère	1.3	5.8	3.9	3.0
Jura	1.2	9.6	4.1	3.5
Loiret	1.2	7.6	3.9	3.0
Var	1.2	7.8	3.1	3.9
Gard	1.2	6.1	4.5	2.1
Indre-et-Loire	1.1	7.5	3.6	2.8
Vaucluse	1.1	9.6	4.0	3.7
Côte-d'Or	1.1	6.5	3.1	3.0
Eure-et-Loir	1.1	7.6	3.4	2.5
Vosges	1.0	4.1	2.9	2.3
Doubs	1.0	4.5	3.0	2.3
Drôme	1.0	7.9	3.5	3.4
Ain	1.0	9.1	3.4	3.0
Allier	1.0	6.7	3.4	3.0
Puy-de-Dôme	1.0	7.1	3.5	3.4
Ille-et-Villaine	1.0	8.7	3.6	2.2
Hautes-Pyrénées	1.0	8.1	3.5	2.6
Haute-Savoie	0.9	5.0	3.6	2.2
Creuse	0.9	17.2	2.9	4.1
Maine-et-Loire	0.9	5.8	2.9	2.1
Nièvre	0.9	6.1	2.8	3.0
Charente-Maritime	0.8	9.0	3.0	2.3
Savoie	0.8	7.4	2.9	1.9
Finistère	0.8	9.1	3.1	1.9
Cher	0.8	4.4	2.4	2.5
Orne	0.8	6.2	2.7	1.7
Yonne	0.8	6.1	2.7	2.3
Sarthe	0.8	6.3	2.7	1.9

Départements	In proportion to total pop'n of both sexes	Unemp't in manufacturing industries	In proportion to active "wage-earning" pop'n by sex	
			Male	Female
Cantal	0.8	7.8	3.5	1.7
Meuse	0.7	4.6	2.3	1.8
Lot-et-Garonne	0.7	7.5	2.5	2.6
Loir-et-Cher	0.7	5.8	2.4	1.7
Tarn	0.7	4.8	2.6	2.2
Saône-et-Loire	0.7	4.3	2.6	1.3
Hautes-Alpes	0.7	7.5	2.5	1.8
Tarn-et-Garonne	0.7	9.1	2.7	2.6
Indre	0.6	5.8	2.1	2.1
Manche	0.6	6.4	2.3	1.1
Charente	0.6	4.8	2.2	1.7
Morbihan	0.6	7.5	2.4	1.0
Vienne	0.6	6.7	2.1	1.9
Haute-Saône	0.6	3.9	2.1	1.5
Haute-Marne	0.6	3.3	1.9	1.2
Ardèche	0.5	4.8	2.2	1.9
Vendée	0.5	6.9	2.2	1.2
Basses-Alpes	0.5	6.0	2.0	1.3
Ariège	0.5	5.1	2.2	1.4
Lozère	0.5	11.2	2.8	0.7
Mayenne	0.5	4.4	1.7	1.1
Corrèze	0.5	5.8	1.9	1.3
Côtes-du-Nord	0.5	6.6	2.1	1.1
Haute-Loire	0.5	5.1	2.1	1.4
Landes	0.4	4.4	1.7	1.0
Deux-Sèvres	0.4	4.4	1.6	1.6
Aveyron	0.4	4.6	1.7	1.4
Dordogne	0.4	4.9	1.5	1.4
Corse	0.3	9.2	1.7	0.7
Gers	0.2	4.9	1.0	0.8
Lot	0.1	2.7	0.7	0.4

Note: Manufacturing industries are defined to include mining and quarrying, transport, and unskilled manual workers not classified by industry (both sexes).
Source: 1936 census.

NOTES

* Robert Salais is Head of the Groupement Scientifique CNRS/INSEE, "Institutions, Emploi et Politique Economique" (GS "IEPE"), Paris. The author would like to thank Maryse Marpsat, Françoise Dumontier and Nicolas Baverez for work made use of to establish some of the results presented here. The population census categories were analysed by Benedicte Reynaud for the book *L'invention du chômage* (Paris, 1986) written by Robert Salais in collaboration with Bénédicte Reynaud and Nicolas Baverez.

1 See the Population Census Archives (INSEE). Terms used in census documents are in inverted commas.

2 This information is taken from Letellier *et al.* (1938, p.197 ff., diagram 1); see Desmarest (1946) for a more general analysis.

3 See *Journal Officiel,* 30 December 1926.

4 In particular individuals could be struck off the register for habitual drunkenness or gambling.

5 This is an application of the *Code Civil:* "When the head of household has no dependent children or dependent grandparents, there exists no reason why he should receive benefits for his partner. The husband is, according to his abilities and state, legally obliged by article 214 of the *Code Civil* to provide his wife with everything necessary for her needs" (Ministry of Labour circular of 25 August). See *Bulletin du Ministère du Travail* (July-August, 1933).

6 See, for example, Mansfield (1987) for the early history of labour exchanges.

7 For further details of the insurance system and its operation, see Beveridge (1930) and Garside (1980).

8 The idea of collecting contributions, by affixing stamps in a book, was taken from the German system.

9 Conditions governing duration of benefit were structured to furnish incentives to workers and employers to control and plan unemployment. Workers formed themselves into "pools" of five or six members who arranged with their employers the rotation of unemployment among the members of the group, one or two of them being unemployed at any given moment. In extreme versions workers on short-time alternated between three days of unemployment and three of work. This practice of rotating unemployment was commonplace among dockers. On the dockside a port works committee maintained registers or preference lists conceived as a means of limiting the number of dockers seeking work. These registers permitted the organisation of work in such a way that the rule of "three days on the hook, three days on the book" was always respected. An excellent description of casual labour in the port transport industry can be found in Philips and Whiteside (1985).

10 See, for this history during the interwar period, Whiteside (1987).

11 This is a bulky collection which, despite some mislaid documents, is rather well preserved. It starts in 1930 and continues through the war years. The aged unemployed were nonetheless underrepresented since fund administrators responsible for verifying entitlement to retirement pensions were in the habit of destroying the files of claimants after verification or invalidation had taken place. These files have since been stocked in the National Archives where they are open to consultation by researchers, subject to conditions of confidentiality.

12 This is a bunched sample, each bunch being a box of files found in the archives and totalling nearly 245 files, opened between 1 January 1930 and 31 December 1939. We randomly extracted twenty-five boxes out of 1,031. The total number of files still preserved for this period can be estimated at a little more than 250,000.

13 An outline of this method can be found in Volle (1981). Here we present only the graphs but the interpretations which they give rise to were verified against the frequency tables.

14 See Marpsat (1983) for an exposition of the problems posed by files relating to the unemployed receiving relief.

15 This analysis was undertaken by Marpsat. Here we describe some of the results published in Marpsat (1984).

16 The first two factorial axes only account for a fifth of the total variation, the diversity of individual situations remaining predominant. The result is similar when we work with individual data. As will be evident, the structures revealed by the diagram of the first two factorial axes seem to be robust, confirming the presence of systematic factors.

17 "Labour regulation" is used not in the sense of the legal codes regulating employment, but in the sense of a coherent ensemble of social and economic relationships: practices, institutions, behaviours and values.

18 Employment is measured here by enterprise staffing levels recorded in population censuses.

19 Typical were L'Ardèche, La Mayenne, Le Maine-et-Loire, La Haute-Saône, and L'Indre.

20 See Hyacinthe Dubreuil, Standards (1929) and Nouveaux Standards (1931), as well as Fine's (1979) commentary on them.

21 For an example of a rationalisation handbook, see Thompson et al. (1926).

REFERENCES

Asselain, J.C. (1974), "Une erreur de politique économique, la loi de 40 heures", Revue économique, July.

Baverez, N. (1986), "Chômages et marchés du travail durant les années 1930 - l'exemple parisien", doctoral thesis, University of Paris I.

Bettelheim, C. and Frère, S. (1950), *Une ville française moyenne: Auxerre en 1950*, Paris: Cahiers de la Fondation nationale des Sciences politiques, Armand Colin.

Beveridge, W. (1930), *Unemployment: A Problem of Industry*, London: Longmans, Green & Co.

Bonnef, L. and Bonnef, M. (1911), *La classe ouvrière*, Paris.

CGTU (Confédération général du travail) (1931), *VIe Congrès national ordinaire*.

CGTU (1933), *VIIe Congrès national ordinaire*.

CGTU (1935), *VIIIe Congrès national ordinaire*.

Chombard de Lauwe, P. (1956), *La vie quotidienne des familles ouvrières*, Paris: Editions du CNRS.

Cohen, Y. (1983), "L'espace de l'organisateur: Ernest Mattern, 1906-1939", *Le mouvement social*, no. 125.

Conseil national économique (1937), "Rapport Brissaud: la pénurie de main-d'oeuvre qualifiée dans ses rapports avec le chômage", *Journal Officiel*, 10 July.

Coutrot, A. (1982), *"Sept" : un journal, un combat: mars 1937 - août 1937*.

Cribier, F. (1980), "Une génération de retraites parisiens du secteur privé", *Consommation*, no. 3.

Deacon, A. (1987), "Systems of Interwar Unemployment Relief", in S. Glynn and A. Booth (eds), *The Road to Full Employment*, London: Allen & Unwin.

Desaunay, E. (1965), "X-Crise, Contribution à l'étude des idéologies économiques d'une groupe de polytechniciens durant la grande crise économique (1931-1939)", thesis, Paris.

Desmarest, J. (1946), *La politique de la main-d'oeuvre en France*, Paris: Presses Universitaires de France.

Dubreuil, H. (1929), *Standards*.

Dubreuil, H. (1931), *Nouveaux standards*.

Eichengreen, B. (1984), "Casual Unemployment in Edwardian Britain: A New Look at Rowntree's York", unpublished manuscript, Harvard University.

"Enquête sur la production" (1937), *Journal Officiel*, 13 December.

Fine, M. (1979), "Hyacinthe Dubreuil: le témoignage d'un ouvrier sur le syndicalisme, les relations industrielles et l'évolution technologique de 1921 à 1940", *Le mouvement social*, no. 106.

Fourcault, A. (1982), *Femmes à l'usine dans la France de l'entre-deux-guerres*, Paris: Editions Maspero.

Frankenstein, R. (1982), *Le prix du réarmement français, 1935-1939*, Paris: Publications de la Sorbonne.

Fridenson, P. (1980), "Le patronat français", in R. Rémond and J. Bourdin, *La France et les Français*.

Fridenson, P. (1981), "La puissance publique et les nationalisations", in *La France en voie de modernisation*, FNSP, Colloquium of 4-5 December.

Friedmann, G. (1946), *Problèmes humaines et machinisme industriel*, Paris: Gallimard.

Friedmann, G. (1953), *Ville et campagne, civilisation urbaine et civilisation rurale en France*, Paris: Centre d'Etudes Sociologiques, Armand Colin.

Garside, W. (1980), *The Measurement of Unemployment in Great Britain 1850-1979: Methods and Sources*, Oxford: Blackwell.

Georges, B., Tintant, D. and Renauld, M.A. (1979), *Léon Jouhaux dans le mouvement syndical*, Paris: Presses Universitaires de France.

Guilbert, M. and Isambert-Jamati, V. (1956), *Travail féminin et travail à domicile*, Paris: Editions du CNRS.

Hatzfeld, H. (1970), *Du paupérisme à la securité sociale, 1870-1940*, Paris: Armand Colin.

Kuisel, R.F. (1981), *Capitalism and the State in Modern France*, Cambridge: Cambridge University Press.

Laroque, P. (1938), *Les rapports entre patrons et ouvriers*, Paris.

Lefranc, G. (1966), *Juin 1936: "L'explosion sociale" du Front Populaire*, Paris: Coll. "Archives", Julliard.

Lefranc, G. (1975), *Histoire du travail et des travailleurs*, Paris: Flammarion.

Lequin, Y. (1979), "La rationalisation du capitalisme français a-t-elle eu lieu dans les années vingt?", *Cahiers d'Histoire de l'Institut Maurice-Thorez*, no. 31.

Letellier, G. *et al.* (1938), vol. 1: *Le chômage en France de 1930 à 1936*, Paris: Librare du Recueil Sirey.

Letellier, G. *et al.* (1941), vol. 2: *Les chômeurs d'après les fiches des fonds de chômage*, Paris: Librairie du Recueil Sirey.

Letellier, G. *et al.* (1949), vol. 3: *Dépenses des chômeurs et valeur énergétique de leur alimentation d'après les budgets de 265 familles*, Paris: Librairie du Recueil Sirey.

Levy-Leboyer, M. (1974), "Le patronat français a-t-il été malthusien?", *Le mouvement social*, no. 88.

Mansfield, M. (1987), "Against the Poorest: The Limits of Social Concern in Turn of the Century Britain", unpublished.

Marpsat, M. (1982), "La statistique des chômeurs secourus en France de 1931 à 1939", in *Journée d'étude "Sociologie et Statistique"*, Société Française de Sociologie et INSEE.

Marpsat, M. (1983), "Chômage secouru des années trente: quelle modélisation? (examen theorique et premiers resultats)", note INSEE, no. 008/930 January.

Marpsat, M. (1984), "Chômage et profession dans les années 1930", *Economie et Statistique*, no. 170, October.

Marseille, J. (1980), "Les origines inopportunes de la crise en 1929 en France", *Revue Economique*, July.

Ministère du Travail (1933), *Bulletin*, July-August, Paris

Ministère du Travail (1939), *Bulletin*, January-March, Paris.

Moscovici, S. (1961), *Reconversion industrielle et changements sociaux*, Paris: Cahiers de la Fondation nationale des Sciences politiques, Armand Colin.

Mottez, B. (1966), *Systèmes de salaire et politiques patronales*, Paris: Editions du CNRS.

Moutet, A. (1983a), "Introduction de la production à la chaîne en France, du début du XXe siècle à la grande crise en 1930", *Histoire, Economie et Société*, January-March.

Moutet, A. (1983b), "La première guerre mondiale et le taylorisme", paper presented to Colloque sur le taylorisme, 4-5 May.

Navel, M. (1945), *Travaux*, Paris: Stock.

Paulin, V. (1938), "Le travail à domicile en France, ses origines, son évolution, son avenir", *Revue internationale du travail*, February.

Perrot, M. (1983), "L'espace de l'usine", *Le mouvement social*, no. 125.

Philipps, G.A. and Whiteside, N. (1985), *Casual Labour: The Unemployment Question in the Port Transport Industry 1880-1970*, Oxford.

Pic, P. (1931), *Traité élémentaire de législation industrielle: les lois ouvrières*, Paris: Editions Rousseau.

Prost, A. (1964), *La CGT à l'époque du Front populaire*, Paris: Cahiers de la Fondation nationale des Sciences politiques, Armand Colin.

Rapport Pouillot (1939), "Recensement qualitatif des chômeurs de la région parisienne", *Bulletin du Ministère du Travail*, January-March.

Rémond, R. and Renouvin, P. (1965), *Léon Blum, chef de gouvernement 1936-1937*, Paris: Presses de la Fondation nationale des Sciences politiques.

Rioux, J.P. (1977), "La conciliation et l'arbitrage des conflits du travail", in R. Rémond and J. Bourdin, *Edouard Daladier, chef du Gouvernement*, FNSP.

Rueff, J. (1931), "L'assurance-chômage, cause du chômage permanent", *Revue d'économie politique*.

Salais, R., Baverez, N. and Reynaud, B. (1986), *L'invention du chômage: histoire et transformations d'une catégorie en France des années 1890 aux années 1980*, Paris: Presses Universitaires de France.

Sauvy, A. (1967), *Histoire économique de la France entre les deux guerres*, Paris: Fayard (2nd edn, Paris: Economica, 1983).

Seidman, M. (1981), "The Birth of the Weekend and the Revolts Against Work: The Workers of the Paris Region during the Popular Front (1936-1938)", *French Historical Studies*, Fall.

Sellier, F. (1984), *La confrontation sociale en France, 1936-1981*, Paris: Presses Universitaires de France.

Thompson, C. *et al.* (1926), *La réorganisation des usines, suivant les méthodes Taylor-Thompson: réorganisation administrative, réorganisation à l'atelier*, Paris: Librairie française de Documentation commerciale et industrielle.

Topalov, C. (1985), *Aux origines de l'assurance-chômage: l'etat et les secours de chômage syndicaux en France, en Grande-Bretagne et aux Etats-Unis: première approche*. Paris: Centre de Sociologie Urbaine.

Touraine, A. (1959), *Histoire générale du travail*, vol. 4, *La civilisation industrielle (de 1914 à nos jours)*.

Valdour, L. (1923), "Ateliers et taudis de la banlieue de Paris", *Observations vécues*, Paris.

Verry, M. (1955), *Les laminoirs ardennais: le déclin d'une aristocratie ouvrière*, Paris, Editions du CNRS.

Volle, M. (1981), *Analyse des données*, 2nd edn, Paris: Economica.

Whiteside, N. (1987), "Social Welfare and Industrial Relations 1914-1939", in C.J. Wrigley (ed.) (1987), *A History of British Industrial Relations, 1914-1939*, Brighton: Harvester Press.

Chapter 8

Interwar Unemployment in Belgium

Martine Goossens, Stefaan Peeters and
Guido Pepermans*

1 Introduction

1.1 Plan of this Chapter

The high level of unemployment in interwar Belgium has, of course, commanded attention from both contemporary and modern writers.[1] But as yet it has not received sophisticated econometric treatment, not least because the statistical groundwork for such an analysis has been wanting. Within the next few years the requisite macroeconomic variables ought to become available as the result of a major research project at the University of Leuven.[2] Here we take some first steps towards understanding Belgian interwar unemployment by describing the system of voluntary unemployment insurance that prevailed during this period, by presenting annual estimates of unemployment, and by examining its incidence along several dimensions.

A system of voluntary unemployment insurance had been introduced in Belgium before the First World War and was further elaborated during the interwar period. In section 2 we describe the nature and functioning of this system.

During the interwar years comprehensive statistics on Belgian unemployment were collected only in February 1937, but sufficient information exists to make annual estimates of the numbers of unemployed manual workers in industry over the period from 1920 to 1939. There exist figures for total unemployment in February 1937 and for unemployment among manual workers and employees in industry and commerce in December 1930. All these estimates and census data are presented in

B. Eichengreen and T. J. Hatton (eds.), Interwar Unemployment in International Perspective, 289–324.
© 1988 by Kluwer Academic Publishers.

section 3, where it is also argued that the statistics for unemployment among manual workers in industry are a good indicator of total unemployment. This group, after all, constituted around 75 per cent of the population without work.

In section 4 we draw upon cross-section data for 1930 and 1937, as well as the annual data underlying our estimates, to examine the characteristics of the unemployed. First, we take up the sectoral and occupational distribution of unemployment. Then its incidence by age and sex is described. Finally, we discuss the duration of unemployment in February 1937.

In order to give a context to our discussion of unemployment we shall first outline briefly the general trends in the Belgian economy in the 1920s and 1930s, and make a few comments on economic policy and the organisation of the labour market. The figures in Table 8.1 illustrate the story.

1. 2 The Historical Background: The Belgian Economy and Labour Market in the Interwar Period

Although the country suffered much during the First World War, with a great part of its productive capacity being destroyed, the Belgian economy recovered relatively quickly during the first two years after the war. Government outlays for reconstruction were high, financed to a great extent by money creation, which led to inflationary pressure. Belgium did not escape from the crisis of 1921-22, which was mainly due to a decrease in foreign demand. Exports, prices and, to a lesser extent, wages fell. From 1923 onwards inflationary pressure recommenced. Government deficits remained high since German reparation payments turned out to be much less than expected. The Belgian franc became overvalued, capital left the country, and industrial production and exports stagnated in 1925. After an unsuccessful devaluation in 1925, the government carried out a monetary reform in 1926 which led to a drastic devaluation in October 1926. Since the currency was now undervalued, capital was repatriated and exports increased.

Belgium, as a small, open economy, took advantage of this successful devaluation and the expansive climate in the rest of the world. As a result the country experienced between 1926 and 1929 a major investment boom. Before 1926 growth was mainly the result of an increase in the labour force, due to a rise in the female participation rate and to a significant movement of low productivity agricultural workers to the better-paid industrial sector.

Although the Belgian economy did not succumb to the Great Depression immediately, its openness meant that it could hardly escape for long.

Table 8.1   Some Index Indicators of the Belgian Economy, 1920-39
(1930=100)

Year	Export (in 1930 prices)	Industrial production (weighted qty)	Nominal hourly wage	Retail prices	Real hourly wage	Nat income (in 1930 prices)
1920	65.0	62.0	36.9	52.1	70.8	59.4
1921	60.8	62.0	39.5	45.7	86.4	67.5
1922	55.8	70.9	38.4	42.7	89.9	78.5
1923	75.9	79.7	44.3	49.0	90.4	84.9
1924	92.5	83.5	51.4	57.3	89.7	85.3
1925	95.5	84.8	51.3	59.3	86.5	85.8
1926	108.1	89.9	58.3	70.7	82.5	89.5
1927	113.5	96.2	71.4	89.9	79.4	84.1
1928	122.9	105.1	79.8	93.8	85.1	92.0
1929	121.7	102.5	93.0	100.1	92.9	102.1
1930	100.0	100.0	100.0	100.0	100.0	100.0
1931	97.0	94.9	93.8	91.3	102.7	96.2
1932	70.2	87.3	85.7	82.4	104.0	96.2
1933	67.7	92.4	83.2	80.7	103.1	93.5
1934	69.2	88.6	79.6	76.2	104.5	92.9
1935	82.4	101.3	76.1	74.8	101.7	98.3
1936	96.3	103.8	82.9	78.4	105.7	103.2
1937	116.0	103.8	92.0	84.1	109.4	108.7
1938	95.1	98.7	96.9	87.1	111.3	105.1
1939	94.6	-	97.6	88.0	110.9	99.7

Sources: Export: Banque Nationale de Belgique (1929), p. 76, and (n.d.), p. 359. Industrial production: Carbonnelle (1959), p. 358. Hourly wage: Cassiers (1980), p. 73. Retail prices: Banque Nationale de Belgique (1929), p. 40, and (n.d.), p. 262. National income: Peeters *et al.* (1986).

Exports and industrial production were already decreasing in 1929 and 1930, though the latter did not fall off dramatically until late in 1930. National income and prices increased in 1929, and remained relatively stable in 1930. The Depression struck hard at the end of 1931 after the devaluation of the pound. The collapse of the international monetary system, successive devaluations by major competitors in export markets, and the general climate of protectionism held the Belgian economy in a deep crisis. The government tried to restore the international competitiveness of industry by a deflationary policy, while also protecting the domestic market. However, government action was not successful since one of the major reasons for the country's weakness, the overvaluation of the national currency caused by an obstinate defense of its position within the framework of the gold bloc, remained.

From 1935 onwards a more Keynesian policy was followed. The devaluation by 28 per cent in March 1935 and the recovery of foreign demand resulted in a sharp increase in exports, industrial production and income from 1935 until the beginning of 1937. This short upward movement did not lead to much new investment, since during the crisis a major part of productive capacity, which had been substantially enlarged in 1926-29, was being underutilised. By the end of 1937 recovery had given way to a new recession as international economic conditions worsened.

A major part of the Belgian interwar labour market was covered by collective wage bargaining on a sectoral basis.[3] Only in 1936 did these sectoral negotiations form part of a national collective agreement. Some, but not all, sectoral agreements included wage indexation and many details differed from sector to sector. Most wages, even those which were not linked to prices, followed the general price level. Since the indexing arrangements involved some lags real wages increased in 1921-22 (because of falling prices) and decreased in 1924-27 (rising prices). Only in 1928-30 was the labour movement strong enough to obtain nominal pay increases that exceeded the rise in prices. Previously industry had been able to draw on labour released from a relatively depressed agricultural sector. During the Depression nominal wages fell, but real wages remained stable or perhaps rose slightly. So, for Belgium the Keynesian notion of wage stickiness holds to a certain extent: nominal wages fell, but not enough to clear the labour market.

2   Institutional Aspects of Unemployment in Belgium, 1920-39: The System of Voluntary Unemployment Insurance[4]

The Belgian system of voluntary unemployment insurance gave certain groups of labourers the opportunity to join an unemployment insurance society. Monthly contributions paid for benefits in times of involuntary unemployment. The working of the system during the interwar period cannot be detached from its historical development. Thus, before discussing the working of the system during the interwar period, we take up the development of the system during its period of origin before the First World War.

2. 1   Origin and Development of the Voluntary Unemployment Insurance System before the First World War[5]

The origin and nature of the Belgian system of voluntary insurance against unemployment emanates from trade unionism. In the second half of the nineteenth century trade unions started unemployment societies, to which trade union members, on a voluntary basis, would contribute regularly and from which benefits were paid in case of involuntary unemployment. Before 1895, the system was not particularly important, being moderately successful only in the luxury-good industries and in other better-paid sectors employing many skilled workers, like the typographic industry. In low wage industries it was extremely difficult for trade unions to persuade labourers to hand over part of their already meagre wages to an unemployment scheme. Moreover, in times of crisis the societies were not always able to fulfil their obligations to affiliated members. This was not only due to the fact that too few members paid too few contributions, but also because the weak organisation and limited character of many local trade unions made it difficult to spread risks.

The system got its most important prewar boost at the end of the 1890s when local authorities started giving financial support to voluntary unemployment insurance schemes. The pioneers were Liège and Ghent, where the local authorities made their first financial contributions to the trade union unemployment associations in 1897 and 1900.[6] Other cities followed very soon and gradually various small towns and communes took part.

Municipal support took two general forms. One followed the practice in Ghent, where the town did not make a general contribution to the union unemployment society but instead oriented its assistance to the individual insured workers. Relief consisted of a supplement to the fruits of the labourer's savings. If the worker was insured at a union unemployment society, this supplement was granted via the union. But a labourer could also bypass the union by opening a savings account at the city hall. If unemployed, he received a benefit from his own savings plus the municipal subsidy. The "Ghent System" was designed to promote unemployment insurance and to assist the individual unemployed without necessarily improving the financial basis of the insurance societies or augmenting the power of trade unions.

Municipal intervention differed where the practice at Liège was followed. In the "Liège System" the town contribution was deposited directly in the insurance funds, so that only members could benefit. Here the aims of financial support were both to promote collective unemployment insurance and, since the trade unions had a quasi-monopoly on such schemes, to strengthen the organised labour movement. Thus, Liège gave subsidies to the unions, Ghent via the unions; the Liège point of view was collectivist, Ghent's individualist.

The choice of system depended on the political colour of the local authorities: socialist authorities preferred the "Liège System", Catholics and liberals favoured the "Ghent System". The minor political power of the socialists before the First World War is one reason for the limited scope of the "Liège System". In 1912 only 1,569 insured unemployed received municipal relief through the "Liège System", compared with 27,081 through the "Ghent System".[7]

Even though subsidies to the unemployed insured labourer in most cases were not conditional on affiliation to a trade union, the majority of insured workers were members of union unemployment societies. In 1912 municipal Unemployment Funds operating under the "Ghent System" awarded 99.48 per cent of their subsidies through union unemployment organisations. Only sixty-two unemployed workers had individual savings accounts. Unemployment insurance and unionism must have seemed indissolubly linked for Belgian workers, and trade unions used unemployment insurance societies as an attraction for new members. The causal relationship between the growing success of the union insurance societies and the increasing power of the trade unions has not been investigated in all its aspects, but both the number of union unemployment funds and the number of union members rose rapidly after 1900. Between 1900 and 1912-13 union affiliation increased from roughly 40,000 to about 210,000.[8] The early growth of union insurance societies cannot be tracked precisely, since we lack statistics concerning their total number and membership, but there is some sporadic data. According to an inquiry by the "Commission Syndical", the socialist coordinating union organisation, in 1900 only twenty-five of the 185 trade unions surveyed had an unemployment insurance fund (13.5 per cent); in 1901 fifty-two out of 142 (36.6 per cent) did; and in 1902 102 out of 200 (51 per cent). After 1905 the number of union unemployment insurance societies increased very rapidly. In 1905, 131 union societies were affiliated to a communal Unemployment Fund, and by 1912 this number had grown to 432.

From 1907 the central government granted a subsidy to unemployment insurance schemes. The amounts were so low, however, that before the First World War the national authorities hardly intervened in the insurance system. This lack of support may be explained by the major role played by the trade unions, which led conservative governments to fear that subsidies would help finance strikes. For the same reason employers were unsympathetic to the system.

Although the system of voluntary unemployment insurance met with increasing approval by the working population, its quantitative impact remained fairly limited before the First World War. In 1910, for instance, only 10 per cent of labourers were insured against unemployment. This does not alter the fact that the fundamental principles of the system, voluntary insurance within the framework of trade-union organisation, would be the basis for further development during the interwar period.

2. 2   Consolidation and Extension of Voluntary Unemployment Insurance in the Interwar Period

During the 1920s and 1930s the prewar system was consolidated and extended. The insurance scheme remained voluntary, mainly through the trade unions, but its financial basis was augmented by the support of the central government. Subsidies from local authorities, which were important before the First World War, continued but became much less significant in the light of this central government support. The link between unemployment insurance and union membership, which existed before the First World War, became even closer during the interwar period. Although non-union funds were created, nearly all workers were affiliated to a union unemployment society. This nearly exclusive link between unions and unemployment insurance would be challenged by the employers during the crisis of the 1930s.

In this section we shall discuss the role of central government, the operation of the system and its coverage.

2. 2. 1 The Role of Central Government.   During the First World War the local unemployment insurance system was abolished and a national system of relief was substituted. Many unemployment insurance societies and trade unions went bankrupt because of a general lack of employment in occupied Belgium. Moreover, the difference between destitution as a result of unemployment and as a consequence of war became so artificial that the organisation of a general relief system was called for.

After the war trade unions were eager for the reintroduction of the prewar system of voluntary unemployment insurance. They had an important ally in the Minister of Labour and Employment, J. Wauters, who as a socialist considered the Belgian insurance system a way to enlarge the influence of the trade unions. He was instrumental in securing a resurrection of the prewar system in the context of beginning central government financial assistance.

Extra benefits and advantages were accorded to those labourers who affiliated to a recognised insurance society. The minister decided, for instance, to pay governmental unemployment benefits immediately to recently affiliated unemployed workers, where previously new members had been required to pay contributions for one year before becoming entitled to benefits (the "probation term"). The minister also extended governmental relief to the "post-statutory period". Since the insurance societies normally paid out benefits only during the first sixty days of unemployment (the "statutory period"), thanks to this government measure, the unemployed received a benefit after the end of financial support by the insurance funds. Wauters did not stop here: in addition to the amount already paid out by the insurance societies, he accorded a supplementary

Table 8.2   Number of Accepted Unemployment Insurance Societies and
             their Membership by Type of Society, 31 October 1930

Type of society	Societies		Membership	
	Number	%	Number	%
Trade union	130	76.9	618,248	96.7
Employers	19	11.3	19,692	3.1
Official	20	11.8	1,334	0.2
Total	169	100.0	639,274	100.0

Source: Kiehel (1932), p. 148.

governmental benefit to the unemployed during the statutory period. He decided that those union organisations whose funds were exhausted could get advances from the government in order to be able to meet their obligations. He also endowed the funds with a state benefit of 50 per cent of the contributions collected from the members. The government's financial commitment to the unemployment insurance system was thus established in 1920, with a "National Emergency Fund" set up to divide state subsidies among the various recognised unemployment insurance societies.

These societies did not have to be of union origin, but in practice the recognition of non-union organisations met with so many difficulties that their number remained very limited. In addition, these non-union insurance societies do not seem to have been very attractive to workers, who considered them to be the bosses' counter-offensive against the rise of union power. Statistics for 1930, shown in Table 8.2, put the share of non-union organisations in the total number of insurance societies at 23.1 per cent, while their share in total membership amounted only to 3.3 per cent. The system of voluntary insurance against unemployment remained a union quasi-monopoly.

Employers found this situation hard to accept. They did not necessarily oppose the idea of unemployment insurance - some even started non-union unemployment organisations, as can be seen in Table 8.2 - but they refused any form of employer contribution to the insured labourer's benefit within a system that explicitly favoured the power of the trade unions. As a result, the employers played almost no direct role in the interwar unemployment insurance system.

In the 1930s employers expressed more and more opposition to the union monopoly. According to the employers, the system of union insurance constituted a severe threat to the normal operation of the labour market. They argued that the associations paid out unemployment benefits that were too high, so that the unemployed had no incentive to present

Table 8.3   **Central Government Expenditure on Unemployment Benefits, 1930-38**

	Total unemp't expenditure (1,000 Belgian francs)	Index of unemp't expenditure	As percentage of state budget (1930=100)
1930	384	100	0.2
1931	422,071	1,097	3.4
1932	749,093	1,947	6.4
1933	560,113	1,455	5.0
1934	675,551	1,755	5.9
1935	662,433	1,721	4.8
1936	688,383	1,789	4.9
1937	602,700	1,566	4.2
1938	895,400	2,327	6.1

Source: Vanthemsche (1987), p. 262.

themselves on the labour market. The wage level in industry was being kept artificially high at a time when, according to the employers, a decrease of the wage level was the only way to get out of the crisis.

Employers suggested alternative forms of organisation in which not the trade union but government would be central. However, it was only after the Second World War that these ideas became reality when a compulsory unemployment insurance system was set up within the framework of social security, and financed by contributions from workers, employers and central government.

The interwar scheme was financed by workers, union funds, local authorities and central government, the last taking a greater and greater role. During the 1920s unemployment was so low that government was able to increase regularly its financial contribution. But in 1931, when the numbers unemployed increased rapidly, expenditure on unemployment benefits became a matter of concern. As can be seen in Table 8.3, the share of the central government budget that went to unemployment benefits rose from 0.2 per cent in 1930 to 6.4 per cent in 1932. Pressure for economies increased, resulting in the 1933 and 1934 "exclusion laws": certain categories of labourers were declared "uninsurable" and some benefits were reduced. Notwithstanding these restrictive measures the outlays for unemployment benefits remained high, illustrating the active participation of central government.

2. 2. 2 Operation of the System.   Here we shall take up some details of the voluntary unemployment insurance system: the conditions for participation and the nature of the benefits. For both features a distinction should be made between the period before and the one after 1933, when the government brought in its economy measures.[9]

Adherence to the system was optional and limited to certain sorts of workers. One major restriction was that the workers had to be linked to an employer by means of an employment contract (as a manual or as a white-collar worker). As a result, craftsmen, professionals, and other self-employed people were not eligible. After 1933 the number of "uninsurable" categories increased considerably, when affiliation was limited to workers and employees between 15 and 65 years old who had been working for at least one year.

It is almost impossible to give an exact picture of the unemployed labourer's benefits during the interwar period. They depended not only on the worker's individual situation (head of the family or not, number of children, etc.) but also on the period of unemployment (probation term, statutory or post-statutory period), his place of residence (for eventual local authority allowances) and the insurance society of which he was a member. Therefore it is only possible to discuss broadly the relationship between unemployment benefits and previous wages.

Before 1933 each insured person had a right to a sixty-day unemployment benefit ("statutory period"). The benefit could at most be two-thirds of the former wage (three-quarters for a head of family). This maximum seems to have been received by only a minority of unemployed. A 1932 questionnaire about the income of 100 unemployed families indicated a more than 50 per cent loss of income in most cases.[10] Big families were favoured by the unemployment system, since they could claim a family allowance, a bonus for a wife and children which increased with the number of children.

After 1933 the benefits decreased severely for most categories of insured unemployed workers and particularly for those with large families. This was principally due to the reduction of the central government's contribution to the scheme. The government decided that the family allowance, which before 1933 had been paid out to every labourer during the statutory period, would only be granted to the unemployed in need. For many families this measure caused an important decrease in income. The most far-reaching governmental decree was the exclusion from benefits of fully unemployed married women who were not heads of households. Although they had paid contributions to the scheme this category of women were no longer eligible for benefits either from the funds or from the government. In 1935 this measure was moderated so that during the statutory period (first sixty days of unemployment) they obtained a fund benefit but no governmental supplement. In the post-statutory period they received nothing at all. Another measure decreasing benefits was the cutback of governmental allowances for the unemployed in the probation[11]

Table 8.4   Average Yearly Number of Insured with Accepted Insurance
Societies, 1913 and 1921-39

	Average insured per year	Growth Rate (%)	Index (1930=100)
1913	126,278	-	19.7
1921	702,211	-	109.5
1922	708,824	0.9	110.6
1923	655,031	-7.6	102.2
1924	654,943	0.0	102.2
1925	606,772	-7.4	94.7
1926	598,251	-1.4	93.3
1927	612,418	2.4	95.5
1928	628,555	2.6	98.1
1929	634,982	1.0	99.1
1930	641,022	1.0	100.0
1931	722,813	12.8	112.8
1932	852,443	17.9	133.0
1933	992,625	16.4	154.9
1934	963,671	-2.9	150.3
1935	921,334	-4.4	143.7
1936	915,068	-0.7	142.8
1937	909,590	-0.6	141.9
1938	945,062	3.9	147.4
1939	1,010,134	6.9	157.6

Sources: Kiehel (1932), pp.334-6, and Banque National de Belgique (n.d.), p. 378.

and post-statutory period. On the other hand the contributions required of the working people were augmented. As a consequence the insurance system became less attractive for the labourers, which resulted in a decrease in affiliation after 1933 (see Table 8.4).

It appears that after 1933 unemployment benefits generally amounted to less than 50 per cent of previous wages. Those insured were still well off compared with the uninsured, who in case of unemployment were totally dependent on public relief.

2. 2. 3 Coverage of the System.   The coverage of the interwar system went well beyond that of its prewar predecessor. We shall examine this expansion from two points of view: the evolution of the number of insured between 1921 and 1939 and the insurance rate of manual industrial workers in December 1930 and February 1937. As can be seen in Table 8.4 and Figure 8.1, the average number of insured with accepted unemployment funds (of union, patronal, or official origin) increased from 126,278 in 1913 to 702,211 in 1921. The measures favouring the insur-

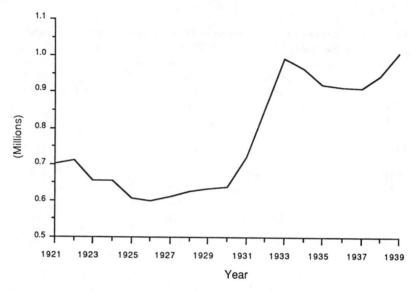

Figure 8.1   **Average Yearly Number of Insured with Accepted Insurance Societies, 1920-39**

Source: See Table 8.4.

ance societies taken immediately after the First World War by minister Wauters were in large part responsible for this growth. Membership reached a first peak in January 1922 with 762,505 affiliates. After 1922, as economic conditions improved, membership fell off somewhat, but during the whole 1923-30 period the level remained relatively stable with about 600,000 to 650,000 insured labourers. When the threat of unemployment became much more serious during the years of economic crisis, membership of insurance societies underwent a new expansion. Between 1930 and 1933 the number of affiliated workers increased by 54.8 per cent. The fall in 1934 is a reflection of the 1933 "exclusion laws" discussed above. This decrease continued in 1935-37 as a result of the economic recovery during this period. Finally, the connection between economic fluctuations and unemployment insurance can once again be illustrated by the figures of 1938-39. In these crisis years the number of affiliated workers rose again and amounted to more than a million members in 1939.

As for the share of industrial manual workers covered by insurance, Table 8.5 shows that in 1930 half (49.8 per cent) were insured against unemployment and in 1937 this share amounted to two-thirds (66.8 per cent). Since more labourers were insured in 1933 than in 1937 (see Table 8.4) the insurance rate may have reached between 70 and 75 per cent during that year.

Table 8.5   **Insurance Rate of Manual Workers in Industry, December 1930 and February 1937**

Industry	December 1930	February 1937
Mines	40.4	53.1
Quarries	73.2	130.0[12]
Metallurgy	67.5	94.2
Ceramics	33.7	21.9
Glass	43.4	72.0
Chemicals	6.6	25.0
Food	20.4	35.3
Textiles	84.4	77.8
Clothing	11.6	14.8
Construction	40.7	74.8
Wood	45.7	99.4
Leather	38.0	48.3
Tobacco	74.1	57.1
Paper	95.6	23.8
Publishing	70.4	69.5
Arts	49.1	54.5
Total	49.8	66.8

Source: Authors' calculations based on *Revue du Travail* (February 1931 and May 1937) and Goossens (1987).

Table 8.5 also shows that the number of insured manual workers was not evenly spread across industries: some industries already had a high insurance rate in 1930, notably export-oriented industries with relatively high unemployment in 1930 (especially metallurgy and textiles). Others, more oriented towards the domestic market and struck by unemployment later in the crisis (e.g. construction and wood), experienced a large increase in the share of workers covered by insurance from 1930 to 1937.

It can be concluded that the voluntary unemployment insurance system was more and more successful in the interwar period, which after the Second World War logically resulted in a compulsory scheme set up within the framework of social security.

3   Quantitative Aspects of Unemployment in Belgium, 1920-39

One product of the voluntary unemployment insurance scheme described in section 2 was monthly statistics by industry of the numbers of affiliated workers and of total and partial unemployment among them. These statistics, based on data recorded by the recognised unemployment schemes, were collected by the Ministry of Labour and Employment, and published in its monthly *Revue du Travail*. They cover a large and growing share of the labour force during the interwar period.

There are problems involved in using this data source: the participation rate in the scheme and variations in its sectoral and industrial coverage. But since only in December 1930 and February 1937 were general censuses of unemployment carried out, the data on insured unemployment must be the basis for any annual estimates of the overall level of unemployment during the other years. The relationship between unemployment as shown by the insurance scheme statistics and the overall level of unemployment will be analysed using the censuses of December 1930 and February 1937.

First, we present annual estimates for unemployment among industrial workers, based on the statistics of insured unemployed. Then we discuss full and partial unemployment among all manual workers and employees in industry and commerce on 31 December 1930 and unemployment for the whole economy on 27 February 1937. Finally, we discuss the evolution of unemployment and the labour force in the 1920s and 1930s.

3. 1 Annual Estimates for Unemployment among Manual Workers in Belgian Industry, 1920-39 [13]

Our estimates for the total numbers of unemployed manual workers in Belgian industry are based, first, upon the assumption that the unemployment rates shown by the insurance statistics, after some adjustment, reflect the overall rate and, second, upon a series we have constructed for the total labour force in industry.

Table 8.6 gives a comparison by industry of the unemployment rates shown by the insurance statistics and those recorded by the industrial and unemployment censuses of 1930 and 1937. While there is, of course, some variation across industries, in part the result of uncertainties in industrial classification, the rates shown by the two sources correspond reasonably well.

A plausible explanation for the lower unemployment rate among insured workers (9.5 per cent) compared to all workers (11.5 per cent) in December 1930 is that during the 1920s and the first months of 1930, when there was almost full employment, low-risk groups were overrepresented in the voluntary insurance system. Since, as we saw, affiliation to the scheme and union membership went hand in hand, and since unionised workers tended to be more skilled than non-union workers, the insured may have been in a stronger position on the labour market than their uninsured colleagues. A related explanation is that the highest-risk groups may have also been lower-paid workers who in a period of full

Table 8.6   Total Unemployment Rate of all Manual Workers in Industry
(UR) (%) and of those Insured Against Unemployment
(UR(Insur.)) (%) in December 1930 and February 1937

Sector	December 1930				February 1937			
	Empl.	Unemp't	UR	UR(Insur.)	Empl.	Unemp't	UR	UR(Insur.)
Mines	164,959	1,633	1.0	0.4	131,630	4,777	3.5	5.2
Quarries	32,122	2,104	6.1	7.3	28,793	2,410	7.7	17.2
Metallurgy	206,758	22,353	9.8	7.1	188,104	21,944	10.4	10.1
Ceramics	32,298	5,564	14.7	27.5	25,160	7,797	23.7	18.7
Glass	26,489	2,781	9.5	10.5	23,156	2,969	11.4	15.5
Chemicals	64,058	2,851	4.3	3.5	55,591	4,561	7.6	16.1
Food	70,668	3,761	5.1	3.0	71,475	10,569	12.9	9.7
Textiles	163,485	16,711	9.3	6.7	150,277	14,384	8.7	9.9
Clothing	44,635	8,712	16.3	10.0	47,410	4,347	8.4	8.9
Construction	93,857	34,360	26.8	19.5	92,156	45,341	33.0	29.3
Wood	55,886	14,115	20.2	17.6	53,222	12,454	19.0	22.9
Leather	32,446	3,808	10.5	6.3	29,436	3,235	9.9	12.8
Tobacco	10,972	629	5.4	3.1	10,991	1,181	9.7	9.3
Paper	15,725	619	3.8	2.1	17,295	1,044	5.7	9.7
Publishing	18,264	875	4.6	2.4	18,130	1,512	7.7	6.8
Arts	19,988	15,435	43.6	52.8	22,268	2,731	10.9	6.4
Total	1,052,610	136,311	11.5	9.5	965,094	141,256	12.8	14.0

Source: Goossens (1987), p. B.4.

employment were not willing or able to hand over part of their incomes
to subscribe to the system.

The inverse situation in February 1937, a higher unemployment rate
among insured workers (14.0 per cent) than among all workers (12.8 per
cent), is probably related to the rise in affiliation to the insurance scheme
that took place during the early 1930s. Between 1930 and 1933 the grow-
ing.threat of unemployment brought an increase of 54.8 per cent in the
numbers insured, with much of this increase undoubtedly coming from
higher-risk groups.

As a result, we have arrived at estimates for the overall unemployment
rate among industrial workers in different ways for the 1920s and the
1930s. For the 1920s, when participation in the insurance scheme was
relatively stable, we simply adjusted the rate shown by the insurance statistics according to the ratio of the rates shown in the two sources in December 1930. For the 1930s we used a linear interpolation on the
differences observed in 1930 and 1937 and for 1938 and 1939 the relative
difference of February 1937 was held constant. This procedure was also
carried out by sector and the detailed results are shown in Table 8.7. Since
the share of the labour force affiliated to an insurance scheme was higher
in the 1930s than in the 1920s our estimates are probably more reliable
for the later decade.

Table 8.7   Estimated Average Full Unemployment Rate among Manual Workers in Industry, 1920-39 (%)

	Mines	Quarries	Metallurgy	Ceramics	Chemicals	Glass	Food	Textiles	Clothing	Construction	Wood	Leather	Tobacco	Paper	Publishing	Arts	Total
1920	3.0	2.4	8.9	8.1	39.1	7.0	6.7	29.0	28.3	14.0	17.2	21.2	47.4	11.5	8.2	44.3	12.6
1921	4.7	2.7	11.4	9.1	32.1	17.2	7.3	22.1	19.4	14.3	10.0	26.8	34.3	22.0	5.4	25.1	12.1
1922	2.0	3.0	5.6	1.8	7.0	8.5	2.4	3.1	4.8	6.1	3.0	6.6	106	3.3	1.9	6.1	3.9
1923	0.0	0.3	1.1	0.3	2.2	1.9	1.0	1.0	3.3	3.6	1.1	2.8	6.5	0.2	1.8	1.2	1.2
1924	0.3	1.0	0.9	1.0	0.9	0.7	0.9	1.2	2.2	4.1	2.0	1.7	8.4	0.3	2.0	2.2	1.3
1925	0.4	1.1	1.6	1.4	1.5	1.0	1.0	1.5	3.0	6.0	3.3	2.8	7.7	1.3	2.9	2.1	1.9
1926	0.4	0.8	2.3	1.2	0.7	1.1	1.3	0.9	2.3	4.9	2.4	1.7	14.8	0.8	9.7	1.1	1.8
1927	0.2	1.2	2.4	2.0	3.6	2.7	1.7	1.1	2.8	7.2	3.8	3.1	10.2	0.5	10.4	3.0	2.3
1928	0.5	0.7	0.9	0.7	2.0	2.4	1.1	0.9	1.8	3.6	1.3	2.2	5.2	0.2	3.9	1.2	1.2
1929	0.1	1.0	1.1	2.6	0.8	3.0	1.3	1.0	1.8	6.6	1.4	1.9	3.5	0.3	2.1	4.9	1.7
1930	0.4	1.2	3.6	3.8	1.3	7.5	2.5	3.6	4.4	7.5	5.9	3.7	6.1	0.9	3.1	22.4	4.3
1931	3.1	7.4	14.2	10.9	9.7	8.9	7.2	11.3	11.3	21.1	17.1	10.5	10.7	5.3	11.6	45.9	12.4
1932	8.5	14.3	23.3	21.6	15.7	13.1	12.5	23.2	15.9	30.2	24.3	21.1	19.8	15.4	20.1	51.9	20.2
1933	9.3	10.3	21.7	33.4	13.7	17.4	12.2	18.9	18.9	30.8	24.4	16.4	17.8	10.1	22.9	39.9	18.8
1934	11.0	10.8	23.4	23.9	15.4	20.4	13.1	19.6	26.3	35.9	26.6	17.0	19.3	12.9	18.1	45.9	20.5
1935	10.1	9.3	21.8	29.2	12.6	21.2	14.2	15.3	17.2	35.6	22.5	14.1	16.1	14.4	14.8	27.3	18.8
1936	6.1	5.4	13.9	32.2	7.3	12.5	12.7	10.3	10.9	28.2	14.1	10.0	10.7	6.6	10.8	17.0	12.9
1937	3.1	6.6	9.1	12.1	5.9	11.7	11.1	7.9	8.5	22.4	19.1	9.1	10.9	5.7	7.4	24.6	10.6
1938	2.5	4.4	11.9	26.6	7.6	12.3	11.7	11.0	8.2	26.8	17.2	10.4	13.6	6.2	9.1	52.7	12.8
1939	3.6	8.6	13.1	33.1	8.0	12.7	14.5	12.5	12.9	36.0	20.2	11.4	14.8	7.6	12.0	48.5	15.6

Source: Goossens (1987, p. B.5).

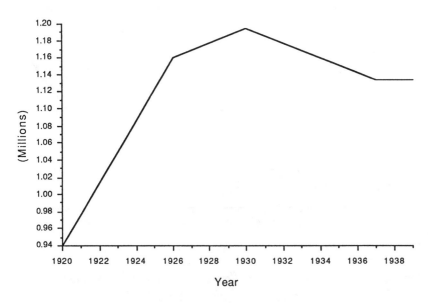

**Figure 8.2   Estimated Total Labour Supply in Industry, 1920-39
(transport excluded)**

Source: Goossens (1987), p. 8.

The second step in estimating total unemployment in industry was to come up with annual estimates for the total labour force, which we defined as the sum of people employed and people officially registered as unemployed. Employment could be taken from the industrial inquiries of December 1920 and October 1926, and from the industrial censuses of December 1930 and February 1937. Unemployment in December 1930 and February 1937 was drawn from the censuses. In December 1920 and October 1926 it was calculated by multiplying the employment figures by the adjusted unemployment rates discussed above. In this way we derived four labour supply benchmarks. The intervening years were linearly interpolated, which means that we started from the hypothesis of constant rates of change in population, and in female, juvenile and old-age participation rates between each two benchmarks. Another assumption was a constant labour mobility between manual work in industry and the other occupational groups and sectors in the economy during each interval.

The results of these calculations are shown in Figure 8.2. We are aware that this interpolation method is rather crude and that the underlying assumptions are difficult to justify. We are therefore working on an alter-

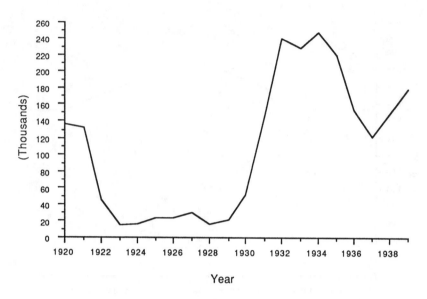

**Figure 8.3   Estimated Total Number of Fully Unemployed Manual
Workers in Industry, 1920-39 (transport excluded)**

Source: Goossens (1987), p. B.6.

native, more sophisticated estimation of the labour force which will be
published later.

Finally, from the estimates for the total industrial labour force and the
overall industrial unemployment rate, the rate of unemployment in Belgian industry may be calculated. The results for manual work in industry
as a whole are shown in Figure 8.3 and Table 8.8. Similar results at industry level are presented in Table 8.9.

What is immediately striking in Table 8.8 is the very low level of unemployment between 1923 and 1929. This is probably due, in part, to
some underestimation of the unemployment rate during the 1920s. The
correction to the rate for uninsured workers, made on the basis of the relatively high level of unemployment that prevailed in December 1930, may
be too low for the 1920s. Even so, the impression of very full employment during most of the 1920s prevails.

The rate of unemployment rose rapidly during 1930 and 1931, and for
the next four years remained at around 20 per cent. The numbers of unemployed industrial workers reached almost 250,000 in 1934. In the late
1930s unemployment fell, but remained far above the level of the mid-
1920s.

Table 8.8   **Estimated Total Average Number of Fully Unemployed**
Manual Workers in Industry, 1920-1939 (transport excluded)

Year	Unemp't rate	Total unemp't	Unemp't index (1930=100)
1920	12.6	135,513	263.4
1921	12.1	132,638	257.8
1922	3.9	44,271	86.1
1923	1.2	15,002	29.2
1924	1.3	15,828	30.8
1925	1.9	23,058	44.8
1926	1.8	22,937	44.6
1927	2.3	30,570	59.4
1928	1.2	16,713	32.5
1929	1.7	22,318	43.4
1930	4.3	51,444	100.0
1931	12.4	147,049	285.8
1932	20.2	239,650	465.8
1933	18.8	228,767	444.7
1934	20.5	247,698	481.5
1935	18.8	220,297	428.2
1936	12.9	153,659	298.7
1937	10.6	120,823	234.9
1938	12.8	149,228	290.1
1939	15.6	179,150	348.2

Note: Annual averages, except for 1920 which are for December only.
Source: Goossens (1987), p. B.6.

The extent to which the labour force was underutilised during the 1930s is understated by these figures, since partial unemployment was also common. Only the industrial census of December 1930 gives a full picture of partial unemployment, but again the insurance statistics, which record partial as well as total unemployment among affiliates, can be brought into play. After a correction for what is apparently a higher incidence of partial unemployment among insured workers, then estimates for the total number of partially unemployed can be made.[14] This has been done for 1930-37 and the results are shown in Table 8.10. It is clear that partial unemployment affected almost as many industrial workers as did full unemployment during the crisis of the 1930s.

The relative importance of partial unemployment increases if one realises that seasonal unemployment (for instance, in construction) was counted as full and not as partial unemployment. In most cases, however, partial unemployment involved a reduction in days worked per week. This means that especially in the first years of the crisis employers

Table 8.9   Estimated Total Average Number of Fully Unemployed Manual Workers by Industry, 1920-39

	Mines		Metallurgy		Chemicals		Food		Clothing		Wood		Tobacco		Publishing		Total
		Quarries		Ceramics		Glass		Textiles		Construction		Leather		Paper		Arts	
1920	5077	730	13564	2126	9805	3187	4305	33772	11822	20431	7952	4106	7189	1077	905	9466	135513
1921	8088	868	18576	2479	8617	8425	4899	27872	8164	20149	4959	5795	5094	2262	661	5730	132638
1922	3456	1019	9752	497	1990	4440	1715	4235	2021	8333	1577	1592	1535	369	250	1491	44271
1923	26	109	2048	86	660	1048	708	1450	1385	4638	598	732	926	27	264	298	15002
1924	532	352	1651	303	288	416	666	1785	929	5111	1195	478	1172	34	316	599	15828
1925	682	428	3305	431	518	626	829	2525	1272	7218	2033	873	1042	173	492	610	23058
1926	730	332	4983	392	251	714	1044	1600	978	5648	1561	570	1956	124	1733	321	22937
1927	279	471	5125	676	1216	1814	1400	1959	1285	8540	2523	1067	1303	73	1905	933	30570
1928	823	265	1998	254	655	1596	837	1616	852	4376	886	761	646	24	714	408	16713
1929	171	361	2430	937	251	2003	1029	1843	918	8242	940	679	419	42	395	1657	22318
1930	666	411	8289	1439	395	5047	1889	6487	2331	9614	4157	1350	711	155	585	7918	51444
1931	5206	2489	32229	4037	2783	5877	5460	20094	5989	27342	11843	3760	1249	885	2220	15586	147049
1932	13769	4759	52126	7862	4462	8538	9586	40800	8390	39523	16739	7448	2329	2597	3883	16839	239650
1933	14602	3377	47954	11936	3839	11140	9449	32866	9974	40651	16642	5698	2109	1734	4435	12363	228767
1934	16639	3498	51001	8363	4239	12881	10325	33649	13775	47965	17957	5799	2303	2257	3519	13527	247698
1935	14773	2994	46900	10025	3399	13136	11335	25930	8998	48019	15036	4753	1930	2550	2882	7636	220297
1936	8703	1704	29537	10836	1932	7631	10251	17203	5666	38455	9325	3314	1299	1191	2105	4509	153659
1937	4247	2049	19095	4001	1531	7043	9148	12988	4384	30843	12517	2987	1333	1053	1461	6143	120823
1938	3343	1374	25025	8768	1993	7409	9564	18160	4267	36881	11280	3400	1660	1132	1792	13180	149228
1939	4881	2697	27519	10905	2100	7664	11928	20583	6670	49504	13291	3734	1797	1401	2363	12112	179150

Source: Goossens (1987, p. B.6).

Table 8.10   Estimation of the Number of Partially Unemployed Manual Workers in Industry, 1930-37

Year	Full unemp't (all workers)	Partial unemp't Full unemp't (insured workers)	Correction rate	Partial unemp't (all workers)
1930	51,444	2.27	0.80	93,422
1931	147,049	1.61	0.80	189,399
1932	239,650	1.12	0.80	214,726
1933	228,767	1.06	0.80	193,994
1934	247,698	0.96	0.80	190,232
1935	220,297	0.78	0.80	137,465
1936	153,659	0.80	0.80	98,341
1937	120,823	0.91	0.80	87,959

Sources: Table 8.8 and Banque Nationale de Belgique (n.d.), p. 378.

preferred to retain as much of their labour force as possible. A parallel development was that the number of hours worked per day also fell.[15] Full employment gradually became more important than partial unemployment, as employers came to believe that the crisis was not temporary.

3. 2   Total Unemployment in the Belgian Economy, 31 December 1930 and 27 February 1937

Information on interwar unemployment is rather sparse for groups other than the industrial workers covered by the voluntary insurance scheme. Comprehensive data on unemployment for the period is found in the censuses of 31 December 1930 and 27 February 1937. The 1930 census covers total and partial unemployment among manual workers and employees in industry and commerce. In 1937 only full unemployment was counted, but in contrast to the 1930 census, data were gathered for the whole economy, including agriculture, the professions, civil servants, employers and the self-employed.

The distribution of the unemployed across sectors, shown in Table 8.11, makes it clear that in 1937 unemployment among manual workers in industry comprised almost three-quarters of the total. It is likely, then, that our annual estimates for industrial manual workers give a good picture of total unemployment.

The census of December 1930 provides somewhat less complete information on unemployment, but gives us some idea of the changes in its sectoral distribution among manual workers and employees in industry and commerce. Table 8.12 shows the numbers unemployed in 1930 and

Table 8.11   Total Full Unemployment in all Sectors, February 1937

Economic sector	Number of unemployed	%
1. Agriculture	10,830	5.45
2. Industry		
(a) Manual workers[16]	145,901	73.37
(b) Employers, self-employed and white-collar workers	7,142	3.59
3. Tertiary sector	34,973	17.59
Total	198,846	100.00

Note: The tertiary sector includes employers, self-employed, white-collar workers and manual workers in commerce and transport; servants; professional people; and civil servants.

Source: Recensement Economique et Social au 27 Février 1937. Recensement des Inoccupés, pp. 54-63.

Table 8.12   Unemployment among Manual Workers and White-Collar Workers in Industry and Commerce, 31 December 1930 and 27 February 1937

Economic sector	Partial unemployment December 1930		Full unemployment December 1930		February 1937	
	Absolute	%	Absolute	%	Absolute	%
Industry						
Manual workers	211,354	90.98	136,334	88.80	145,901	82.75
White-collar workers	1,937	0.83	2,621	1.71	4,764	2.71
Commerce (inclusive of transport)						
Manual workers	17,448	7.51	10,752	7.00	18,397	10.43
White-collar workers	1,573	0.68	3,829	2.49	7,250	4.11
Total	232,312	100.00	153,536	100.00	176,312	100.00

Sources: Recensement de l'Industrie et du Commerce au 31 Décembre 1930. Recensement Professionnel, pp. 758-9, and *Recensement Economique et Social au 27 Février 1937. Recensement des Inoccupés,* pp. 54-63.

1937 in comparable categories. The share of industrial manual workers falls over the period. This is not particularly surprising since it might be supposed that enterprises laid off first blue-collar, then white-collar workers and that the effects of decreased purchasing power took some time to hit the commercial sector.

Starting from the assumption that in 1934 manual workers in industry represented 75 per cent of total unemployment (in 1937 it was 73.37 per cent), we arrive at a rough estimate of total full unemployment of 330,000 persons, which was roughly 10.6 per cent of the labour force as a whole.[17] If we suppose that partial unemployment among manual workers in industry counted for 80 per cent of all partial unemployment in 1934, we get a partial unemployment figure of somewhere about 240,000 persons or 7.7 per cent of the total labour force. This means that at the peak of the crisis 18 per cent of the labour force was hit by unemployment.

3. 3 Evolution of Unemployment and the Labour Force, 1920-39

The 1920s were generally a period of full employment. Only during the recession from the end of 1920 until the beginning of 1922 was unemployment a problem. Between 1923 and 1929 the unemployment rates were so low that nearly all people without work could be considered either frictionally or seasonally unemployed. The economic recession of 1925, which was due to monetary and fiscal difficulties, had no significant influence on unemployment.

The extremely low unemployment rates in the 1920s are even more remarkable since the industrial manual labour force increased enormously during this period, especially between 1920 and 1926, when it grew by 23.3 per cent (from 941,000 to 1,160,000). Besides population growth (5.5 per cent), this expansion can be explained by two structural changes: a shift from the agricultural to the industrial sector and a rise in female labour force participation. Although the number of farmers remained fairly constant between 1920 and 1930, many agricultural labourers left the low-paid agricultural sector. Their number fell from 219,000 in 1920 to 125,000 in 1930.[18] Between 1920 and 1926 female employment in industry rose by about 100,000, an increase of two-thirds.

Between 1926 and 1930 the industrial labour force increased only modestly (3.0 per cent), primarily as the result of population growth (2.8 per cent). During this period, it was not labour but capital which made the greatest contribution to economic growth.

Mass unemployment appears in the statistics only in 1931. The figures for partial unemployment suggest that in the first instance employers adjusted in part by short-time working. The Depression was deepest from 1932 until the first months of 1935. During these black years about 20 per cent of all industrial manual workers had no work and many others were partially unemployed. For the labour force as a whole full unemployment came to about 10 per cent.

From 1935 the Belgian economy began to recover so that by 1937 industrial unemployment had fallen to just over 10 per cent. This recovery was short-lived, and unemployment worsened in 1938 and 1939.

Our estimates for the industrial manual labour force show a decline during the 1930s. Since the population was increasing, the labour force in other sectors must have been growing. This was indeed the case for the self-employed: between 1930 and 1935 this group increased by over 100,000 (from 446,000 to 547,000), which exceeded the decline of 88,000 (from 1,194,000 in 1930 to 1,106,000 in 1937) in the industrial labour force. The growth of self-employment, especially in retailing, is frequently observed in periods of crisis.

4 Structural Aspects of Unemployment in Belgium, 1930-37

We now take a closer look at the structure of Belgian unemployment during the 1930s: its incidence by economic sector, occupation, educational attainment, sex and age, and its duration. At the outset we take a necessarily brief look at the characteristics of unemployment in the economy as a whole. For this we use the rich and uniquely comprehensive census of 1937. Then we shall delve more deeply into the nature of unemployment among industrial workers, the group most hard hit and that about which we have the best information. Here we can draw on the census of 1930 as well as that of 1937 and on our estimates for unemployed industrial workers. Unless indicated explicitly, all the figures mentioned in this section refer to full unemployment.

4. 1 Unemployment on 27 February 1937 by Economic Sector and by Occupation

4. 1. 1 Unemployment by Economic Sector.   As has already been indicated in Table 8.11, unemployment in the 1930s was predominantly industrial. In February 1937 77 per cent of the unemployed were classed as industrial labour (employers, self-employed, white- and blue-collar workers), and we have argued that this share was probably higher at the beginning of the crisis. But to get a proper notion of the sectoral incidence of unemployment it is necessary to know the distribution of the labour force. Table 8.13 shows the occupational distribution in 1930 compared with the spread of unemployment in 1937. Since we have no data for the total labour force and total unemployment at the same date, it was not possible to compute unemployment rates. Table 8.13 confirms the industrial character of unemployment: the share of industry in unemployment was much higher than its share of the labour force.

4. 1. 2 Unemployment by Occupation and Educational Attainment. The unemployed are also classified in the 1937 census according to whether they are self-employed (self-employed, employers and professionals), sa-

Table 8.13 Share of the Various Economic Sectors in the Labour Force (1930) and Unemployment (1937)

Sector	Share in labour force (%)	Share in unemployment (%)
Agriculture	17.1	5.4
Industry	54.9	77.0
Tertiary sector	28.0	17.6
Total	100.0	100.0

Sources: Population. Recensement Général du 31 Décembre 1930. Recensement des Professions, pp. 44-5, and *Recensement Economique et Sociale au 27 Février 1937. Recensement des Inoccupés*, pp. 54-63.

Table 8.14 Share of the Various Occupational Categories in the Labour Force (1930) and Unemployment (1937)

Occupational category	Share in labour force (%)	Share in unemployment (%)
Self-employed	26.6	2.1
Salaried employees	19.3	8.0
Manual workers	54.1	89.9
Total	100.0	100.0

Source: See Table 8.13.

Table 8.15 Unemployment and Educational Attainment, 27 February 1937 (%)

Educ'al attainment of the unemp'd	Self-employed	Employees	Manual workers	Share in total unemployment
No studies	11.5	--	17.0	15.5
Primary school	62.5	30.8	77.6	73.6
Technical school	4.6	8.7	2.1	2.7
High school	18.8	53.2	3.2	7.5
University	2.6	7.3	0.1	0.7
Total	100.0	100.0	100.0	100.0

Note: "High school" includes normal schools and teacher training colleges.
Source: Recensement Economique et Social au 27 Février 1937. Recensement des Inoccupés, pp. 42 and 136-9.

laried employees, or manual workers. Table 8.14 compares this distribution with that for the entire population in 1930. As might be expected, the self-employed and salaried employees account for a disproportionately small share of the unemployed.

One reason for this result is that wage earners were concentrated in industry, the sector hardest hit by the crisis. A related reason may be that manual workers had a lower level of education. Table 8.15 shows a cross-tabulation of the unemployed by economic status and educational attainment. In all three groups the unemployed were characterised by a relatively low level of schooling. The correlation between unemployment and educational attainment could not be measured, since we lack data concerning the latter for the entire labour force.

4.2 Industrial Distribution of Unemployment among Manual Workers, 1930-37

Estimates for unemployment rates and for the numbers of unemployed manual workers by industry may be found in Table 8.7 and Table 8.9. Unemployment in all industries rose during the crisis of the 1930s. Rates of 20 per cent and more were not exceptional in some export-oriented industries, such as metallurgy, textiles and arts, but were also observed in sectors more oriented to the home market, like ceramics, clothing, construction and wood. The rather low unemployment rate in the mining sector can be explained by state subsidies and protectionist measures which maintained coal production at a relatively high level. [19]

The way in which unemployment spread through the industrial sector may be seen in Table 8.16. The crisis was felt first and hardest in the major export industries: metallurgy, textiles and arts (which included the important diamond industry) show very large increases in 1930. In 1931 unemployment began to rise very rapidly in other, less export-oriented industries and continued to increase in 1932. By the mid-1930s industries catering to the home market were being hit harder than the export-oriented ones. This gradual shift of the unemployment burden illustrates the extent to which the Great Depression in Belgium was a phenomenon imported from abroad.

The openness of the Belgian economy can also be seen in the recovery from 1935 to 1937, when unemployment in the export-oriented industries fell noticeably. Unemployment in the industries catering for the home market, such as food, construction and ceramics, fell later and to a lesser extent.

4.3 Unemployment by Sex and Age, 31 December 1930 and 27 February 1937

4.3.1 Female Unemployment. Female employment in industry had increased markedly in the early 1920s, with the share of women in the industrial manual labour force rising from 17.2 per cent in 1920 to 21.1 per

Table 8.16 Growth Rates of Unemployment among Manual Workers in Industry, 1920-39 (%)

	Mines	Quarries	Metallurgy	Ceramics	Chemicals	Glass	Food	Textiles	Clothing	Construction	Wood	Leather	Tobacco	Paper	Publishing	Arts	Total
1921	59.3	18.9	37.0	16.6	-12.1	164.4	13.8	-17.5	-30.9	-1.4	-37.6	41.1	-29.1	110.1	-26.9	-39.5	-2.1
1922	-57.3	17.4	-47.5	-80.0	-76.9	-47.3	-65.0	-84.8	-75.2	-58.6	-68.2	-72.5	-69.9	-83.7	-62.2	-74.0	-66.6
1923	-99.2	-89.3	-79.0	-82.7	-66.8	-76.4	-58.7	-65.8	-31.5	-44.3	-62.1	-54.0	-39.7	-92.8	5.4	-80.0	-66.1
1924	1919.0	223.2	-19.4	253.4	-56.4	-60.3	-5.9	23.1	-32.9	10.2	99.9	-34.7	26.5	26.7	20.0	100.8	5.5
1925	28.3	21.4	100.1	42.2	80.1	50.4	24.5	41.5	36.9	41.2	70.2	82.7	-11.0	412.5	55.5	1.9	45.7
1926	7.0	-22.4	50.8	-9.0	-51.7	14.0	25.9	-36.6	-23.1	-21.7	-23.2	-34.7	87.7	-28.4	252.4	-47.3	-0.5
1927	-61.7	41.9	2.9	72.4	385.4	154.2	34.2	22.4	31.4	51.2	61.6	87.1	-33.4	-41.2	9.9	190.3	33.3
1928	194.4	-43.8	-61.0	-62.4	-46.1	-12.0	-40.2	-17.5	-33.7	-48.8	-64.9	-28.7	-50.4	-67.3	-62.5	-56.2	-45.3
1929	-79.2	36.5	21.6	268.6	-61.7	25.5	22.9	14.0	7.7	88.3	6.1	-10.7	-35.2	78.4	-44.7	305.8	33.5
1930	288.8	13.7	241.1	53.6	57.6	152.0	83.6	252.0	154.0	16.6	342.2	98.7	69.6	265.9	48.0	377.8	130.5
1931	682.3	505.4	288.8	180.4	604.4	16.4	189.0	209.8	156.9	184.4	184.9	178.6	75.8	470.0	279.7	96.9	185.8
1932	164.5	91.2	61.7	94.8	60.3	45.3	75.6	103.0	40.1	44.6	41.3	98.1	86.4	193.4	74.9	8.0	63.0
1933	6.0	-29.0	-8.0	51.8	-14.0	30.5	-1.4	-19.4	18.9	2.9	-0.6	-23.5	-9.5	-33.2	14.2	-26.6	-4.5
1934	14.0	3.6	6.4	-29.9	10.4	15.6	9.3	2.4	38.1	18.0	7.9	1.8	9.2	30.2	-20.6	9.4	8.3
1935	-11.2	-14.4	-8.0	19.9	-19.8	2.0	9.8	-22.9	-34.7	0.1	-16.3	-18.0	-16.2	13.0	-18.1	-43.5	-11.1
1936	-41.1	-43.1	-37.0	8.1	-43.2	-41.9	-9.6	-33.7	-37.0	-19.9	-38.0	-30.3	-32.7	-53.3	-27.0	-41.0	-30.2
1937	-51.2	20.3	-35.4	-63.1	-20.7	-7.7	-10.8	-24.5	-22.6	-19.8	34.2	-9.9	2.6	-11.6	-30.6	36.3	-21.4
1938	-21.3	-32.9	31.1	119.1	30.2	5.2	4.6	39.8	-2.7	19.6	-9.9	13.8	24.5	7.5	22.7	114.5	23.5
1939	46.0	96.2	10.0	24.4	5.4	3.4	24.7	13.3	56.3	34.2	17.8	9.8	8.3	23.8	31.8	-8.1	20.1

Source: Table 8.9. Each row of data represents percentage change since previous year.

Table 8.17   Share of Female Industrial Manual Workers in the Labour Force, and Unemployment Rates by Sex, 31 December 1930 and 27 February 1937

Industry	Female share in labour force (%)		Unemployment rates by sex								
			1930						1937		
			Fully unemployed			Partially unemployed			Fully unemployed		
	1930	1937	Men	Women	Total	Men	Women	Total	Men	Women	Total
Mines	3.0	2.1	1.0	0.3	0.9	1.0	1.0	1.0	3.2	1.3	3.1
Quarries	1.1	1.6	6.3	3.8	6.2	19.0	11.4	18.9	7.5	2.4	7.4
Metallurgy	4.4	7.6	10.1	4.7	9.8	21.8	17.8	21.5	12.6	2.0	11.8
Ceramics	10.7	10.4	15.8	8.1	14.7	16.8	15.6	16.6	24.5	3.9	22.4
Glass	16.3	16.1	11.2	2.4	9.5	19.2	7.3	17.0	13.5	2.1	11.6
Chemicals	21.2	20.6	4.7	2.7	4.3	6.6	14.6	8.5	6.6	1.7	5.6
Food	15.2	17.1	5.4	3.7	5.1	4.0	8.6	4.9	10.4	3.3	9.2
Textiles	52.4	48.6	10.0	8.6	9.3	38.1	40.1	39.2	14.6	2.8	8.9
Clothing	75.7	76.3	17.9	15.9	16.3	16.6	18.5	18.1	17.2	7.4	9.7
Construction	0.3	0.2	26.9	8.4	26.8	14.1	10.8	14.1	34.3	36.8	34.4
Wood	4.2	6.2	20.9	10.6	20.2	20.1	18.5	20.0	24.1	4.4	22.9
Leather	33.3	34.1	10.7	10.1	10.5	29.5	28.5	29.1	14.9	2.9	10.8
Tobacco	57.1	63.8	6.7	4.6	5.4	12.1	9.0	10.2	20.3	3.3	9.4
Paper	32.8	33.1	3.9	3.5	3.8	12.7	16.1	13.8	6.6	1.8	5.0
Publishing	18.2	19.7	5.0	3.3	4.6	3.4	3.9	3.6	9.0	2.6	7.7
Arts	15.3	18.7	48.8	21.3	43.6	18.6	15.0	17.9	11.7	3.4	10.2
Total	19.5	19.0	12.1	8.7	11.4	15.8	25.0	17.7	15.4	3.6	13.1

Sources: Recensement de l'Industrie et du Commerce au 31 Décembre 1930. Recensement Professionel (1934), pp. 758- 9, and Recensement Industriel et Commerciel (1935), p. 1343; *Recensement Economique et Social au 27 Février 1937*, part II, pp. 8-99. *Recensement des Inoccupés*, pp. 58-61.

Table 8.18 **Share of Various Age Groups of Manual Industrial Workers in the Labour Force, and Rates of Full Unemployment by Age and Sex, 27 February 1937**

Age group	Share in labour force (%)			Unemployment rate (%)		
	men	women	total	men	women	total
... 15	1.4	4.3	1.9	7.3	2.7	5.5
15-20	9.8	24.6	12.5	8.1	3.2	6.3
20-25	11.5	20.3	13.1	12.0	3.2	9.5
25-30	14.9	15.8	15.1	11.5	2.8	9.8
30-35	14.9	11.9	14.3	12.2	2.7	10.7
35-40	12.8	8.7	12.0	12.6	3.2	11.4
40-45	9.4	5.8	8.7	13.8	4.5	12.7
45-50	7.7	3.6	6.9	16.6	5.9	15.6
50-55	6.9	2.3	6.1	21.2	8.5	20.3
55-60	5.4	1.4	4.6	29.6	12.8	28.6
60-65	4.1	0.9	3.5	40.1	16.1	39.0
65 ...	1.2	0.4	1.1	12.1	2.4	11.5
Total	100.0	100.0	100.0	14.9	3.6	12.8

Source: Recensement Economique et Sociale au 27 Février 1937, part IV, p. 20. *Recensement des Inoccupés*, pp. 60-1.

cent in 1926. During the late 1920s this share remained fairly stable. We will now consider the impact of the crisis of the 1930s on this segment of the labour force.

Table 8.17, which summarises the data for 1930 and 1937, displays two interesting results. First, one can see the differing incidence by sex of full and partial unemployment in 1930. Although there is some tendency for women to have lower rates of full unemployment and higher rates of partial unemployment by industry, the differences in the industry-wide rates are primarily due to the differences in the distributions of men and women workers across industries. The high rate of partial unemployment among women is mostly due to their concentration in the textile industries, where short-time working, among both men and women, was common in 1930. Of all partially unemployed women 62 per cent worked in textiles.

The second striking feature shown in Table 8.17 is the fall in the rate of unemployment among women from 1930 to 1937, during which time male unemployment rose. This was not due to an increase in the women's share in industrial employment, which remained constant at 21.0 per cent. What seems to have happened is that many women left the labour market, that is, they did not declare themselves as unemployed to the census takers. This withdrawal from the labour force was probably abetted by the economy measures of 1933-34, which denied unemployment benefits to married women. Other women must have shifted from industrial work to the service sector. Many undoubtedly were occupied in running the much greater numbers of cafés and small shops that appeared during the 1930s. Together these changes help account for the fall in the female share of the industrial labour force.

4.3.2 Unemployment by Age. The higher incidence of unemployment with age in 1937 can be seen in Table 8.18. Late in the crisis of the 1930s youth unemployment appears to have been relatively unimportant. Those hardest hit were people aged between 50 and 65. In this age group 20 to 40 per cent of all manual industrial workers were without work. Unemployment rates among women also increased at the upper age groups, but since women workers were heavily concentrated at younger ages, the average age of unemployed women was lower than that for men.

There is some indication that youth unemployment during the early years of the crisis must have been relatively more important than it was in 1937. Fragmentary evidence for 1935-38 shows that the share of younger workers unemployed fell during the recovery of 1935-37, then rose again as economic conditions worsened in 1938.[20] This suggests that older workers, perhaps because of their experience, were laid off later, but that once out of work, their chances for re-employment were smaller.

4.4 Duration of Unemployment

Table 8.19 **Total Full Unemployment in the Belgian Economy: Average Duration among Unemployed who had Already Worked, 27 February 1937**

Age group	Average duration
... 16	4 months
16-18	5 months
18-20	8 months
20-25	1 year 2 months
25-30	1 year 5 months
30-40	1 year 8 months
40-50	2 year 1 month
50-55	2 year 4 months
55-60	2 year 7 months
60-65	2 year 11 months
65 ...	2 year 10 months
All	1 year 11 months

Source: Recensement Economique et Social au 27 Février 1937. Recensement des Inoccupés, pp. 38-9.

**Table 8.20   Total Full Unemployment in the Belgian Economy:
Unemployed Having Already Worked and Unemployed
Having Never Worked, 27 February 1937**

	Men		Women		Total	
	Number	%	Number	%	Number	%
Having already worked	178,315	96.6	12,686	88.7	191,001	96.1
Having never worked	6,235	3.4	1,610	11.3	7,845	3.9
Total	184,550	100.0	14,296	100.0	198,846	100.0

Source: Recensement Economique et Social au 27 Février 1937. Recensement des Inoccupés, p. 17.

**Table 8.21   Total Full Unemployment in the Belgian Economy: Average
Duration by Sex, 27 February 1937**

Duration	Men		Women		Total	
	Number	%	Number	%	Number	%
less than 1 month	11,968	6.5	1,321	9.3	13,289	6.7
1-2 months	11,857	6.4	1,337	9.4	13,194	6.6
2-3 months	15,116	8.2	1,174	8.2	16,290	8.2
3-6 months	32,756	17.7	1,997	14.0	34,753	17.5
6-12 months	19,671	10.7	2,220	15.5	21,891	11.0
Subtotal, less than 1 year	91,368	49.5	8,049	56.4	99,417	50.0
12-14 months	5,062	2.7	572	4.0	5,634	2.8
since 1935	20,646	11.2	1,909	13.4	22,555	11.3
since 1934	16,712	9.1	1,263	8.8	17,975	9.0
since 1933	15,020	8.1	791	5.5	15,811	8.0
since 1932	15,375	8.3	649	4.5	16,024	8.1
since or before 1931	20,229	11.0	1,043	7.3	21,272	10.7
Subtotal, 1 year & more	93,044	50.4	6,227	43.5	99,271	49.9
Not known	138	0.1	20	0.1	158	0.1
Total	184,550	100.0	14,296	100.0	198,846	100.0

Source: Recensement Economique et Social au 27 Février 1937. Recensement des Inoccupés, pp. 78-83.

That the older unemployed found it harder to get a new job is confirmed by the average duration of unemployment by age in 1937 (Table 8.19).[21] Age and unemployment spells were positively correlated. The long average duration of unemployment for all age groups at the end of the recovery period suggests that a large share of those without work in 1937 were structurally unemployed. Young people seem to have had fewer problems finding a job, for the 1937 census recorded that only 3.9 per cent of the unemployed had never worked (Table 8.20). This low figure is another indication that in a period of economic recovery employers preferred to engage young people who had recently entered the labour market rather than to reinstate older workers.

It is also interesting to compare unemployment duration between men and women. Table 8.21 shows that men remained for relatively longer periods without a job: 27.4 per cent of the men who were unemployed in February 1937 had been jobless since 1933 compared with 17.3 per cent of the female unemployed. This may be another indication of the tendency for unemployed women to leave the labour market.

5 Conclusion

Most of what we know about unemployment in interwar Belgium is based on statistics generated by a voluntary insurance system set up within the framework of unionism, but financially supported by the government. This system covered a large and generally increasing share of industrial workers: on the eve of the crisis of the 1930s 50 per cent of industrial manual workers were insured; by 1937 this share had risen to 66 per cent, despite restrictions brought about by government economy measures.

The insurance statistics have been used to make annual estimates for industrial unemployment, which display a marked contrast between the 1920s and the 1930s. Except during the 1920-22 recession, the 1920s were a period of full employment in Belgium. But, as a small open economy, the country could not escape from the Great Depression which was heralded by falling exports in 1929. From the end of 1930 onwards the unemployment rate for manual workers in industry went from an extremely low level compatible with full employment to about 20 per cent at the peaks of the crisis (1932 and 1934). This rate corresponds to almost 250,000 workers. For the economy as a whole unemployment must have come to about 330,000, which is roughly 10 per cent of the total labour force. Many other workers felt the crisis through partial unemployment.

During the crisis of the early 1930s the nature and incidence of unemployment changed. Partial unemployment was very important at the outset, but gave way to full unemployment by the mid-1930s. Unemployment was initially concentrated in the export-oriented industries, then spread to those catering more for the home market.

During the economic recovery in 1935-37, the number of unemployed remained high, which indicates that Belgian unemployment in the 1930s was not only cyclical, but also structural. In contrast to the late 1920s Belgian productive capacity hardly changed in the 1930s. The most important structural change caused by the crisis was a shift towards self-employment in the commercial sector, activity which may have been characterised by low productivity.

In 1937 the majority of the unemployed were male, and large numbers were found in older age groups with little chance of re-employment. The female rate of full unemployment was lower than that for men, but this does not mean that women were less hard hit by the crisis. Many women simply left the labour force, a movement fostered by government measures excluding married women from unemployment benefits.

NOTES

* Martine Goossens is a Fellow of the National Fund for Scientific Research of Belgium. Stefaan Peeters and Guido Pepermans are research assistants at the Katholieke Universiteit Leuven. All three are members of the Workshop on Quantitative Economic History under the direction of Herman Van der Wee. The authors are very grateful to Bradford Lee for his valuable comments on the original draft. They would also like to express their gratitude to Peter Solar for editorial assistance in preparing the English translation of the present essay. Finally, they thank Herman Van der Wee and the members of his Workshop for their inspiring comments.

1 See e.g. Baudhuin (1946); Cassiers (1986); Hogg (1986); Leën (1933); Scholliers (1985); and Veraghtert (1979).

2 H. Van der Wee and his collaborators of the Workshop on Quantitative Economic History are reconstructing the statistics for National Product, National Income, National Expenditure and employment between 1920 and 1953.

3 See Scholliers (1985).

4 The seminal work on the institutional and social aspects of Belgian unemployment during the crisis of the 1930s is undoubtedly the PhD thesis of Vanthemsche (1987). Our discussion of the voluntary unemployment insurance system that prevailed in the interwar period draws mainly on chapters 1 and 3 of this thesis.

5 Based on Vanthemsche (1985).

6 In Liège subsidies were granted by the provincial council, in Ghent by the municipality. See Vanthemsche (1985), p. 133.

7 Vanthemsche (1985), p. 154; and *Les Fonds* (1913), pp. 12-13.

8 Vanthemsche (1985), p. 159; Rutten (1912), p. 27; and Vandervelde (1925), pp. 340-41.

9 De Leener (1934).

10 Vanthemsche (1987), p. 304; and Jacquemyns (1932-34).

11 There was a period of one year during which new affiliates of unemployment insurance funds had to pay contributions without being entitled to benefits.

12 This impossible insurance rate (more than 100 per cent) is due to the fact that the classification in the industrial censuses (all workers) and in the insurance fund statistics (insured workers) differs for some categories.

13 Based on Goossens (1987).

14 The estimates for partial unemployment take account of its higher incidence among the total industrial labour force than among insured workers in December 1930 (partial/full unemployment from the industrial census was 1.49; for insured workers 1.85). We did not find an explanation for this discrepancy.

15 Scholliers (1985), pp. 269-78.

16 The difference between the number of unemployed industrial workers according to the February 1937 census and our estimates in Tables 8.8 and 8.9 is due to the fact that our data are annual averages. In February seasonal unemployment tends to be high, which largely explains the observed discrepancy.

17 Only in 1930 is total labour force of all sectors available; see *Population* (1930). The 1930 figure was augmented by the population growth percentage between 1930 and 1934 to estimate the total labour force in 1934.

18 Veraghtert (1979), p. 91.

19 Hogg (1986), pp. 81-95.

20 Vanthemsche (1987), pp. 128-37; and Roger (1937).

21 It must be clear that our figures concern interrupted durations of unemployment at a certain point in time. For Belgium no data are available on complete periods of employment and unemployment. Therefore it is impossible to calculate rates of flow between employment and unemployment.

REFERENCES

Banque Nationale de Belgique (1929), *Statistiques Economiques Belges 1919-1928,* special issue of *Bulletin d'Information et de Documentation* (April).

Banque Nationale de Belgique (n.d.), *Statistiques Economiques Belges 1929-1940,* special issue of *Bulletin d'Information et de Documentation.*

Baudhuin, F. (1946), *Histoire Economique de la Belgique 1914-1939,* 2 vols, 2nd edn, Brussels: Bruylant.

Carbonnelle, C. (1959), "Recherches sur l'Evolution de la Production en Belgique de 1900 à 1957", *Cahiers Economiques de Bruxelles* 3, pp. 353-79 (April).

Cassiers, I. (1980), "Une Statistique des Salaires Horaires dans l'Industrie Belge, 1919-1939", *Recherches Economiques de Louvain* 46, pp. 57-85 (March).

Cassiers, I. (1986), "Croissance, Crise et Regulation en Economie Ouverte: la Belgique entre les Deux Guerres", Université Catholique de Louvain. Unpublished doctoral dissertation, 2 vols.

De Leener, G. (1934), "Les Réformes de l'Assurance-Chômage en Belgique", Banque Nationale de Belgique. *Bulletin d'Information et de Documentation* 9, pp. 285-9 (November).

Goossens, M. (1987), "Reconstructie van Werkgelegenheidscijfers voor het Interbellum. Methodologie en Resultaten", Katholieke Universiteit Leuven, Workshop on Quantitative Economic History, Discussion Paper 87.01.

Hogg, R.L. (1986), *Structural Rigidities and Policy Inertia in Inter-War Belgium*, Verhandelingen van de Koninklijka Academie voor Wetenschappen, Letteren en Schone Kunsten van België, Brussels: Klasse der Letteren.

Jacquemyns, G. (1932-34), *Enquête sur les Conditions de Vie des Chômeurs Assurés*, 5 vols, Etudes Sociales, Travaux de l'Institut de Sociologie, Liège: Instituts Solvay.

Kiehel, C.A. (1932), *Unemployment Insurance in Belgium. A National Development of the Ghent and Liège Systems*, New York.

Leën, W. (1933). *Werkeloosheidsverzekering en Werkelozensteun in België*, Brussels: Standaard.

Les Fonds Communaux et Provinciaux d'Encouragement à la Prévoyance contre le Chômage Involontaire (1913), Publications du Ministère de l'Industrie et du Travail, Brussels: Office du Travail.

Peeters, S. *et al.* (1986), "Reconstruction of the Belgian National Income, 1920-1939, Methodology and Results", Katholieke Universiteit Leuven, Workshop on Quantitative Economic History, Discussion Paper 86.01.

Population. Recensement général du 31 Décembre 1930, vol. 5. Recensement des Professions.

Recensement de l'Industrie et du Commerce au 31 Décembre 1930. Recensement Industriel et Commerciel (1935), *Revue du Travail*, pp. 1329-1497 (November).

Recensement de l'Industrie et du Commerce au 31 Décembre 1930. Recensement Professionel (1934), *Revue du Travail*, pp. 719-771 (June).

Recensement Economique et Social au 27 Février 1937, 5 vols. Recensement des Inoccupés.

Roger, C. (1937), "Analyse de la Répartition du Chômage Complet d'après l'Enquête Spéciale de Mars 1936", *Bulletin de l'Institut des Sciences Economiques* 8, pp. 327-43 (May).

Rutten, G.C. (1912), *Rapport Général sur le Mouvement Syndical Chrétien en Belgique*, Ghent: Publications des Unions Professionelles Chrétiennes.

Scholliers, P. (1985), *Loonindexering en Sociale Vrede. Koopkracht en Klassenstrijd in Belgitijdens het Interbellum*, Brussels: Vrije Universiteit Brussel, Centrum voor Hedendaagse Sociale Gerschiedenis.

Vandervelde, E. (1925), *Le Parti Ouvrier Belge*, Brussels: L'Eglantine.

Vanthemsche, G. (1985), "De Oorsprong van de Werkloosheidsverzekering in België: Vakbondskassen en Gemeentelijke Fondsen (1890-1914)", *Tijdschrift voor Sociale Geschiedenis* 11, pp. 130-64 (May).

Vanthemsche, G. (1987), "De Werkloosheid in Belgitëjdens de Krisis van de Jaren 1930", Vrije Universiteit Brussel, Fakulteit der Letteren en Wijsbegeerte. Unpublished doctoral dissertation, 2 vols.

Veraghtert, K. (1979), "Het Ekonomisch Leven in België 1918-40", *Algemene Geschiedenis der Nederlanden*, vol. 14, pp. 51-101.

Chapter 9

Interwar Unemployment in the United States: Evidence from the 1940 Census Sample

Robert Margo*

1 Introduction

Unemployment in the 1930s is a central issue in macroeconomics, and it is the persistence of high unemployment that makes the Great Depression unique in American history. Why were rates of unemployment so high for so long? How can one reconcile persistent unemployment with the rise in real wages throughout much of the decade?

In a Keynesian model of the labour market persistent unemployment is traced to a failure of real wages to adjust downwards. According to Martin Baily (1983, p.59) "an eclectic version of contract theory" combined with the effects of various legal and institutional changes during the decade provides the reason why wages were rigid in the 1930s. Firms did not follow "a policy of aggressive wage cutting" when unemployment was high because the policy would hurt worker morale and thus the reputation of the firm. The passage of the National Industry Recovery Act, the National Labor Relations Act, the Fair Labor Standards Act, and growing unionisation, created a legal and moral climate in which wage cutting was difficult. The availability of work relief and other forms of assistance "permitted the economic system to operate despite the presence of a large group of hard-core unemployed and non-employed", thereby reducing any downward pressure on real wages (ibid., p.53).

The New Classical Macroeconomics provides a different answer. Its hallmarks are the assumptions of rational expectations, market clearing, and the intertemporal substitution of labour. According to Lucas and Rap-

B. Eichengreen and T. J. Hatton (eds.), Interwar Unemployment in International Perspective, 325–352.

Table 9.1   Unemployment Rates, 1930-41

Year	BLS	Darby
1931	15.9	15.3
1932	23.6	22.9
1933	24.9	20.6
1934	21.7	16.0
1935	20.1	14.2
1936	16.9	9.9
1937	14.3	9.1
1938	19.0	12.5
1939	17.2	11.3
1940	14.6	9.5

Source: Darby (1976). "BLS" refers to official Bureau of Labour Statistics estimates which count relief workers as unemployed; "Darby" refers to Darby's corrected BLS estimates which count relief workers as employed.

ping (1972), a model of labour markets incorporating these assumptions does a credible job in explaining wage, price and employment changes from 1929 to 1933. The model fails to explain the persistence of high unemployment after 1933. But according to Michael Darby (1976), the persistence of high unemployment is part illusion - the standard unemployment series includes persons on work relief. By today's convention a worker is unemployed if the worker is looking for work but unable to find a job. Relief workers had jobs and so were employed. Darby argues that counting relief workers as employed not only correctly adjusts aggregate unemployment rates downwards in the late 1930s (see Table 9.1) but also improves the fit of the Lucas-Rapping model (for a contrary view see Kesselman and Savin, 1978).

Another framework to explain high unemployment appeals to the notion of hysteresis, or that high unemployment today causes high unemployment tommorrow. A key symptom of hysteresis is long-term unemployment, either because of duration dependence (the longer a worker is unemployed the lower the chances of being re-employed) or because some workers, once unemployed, have very low chances of re-employment. According to Blanchard and Summers (1986, p.14), a long spell of unemployment causes "the atrophy of skills ... [and] disaffection from the labour force", thereby reducing "the effective supply of labour". If, for a variety of reasons, employers prefer workers who would remain with the firm for a long time, "it may be very difficult for middle-aged workers to find new jobs" (ibid., p.15). And, if workers with jobs - "insiders" - bargain over wages so as to keep their jobs, unemployed "outsiders" will stay unemployed. Although the solution to hysteresis may be structural, Blanchard and Summers emphasise the value of strong and persistent aggregate demand shocks in reducing long-term unemployment.

The potential relevance of hysteresis to the 1930s is easy to see. By comparison with later decades the proportion of individuals with long spells of unemployment (for example, over a year) seems much higher.[1] Hysteresis evidently disappeared in the early 1940s, when the United States entered the Second World War and the economy expanded greatly.

Whatever the differences among them, the various macroeconomic theories share a common goal: the explanation of aggregate unemployment rates. Knowledge about labour markets in the 1930s is knowledge gleaned from aggregate time series data.[2] The method and evidence differ sharply from that of the labour historian - or, for that matter, the labour economist - whose focus is on unemployed people: who was unemployed, why they were unemployed, what the consequences were for individual and household behaviour, and how the who, why and what were influenced by economic and social change.[3] Given the overwhelming importance of the Great Depression in the economic history of the United States, one might suspect the microeconomics of interwar unemployment to be old hat, but the opposite is true: the issues have scarcely been addressed.

By using a new body of microeconomic evidence on interwar unemployment - the public use sample of the 1940 census - this chapter serves to remedy some of the neglect. The analysis in the chapter provides information about the correlates of employment status and the duration of unemployment that cannot be gleaned from published sources. The results also provide insights, I believe, into the various macroeconomic theories, particularly the implications of Darby's adjustments to measured unemployment and the effects of work relief and hysteresis in labour markets in the late 1930s.

1.1   Plan of the Chapter

Section 2 of the chapter reviews some aggregate statistics from the sample on the incidence and duration of unemployment for male heads of households. I show that the employed, the unemployed, and persons on work relief differed in demographic and other characteristics; that the distribution of incomplete spells of unemployment differed between unemployed, experienced workers and persons on work relief; and that many persons on work relief held relief jobs for a long time. Section 3 extends the results through multivariate analyses of employment status, the probability of holding a relief job, the length of incomplete spells of unemployment, and a proxy for the probability of re-employment. Section 4 discusses the implications of the findings for understanding labour markets in the 1930s and the various macroeconomic theories of interwar unemployment. Section 5 presents some preliminary results from the sample on the so-called "added-worker" effect, and section 6 concludes.

2 The Data

The Census Bureau's public use sample of the 1940 census is a large, newly available source of microeconomic evidence on unemployment in the Great Depression.[4] The sample has information on employment status in the survey week (24-30 March 1940), the number of weeks of unemployment for those currently unemployed in the survey week, and weeks worked in 1939.

By historical standards the information is rich. Employment status has nine categories. A person can: be employed in a private sector or non-relief government job; be working on a relief job; be an unemployed, experienced worker; have a job, but be temporarily not working; be a new entrant; or be in one of four additional categories referring to people out of the labour force (for example, in school).[5] Duration of unemployment means the number of weeks since the person last held a private sector or non-relief government job, or, if he never held such a job, the number of weeks since he began looking for work. Weeks worked is a full-time equivalent measure, that is, part-time workers report the number of weeks worked as if they worked full-time for part of the year. Weeks worked includes time spent working on relief jobs, even though workers on relief officially were counted among the unemployed.

The sample, though, is no panacea. March 1940 was not March 1931 or March 1935. Whatever one learns about unemployed people near the end of the Depression differs from what one learns about the beginning or the middle. The initial shock was over, legal and institutional changes had taken place, and the war in Europe had begun. The sample is cross-sectional, so the duration of unemployment refers to *incomplete* spells of unemployment at the time the census was taken. Serious questions were raised in the early 1940s about errors of measurement of employment status, the duration of unemployment, and weeks worked.[6]

Furthermore, the census provides no information on which agency (for example, the Works Progress Administration (WPA) or a state agency) employed a sample member who was on work relief. The information is not crucial for evaluating the macroeconomic issues raised by Darby. The information would be crucial, however, for evaluating how the policies of specific relief agencies may have affected the labour market. In fact, by the late 1930s the vast majority of persons on work relief (and presumably the same is true of the sample) were employed by the WPA (see Howard, 1943, pp. 633-40, 856-9).

Table 9.2   Employment Status and Duration of Unemployment: Male Heads of Households, 1940 Census Sample (continued over)

	Emp'd (%)	Unemp'd (%)	Relief	Unemployment rate Official	Unemployment rate Darby
Total	83.8	6.2	5.0	11.1	6.2
Age:					
18-24	4.7	3.9	6.7	12.7	5.3
25-29	11.7	9.0	10.3	9.8	5.1
30-34	14.8	9.2	14.1	9.3	4.1
35-44	25.5	23.5	36.8	13.3	5.9
45-54	29.1	28.9	23.2	10.7	6.5
55-59	8.3	10.4	8.3	13.2	8.0
60-64	5.6	8.9	5.5	14.8	9.9
65+	6.2	6.5	3.5	10.0	7.0
White	91.5	91.3	83.8	10.7	6.2
Foreign	15.0	23.8	8.7	12.9	10.0
Married	93.3	89.2	95.4	11.0	5.9
Urban	61.1	71.8	59.2	12.1	7.3
Migrant across state lines	6.9	5.4	5.0	8.7	4.9
Has non-wage income	8.7	10.4	10.5	13.4	7.2
Years of schooling (mean)	8.6	7.4	7.2		
Value of owner-occupied housing $x\ 10^{-2}$ (mean)	14.2	7.5	4.2		
Region:					
North-east	29.6	40.5	22.0	12.6	8.8
North central	31.7	25.3	34.7	11.0	5.2
South	33.3	21.4	30.9	9.3	4.3
West	11.4	13.1	12.4	13.0	7.4

Table 9.2 reports aggregate statistics from the sample on employment status and the duration of unemployment for male heads of households.[7] I focus on male heads of households throughout (except in section 5) because they were less likely to have been new entrants or out of the labour force, and so their behaviour is easier to categorise.[8] According to the official definition of unemployment (relief workers were unemployed), 11.1 per cent of male heads of households in the labour force were unemployed at the time of the survey. Forty-five per cent of the unemployed had relief jobs, 55 per cent were unemployed experienced workers, and very few (0.1 per cent) were new entrants (not surprising for heads of households). That nearly half of the "unemployed" were on work relief illustrates one implication of Darby's argument. Counting relief workers

Table 9.2 (continued)

	Emp'd (%)	Unemp'd (%)	Unemp't rate
Industry:			
Agriculture	24.0	9.3	2.8
Mining	2.5	3.1	8.1
Construction	6.3	28.9	25.2
Light manufacturing	15.2	13.0	5.9
Heavy manufacturing	12.5	9.9	5.5
Service	45.3	33.7	5.5
Occupation:			
Professional	6.0	2.1	2.5
Managers	31.8	5.9	1.3
Clerical	11.9	8.6	5.0
Craftsmen	17.8	24.1	9.1
Service	19.6	18.2	6.4
Labourers	18.8	41.2	13.9

Distribution of Weeks Unemployed of Currently Unemployed (%)

Weeks	Total	Exp. work.	Relief
0-13	21.4	30.2	10.6
14-26	16.8	18.6	14.5
27-39	10.9	11.4	10.3
40-52	9.4	9.8	9.0
52+	41.5	30.0	55.6

Source: First random subsample, 1940 Census Public Use Tape. Percentages may not add up to 100 due to rounding. Light manufacturing: food; textiles and related; lumber; paper; printing. Heavy manufacturing: chemicals; petroleum; coal; rubber; stone, clay, and glass; iron and steel; non-ferrous metals; machinery; transportation; plus unspecified manufacturing. Service sector: transportation; wholesale and retail trade; finance, insurance, real estate; business and other services; government. Occupation: Professional: includes semi-professionals. Managers: includes proprietors, officials and farm managers. Service: includes protective service (e.g. police) and others.

as employed gives a total unemployment rate of 6.2 per cent among male heads of households: very low by Depression standards, and hardly shocking to Americans in the 1980s.

Employment status varied by age and other personal characteristics. Compared with the employed, unemployed experienced workers were more often middle-aged or older (over age 45), foreign-born, single, urban, less geographically mobile, as measured by the proportion migrating across state lines from 1935 to 1940, and living in the north-east or west rather than in the north central states or the south.[9] The unemployed had 1.2 fewer years of schooling than the employed, and far less wealth, as measured by the value of owner-occupied housing. Non-wage income includes payments of direct relief, which probably explains the greater incidence of non-wage income among the unemployed (and relief workers).

Persons on work relief differed from the employed and the unemployed. Sixty per cent of persons on work relief were under age 45, compared with 51 per cent of the employed and 45 per cent of the unemployed. Twenty-two per cent of persons on work relief were residents of the northeast, far less than the percentages among the employed or the unemployed; 65 per cent were residents of the north central states or the south, much greater than the percentage among the unemployed (47 per cent). Compared with the unemployed, persons on work relief were less often foreign, but more likely to be non-white. A larger fraction were married (95 per cent) than was the case with either the employed or unemployed. Like the unemployed, however, persons on work relief had fewer years of schooling and considerably less wealth than the employed.

Most of the differences between persons on work relief and the rest of the labour force can arguably be traced to the policies of the WPA and other relief agencies. In the case of the WPA, persons on work relief were selected from local rolls of direct relief, and then certified as acceptable or unacceptable for WPA jobs. The specific criteria varied enormously, but certain aspects were common throughout the country. Most relief jobs involved heavy physical labour and that, along with a general tendency not to certify elderly men (who were often eligible for other types of assistance like social security), accounts for the age distribution of relief workers. Persons on work relief had to satisfy a means test, which would explain their lower schooling levels (lower incomes) and lower values of owner-occupied housing (lower wealth). There was a general preference for married heads of households and a greater willingness in some parts of the country to certify non-whites. Employment of aliens was restricted, which explains the smaller fraction of foreign-born persons among relief workers. Although the WPA did not have a residency requirement, many state and local relief agencies did, which may explain the lower level of geographic mobility among relief workers.[10]

Employment status varied by industry and occupation. The data refer to the worker's current industry and occupation, so I cannot compare Darby's and the official definition of unemployment across industries and occupations. A fair comparison requires information on the usual industry and occupation of workers on relief, which is not available in the current sample.[11] Unemployment rates - the fraction of experienced workers who were unemployed - were lowest in agriculture (not surprisingly); higher in mining (8.1 per cent) than in light manufacturing, heavy manufacturing, and the service sector (5.5 to 5.9 per cent); and extraordinarily high in construction (25.2 per cent).[12]

Unemployment rates were lowest among professionals (2.5 per cent) and managers (1.3 per cent); slightly below average for clerical and kindred workers (5 per cent); slightly above average for service workers (6.4 per cent); significantly above average for skilled craftsmen, foremen, and kindred workers (9.1 per cent); and highest among unskilled labourers (13.9 per cent). Indeed, unskilled labourers accounted for 41.1 per cent of all unemployed experienced workers in the sample.

The final part of Table 9.2 gives information on the distribution of incomplete spells of unemployment. The column labelled "Total" under "Distribution of Weeks Unemployed" aggregates the distribution of incomplete spells across relief workers and unemployed experienced workers - that is, it shows the distribution of incomplete spells counting relief workers among the unemployed. According to the "Total" distribution, 21 per cent were out of work thirteen weeks or less, and 38 per cent for six months or less. The distribution looks similar to others from the 1930s: the fraction of incomplete spells declines as the length of the spell increases but at a decreasing rate (compare the relative percentages at 0-13 weeks versus 14-26 weeks and again at 27-39 weeks versus 40-52 weeks), and the fraction out of work a year or longer (42 per cent) looks enormous by postwar standards. The evidence on incomplete spells suggests that long-term unemployment was indeed a serious problem in the Great Depression.

Disaggregating the distribution, however, gives a somewhat different picture. Among unemployed experienced workers the fraction of incomplete spells declines regularly as the length of the spell increases. The fraction out of work over a year is 30 per cent, still quite high. The fraction of relief workers with incomplete spells less than three months is only 10 per cent, and *less* than the fraction with spells from three to six months, quite the opposite of the pattern among experienced workers. Furthermore, the fraction of relief workers with incomplete spells of a year or longer is 56 per cent, nearly twice the fraction among experienced workers. The results suggest that had relief work not been available, far more experienced workers would appear among the long-term unemployed (with incomplete spells over a year).

That more than half of all relief workers were unemployed a year or longer raises another question. Did people find relief jobs after being out of work for a long time, or were they "employed" on work relief for a long time? The information in the sample cannot answer the question definitively, but the data on weeks worked are suggestive. Among those on work relief who had not held a private sector job in both 1940 *and* 1939, 28 per cent worked thirty-nine weeks or more in 1939. Since by definition they could not have been doing anything else, they must have been employed full-time - or nearly full-time - on work relief. The vast majority of relief jobs, however, were part-time; hours worked were less than in the private sector. Recall that weeks worked means full-time equivalent weeks. If the cut-off point is twenty-six weeks worked, over half of relief workers held relief jobs for the whole of 1939.

In summary, employed and unemployed workers, and workers with relief jobs, differed in their personal characteristics. Furthermore, the distribution of interrupted spells of unemployment differed between unemployed experienced workers and persons on work relief. Long-term unemployment was common among persons on work relief, but so was long-term attachment to a relief job. The multivariate analyses in section 3 extend these findings, but the evidence in Table 9.2 is sufficient to establish a basic point. Counting relief workers as unemployed affects more than the aggregate rate of unemployment; it affects the interpretation of relationships among employment status and individual characteristics, and the interpretation of the distribution of unemployment durations.

3   Multivariate Analysis

Section 2 demonstrated that the census sample has a rich array of information on the characteristics of individuals and their families, which can be related to employment status. Here I extend the analysis by controlling simultaneously for the characteristics discussed previously and by examining the determinants of the duration of unemployment, the probability of long-term attachment to a relief job, and a proxy for the probability of re-employment.

Table 9.3 reports two logit regressions on employment status. For ease of interpretation I have converted logit coefficients throughout the paper to marginal changes in probabilities, evaluated at sample means.[13] The dependent variable in column 1 of Table 9.3 takes the value 1 if the individual is an unemployed experienced worker, 0 if the individual is employed. The dependent variable in column 2 takes the value 1 if the individual is on work relief, 0 if he is an unemployed experienced worker. I analyse unemployment and relief separately, in order to control for industry and occupation (which cannot be done for the employed and relief workers simultaneously because the data for relief workers refer to the worker's current industry and occupation, not usual industry and occupation). The discussion focuses on variables whose regression effects differ from those in Table 9.2.

The differences in the unemployment regression involve the effects of race, ethnicity, population density, industry, and occupation. In contrast to Table 9.2, non-whites have slightly lower unemployment rates than

Table 9.3   Logit Regressions of Employment Status: Male Heads of Households, 1940

Regression Number Variable	Mean	(1) dP/dX	Mean	(2) dP/dX
Constant		0.138[a]		0.450[a]
Age:				
18-24	0.044	-0.013	0.052	0.088
25-29	0.109	-0.015[b]	0.095	-0.002
30-34	0.136	-0.025[a]	0.111	0.077
45-54	0.241	0.002	0.247	-0.011
55-59	0.080	0.017[b]	0.095	-0.016
60-64	0.055	0.044[a]	0.076	-0.093[b]
65+	0.059	0.022[a]	0.053	-0.121[b]
White	0.915	0.019[a]	0.879	-0.106[a]
Foreign	0.156	0.003	0.171	-0.196[a]
Married	0.931	-0.025[a]	0.919	0.190[a]
Yrs. schooling x 10^{-2}	0.085	-0.273[a]	0.072	-1.310[a]
Value of house x 10^{-5}	0.138	-0.547[a]	0.061	-1.953[a]
Non-wage income	0.088	-0.0003	0.104	-0.043
Migrant	0.068	-0.008	0.052	-0.065
Region:				
North central	0.296	-0.027[a]	0.306	0.204[a]
South	0.307	-0.040[a]	0.224	0.123[a]
West	0.109	-0.009	0.133	0.111[a]
Urban	0.618	0.004	0.658	-0.070[a]
Industry:				
Agriculture	0.218	-0.008		
Mining	0.024	0.039[a]		
Construction	0.075	0.208[a]		
Heavy manufacturing	0.117	-0.003		
Service sector	0.423	0.003		
Occupation:				
Professional	0.053	-0.076[a]		
Managerial	0.285	-0.107[a]		
Clerical	0.111	-0.070[a]		
Craftsmen	0.172	-0.086[a]		
Service	0.185	-0.067[a]		
N		12,602		1,417
Dependent variable mean	0.065		0.442	
% classified correctly		79.3		63.6

Notes: (a) Significant at 5% level. (b) Significant at 10% level.
Left-out dummy variables are: Age (35-44), Region (North-east), Industry (Light manufacturing), Occupation (Labourer). Dependent variables: Regression (1): =1 if worker is unemployed, 0 otherwise. Regression (2): = 1 if person holds a relief job, 0 otherwise. Calculation of "% classified correctly": linearised discriminant

Table 9.3 (continued)

scores were evaluated for each observation and the observation was assigned to the category (for example, unemployment or relief work) with the highest discriminant score. A figure of 79.3 means 79.3 per cent were assigned correctly. See Rao (1973) for further discussion of this procedure.

whites; foreigners have unemployment rates identical to the native-born; and unemployment rates are no longer higher in urban areas. Furthermore, rates of unemployment in agriculture and in the service sector are similar to the average rate once other factors are controlled for. Controlling simultaneously also reduces the differences in unemployment rates between unskilled labourers and other occupations (except for craftsmen, foremen and kindred workers), although the occupational differences are still large and highly significant. In contrast, there is one minor difference in the relief regression: unemployed persons with non-wage income were less likely to become relief workers even though the percentage of relief workers with non-wage income was slightly higher than among unemployed experienced workers (see Table 9.2).

The regressions show that employment status varied with the characteristics of workers. Can the same be said for the duration of unemployment?

There is a sophisticated econometric technique for estimating transition probabilities from information on incomplete spells of unemployment. But because this analysis is exploratory, I have relied instead on regressions of incomplete spells. I am mindful, however, that regressions of incomplete spells can give highly misleading information about the duration of completed spells of unemployment.[14] As a substitute for now, I also report a regression of a proxy for the probability of re-employment, which I constructed from the data on weeks worked (see below).

Tables 9.4 and 9.5 report logit regressions of the duration of incomplete spells of unemployment for experienced workers and relief workers. The dependent variables are the log of weeks unemployed and a dummy variable that takes the value 1 if the worker was unemployed longer than a year, 0 otherwise. The final column in Table 9.5 reports a regression in which the dependent variable takes the value 1 if the worker was unemployed longer than a year and also employed full-time on work relief in 1939; that is, if the worker had a long-term attachment to a relief job.

The duration of incomplete spells and the probability of long-term unemployment was lowest under age 30 and highest over age 60 among unemployed experienced workers, but was unrelated to race, marital status, or schooling. Native-born workers had shorter interrupted spells, as did the geographically mobile, those with non-wage income, and residents of the western states. Urban residents, however, had longer interrupted

Table 9.4   Regressions of Duration of Unemployment and Probability of Long-Term Unemployment: Experienced Workers

Regression Number Variable	Mean	(1) β	(2) dP/dX
Constant		3.036[a]	0.203[a]
Age:			
18-24	0.041	-0.070	-0.161[b]
25-29	0.087	-0.281[b]	-0.074[b]
30-34	0.093	0.026	-0.115[b]
45-54	0.254	0.066	0.002
55-59	0.104	0.128	-0.038
60-64	0.091	0.623[a]	0.144[a]
65+	0.066	0.235	0.045
White	0.913	0.208	0.040
Foreign	0.238	0.186[b]	0.106[a]
Yrs. school x 10^{-2}	0.074	-1.000	-0.188
Value of house x 10^{-4}	0.075	0.115	0.037
Non-wage income	0.104	-0.211[c]	-0.115[a]
Married	0.892	-0.110	-0.010
Migrant	0.054	-0.267[c]	-0.135
Urban	0.708	0.169[b]	0.068[b]
Region:			
North central	0.260	0.083	0.038
South	0.185	-0.074	0.0004
West	0.136	-0.247[b]	-0.076
Industry:			
Agriculture	0.094	0.211	-0.004
Mining	0.028	0.735[a]	0.261[a]
Construction	0.289	0.265	0.147[a]
Heavy manufacturing	0.101	0.404[a]	0.192[a]
Service	0.360	0.212[c]	0.115[b]
Occupation:			
Professional	0.022	-0.057	-0.077
Managerial	0.056	-0.032	0.001
Clerical	0.087	0.298[b]	0.104
Craftsmen	0.243	-0.319[a]	-0.127[a]
Service	0.183	-0.428[a]	-0.139[a]
N=789			
Dependent variable mean		3.340	0.329
R^2		0.072	
% classified correctly			63.4

Notes: (a) Significant at 5% level. (b) Significant at 10% level. (c) Significant at 15% level. Dependent variable in regression (1) is log of weeks unemployed. Dependent variable in regression (2) =1 if unemployed fifty-two weeks or more, 0 otherwise. % classified correctly: see Table 9.3.

Table 9.5   Regressions of Duration of Unemployment, Probability of Long-Term Unemployment, and Probability of Having a Permanent Relief Job: Relief Workers

Regression Number Variable	Mean	(1) β	(2) dP/dX	(3) dP/dX
Constant		3.714[a]	0.546[a]	0.158
Age:				
18-24	0.065	-0.316[b]	-0.112[b]	-0.161[a]
25-29	0.104	-0.227[c]	-0.059	-0.094[c]
30-34	0.134	0.033	0.041	-0.066
45-54	0.238	0.031	0.042	0.094[c]
55-59	0.083	0.092	0.111	0.036
60-64	0.056	-0.052	0.024	0.062
65+	0.037	-0.222	-0.204[b]	-0.074
White	0.837	0.228[b]	-0.006	0.099[b]
Foreign	0.087	0.100	0.027	-0.057
Married	0.954	-0.138	-0.045	-0.015
Value of house $x\ 10^{-4}$	0.042	-0.890[a]	-0.539[a]	-0.122
Non-wage income	0.105	-0.060	-0.040	-0.245[a]
Yrs. schooling $x\ 10^{-2}$	0.072	1.400	0.439	0.284
Migrant	0.050	-0.401[a]	-0.142[b]	-0.071
Urban	0.592	0.503[a]	0.172[a]	0.112[a]
Region:				
North central	0.366	0.124	0.015	0.091[b]
South	0.272	0.010	0.006	0.092[b]
West	0.131	0.325[a]	0.088	0.042
Job assignment:				
Construction	0.757	0.109	0.094[c]	0.037
Unskilled	0.780	-0.249[a]	-0.138[a]	-0.125[a]
N=661				
R^2		0.073		
% classified correctly			62.2	61.4
Dependent variable mean		4.065	0.578	0.286

Notes: (a) Significant at 5% level. (b) Significant at 10% level. (c) Significant at 15% level. Dependent variables: Regression (1): log of weeks unemployed. Regression (2): =1 if relief worker has been unemployed for fifty-two weeks or longer, 0 otherwise. Regression (3): =1 if relief worker has been unemployed all of 1939 and 1940 *and* worked thirty-nine weeks or more in 1939, 0 otherwise.

spells and a higher probability of long-term unemployment. Compared with workers in light manufacturing, incomplete spells were longer among workers in mining, construction, heavy manufacturing, and services. Compared with unskilled labourers, clerical and kindred workers

Table 9.6   Logit Regression of Re-employment Probabilities

Variable	Mean	dP/dx
Constant		0.615[a]
Age:		
18-24	0.043	0.169[c]
25-29	0.094	0.201[a]
30-34	0.104	0.127[a]
45-54	0.246	-0.060
55-59	0.102	-0.038
60-64	0.089	-0.132[a]
65+	0.077	-0.131[a]
White	0.909	-0.049
Foreign	0.227	-0.023
Married	0.896	0.028
Value of house $x\ 10^{-4}$	0.087	0.183[a]
Non-wage income	0.094	-0.199[a]
Yrs. of schooling $x\ 10^{-2}$	0.073	-0.133
Migrant	0.073	0.077
Urban	0.406	-0.039
Region:		
North central	0.264	0.052
South	0.256	0.117[a]
West	0.128	0.119[a]
Industry:		
Agriculture	0.174	0.039
Mining	0.029	-0.264[a]
Construction	0.179	-0.294[a]
Heavy manufacturing	0.139	0.101[b]
Service	0.366	-0.055
Occupation:		
Professional	0.028	0.394[a]
Managerial	0.171	0.544[a]
Clerical	0.078	0.175[a]
Craftsmen	0.216	0.290[a]
Service	0.188	0.159[a]
Long	0.400	-0.355[a]
N=1,244		
Dependent variable mean	0.621	
% classified correctly		70.9

Notes: (a) Significant at 5% level. (b) Significant at 10% level. (c) Significant at 15% level. Dependent variable =1 if person was employed on a full-time private or non-emergency job in March 1940, 0 if unemployed experienced worker. Sample consists of all individuals who worked six months or less in 1939. Long=1 if person did not work at all in 1939. % classified correctly: see Table 9.3.

had slightly longer incomplete spells and were more likely to be unemployed for over a year, while service workers and craftsmen, foremen and kindred workers had shorter interrupted spells and were less likely to be unemployed for over a year.

Among relief workers, the duration of incomplete spells and the probability of long-term unemployment tended to be lower under age 30 and over age 65 than at other ages. White heads of households had longer incomplete spells, apparently because they were more likely than non-whites to have a long-term relief job. Wealth was negatively related to the length of the incomplete spell and the probability of a long-term relief job, as was geographic mobility. Residents of the north central states and the south were more likely to have a long-term relief job than residents of the north-east or the west, even though the duration of incomplete spells was longer in the west. But the key effects were an urban location and the occupation the relief worker reported to the census. Residents of urban areas or persons reporting skilled jobs were far more likely to have a long-term relief job than rural residents or persons assigned to unskilled jobs.

The re-employment regression is shown in Table 9.6. The sample consists of all people who reported twenty-six or fewer weeks of work in 1939, and who were either employed or an unemployed experienced worker at the time of the census. There is an obvious problem with part-time workers, so I also exclude anyone who worked part-time in the census survey week. The dependent variable takes the value 1 if the person held a full-time private or non-emergency government job at the time of the census, 0 if the person was an unemployed experienced worker.

The probability of re-employment varied sharply by age. Compared with persons between the ages of 35 and 59, the probability of re-employment was higher at younger ages and lower at older ages. The probability of re-employment did not vary by race, ethnicity, marital status, schooling, or urban-rural status, but was higher for the geographically mobile, and lower for residents of the north-east. The probability of re-employment rose with the value of owner-occupied housing, but was lower among persons with non-wage income, which conflicts with the evidence on interrupted spells. Compared with workers in light manufacturing, the probability of re-employment was far lower in mining and construction, but somewhat higher in heavy industry. The probability of re-employment was higher for every other occupation than for unskilled labourers, but especially so for occupations requiring schooling or training (for example, professional and managerial jobs).

The final variable in Table 9.6 is Long, which takes the value 1 if the person did not work at all in 1939, 0 otherwise. A large negative coefficient is suggestive of duration dependence or some unobserved charac-

Table 9.7   **Coefficients of Per Capita Expenditures on Work Relief and Employment Growth**

Equation	Per capita expenditure Mean x10^{-2}	β	Employment growth Mean x10^{-2}	β
Unemp'd exp. workers:	0.143		0.035	
LWKUNEM		0.290		-2.550[a]
LTERM		-0.144		-0.850[a]
Relief workers:	0.155		0.042	
LWKUNEM		0.510		-0.756
LTERM		0.091		-0.195
PERM		0.541		0.407[b]
Re-emp't probability	0.143		0.045	
		0.346		0.308
Emp't growth *x* Long				0.803[a]

Notes: (a) Significant at 5% level. (b) Significant at 15% level. LWKUNEM: log of weeks unemployed. LTERM: probability of being out of work over a year. PERM: probability of holding a permanent relief job.

teristic associated with a low re-employment probability. The coefficient is indeed negative, large and statistically significant.

For the most part the results on re-employment probabilities are consistent with the results on interrupted spells among unemployed, experienced workers. The differences involve ethnicity, non-wage income, industry and occupation. Foreigners had longer incomplete spells but their probability of re-employment was no lower than that of native-born workers. Persons with non-wage income had shorter incomplete spells, but lower re-employment probabilities, while the reverse was true for persons in heavy manufacturing (relative to light manufacturing) or with clerical or kindred occupations (relative to unskilled labourers). The definition of the "probability of re-employment" is non-standard, and different from the definition implied by the duration regressions. I suspect the discrepancies between coefficients reflect the different concepts, but verifying the suspicion is a subject for future research.

Up to this point I have only included variables that can be constructed from information in the sample. Table 9.7 reports the coefficients from the various duration regressions for two state-level variables (state refers to state of residence in 1940): per capita expenditures on work relief, and the percentage growth of employment in the state from 1930 to 1940.[15] A higher level of relief spending was associated with longer incomplete spells of unemployment among relief workers, but the effects were small and statistically insignificant. Relief spending did not lengthen incomplete spells among unemployed experienced workers and may have increased the probability of re-employment. More rapid employment growth significantly reduced the length of incomplete spells and the probability of long-term unemployment among unemployed experienced workers. Employment growth slightly reduced the length of incomplete spells among relief workers but did not reduce (if anything the effect was positive) the probability of long-term attachment to a relief job. Perhaps the most striking result, however, is that more rapid employment growth significantly raised the probability of re-employment for persons who did not work at all in 1939.

3.1 Discussion

In interpreting the results in sections 2 and 3 it is useful to consider why a worker would be employed, unemployed, or on work relief if the labour market in the late 1930s were in steady state. Consider a simple dynamic model with three categories of employment status: employment (e), unemployment (u), and work relief (r). The transition rates from one category to another are: β^{eu}, β^{er}, β^{ur}, β^{ru}, β^{re}, β^{ue}. I shall assume the rates are constant over time, although the rates may vary across individuals. I also assume that $\beta^{er}=\beta^{ru}=0$, that is, the employed cannot enter directly into relief work from employment, and persons leave a relief job only to take a private or non-emergency job. Neither assumption is innocuous (the second is factually incorrect), but they are defensible as rough approximations.

Under the above assumptions, then, the steady state probabilities are:

$$p(e) = \beta^{re}(\beta^{ue}+\beta^{ur})/DEN \qquad (1)$$

$$p(u) = \beta^{re}\beta^{eu}/DEN \qquad (2)$$

$$p(r) = \beta^{ur}\beta^{eu}/DEN \qquad (3)$$

where

$$DEN = [\beta^{eu}\beta^{re} + \beta^{eu}\beta^{ur} + \beta^{re}(\beta^{ue}+\beta^{ur})].$$

Consider the probability of being employed at any instant, $p(e)$. The probability of employment is higher if: the person has a higher probability of re-employment if unemployed; he has a small probability of getting on to work relief and the transition rate from relief to employment is lower than the transition rate from unemployment to employment (or there is a

Table 9.8   Qualitative Guesses About Transition Probabilities: Male
Household Heads, 1940

Variable	β^{eu}	β^{ur}	β^{re}	β^{ue}
Age:				
18-45	A	H	H	H
45+	A,H	L,A	L	L
White	A	A,L	L	A
Foreign	A	L	A	A,L
Married	L	H	A	A
Wealth	L	L	H	A,H
Schooling	L	L	A	A
Migrant	A	L	H	H
Region:				
North-east	A,H	L	A	L,A
North central	A,H	H	L	A
South	L,A	H	A	A,H
West	H	A	L	A,H
Industry:				
Agriculture	A			A
Mining	H			L
Construction	H			L
Heavy manufacturing	L,A			L,A
Light manufacturing	A,H			A,H
Service	L			L,A
Occupation:				
Professional	L			A,H
Managerial	L			A,H
Clerical	L			L,A
Craftsmen	A,H			A,H
Service	A			A
Unskilled	H			L

Note: A: average. L: below average. H: above average.

higher transition rate from unemployment to relief work and a higher
transition rate from relief to employment); or there is a low transition rate
from employment to unemployment.

In a similar manner one can unravel the factors affecting p(u) and p(r).
By comparing the coefficients across regressions one can get a sense of
the relative importance of the various factors for any particular characteristic. For example, married men were likely to be employed or on work
relief, but there is no evidence that their duration of unemployment was
longer, whether or not they held relief jobs. Evidently some combination
of a lower probability of entering unemployment (perhaps a reluctance

among employers to lay off or fire married men, or lower quit rates) and
a higher transition rate from unemployment to relief explains the lower
unemployment rate among married men.

For unskilled labourers, however, in hard-hit industries or regions, all
effects appear to matter. Unskilled labourers in construction, for example,
surely faced a higher risk of becoming unemployed and a lower probability of re-employment from unemployment. Without knowing a person's usual occupation one cannot link current occupations to the
probability of finding a relief job or the probability of leaving relief for
employment. However, the probability of finding a relief job among unskilled labourers in construction must have been higher than average
since the vast majority of relief jobs, in fact, were unskilled jobs in construction.

My qualitative guesses about the magnitudes of the various effects are
summarised in Table 9.8. Perhaps the most interesting are the effects of
schooling and geographic mobility. Higher levels of schooling and geographic mobility lead to higher steady state probabilities of employment
and lower probabilities of work relief. Schooling did not lower the duration of unemployment but schooling did lower the probability of becoming unemployed and the likelihood that a person would be on work relief.
Geographic mobility, on the other hand, arguably raised the probability
of re-employment. The effects of schooling and geographic mobility raise
important questions about the efficiency of interwar labour markets.
What explains the differences among individuals in their schooling and
their geographic mobility? If higher aggregate levels of schooling and
geographic mobility would have helped reduce unemployment in the
1930s, why were the levels not higher? These are questions on which the
sample can shed light in future research.

4   Implications

Discussions of interwar unemployment often begin and end with aggregate unemployment rates. I have shown, however, that the incidence and
duration of unemployment and relief work in the late 1930s varied trem-
endously within the labour force. The heterogeneity has several implications for understanding the macroeconomics of interwar unemployment.

The behaviour of real wages in the 1930s has puzzled many scholars.
Why should real wages rise with unemployment rates so high? The evidence on real wages in the 1930s, however, is aggregate in nature. Because the unemployed were not a random sample of the labour force,
changes in the composition of the labour force could affect the average
wage in, for example, manufacturing. Low-wage workers were at greater
risk of becoming unemployed than high-wage workers, and tended to be

unemployed longer. Depending on how the characteristics of the unemployed evolved over the 1930s (which is not known at present) the behaviour of the average wage may be highly misleading about the behaviour of wages at the individual level.

What about the debate over work relief? As I read the evidence - which, admittedly, is preliminary - the truth lies somewhere between Baily and Darby. Persons on work relief had longer incomplete spells than other unemployed persons. Persons on work relief, unlike unemployed experienced workers, were not particularly responsive to improved economic conditions, which together with the evidence on duration suggests hardcore unemployment.

But many relief workers held relief jobs for a long time. Some characteristics associated with a long-term relief job were also associated with long-term unemployment or low re-employment probabilities among unemployed, experienced workers. For example, a long-term relief job was uncommon among persons under age 35 or persons with non-wage income, groups with shorter unemployment spells and higher probabilities of re-employment.[16] Urban residents had longer spells and they, too, were more likely to have long-term relief jobs. But the link between long-term unemployment and long-term relief was far from perfect. Relief workers reporting a skilled occupation in the census were more likely to hold a relief job for a long time, even though their chances of finding a private or non-emergency government job were higher than average.[17]

However one feels about Darby's aggregate adjustments, then, it may be appropriate to count some fraction of long-term relief workers among the employed. 1940 is not the only year potentially affected. According to a study by the WPA in 1939, 59 per cent of all persons holding relief jobs in September of 1937 held relief jobs continuously through to February of 1939. Furthermore, 16 per cent of all persons with relief jobs in February of 1936 worked continuously through to February of 1939. Mindful of the political costs it had incurred because so many people held relief jobs for so long, the WPA summarily dismissed 783,000 of them in August 1939. Half a year later a majority (57 per cent) had found new relief jobs, a practice the WPA encouraged (US Federal Works Agency, 1943, p.41)!

For many workers, then, a relief job frequently meant more than a few weeks of digging ditches or planting trees: it was stable employment. Critics of Darby have often pointed to the low pay of relief jobs compared with average wages in private employment, implying that relief jobs were relatively unattractive and that the disincentive effects of relief programmes could not have been large. Because the majority of persons on work relief were low-wage workers to begin with, however, comparisons with average wages are misleading. Furthermore, the greater stability of relief work may have compensated for the lower pay. A relief worker makes the point better than the scholar:

> "Why do we want to hold onto these [relief] jobs? Well, you know, we know all the time about persons who are on direct relief ... just managing to scrape along [.] ... My advice, Buddy, is better not take too much of a chance. Know a good thing when you got it." (quoted in Bakke, 1940, pp. 421-2)

One objection to my argument that relief jobs were generally stable is that rates of assignment to and separations from WPA projects in the late 1930s suggest a high rate of labour turnover. For example, from July 1938 to June 1939 the rate of assignment (new relief workers per 100 employed) averaged 6.9 per cent per month and the voluntary separation rate averaged 4.3 per cent per month. The total separation rate, which includes discharges, lay-offs, and quits, averaged 8.1 per cent per month. But the data on continuous relief employment suggest a far lower separation rate: 2.3 per cent per month after 1937.[18]

The solution to the paradox, I believe, is that the evidence on assignments and separations refers to projects, not WPA employment. Put another way, there were two types of relief workers: intermittent and permanent. Intermittent workers moved on and off work relief at a higher rate than permanent workers. The WPA clearly knew about intermittent workers:

> Accessions to [WPA] project employment were made up of initial assignments and reassignments. ... Since persons who had left the program to take private employment were entitled *by law to immediate reassignment if they had lost their jobs through no fault of their own and if they were still in need*, a large portion of the reassignments was regularly made up of workers who had left project employment for seasonal or other temporary private jobs. (US Federal Works Agency, 1943, p.32)

For an intermittent worker, the duration of a single completed spell of relief work was far less than the completed spell of a permanent worker. Thinking about completed spells, however, may be misleading. More relevant would be the sum of the intermittent worker's completed spells, which could be quite close to the completed spell of a permanent worker. The point is, most relief workers - intermittent and permanent - had difficulty finding stable private or non-emergency jobs in the late 1930s, comparable to their relief jobs.

The coexistence of intermittent and permanent relief workers may shed light on another puzzle. In his analysis of the labour market in the 1930s

Baily expressed surprise at the "very large labour turnover relative to the changes in the stock of workers" (1983, p.31). He conjectured that "layoffs followed by rehires ... were very important relative to layoffs followed by search and labour mobility" (ibid., p.48). He explained the high lay-off rate - rightly I believe - by appealing to the theory of implicit contracts, but the WPA may have had an independent effect on lay-off rates, in a manner similar to unemployment insurance today. The key parameter in a system of unemployment insurance is the firm's experience rating, the value of the marginal tax liabilities paid by employers (for unemployment insurance) per dollar of unemployment benefits paid to workers. If the experience rating is incomplete, lay-offs are subsidised (see Feldstein, 1976 and Topel, 1983).

I have not investigated the matter, but I doubt seriously that a typical firm in the late 1930s had an experience rating anywhere near 1, in the case of work relief. Project costs were shared by communities and the WPA, and the WPA's share was frequently high. In such cases, the local share - and by inference the share of taxes paid, directly and indirectly, by a typical firm - would be too low for full experience rating, even though the probability that a laid-off worker could get a WPA job was less than 1 and WPA wages were lower than comparable private wages. If I am correct, industries in areas with a disproportionate share of WPA projects would have higher lay-off and higher rehire rates.[19] Evaluating the conjecture is beyond the scope of this chapter, but a test could be devised by comparing state-level data on industry lay-off and rehire rates (if such data could be found) to the distribution of WPA jobs.

Finally, my results shed some light on hysteresis. Accepting for the moment the results on re-employment probabilities, then hysteresis in the late 1930s was a serious problem. Consistent with Blanchard and Summers's emphasis on aggregate demand, more rapid employment growth would have lowered the probability of long-term unemployment and increased employment rates, especially among persons who did not work at all in 1939. As John Wallis has emphasised, employment growth - and more generally, economic performance - varied sharply across states in the late 1930s (see Wallis, 1986). My results suggest the value of studying further the reasons behind the geographic differences in employment growth, and whether a different set of government policies could have increased employment growth overall.

5 The Added Worker Effect: Labour Force Participation of Married Women

The determination of aggregate unemployment depends not only on the number of persons unemployed but also on the level of employment. Business cycle fluctuations can influence employment through the "added worker" or "discouraged worker" effects. When the head of the household is unemployed family members who would not ordinarily work seek jobs. Alternatively, such persons could be "discouraged" from looking for work when business conditions are poor. For the United States in the 1930s, it has been suggested that discouraged workers predominated over added workers, despite evidence of a strong added worker effect early in the decade.[20]

This section re-examines the added worker effect in the Great Depression, based on a sample of married women drawn from the 1940 census tape. I show that a married woman was more likely to work if her husband was an unemployed, experienced worker than if he was employed, but less likely to work if her husband was on work relief.

Table 9.9 reports a logit regression of labour force participation of married women. The dependent variable takes the value 1 if the wife was in the labour force at the time of the census, 0 otherwise. The effects of demographic and other personal characteristics are similar to those found in other studies of labour force participation, and are not discussed here.

The key findings are the effects of the husband's employment status. Evaluated at the sample means, a wife whose husband was an unemployed, experienced worker was 59 per cent more likely to be in the labour market than if the husband held a full-time job. Wives were also more likely to work if the husband was out of the labour force or if he had a part-time job, although the magnitude of the increase in participation was smaller than if the husband were unemployed. The most striking result, however, is the negative effect of work relief. A wife whose husband held a relief job was 43 per cent less likely to be in the labour force than if the husband was employed full- time.[21]

Roughly half of unemployed heads of households held relief jobs in the late 1930s. A simple average of the (positive) unemployment and (negative) relief coefficients in Table 9.9 gives an added worker effect of 2.3 percentage points, or approximately 17 per cent of the sample mean participation rate (13.7 per cent). The availability of relief jobs did not eliminate the added worker effect in the late 1930s, but clearly did reduce its magnitude. The results suggest, then, that in the absence of work relief, more married women would have entered the labour market in the late 1930s, and the added worker effect would have been larger.

Table 9.9   Labour Force Participation of Married Women: 1940 Census Sample

Variable	Sample Means		Prob (in LF)
	Out of LF	In LF	dp/dX
Constant			0.301[a]
Age:			
18-24	0.110	0.138	-0.026[a]
25-29	0.140	0.204	0.008
30-34	0.141	0.188	0.016
45-54	0.184	0.144	-0.039[a]
55-59	0.062	0.027	-0.110[a]
60-64	0.044	0.018	-0.127[a]
65+	0.058	0.004	-0.187[a]
Foreign	0.146	0.099	0.010
White	0.931	0.840	-0.156[a]
Yrs. schooling $x\ 10^{-1}$	0.857	0.938	0.073
No. of children present	1.978	1.230	-0.028[a]
Value of house $x\ 10^{-4}$	0.135	0.094	-0.052[a]
Non-wage income	0.104	0.106	-0.009
Region:			
North central	0.305	0.245	-0.056[a]
South	0.262	0.309	-0.006
West	0.110	0.109	-0.077[a]
Migrant	0.080	0.074	-0.030[a]
Urban	0.693	0.717	0.007
Husband:			
Unemployed	0.059	0.095	0.083[a]
On work relief	0.064	0.030	-0.060[a]
Out of labour force	0.115	0.071	0.034[a]
Part-time job	0.057	0.060	0.026[b]
Weekly earnings $x\ 10^{-2}$	0.285	0.245	-0.012[a]
N=10,077			
% classified correctly			63.6

Predicted probabilities of wife's labour force participation
(evaluated at sample means):

Husband has full-time job:	0.131
Husband has part-time job:	0.155
Husband has relief job:	0.075
Husband unemployed:	0.208
Husband out of labour force:	0.163

Notes: (a) Significant at 5% level. (b) Significant at 10% level. The sample consists of all married women with husbands present and whose husbands are wage or salary workers. Dependent variable = 1 if the woman is in the labour force (employed; looking for work; has job, temporarily not working; or has relief job), 0 otherwise. LF: labour force.

6 Concluding Remarks

The 1940 census was, and is, a remarkable document. The questions on employment status, the duration of unemployment, and many others, were valuable and durable innovations. The availability of a public use sample, for the first time, allows scholars to tap the census's full riches.

The study of unemployment in the 1930s has, until now, been the study of aggregate phenomena. The value of such studies cannot be disputed or underestimated, but I believe it is time to look under the microscope. With microeconomic evidence like the census sample we can paint more detailed portraits of unemployed people in the Depression. With microeconomic evidence we can illuminate, if not settle, important controversies in macroeconomics. Nor should the analysis stop with the census sample, for there are other sources like it, awaiting rediscovery.

NOTES

* I am grateful to Martin Baily, Barry Eichengreen, Stanley Engerman, David Feldman, Claudia Goldin, Tim Hatton, Takao Kato, Tom Michl, Mark Rockel, Charles Trout, John Wallis, and participants at the Conference on Interwar Unemployment in International Perspective for helpful comments. Errors are my own.

1 For example, the fraction of unemployed people in Philadelphia in 1937 with incomplete unemployment spells of longer than a year was 62 per cent (Woytinsky, 1943). According to Blanchard and Summers (1986), 15 per cent of completed spells of unemployment in 1980 were a year or longer. The figures are not comparable strictly but the point is the same.

2 There are some exceptions; see Bernanke (1986) and Wallis (1986).

3 The pioneering study by a labour historian is Keyssar (1986).

4 US Bureau of the Census (1983). The sample was made available to me by the Inter-University Consortium for Political and Social Research at the University of Michigan.

5 The category "Has job, temporarily not working" is problematic. It includes some workers on short-term lay-off (less than four weeks) as well as persons who were at home sick, on paid or unpaid vacation, or on strike. Because there is no way to separate out persons on temporary lay-off, I have arbitrarily excluded the category from the analysis.

6 There was an undercount of persons on work relief, and the answers to the questions on unemployment duration and weeks worked were "largely approximate" in many cases; see Jenkins (1983, pp. 96, 101).

7 The tape is arranged into twenty random subsamples. The analysis is based on the first random subsample.

8 Preliminary analysis suggests, however, that none of the substantive results - particularly regarding relief work - change when the analysis is extended to include all males over age 14.

9 Using Darby's definition (persons on work relief were unemployed), the unemployment rate follows an inverted U-shape by age, similar to the pattern observed in postwar samples; see Sinclair (1987, pp. 21-2).

10 See Howard (1943) and US Federal Works Agency (1946) for general discussions of eligibility for work relief. The under representation of relief workers in the north-east, however, is a puzzle. According to the WPA, "the available evidence points to a close correspondence between the distribution of WPA employment and a similar distribution of the population" (US Federal Works Agency, 1946, p. 36).

11 Because three-quarters of relief workers in the sample held construction jobs, allocating by current industry and occupation would make the unemployment rates in construction and among unskilled workers unbelievably high. Information on usual industry and occupation is available for a small fraction of the sample (so-called "sample-line people") but the number is too small to permit analysis.

12 One reason why the unemployment rate in construction was so high may be seasonal. The census was taken in late March.

13 Because of the large sample sizes and the number of estimations, discriminant analysis was used. Discriminant estimates of logit coefficients are biased, but the bias is usually small (see Amemiya, 1981, pp. 1508-10) and the discriminant estimates are much cheaper to compute than maximum likelihood.

14 Salant (1977). For example, the average incomplete spell among older workers may be longer than the average incomplete spell among younger workers, but the reverse could be true for complete spells, if the variance of completed spells was larger among older workers.

15 Relief expenditures were taken from US Federal Works Agency (1943, p. 120) (fiscal year ending 30 June 1940). The data on employment growth are from Wallis (1986).

16 According to the WPA, "the age of ... WPA workers affected greatly their opportunities for employment" (US Federal Works Agency, 1946, p. 41). My results also suggest that clerical workers had longer unemployment spells than other skilled workers (see Tables 9.4 and 9.5). To the extent that clerical workers on the WPA payroll were more likely to hold relief jobs for a long time, it may have been due to a lower probability of re-employment (see US Federal Works Agency, 1943, p. 33).

17 The effect of occupation may reflect the structure of WPA wages. Because wages in skilled WPA jobs were quite close to prevailing rates of pay in the private sector (see US Federal Works Agency, 1943, p. 24), such jobs may have been especially attractive.

18 Rates of assignments and separations were calculated from data in US Federal Works Agency (1943, p. 31). The calculation of the separation rate from continuous relief employment assumes that the rate was constant over the course of such employment. That is, I assume that the distribution of incomplete spells of relief employment was negative exponential. Thus $1-F(T) = 0.59 = \exp(-\beta T)$ where β is the separation rate and $T = 18$ months (September 1937 to February, 1939). Solving for β gives $\beta = 0.023$, or a separation rate of 2.3 per cent per month from WPA employment.

19 In addition, persons who had been relief workers or who were eligible for relief jobs would be more likely to be laid off and rehired. For a similar effect today involving unemployment insurance, see Katz (1986).

20 For further discussion see the introduction to this volume by Eichengreen and Hatton, and Woytinsky (1943).

21 Exactly why the effect is negative is unclear. One possible explanation is the means test persons on work relief had to satisfy. In some cases, a working wife may have pushed the family over the limit. Policies towards allocating WPA jobs when other persons in the family were employed varied across states; see Howard (1943), pp. 208, 394.

REFERENCES

Amemiya, T. (1981), "Qualitative Response Models: A Survey", *Journal of Economic Literature* 4, pp. 1483-536 (December).

Baily, M.N. (1983), "The Labor Market in the 1930s", in J. Tobin (ed.), *Macroeconomics, Prices and Quantities: Essays in Honor of Arthur Okun*, Washington, DC: Brookings Institution.

Bakke, E.W. (1940), *The Unemployed Worker*, New Haven: Yale University Press.

Bernanke, B. (1986), "Employment, Hours, and Earnings in the Depression: An Analysis of Eight Manufacturing Industries", *American Economic Review* 76, pp. 82-109 (March).

Blanchard, O. and Summers, L. (1986), "Hysteresis and the European Unemployment Problem", Cambridge, Mass.: National Bureau of Economic Research, Working Paper no. 1950.

Darby, M. (1976), "Three and a Half Million US Employees Have Been Mislaid: Or, An Explanation of Unemployment, 1934-1941", *Journal of Political Economy* 84, pp. 1-16 (February).

Feldstein, M. (1976), "Temporary Layoffs in the Theory of Unemployment", *Journal of Political Economy* 84, pp. 937-58 (October).

Howard, D. (1943), *The WPA and Federal Relief Policy*, New York: Russell Sage Foundation.

Jenkins, R. (1983), *Procedural History of the 1940 Census of Population and Housing*, Madison: Center for Demography and Ecology, University of Wisconsin.

Katz, L. (1986), "Layoffs, Recall, and the Duration of Unemployment", Cambridge, Mass.: National Bureau of Economic Research, Working Paper no. 1825.

Kesselman, J. and Savin, N.E. (1978), "Three and a Half Million Workers Were Never Lost", *Economic Inquiry* 16, pp. 186-191 (April).

Keyssar, A. (1986), *Out of Work: The First Century of Unemployment in Massachusetts*, Cambridge: Cambridge University Press.

Lucas, R. and Rapping, L. (1972), "Unemployment in the Great Depression: Is There a Full Explanation?", *Journal of Political Economy* 80, pp. 186-191 (January/February).

Rao, C. (1973), *Linear Statistical Inference and Its Applications*, New York: John Wiley.

Salant, S. (1977), "Search Theory and Duration Data: A Theory of Sorts", *Quarterly Journal of Economics* 91, pp. 39-58 (January).

Sinclair, P. (1987), *Unemployment: Economic Theory and Evidence*, Oxford: Basil Blackwell.

Topel, R. (1983), "On Layoffs and Unemployment Insurance", *American Economic Review* 83, pp. 541-559 (September).

US Bureau of the Census (1983), *Census of Population, 1940: Public Use Microdata Sample*, Washington, DC: US Bureau of the Census.

US Federal Works Agency (1946), *Final Report of the WPA Program, 1935-43*, Washington, DC: US Government Printing Office.

Wallis, J. (1986), "Employment in the Great Depression", mimeo, College Park, University of Maryland.

Woytinsky, W.S. (1943), *Three Aspects of Labor Dynamics*, Washington, DC: Social Science Research Council.

Chapter 10

Unemployment and Relief in Canada

Alan Green and Mary MacKinnon*

1 Introduction

The structure of the Canadian economy in the interwar era made it particularly vulnerable to the shocks generated in the international economy during the Depression. As a result, the labour market experienced massive dislocation. This chapter examines the impact of the Depression on the labour force, and the nature of government responses to these conditions.

We argue that unemployment by region, occupation and industry was largely determined by the extent of decline in the demand for output. Where output contracted most sharply, so did employment. The effect of the Depression on income was highly regionalised but its effects on unemployment were more evenly spread. Although there are considerable differentials in regional unemployment rates, on the basis of intertemporal or international comparisons, they are not unusually large.

The impact of the Depression was transmitted across regions to a greater degree than it was across occupations. Because the labour force was occupationally segmented according to sex, women workers experienced much less unemployment than men. Immigrant workers from continental Europe were concentrated in the riskiest occupations, and therefore suffered extremely high unemployment rates. Segmentation by age also had some effect in producing unemployment differentials by age. Early in the Depression, unemployment rates were quite similar across age groups. Later in the 1930s, however, juvenile unemployment increased strikingly, and the long-duration unemployed were disproportionately drawn from older workers. The recovery of the late 1930s benefited prime-aged workers, apparently at the expense of the young and old.

This chapter is divided into three parts. In the first section, we briefly discuss the structure of the Canadian economy and labour market. The

B. Eichengreen and T. J. Hatton (eds.), Interwar Unemployment in International Perspective, 353–396.
© 1988 by Kluwer Academic Publishers.

second section examines the incidence of unemployment by region, occupation, age, sex, and immigrant status. In the final part, we examine responses to the Depression - the effects of the Depression on occupational and regional mobility and labour force participation, and the nature of government programmes (particularly relief measures) implemented to alleviate destitution and unemployment.

1.1 The Canadian Economy During the Great Depression

To a large extent, the Depression was imported to Canada. By the late 1920s Canada had become highly integrated into the international economy, with a large proportion of its exports concentrated in a narrow range of goods, especially wheat, lumber and paper, and non-ferrous minerals. Commodity exports had been fairly stable at about 15-17 per cent of GNP from the 1870s to 1914, but by 1929 they were approximately 25 per cent of GNP (Green and Urquhart, 1988). The collapse in world commodity markets in 1929 thus hit the Canadian economy extremely severely, with the drop in raw material prices exerting strong downward effects on Canadian income.

The contribution of autonomous expenditures to the annual change in GNE has been estimated by Green and Sparks using a Keynesian-type model of the Canadian economy.[1] Component analysis demonstrates that the downturn in Canada after 1929 was related to conditions in the foreign sector. The steep fall in US real income exerted a strong negative influence on the Canadian economy as exports of primary products declined sharply. The drop in American demand was exacerbated by the passage, in 1930, of the Smoot-Hawley Tariff which increased protection for US raw material producers. Income loss was greatest in Canada in the farm sector. Farm income was 17-18 per cent of GDP in the late 1920s; it dropped to 8-9 per cent in the early 1930s, and settled at 10-12 per cent for the rest of the decade (Butlin, 1984, series C7(a) and (m)). Canadian farmers suffered both from low prices and, on the prairies, from a succession of devastating droughts.

Investment expenditure fell even more dramatically in the early 1930s than did exports. The late 1920s had seen a boom in investment, largely financed by foreign borrowing, so that the industries which had expanded in the 1920s (especially newsprint, mining, utilities and automobiles) had ample, if not excessive capacity by 1929. With the collapse of exports, almost all further investment appeared unprofitable, and a substantial debt burden, which increased as the price level fell, had to be paid off (Safarian, 1959, pp. 45-54).

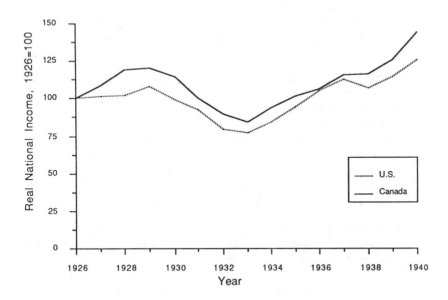

Figure 10.1   Real National Income, Canada and the United States, 1926-40

Source: Butlin (1984). Series C2(W) GNE in constant 1971 dollars, U2(H) Gross National Product, commerce concept in constant 1929 dollars.

The Depression is usually believed to have been most severe in the United States. By the late 1920s, the US was Canada's major trading partner, and major source of foreign capital. Thus the broad similarity in real income trends in the two countries, shown in Figure 10.1, is to be expected. The Canadian economy grew more quickly in the late 1920s, and contracted a little faster in the first two years of the Depression. According to national income figures, 1933 was the low point of the Depression in both countries, and by 1937, income had returned to the level of the late 1920s.

Economic recovery was driven by several factors. The most prominent was the rebound in US real income growth, which raised demand for Canadian exports, although by international standards recovery in both countries was fairly weak. Increased tariff protection also helped raise production of some manufactured goods. Despite the close ties between the Canadian and American economies, the patterns of depression and recovery show some substantial differences. Mining and refining of metals, especially gold and nickel, were more important for Canada. Imperial preference encouraged trading links with Britain, and the relatively strong recovery in the UK thus helped the Canadian export sector more than the American. The agricultural sector was larger in Canada than the US and, in particular, wheat production on the prairies was much more important. The persistent drought conditions on the great plains therefore had a greater impact in Canada, and as Safarian (1959, p.144) points out,

> The similarity in aggregate behaviour ... conceals quite different recoveries in some sectors, differences which cannot be closely related to current developments in the United States. Some sectors of the Canadian economy recovered more strongly, partly because of a strong recovery in non-agricultural exports to the United Kingdom. But the relatively larger agricultural sector remained more depressed than that in the United States, the recovery in durable investment (except housing) was poorer, and direct government expenditure contributed more to recovery in the United States than in Canada.

The national figures outlined above mask substantial differences in regional income responses to the Depression. For example, between 1928 and 1931 nominal per capita income in Saskatchewan plummeted from $525 to $178, while in Ontario it fell from $541 to $435, and in New Brunswick the already low income level was reduced rather little, from $284 to $243.[2] The large cut in Saskatchewan income reflects the disastrous impact on the province of falling wheat prices, coupled with widespread drought. By 1933, per capita money income in Saskatchewan was only a quarter of its 1928 level, while at the other extreme, in New Brunswick and Nova Scotia, it was about 60 per cent. For the country as a whole, per capita money income was about 50 per cent of its 1928 peak (Mackintosh, 1939, p. 137).

1. 2   The Labour Force and the Structure of Employment in Interwar Canada

In 1931, most wage earners (about 80 per cent) were male. Over half of all female wage earners were aged less than 25, and almost all women in the workforce were single or widowed. The sex and age composition of wage earners changed little between 1921 and 1931, with the main change being a small reduction in the proportion of teenaged wage earners. Over a third of all wage earners were foreign-born. The largest wave of immigrants arrived before the First World War, but there was a second peak in the late 1920s. When the economy collapsed, this latter group of immigrants was especially vulnerable.

Unions had limited influence in Canada in the late 1920s and the 1930s. Union membership fell sharply in the early 1920s, rose slowly to 1930, and slumped again until the mid-1930s. Although unions did not receive the kind of support New Deal legislation gave in the US (Chandler, 1970, pp. 223-40), union membership rebounded considerably in the late 1930s, but even then the unions appear to have possessed little power. At the end of the decade, about 18 per cent of employed wage earners in the non-agricultural sector (and virtually no agricultural wage earners) were unionised, which was the highest rate since 1920 (Leacy, Urquhart and Buckley, 1983, E175 and E176). Apart from coal mining, there was little strike activity from the mid-1920s on (Palmer, 1983, pp. 185-228). In Canada, it seems safe to conclude, union activity had a negligible impact on the employment and unemployment experience of most workers.

Although Canada became urbanised rapidly in the 1920s, the composition of employment in 1931 still shows the importance of the rural economy. Relative to the US, primary industries provided a higher proportion of employment. Since agriculture and logging were more important for men, and service occupations more important for women, manufacturing and construction were rather less important sources of employment in Canada than in the US. The unemployment effects of the Depression were particularly large in manufacturing and construction. Similar increases in unemployment in these sectors in both countries would thus have a rather smaller aggregate effect north of the border.

One would expect the nature of unemployment in different parts of Canada to depend on the regional composition of employment. The regional differences in the occupational composition of the wage earning labour force are seen most clearly by considering the distribution of the workforce by cities. Table 10.1 shows employment by occupational sector for eight of the largest cities (see map for locations) and for Canada as a whole.

The distributions in Table 10.1 are for workers classified by occupational sector, not by industry, and are only for wage earners. The high proportion of men classified as labourers occurs because their occupations were not considered to be specifically tied to the production of particular goods or services. Many general labourers normally worked in manufacturing, construction, or transport, but the occupational classification of the 1931 census does not assign them to these categories. Most of the occupations assigned to particular sectors were semi-skilled or skilled.

Manufacturing employment was heavily concentrated in the central provinces of Ontario and Quebec, with a high proportion of workers in the large cities in manufacturing. Since the largest cities were in central Canada, most manufacturing workers lived there. For women, manufacturing was most important in Montreal and Hamilton since both were centres of textiles and clothing production.

Table 10.1   Distribution of Male and Female Wage Earners, by Occupational Group, 1931

	Halifax M	F	Montreal M	F	Ottawa M	F	Toronto M	F	Hamilton M	F	Winnipeg M	F	Calgary M	F	Vancouver M	F	Canada M	F
Primary %	1.2	-	0.7	-	1.4	-	1.0	-	1.1	-	3.2	-	4.9	-	7.5	-	15.2	0.3
Manufacturing %	9.6	3.9	19.1	25.8	14.2	4.7	23.7	17.8	30.8	25.3	16.2	7.7	14.1	2.9	14.5	5.7	16.9	13.8
Construction %	9.1	-	12.1	-	7.9	-	8.8	-	8.7	-	9.2	-	9.7	-	9.2	-	8.1	-
Transport %	18.8	2.8	12.2	3.0	11.4	3.8	10.3	3.3	8.5	2.9	12.4	1.7	11.8	2.2	12.8	6.2	11.3	3.1
Trade %	13.8	12.9	13.2	10.7	13.5	7.8	17.4	11.7	12.7	12.7	15.1	12.7	16.9	11.9	13.2	12.9	10.7	9.9
Service %	16.8	48.0	12.3	33.3	18.9	40.3	15.1	33.9	9.3	31.1	13.7	43.5	13.1	44.5	14.8	44.8	10.8	49.5
Clerical %	8.6	27.8	9.0	22.3	17.5	41.0	9.7	31.7	5.8	22.6	10.8	31.9	10.4	35.7	7.3	28.1	6.1	21.2
Labourer %	17.8	0.5	21.3	4.4	13.4	0.6	13.8	1.1	22.0	3.3	18.6	0.9	16.9	0.4	20.2	0.8	20.9	2.1
Total workforce (000)	14.2	5.2	216.5	70.8	29.8	13.9	170.7	68.1	43.6	12.7	61.2	21.7	24.6	6.4	72.3	18.4	2022.0	548.0

Note: Occupational groups defined as follows: primary: agriculture, logging, fishing and mining; manufacturing: manufacturing and electric power; transport: transport and communication; trade: trade, warehousing, finance and insurance; labourer: not in primary industry.
Source: DBS (1934), 1931 census, vol. 5 (cities, Tables 34 and 36, pp. 388-485, 544-649; Canada, Table 28, pp. 116-29).

This geographical concentration of manufacturing activity has important consequences for our analysis of unemployment and policy responses to unemployment. Decreased demand for manufactured goods, especially durable goods, is a hallmark of the Depression in every industrialised country. Thus the cities of central Canada, especially Hamilton (with large steel, farm implement and railway repair industries) and Windsor (the centre of automobile production) were extremely vulnerable. Tariff levels, which rose sharply in 1930, protected some workers in the industries located in this region. While manufacturing employment varied widely across the country, the other extremely vulnerable sector, construction work, employed a much more even proportion of men, about 8 to 12 per cent, in each of the major cities. The service, clerical and trade sectors, which, as we will discuss below, offered relative security of employment, were most important for men in Quebec and Ottawa. Especially in Ottawa, the civil service accounts for a large share of service and clerical employment. For women, the importance of the service (mainly personal service) sector is inversely related to the proportion of women in manufacturing. Only in Montreal, Toronto and Hamilton were fewer than 40 per cent of women workers employed in the service sector. The other important source of employment for women was the clerical sector, where 20 to 40 per cent of women found jobs.

2   The Incidence of Unemployment

Evidence about employment and unemployment comes from two main sources. The Dominion Bureau of Statistics (DBS) both collected information furnished by trade unions about the unemployment of their members, and conducted nationwide employer surveys to determine trends in employment. These data can thus be used to consider the rate of contraction or expansion in various sectors of the economy. This time series evidence about labour market conditions, however, is seriously incomplete. Union membership was relatively low in Canada, fell in the early 1930s, and was concentrated in a narrow range of industries and occupations. Surveys of employment trends were more comprehensive, although there is a definite bias towards larger firms. Much more detailed information is given in the national censuses of 1 June 1931 and 2 June 1941, and the Prairie census of 1 June 1936. Some census material is cross-classified so the employment experience of the labour force can be divided by sex, age, region, occupation, industry and ethnic origin.

Census definitions do not fully correspond with current definitions of labour force status or employment. To be counted as a member of the labour force in the Canadian census, one had to be "gainfully occupied".[3] The gainfully occupied included employers, the self-employed, and employees, who were further subdivided into wage earners and "no pay" workers. To be counted as gainfully occupied, one had to be principally engaged in one of these categories. Hence part-time workers were typically excluded. In 1931, for the country as a whole, about 60 per cent of gainfully occupied men and 80 per cent of gainfully occupied women were wage earners. Most men who were counted as employers or "own account" workers were farmers and, typically, no pay workers were farmers' sons. The discrepancy between the gainfully occupied and wage earners is much smaller for cities than for provinces or for the country as a whole. In cities, only about 15 per cent of gainfully occupied men and women were not wage earners as outside the agricultural sector, relatively few people were employers or self-employed. Women engaged in unpaid domestic duties were not classed as gainfully occupied. Labour force entrants could not be counted as gainfully occupied until they had found work or set up a business. The census gathered information about employment and unemployment only from wage earners. An "own account" worker, for example, a professional such as a lawyer or architect, might have no clients or customers, and thus not be at work, but he could not be counted as unemployed.

The information collected about employment and unemployment varied somewhat across censuses. Wage earners were always asked how many weeks they had worked in the census year (June to June). They were also asked to state whether they had "lost time" for any reason - because they had no job, were on temporary lay-off, were ill, on strike, etc. The total number of wage earners not at work at some time during the year is often the only statistic given, and it closely approximates an estimate of unemployment, as illness and strikes accounted for very little time lost. The category "losing time" was purged of double entries for those who were, for example, both jobless for some period and also absent from work because of illness. The causes of time lost, where they are separately listed, however, were not,[4] so the sum of wage earners who lost time because they had no job or were on lay-off is slightly greater than the total number who were unemployed at some time during the year. The distinction between being jobless and on lay-off was entirely self-defined; anyone who believed that he would be recalled to work was told to consider himself on lay-off.

Similar information was collected from wage earners for census day. As one would expect, the proportion of wage earners not at work at some time over the year was much higher than the proportion not at work on a single day at the beginning of June. It is important to note, therefore, whether tables refer to the census year or the census day. For 1931, there is limited information about the distribution of the duration of total time lost, but it is not possible to separate completed from interrupted spells, nor is any information given about the lengths of spells over one year. In 1936, the Prairie census asked how long wage earners unemployed on census day had been without work, so that for the later years of the Depression, there is some evidence about long-duration unemployment.

Using the available evidence, the main questions we wish to address in this section are:
(1) What was the regional distribution of unemployment?
(2) How did unemployment vary by occupation and industry?
(3) How was unemployment spread across age groups and by sex?
(4) How did immigrants fare relative to the native-born?

2. 1   Unemployment by Region

There are two main ways of characterising the Canadian economy in the interwar era. One can see it as three or perhaps four distinct regions (the Maritimes, Central Canada, and the West, or the Prairies[5] and British Columbia) which produced different commodities and thus responded largely independently to exogenous shocks. Alternatively, one can argue that most of the country was dependent on the production and export of a few commodities, most notably wheat and timber. When export markets collapsed, the employment effects were felt across the country. It is this second view which we feel is most useful in gaining an understanding of the Canadian economy, particularly the labour market. This is consistent with Mackintosh's claim that the Canadian economy had become highly integrated by the early 1920s with the export industries relying heavily on domestic sources for all types of supplies. Estimates by Green suggest that a major structural reorientation of regional output had occurred by 1911, which is shown by an increase in the concentration of manufacturing output in Ontario and Quebec (Mackintosh, 1939, pp. 49ff.; Green, 1971, p. 57). In most industries, production was principally based in one economic region, but domestic demand for the output was spread across the country. A study of the transmission mechanisms linking the interwar economy of British Columbia to that of the rest of Canada also suggests that while regional cycles were more severe than national cycles, aggregate economic conditions in British Columbia were very sensitive to cycles in the rest of the country (Blain, Paterson and Rae, 1974, pp. 381-401).

Our conclusion is that a considerable part of the fall in incomes caused by the world slump in raw materials prices was transmitted throughout the country. For example, heavy unemployment occurred in eastern railway shops as demand for transportation services fell with declining export volumes, and farm implement production declined drastically as prairie farmers suffered the effects of falling wheat prices. As we have noted, the contraction in provincial income was greatest on the prairies.

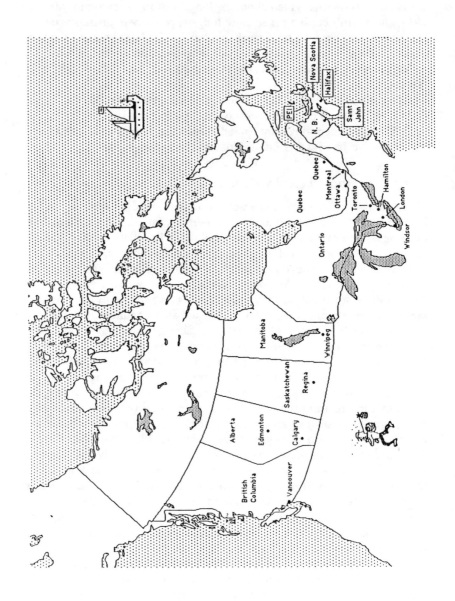

Figure 10.2   Provinces and Major Cities of Canada

Note: Verdun is a suburb of Montreal.

Table 10.2   Employment and Unemployment, 1920-21 and 1930-31

	Wage earners[a] % not at work 1 June 1931		% losing time[a] 1 June 1930- 1 June 1931		Average weeks[a] lost by those losing time		Average weeks worked[b]			
							1921		1931	
	M	F	M	F	M	F	M	F	M	F
Canada	20.8	8.2	44.0	22.9	24.1	20.2	46.5	48.3	41.1	46.6
Vancouver	34.3	11.4	49.4	25.6	30.7	23.1	44.5	48.5	36.9	47.1
Edmonton	27.1	9.5	43.3	22.6	26.7	21.9	47.7	49.2	40.4	46.7
Calgary	29.0	12.7	47.3	25.6	27.1	23.5	46.1	48.6	39.2	45.0
Regina	27.3	8.4	42.2	20.6	29.3	22.3	48.9	49.9	39.8	46.5
Winnipeg	27.7	11.7	44.9	27.3	28.4	21.6	46.5	47.8	39.0	45.2
Windsor	27.7	10.0	58.9	31.0	30.8	23.0	44.1	47.1	33.7	43.7
London	13.8	5.5	34.2	20.8	21.7	17.6	47.6	48.5	44.3	47.8
Hamilton	23.9	7.9	39.8	31.0	32.5	19.4	45.4	47.0	38.8	45.2
Toronto	19.4	9.2	40.2	26.1	24.6	19.2	46.2	48.1	42.0	46.4
Ottawa	14.2	5.1	28.7	15.1	23.1	17.7	48.5	50.3	45.3	49.1
Montreal	20.3	9.7	45.4	28.6	23.6	19.1	45.9	47.7	41.2	45.8
Verdun	11.7	8.1	34.3	25.5	19.6	18.6	-	-	44.6	46.8
Quebec	20.4	6.8	34.7	20.0	22.7	19.3	47.9	48.4	44.0	47.5
Saint John	22.1	7.4	43.4	24.0	22.6	19.2	45.1	48.5	42.0	47.1
Halifax	19.6	6.2	39.4	21.4	21.5	17.6	46.9	49.2	43.4	47.8

Note: (a) Aged 20+; (b) aged 10+.
Sources: For cities: % not at work 1 June 1931 from DBS (1934), 1931 census, vol. 6, Table 2, p.1268; % losing time and average weeks lost from Table 6, p.1280; average weeks worked 1921 and 1931 from 1931 census, vol. 5, pp. 18, 24-5, 388-485, 544-649. For Canada: % not at work 1 June 1931 from 1931 census, vol. 6, Table 6, p.8; % losing time and weeks lost, Table 28, pp.380-81; average weeks worked, 1931 census, vol. 5, Table 1, pp.2-3.

Prairie cities, which were largely service centres for the agricultural sector, did not however experience unemployment rates markedly higher than those found in some other cities in 1930-31 (see Table 10.2). The differentials in employment and unemployment in the early 1930s appear fairly modest when compared to the very much greater differentials in provincial per capita income decline. Western cities, plus Windsor and Hamilton, were the worst hit, both in terms of the proportion of workers not at work on 1 June, and weeks worked during 1930-31. The differential across cities is greater for 1 June than for the year as a whole, suggesting that in the better-off cities, a considerable portion of winter unemployment was indeed temporary. In early 1931, despite the continuing deterioration of the economy, the arrival of spring brought some vacancies. The degree of variation in employment and unemployment in 1931 was, however, considerably greater than in 1921, also a depression year. As Table 10.2 shows, the distribution of weeks worked by city is substantially wider in 1930-31 than it had been ten years previously. From the perspective of the 1930s, regional unemployment could be seen to have increased substantially.

Evidence about income declines emphasises the regional component of the Depression in Canada. However, the employment effects of the disastrous fall in prairie agricultural incomes were not concentrated exclusively in western Canada. Further evidence about the cohesiveness of the economy comes from the DBS employment indices. Employment contracted most in Windsor and Hamilton, sinking to 50-60 per cent of its 1929 level by 1933, while in the other major cities it fell to 70-75 per cent. Later in the decade, expansion was most rapid where the slump had been most severe. By 1937, employment in Windsor and Vancouver stood at roughly the 1929 level, elsewhere it was still somewhat lower. Here as well, the impression is that the timing and extent of contraction and expansion were similar across the country, with the most vulnerable cities being those dependent on the production of durable goods.

If provinces rather than cities are used as the unit of comparison for rates of unemployment, regional differences appear fairly small in the early 1930s. Excluding Prince Edward Island (where the total labour force was only 18,000, and the economy was almost exclusively based in rural areas and small towns) the percentage of wage earners not at work ranges from about 16 per cent in Ontario to 25 per cent in British Columbia on 1 June, and over the census year, from 35 per cent in Saskatchewan to 47 per cent in British Columbia.

The postwar period can be used as a yardstick to compare the extent of regional unemployment in interwar Canada. By the standards of modern Canada, the variations existing in 1931 do not seem particularly large. Unemployment rates by province are typically two to three times higher in the worst than best province. The 1981 census, for example, which gives unemployment rates for the average of urban areas in each province for the last week of May, indicates that unemployment rates ranged from 3.4 per cent (for males) and 4.3 per cent (for females) in Alberta, to 9.3 per cent and 11.9 per cent in New Brunswick. This is not simply a feature of the 1980s; similar disparities are evident in the 1951 census (Statistics Canada, 1984, 1981 census, nos.92-915, Table 1; DBS, 1953, 1951 census, vol. 5, Table 3, pp. 3.1-3.22). While changing definitions of unemployment make intertemporal comparisons of levels virtually impossible, it is not clear that they invalidate regional comparisons. To the extent that such observations are relevant, they suggest that regional unemployment is a normal feature of Canadian labour markets, and that it was not particularly severe during the early years of the Depression.

Great Britain is typically thought of as a country which experienced serious regional unemployment problems. Throughout the 1930s, the unemployment rate in the worst region was at least two and a half times higher than in the best region, with the differentials at a minimum early in the decade. The Canadian experience thus does not appear extreme in the light of conditions at the same time in Britain.[6] In both countries in the early 1930s, unemployment rates were high everywhere, and extremely high in some areas. We have considered the multiple between the worst and best region as the appropriate measure of regional unemployment. Another way of looking at these disparities is to consider the absolute difference between levels. Canada and Britain appear broadly similar using this criterion as well, with about a 20 percentage point spread between the south-east and Wales in 1931. Using data for individual cities in Britain would show greater differences between those with the most and the least unemployment than we find for Canada.

2. 2   *Unemployment by Occupation and Industry*

The main determinant of the industrial distribution of unemployment was the extent of output decline. Thus workers in logging, pulp and paper, construction, and durable manufacturing were extremely vulnerable. Although agricultural labourers experienced high unemployment, they were somewhat protected because prices fell more sharply than quantities produced. The most secure sectors to work in were trade, finance and services. Thinking of the labour force in terms of occupational rather than industrial divisions, there are again very great differences in unemployment. Manual workers, including skilled tradesmen, were very likely to lose their jobs. At the other extreme, professional and managerial workers had high employment rates, and clerical, sales and service workers were also relatively secure. Table 10.3 shows the percentage of Toronto wage earners in selected occupations who were in the no job category at some time during 1930-31, with the average weeks they spent in that state, and for all workers in each occupation, average weeks worked by age. The occupations chosen were selected to cover some of the largest occupational groups in a variety of sectors.[7]

The pattern of unemployment incidence observed in 1930-31 remains very similar throughout the 1930s, according to the DBS employment indeces and the 1936 Prairie census. In 1937, employment in trade and services was very close to its 1929 level. Manufacturing had recovered considerably, at least partly due to the effects of the tariff, while employment levels in transport and construction were still only 80 per cent of their 1929 levels. After the disastrous decline of the early 1930s, employment in logging rebounded, and the boom in mining (especially gold mining) also led to a sustained increase in employment.

Why should clerical, sales and service workers enjoy a much higher degree of job security than other workers? One might suspect these recorded differences in employment to be more apparent than real, as in these sectors work might have been most commonly rationed by cutting hours, not

Table 10.3   Employment and Unemployment, Selected Occupations, Toronto, 1930-31

| | % no job | Average weeks lost by jobless | Average weeks worked by age group | | | | | | |
			<20	20-4	25-34	35-44	45-54	55-64	65-9
MALES									
Retail store									
managers	6.0	26.5	45.0	48.5	50.5	50.5	50.0	50.0	51.0
Mechanics	33.0	27.5	38.0	38.5	40.5	42.5	41.0	43.5	36.5
Carpenters	61.0	29.0	38.0	33.5	32.5	33.0	32.5	29.5	27.0
Truck drivers	30.0	27.5	35.5	39.0	42.0	45.5	44.5	46.0	46.5
Labourers	54.5	32.5	31.5	30.5	29.5	32.5	34.5	32.5	31.0
Janitors	13.0	27.5	-	45.5	46.0	48.0	48.0	48.0	46.0
Cooks	32.0	28.0	-	44.0	43.0	41.0	39.0	38.0	42.0
Salesmen	19.0	27.0	44.5	44.5	47.0	46.5	45.5	43.5	42.5
Office clerks	10.5	28.5	47.5	47.5	49.0	49.5	49.0	48.0	46.5
FEMALES									
Sewing machine									
operators	27.0	24.0	38.0	40.0	40.5	41.0	42.0	40.5	42.5
Waitresses	25.0	21.0	44.5	46.0	44.5	46.5	46.5	45.5	44.5
Domestic servants	14.5	23.5	46.0	48.5	48.5	47.5	46.0	45.5	44.5
Saleswomen	17.5	25.5	42.5	46.0	47.0	47.0	46.5	45.0	48.5
Stenographers									
and typists	12.5	26.0	45.5	48.5	49.0	48.5	48.5	47.5	49.5

Source: DBS (1935, 1934), 1931 census, vol. 5, Table 34, pp.440-458 and vol. 6, Table 36, pp.688-701.

weeks. However, it appears that the occupations recorded in the census as having the fewest weeks worked also had a great deal of short-time working. The *Labour Gazette* gives hourly wages and standard hours worked for a few occupations. Comparing average earnings per week worked (recorded in the census) with earnings for a standard week suggests that short-time working was widespread.[8] Manual workers in the building trades (both skilled and unskilled) worked from half to three-quarters of their standard hours in 1930-31. By contrast, truck drivers, who can be seen from Table 10.3 to experience much lower unemployment rates, worked only slightly less than standard hours. While the *Labour Gazette* does not provide any information about wages and standard hours of clerical, sales and service workers, for annual hours worked in these areas to have fallen by an amount approaching that observed for (say) construction workers, there would have had to have been implausibly large cuts in weekly hours.

Two explanations can be advanced for the superior employment chances of workers in the clerical, sales and service sectors. As claimed above, the demand for the services they performed might have fallen relatively little. Alternatively, wages in these sectors might have been very flexible, and declining demand could have been largely offset by considerable wage reductions. Available evidence suggests the first story is more plausible than the second. On the whole, the occupations and industries which contracted least were those in which the demand for output stayed highest. It is hard to find much evidence at a disaggregated level that wage cutting led to higher employment, or that groups with very rigid wages *(ceteris paribus)* experienced the highest unemployment.

The security of jobs in the sales and service sectors highlights the fact that those who remained in employment had stable or rising real incomes. The impact of the Depression was in large part borne by those already relatively disadvantaged, as general labourers and other unskilled workers were the largest share of the high unemployment group. Whether employed or unemployed, their purchasing power had little impact on the number of jobs in the trade and service sector. Clerical jobs appear to have been largely indivisible. Despite a reduced volume of business activity, most clerical staff had to be kept on. Some service and trade jobs were probably similarly protected; if a store or restaurant was to remain open, some minimum number of workers was needed.

Wage flexibility appears to explain very little of the differential decrease in employment. In 1921 and 1931, average money wages per week worked were roughly equal (which implies a substantial increase in real wages, as 1931 prices were roughly 75 per cent of 1921 prices). For general labourers, and workers in agriculture and logging, money wages fell - for the workers in primary industry by enough to cut real wages slightly.[9] In the early 1930s, logging was a very high unemployment occupation; agricultural labourers faced about average risks. Weekly wages in manufacturing and building were virtually unchanged, as were those in the personal service, trade and clerical sectors. Between 1931 and 1936 (in the Prairie provinces), agricultural wages fell by more than the average, as did wages for salesmen and service workers. The pattern is far from clear-cut; in some high unemployment sectors, wages fell; in some low unemployment sectors wages fell. It is thus difficult to attribute a very great role in explaining unemployment to wage rigidity. For a similar decrease in demand for labour, wages were more likely to fall in non-unionised occupations, but wage cutting does not appear to have had much impact on employment levels. Where wages were cut, unemployment rates may have been somewhat modified, but output determined the basic pattern of employment reduction. In the short to medium term, the demand for labour was quite inelastic.

Part of the downward pressure on wages in occupations such as agricultural labour and domestic service came from increased labour supply. As alternative, higher wage opportunities disappeared, these traditional low wage jobs attracted or retained more workers. If increased labour supply put downward pressure on wages, this would be a further reason why falling wages might not be associated with an increase in average weeks worked. While lower wages would lead to greater total employment, the increased labour supply would reduce average employment per employee.

Between 1931 and 1936, agriculture (for men) and domestic service and manufacturing (for women) absorbed some workers displaced from other occupations. On the prairies, the proportion of the labour force in agriculture increased substantially, with the number of farmers, and of unpaid family workers, rising faster than the number of wage earning labourers. Clearly, despite the low prices and poor crop yields, staying on, or moving to, a farm, was often the best strategy available.[10] Women increasingly found domestic service to be their only possible form of employment. For both sexes, employment in food processing and textiles expanded, but for men, declines in other types of manufacturing cancelled out any net expansion in manufacturing employment.

Most attention has so far been focused on explaining the differential probabilities of being jobless during the Depression, not on the length of time spent unemployed. Baily (1983, p.48) suggests that in the US short-term lay-offs most likely accounted for a high proportion of unemployment. He points to high turnover rates, and argues that the same workers may have been hired and fired repeatedly. Turnover data are not available for Canada, but 1931 census evidence suggests this story is inappropriate, at least outside the manufacturing sector. Workers in manufacturing were much more likely than the average to be on lay-off during 1930-31, with unemployment distributed somewhat more evenly across employees than is typical in other sectors. Manufacturing employment was less important in Canada than in the US however, so the role of lay-offs in an explanation of Canadian unemployment is correspondingly smaller. It is unusual for more than one quarter of workers losing time to have been on lay-off during the year and those in the no job category were out of work for substantial periods. Their joblessness may have been made up of more than one spell, but when average time lost per worker losing time amounts to half the year (as in Table 10.2), spells between jobs must have been considerable.

Average weeks lost per jobless individual are surprisingly constant across occupations and cities in 1930-31. For example, 19 per cent of salesmen in Hamilton had no job, on average for twenty-eight weeks; 61 per cent of Toronto carpenters were jobless, on average for twenty-nine weeks; 28.5 per cent of Winnipeg sewing machine operators were jobless, for an average of twenty-seven and a half weeks. There is a weak positive relationship between weeks lost per jobless worker and the proportion of workers in the no job category, but the correspondence is far from exact.[11]

To a very great extent, once jobless, in whatever occupation or city, chances of finding a long-term job were slim. Since the economy was deteriorating over the year, the prevalence of six- and seven-month spells partly reflects a sharp drop in employment at the end of 1930 (Marsh, 1940, p.327). It is also possible that some high unemployment individuals were fired earlier in the Depression and were able thereafter to pick up short-term jobs. Clearly, however, once fired, prospects for rapid re-employment, especially for men, were slight (see Tables 10.2 and 10.3). The preponderance of six-month spells is to some extent an artefact of the data, as some respondents bunched their answers at a convenient approximation. However, unless exaggeration was common, that would suggest more spells slightly above or below six months, which would not much affect the average.

Although average weeks lost in 1930-31 are very similar across occupations, the distribution of weeks lost by occupational sector indicates a more varied pattern of time lost. The census provides information on the distribution of weeks lost only for broad occupational sectors, not for individual occupations. While the highest proportion (a third) of workers losing more than thirty-three weeks were in the highest unemployment sector (general labour), nearly as high a proportion of the relatively few workers in finance and professional service jobs who lost time were out for more than thirty-three weeks, which is rather greater than in sectors such as construction. This evidence suggests that unskilled workers were the first fired, and the least likely to pick up any subsequent employment. More skilled manual workers were fired later in the year or had more chance of finding a short-term job. In manual trades, especially construction and transport, seasonal unemployment was normal, and vacancies for temporary workers were also common. The Depression increased the instability and reduced the number of jobs in these sectors, but the short-term nature of this work meant that there was some chance for the unemployed to pick up temporary jobs. By contrast, in finance and professional service, virtually all jobs were permanent jobs. Not many workers lost their place, but once out, they were likely to stay out for protracted periods because there were no temporary jobs to fill.

In 1931, and to an even greater extent in 1936, even where only a small proportion of workers in an occupation lost their jobs, turnover was low, so that most of those out of work were so for a sustained period. In the higher unemployment occupations, most workers were unemployed for part of the year, and none had much chance of finding further steady employment. In many of the low unemployment occupations, those who lost their places were unlikely to find another. While workers in some occupations and industries were much more prone to unemployment than others, once a job had been lost, occupational and regional factors seem to have played a relatively minor role in affecting chances of steady re-employment.

2. 3   Unemployment by Age, Sex and Marital Status

Because clerical, sales, and service jobs were the low unemployment occupations, and almost all women worked in these sectors, average female unemployment rates were well below male rates (Table 10.2). Within occupations, however, a female advantage is not so clear-cut. For example, in 1930-31, male and female sales clerks had roughly equal rates of joblessness (Table 10.3), although up to twice as many females experienced temporary lay-offs. In clerical jobs, jobless and lay-off rates were similar, and the same was true for service work. Very few women were employed in manual labour, and those few were in a narrow range of trades. As noted above, in the manufacturing sector they were concentrated in food processing and textiles, so were somewhat insulated from the declines in durable manufacturing, and were also well placed to benefit from tariff protection. That almost all contemporary concern was focused on male unemployment is therefore not simply a result of prevailing attitudes about women's role in the workplace, but also a function of the differential decrease in demand for the types of jobs men and women held.

The Depression's employment effects were greatest in predominantly male occupations. Thus men in the most vulnerable occupations worked an average of ten to fifteen weeks less in 1930-31 than in 1920-21, while even in the riskiest female jobs, reductions of more than six weeks were unusual. These patterns persist throughout the 1930s. In Manitoba from 1921 to 1941,[12] women worked more weeks than men (Table 10.5), were less likely to have been jobless on census day, and in 1936, if without work, tended to have been out for a shorter time (Table 10.4). About 20 per cent of jobless male wage earners in Manitoba reported that they had been without work for over two years, which is about twice as great as the proportion among women.[13] It is doubtful that labour force withdrawal accounts for the differences between men and women. While the number of men in Manitoba reporting themselves as wage earners fell by 15 per cent between 1931 and 1936, the number of female wage earners remained virtually constant. Any added worker effect among women would tend to lower, not raise, their average weeks worked. For the country as a whole, although a female advantage is evident in all censuses from 1921 to 1941, it is quite small in 1921 and 1941 (Table 10.6). In these years, women in each age group worked only one to two weeks more, on average, than did men.[14] Thus one of the most striking features of the Depression on Canadian labour markets is that it created a large differential between the stability of male and female employment.

Table 10.4   Duration of Joblessness by Age, Manitoba, 1 June 1936

Age	% "no job", 1 June 1936	Duration of joblessness (% distribution)		
		<12 weeks	1-2 years	2 years +
MALES				
<20	14.9	39	4	1
20-24	17.5	29	12	8
25-34	19.2	23	12	16
35-44	18.5	19	13	22
45-54	17.3	16	14	28
55-64	21.4	14	14	32
FEMALES				
<20	8.4	45	7	3
20-24	8.7	34	12	6
25-34	8.0	25	16	19
35-44	7.7	20	19	25
45-54	8.2	18	25	25
55-64	11.4	17	20	27

Source: DBS (1938) (Census of Manitoba), vol. 2, Table 23, pp.152-3.

Table 10.5   Average Weekly Wages and Weeks Worked, All Occupations, Manitoba

Age	1920-21	1930-31	1935-36	1940-41
Weeks worked				
Males: <20	46.4	39.6	29.8	28.8
20-24	46.7	39.5	34.9	36.8
25-44	47.4[a]	40.2	37.2	42.5
Females: <20	46.9	42.5	31.3	29.2
20-24	48.7	45.9	39.2	39.4
25-44	48.7[a]	47.3	43.8	44.4
Wage earnings per week worked				
Males: <20	12.11	7.94	5.94	9.24
20-24	18.20	13.90	10.48	14.10
25-44	27.38[a]	24.46	20.62	23.26
Females: <20	10.52	6.50	4.10	6.28
20-24	15.13	11.09	7.65	9.11
25-44	16.50[a]	16.02	12.99	13.26

Note: (a) 1921, age group 25-49.
Sources:
1921: DBS (1935), 1931 census, vol. 5, Table 9, p.18
1931: DBS (1935), 1931 census, vol. 5, Tables 31-32, pp. 248-9, 260-1, 351, 357.
1936: DBS (1938), (Census of Manitoba), vol. 2, Table 39, pp.210-11.
1941: DBS (1946), 1941 census, vol. 6, Table 5, pp.82-3.

Table 10.6 Employment and Unemployment by Age, Canada, 1920-21 to 1940-41

Age	Per cent losing time[a], 1930-31 M	F	Ave. no.weeks lost by workers losing time, 1930-31 M	F	Average no. weeks empl'd, 1930-31 M	F
16-17	42.44	36.13	27.06	24.28	40.2	43.0
18-19	45.86	31.17	26.28	22.14	39.7	45.0
20-24	46.48	24.98	24.66	19.96	40.3	46.9
25-34	45.05	21.65	23.54	19.59	41.2	47.7
35-44	41.55	21.42	22.90	20.53	42.3	47.5
45-54	42.70	21.48	23.92	21.33	41.5	47.2
55-64	44.72	20.73	25.93	22.94	40.1	47.0
65-69	46.71	20.47	28.39	24.66	38.3	46.6
70+	42.70	13.17	29.26	23.37	38.7	48.6
Total	44.00	25.14	24.28	21.05	41.1	46.6

Age	Average no. of weeks employed, 1920-21 M	F	Age	Average no. of weeks employed, 1940-41 M	F
15-19	45.7	47.0	16-17	27.9	27.2
			18-19	33.5	34.1
20-24	46.1	48.7	20-24	38.8	40.9
25-49	46.9	48.9	25-34	43.3	44.1
			35-44	43.7	44.7
50-64	46.1	48.7	45-54	43.0	44.1
			55-59	41.5	43.0
			60-64	40.0	42.2
65+	44.8	49.1	65-69	36.6	41.3
			70+	37.8	42.5
Total	46.5	48.3	Total	41.3	40.7

Notes: (a) for older age groups, and for women, a higher proportion lost time due to illness and accident.

For 1920-21 and 1930-31 the total is for all employees over 10, for 1940-41 the total is for all employees over 14.

Sources: % losing time and average weeks lost 1930-31, DBS (1934), 1931 census, vol. 6, Table 28, pp.380-81; average weeks worked 1930-31, 1931 census, vol. 5, Table 8, p.16; average weeks worked 1920-21, 1931 census, vol.5, Table 9, p.18; average weeks worked 1940-41, DBS (1946), 1941 census, vol. 6, Table 5, p. 70.

    The extent to which better employment prospects for women could off-set the impact of male unemployment on family income was probably fairly small. Very few married women were in the labour force.[15] Daughters living at home were much more likely to be employed, but their wage rates were low; the weekly wage of a women in her early twenties was less than half that of the average man in his forties. The poor employment prospects for men, and the rather better chances for single women to remain in work, combined to reduce the marriage rate, and thus to raise female participation rates somewhat, although changes in the marriage rate alone are not sufficient to explain fully the increase over the interwar years in the number of female wage earners in their twenties.

In 1930-31, married men were somewhat less likely to lose time than single men, and less likely to be out for more than eight months. This is partly due to the different age composition of married and single men. It is also possible that employers were less willing to fire married men because they had dependants, or that married men were more willing to accept any available job. Single men thus show up as the group most likely to be unemployed and in need of relief, but municipalities attempted to avoid giving them any assistance. By contrast, married women were more likely to lose time than single women, and longer spells were a little more prevalent among the former group. These differences may reflect time lost due to family responsibilities, but they are also consistent with the existence of some policies to fire or refuse to hire married women.

While patterns of unemployment by region, occupation and sex remain quite stable throughout the Depression, the pattern of unemployment by age alters considerably. In 1931, prime-aged adults typically worked a few weeks more than did those under 25 or over 55, but, especially for men, age-employment profiles are very flat, and flatter in aggregate than for individual occupations because the composition of the male labour force changed with age (compare Tables 10.3 and 10.6). Young men, like young women, were concentrated in the clerical and sales sectors of the economy, which offered relatively stable employment. Prime-aged and older men were much more likely to be skilled or unskilled manual workers, and therefore more likely to be unemployed. Women were concentrated in sales, service and clerical jobs (with the proportion in service jobs rising with age) so the occupational composition effect for them is less important, and therefore youth unemployment is more pronounced.

Generally, older workers are believed to have been at a disadvantage during the Depression. In Britain, high unemployment rates among the elderly appear to have been a product more of low re-employment probabilities than of higher likelihood of separation (Pilgrim Trust, 1938, p.21). Canadian evidence for 1930-31 is consistent with this finding, as the country was not yet deep enough into the Depression for a large pool of long-term unemployed to have built up.

In 1930-31, young men and (more markedly) young women were more likely to lose time, and for a longer period, than prime-aged adults, but the differences early in the Depression are far smaller than the existing literature would lead one to suspect (e.g. Horn, 1984, p. 9). The weak relationship between age and weeks worked is perhaps typical of the 1920s; a very similar pattern is observed in the 1921 census (see Table 10.6). Early in the Depression, young people classified as wage earners were not much more likely to lose time than their elders, but the proportion of teenaged wage earners fell sharply between 1921 and 1931. In 1921, in the larger cities, 25-35 per cent of boys and 18-29 per cent of girls aged 10 to 19 were wage earners, while in 1931, the proportions ranged from 15-27 per cent for boys and 14-21 per cent for girls. It is not clear how much of this decrease was due to a discouraged worker effect. School attendance rates for teenagers increased substantially in the early 1920s. They rose again in the early 1930s, although in many provinces they had dropped in the late 1920s, so the proportion of teenagers in school in 1931 was not always much above the 1921 level. How many children stayed in school simply because they could not find a job is not clear. Rates of unemployment for wage earners thus understate unemployment for teenagers because to be counted as a wage earner, one had to have held a job at some time. While the proportion of teenaged wage earners fell between 1921 and 1931, for reasons which cannot be fully divided into unemployment and other causes, the proportion of 20- to 24-year-olds who were wage earners increased between 1921 and 1931 (more for females than males), so it seems improbable that many potential workers in this age group were excluded from the 1931 census. The young did bear a larger share of the burden of the Depression than can be inferred from the 1930-31 census, but undercounting appears to be restricted to those under 20.

By 1936, variation in employability across age groups was much more pronounced. Long-term unemployment was concentrated among the elderly; in Manitoba, over a quarter of men over 45 without work on 1 June 1936 had been jobless for more than two years, compared to 16 per cent for 25- to 34-year-olds (see Table 10.4). Older workers were grouped at both ends of the employment spectrum. They were more likely to work either most of the year or not at all (see Table 10.7). The inference is that job turnover was much lower for older workers. If employed, their jobs tended to be secure, but if that job was lost, their chance of finding further steady employment was very poor. Younger workers were less likely to be employed all the year round (and their average weeks worked were thus lower than for prime-aged adults), but they were overall more likely to be employed, at least sporadically, than were the oldest members of the labour force.

Not only had the position of young relative to prime-aged workers deteriorated between 1931 and 1936 in terms of the average number of weeks worked, but a high proportion of potential wage earners are also excluded

Table 10.7   Weeks Worked by Age, Manitoba, 1935-36 (% of wage earners)

Weeks	Males		Females	
	25-34	55-64	25-34	55-64
0	7.5	13.4	4.4	7.1
1-15	12.8	9.5	6.5	5.5
16-31	17.3	13.5	8.6	7.1
32-47	11.1	8.4	8.7	6.2
48-52	51.1	55.2	71.8	74.2

Source: DBS (1938) (Census of Manitoba), vol. 2, Table 37, pp. 206-207.

from these statistics because they had never been employed. Over a third of 18- and 19-year-olds in Manitoba were in this position, and almost 20 per cent of 20- to 24-year-olds. Young people on the prairies were much less likely to find any work in 1936 than in 1931, and if employed, were likely to have only temporary jobs.

By 1936, there had been a drastic reduction in the proportion of teenagers working in what in 1931 were sectors employing a lot of young people. Even where overall employment remained nearly constant, as in clerical occupations, teenage employment fell. The number of wage earning males in Manitoba fell by 15 per cent between 1931 and 1936, but by 40 per cent for teenage boys. In 1936, young adults often held jobs - as messengers, for example - which would previously have been filled by adolescents.

Declining wages were associated with poor initial employment possibilities, and short-term jobs. The shift in occupational composition towards low wage domestic service and agriculture is partly responsible for the decline in youth relative to adult wages shown in Table 10.5. However, similar declines are observable in individual occupations. Young people's wages fell between 1921 and 1931, and between 1931 and 1936. Wage flexibility may partially account for the reasonably high employment rates of young workers in 1930-31. By 1936, however, employers had shifted away from hiring young workers, despite the fact that they were becoming relatively cheaper to employ.

The experience of young workers on the prairies in 1936 may not be typical of the whole country. In central Canada, the recovery of import-competing industries (most notably textiles) probably boosted youth employment somewhat, since considerable contemporary concern was expressed about the substitution of cheap young workers for adults. Because in the early 1930s males were usually not affected by minimum wage laws, minimum wage legislation probably tended to reduce female employment somewhat by encouraging the substitution of young male workers for women. Certainly in the early 1930s in the textiles industry, employment of females fell relative to males. In 1934 Ontario and Quebec minimum wage laws were amended so that men could not be paid less than women when they were performing the same work (DBS, *Canada Year Book, 1934-5*, p.846), which halted male-female substitution. However, the extension of minimum wage legislation by some provinces in the early 1930s may have tended to reduce employment of very young workers of both sexes in a variety of occupations. The tariff was stimulating employment growth, but minimum wages were probably slowing it down. Unfortunately we do not have census evidence about youth employment in central Canada in 1936.

However, evidence from 1940-41 indicates that throughout the country, juvenile employment did not recover at the rate adult employment did. In 1930-31, teenagers worked about the same number of weeks in the year as adults. In 1940-41, by contrast, 16- and 17-year-olds worked one-third fewer weeks than adults ages 25 to 34, and 18- and 19-year-olds worked about 20 per cent fewer weeks (see Table 10.6). In addition, there was a substantial group of teenagers in 1941 not included as wage earners because they had yet to find their first job. Over the decade, juvenile weekly wages rose somewhat relative to adult weekly wages; how much of this was due to the impact of minimum wages remains an open question. Clearly further research on this point is necessary.

Young people entering the labour market in 1929-31 appear to have had considerable difficulty finding their first job. Once employed, however, their employment chances were quite similar to those of older workers in the same occupation. As the Depression continued, labour force entrants found it very much more difficult to find work, with employers preferring to hire those with some job experience. Even in agricultural labour and domestic service, the number of teenagers employed fell in the mid-1930s. Despite the economic recovery of the early war years[16] teenaged wage earners were worse off than their counterparts ten years before. The situation in Canada is thus quite different from that in Britain, where juvenile unemployment was substantially lower than adult unemployment throughout the Depression.[17]

2.4 Unemployment by Country of Birth

In 1931, over a third of all wage earners were immigrants, and almost a quarter of these had arrived since 1925 (DBS, *Canada Year Book, 1936*, p. 125; DBS, 1934, 1931 census, vol.6, pp.4, 1174). Immigrants were unevenly spread across the country, with over half the wage earners in the four western provinces born abroad, and the lowest proportion of immi-

**Table 10.8   Immigrants Losing Time and Average Weeks Lost, Toronto
1930-31**

	% losing time[a]		weeks lost by those losing time	
Date of Arrival	M	F	M	F
Immigrants Born in British Isles and British Possessions				
1930-31	50	21	24	19
1926-29	46	22	23	16
1921-25	42	27	23	18
1911-20	36	30	23	19
1901-10	40	31	23	19
pre-1901	38	28	26	20
Immigrants Born in Europe				
1930-31	71	32	30	22
1926-29	69	37	30	21
1921-25	61	51	27	22
1911-20	61	51	27	22
1901-10	59	50	27	22
pre-1901	52	40	28	20

Note: (a) Wage earners 10+.
Source: DBS (1934), 1931 census, vol. 6, Table 46, pp. 1242-1249.

grants in the Maritimes. If unemployed, immigrants could be expected to
be in severe financial difficulties, as they were unlikely to have many
friends or family able to support them. Immigrants born in Britain or the
US fared relatively well in 1930-31, with overall rates of time lost similar to those for the workforce as a whole. Males who had arrived since
1920 were the most vulnerable, while those who came between 1911 and
1920 were best off. Presumably, a high proportion of earlier immigrants
were elderly by 1931 and, in common with native-born wage earners,
were somewhat more likely to lose time. It seems most unlikely that English-speaking immigrants who had come to Canada as children before the
First World War would fare any worse than the average during the Depression. The benefits of longer residence in Canada are not so clear for
women, as no downward trend is apparent in the proportion of wage earners losing time by length of residence. (Table 10.8 shows the percentage
losing time and weeks lost for immigrants in Toronto.)

While the experience of English-speaking immigrants was not markedly different from the average for all wage earners, European immigrants
(most from central or eastern Europe) were at a considerable disadvantage. Both men and women were more likely to lose time, and for longer

periods than the average worker. The male disadvantage shrinks with length of time in the country (unlike the British immigrant, minimum disadvantage does not generally occur in the 1911-20 arrival category) but European immigrants were always far more likely to be without work than British immigrants.

Europeans were unlikely to possess the skills necessary to obtain clerical, sales, or service work, and were therefore unavoidably concentrated in the most vulnerable occupations. The presence of a high proportion of the foreign-born among the jobless may help to account for the attitudes of all levels of government towards unemployment relief. In fact, it would be quite surprising if unskilled workers, unable to speak much English or French, and recently arrived in Canada, were thought to deserve anything but minimal assistance.

3 Coping with the Depression

The previous section described the employment effects of the Depression in Canada. How did individuals adapt to the environment they were thrust into? Did changing occupations, or migrating to a different part of the country, offer much hope of greater employment security? How did government policies mitigate the effects of income declines?

3.1 Individual Responses

Retraining and migration offered little hope for most workers. Older men were unlikely to be able to become clerical or sales workers. For young men entering the labour force early in the Depression, the clerical and trade sectors offered the best chances of security. However, we have noted that as the decade continued, although overall employment in these sectors remained relatively high, openings for teenagers fell dramatically. Thus staying on at school is both a sign of abysmal employment prospects and of the need to obtain a high school education if there was to be any hope of obtaining a clerical job. School attendance rates rose quite sharply in the mid-1930s.

The service sector, which might be expected to absorb male unskilled workers, was relatively small. There were between five and ten unskilled labourers for every unskilled service job (as a janitor, watchman, porter, or similar). Once unemployed, workers in any occupation tended to remain in that state for protracted periods. Even in relatively secure occupations, there was always a pool of experienced unemployed who would probably be hired in favour of applicants without any background in that type of work, so the scope for changing occupations was very limited.

The 1941 census offers limited information about occupational change between 1931 and 1941. The gainfully occupied aged over 25 were asked to list their occupation in 1931, which was matched to their 1941 occupation (DBS, 1946, 1941 census, vol. 7, Table 15, pp.486-93). Only those workers who had a gainful occupation in both 1931 and 1941 are included. Some workers may have changed their occupations during the Depression, but reverted to their 1931 occupation by 1941, so this evidence relates mainly to long-term changes, and may also be somewhat confused by the impact of the early years of the war. Over 90 per cent of male workers in agriculture had been there ten years previously. For most other occupational sectors, 70-80 per cent of male workers were still in the same broad occupational group. General labourers, with 65 per cent unchanged, were least likely to have been in the same category in 1931. Although manufacturing took the largest number of men from the agricultural sector, they were only about a quarter of the total male entrants to manufacturing. In contrast, over two-thirds of those who switched into logging, mining and general labour came from the farm. In manufacturing, construction, transport, trade and service work, job changers had a wider variety of backgrounds, with a much lower concentration from agriculture, although the farm was still normally the largest single source of recruits. Only in the clerical sector were former farm workers relatively uncommon, which is to be expected, given the higher educational qualifications needed for such jobs. Workers from trade and finance were most likely to shift over to clerical work.

Between 1931 and 1941, the connection between agriculture and the rest of the economy was a one-way street. For the country as a whole, agriculture was a declining sector. Workers left the farm, and entered a wide variety of occupations, but it was rare for workers from any other sector to move into farming. Jobs in mining and lumbering, which were often physically demanding, unskilled, and geographically isolated, appear to have been acceptable mainly to men from the agricultural sector. Urban jobs, while drawing in many workers from the land, also permitted some reshuffling across other occupational sectors.

As we discussed in section 2, women were concentrated in a very narrow range of jobs. They were also more likely to remain in the same sector (if they remained in the labour market), with 80-90 per cent or more not changing between 1931 and 1941. Most gainfully occupied men over 25 in 1941 would have been gainfully occupied ten years earlier, but this is less true for women, making comparisons of persistence rates across the sexes more difficult. In particular, very few women on farms were classed as being gainfully occupied in 1931. Women who moved off the farm during the Depression are thus not included in the intercensal comparison. If men who shifted from agriculture to another sector of the economy are excluded from the 1941 labour force, persistence rates for the two sexes are quite close.

The evidence discussed above bears only indirectly on the question of the scope for occupational change in the 1930s to reduce unemployment. Clearly, for the country as a whole, very few men moved into agriculture during the 1930s and stayed there until 1941. Although different occupational sectors had very different risks of unemployment during the Depression, the proportion of workers in the same sector in 1931 and 1941 was broadly similar. Relatively secure occupational sectors in 1931 have virtually the same proportion of sector changers in 1941 as do the most vulnerable sectors. If safe jobs had been associated with expanding employment, and risky jobs with contracting employment, one would expect the safe sectors to have drawn in workers from other areas, thus raising the proportion of sector changers in the safe sectors. Workers would have fled from the vulnerable jobs, resulting in a low proportion of sector changers. Since the census was not taken until 1941, however, such a pattern would be blurred by wartime expansion.

Disaggregating further, to the level of the individual occupation, indicates that, as one would expect, unskilled jobs had lower persistence rates than highly skilled jobs. For example, virtually all printers, and men working in the railway running trades, had been in the same sector ten years earlier. Within the manufacturing sector, persistence rates were lower in metal manufacturing than in textiles or wood. The development of the war economy led to very rapid growth in the metal trades; it is also likely that textiles relied more heavily on young labour market entrants for its new employees, which would help to explain the difference across types of manufacturing. Old men's jobs - as caretakers, watchmen, and janitors - had low persistence rates (less than 50 per cent), which is also understandable. Without a standard for comparison (the 1941 census is the only one for which this question was asked), it is difficult to say whether occupational change over the decade was unusually high or low. The similarity of persistence rates across very different occupational sectors, however, suggests that the differential incidence of unemployment during the Depression did little to cause occupational mobility.

For Canada as a whole, the absolute number of men in agricultural occupations declined between 1931 and 1941, unlike from 1921 to 1931. During both decades, agricultural workers fell as a proportion of the gainfully occupied, more slowly during the Depression, because the total male labour force remained nearly constant over the 1930s. According to the evidence discussed above about occupational persistence rates from 1931 to 1941, few men returned to agriculture and stayed there. Despite the bleak situation in prairie agriculture in the 1930s, the number of men in agriculture rose 6-9 per cent in each of the Prairie provinces between

1931 and 1936, with the lowest growth in Saskatchewan. By 1941, however, numbers in agriculture were below 1931 levels, very slightly in Manitoba and Alberta, but by about 9 per cent in Saskatchewan. Staying on, or moving to, the farm was a strategy used to cope with the Depression, but the movements of workers were fairly short-term.[18] The proportion of gainfully occupied men in prairie agriculture was greater in 1941 than in 1931, with the highest observed rate in 1936. Since the number of men on farms fell between 1936 and 1941, this could occur only if numbers in the non-agricultural sector fell faster than in the agricultural sector. It therefore appears that the men who left prairie farms typically did not move to urban areas on the prairies; rather, they moved to British Columbia or Ontario. In Quebec, agricultural occupations were followed by virtually the same proportion of men in 1941 as in 1931, and it was the only province where more men worked in agriculture in 1941 than in 1931. It seems quite possible that in Quebec, as on the prairies, agricultural employment would have been yet more important in the mid-1930s. In the rest of the country, the agricultural sector contracted in both absolute and proportional terms between the two censuses, suggesting that in the mid-1930s, the farm sector probably absorbed very few workers displaced by the effects of the Depression. There was a trend to move back to the land during the Depression, but it was limited to specific regions, and the trend was reversed within a few years.

Marriage rates fell until the mid-1930s, so that more women in their twenties were in the labour force. While female occupations contracted less than male ones, women became much more concentrated in domestic service. Much of the shift into the personal service sector had taken place by 1931, with the proportion of women working in that sector rising by about a quarter between 1921 and 1931. On the prairies at least, the proportion rose still higher by 1936. While personal service occupations were a little less important for women in 1941, they still accounted for a higher fraction of employment than in 1921. In the later 1930s, the growth in tariff-protected industries, especially textiles, was of considerable benefit to women, but the textile factories were concentrated in Ontario and Quebec. Even there the proportion of women employed in manufacturing in 1941 was no higher than it had been in 1921.

The scope for occupational mobility to reduce unemployment risks was quite limited. Much the same story must be told for regional mobility between cities and provinces. Even in very sheltered cities, such as Ottawa, men who lost time in 1931 were out for over five months, women for four months. The cities with the least unemployment generally had the fewest unskilled workers, and a small manufacturing sector, so that possible vacancies were restricted to a fairly narrow range of occupations. Migrants were at the end of the queue in any search for jobs. Even if the queue was shorter in central or eastern cities, progress along it was very likely to be slow anywhere. According to the 1931 census, there were few occupations where the difference in average weeks worked is great enough to justify the costs of moving and the loss of relief entitlements, assuming migrants would be able to work for the average period in their new city. Young single men had the lowest moving costs, and were very often excluded from municipal relief schemes. Therefore, they were most likely to travel in search of any work, however short-term.

Between 1931 and 1941, migration of the gainfully occupied was low, except to British Columbia. In 1941, about 6 per cent of the total labour force had lived in their current province for less than ten years. As with the evidence on sectoral mobility, there may have been some reverse migration by 1941.[19] Quebec, the Maritimes and Saskatchewan had very few immigrants (3-5 per cent of gainfully occupied males, slightly more females.) Ontario, Manitoba and Alberta attracted more migrants, but they were a small proportion of the gainfully occupied - 6-7 per cent for men, up to 11 per cent for women. In British Columbia, however, 16 per cent of gainfully occupied males and 22 per cent of females had been in the province less than ten years. Most Canadian workers who moved across provincial borders during the decade lived in the Prairie provinces in 1931. Over a quarter of these stayed on the prairies, close to 40 per cent went to British Columbia, and about a third to Ontario; virtually none moved to Quebec or the Maritimes. Those who moved around the prairies were mostly leaving Saskatchewan; it was the only province in Canada to experience a net population decrease over the decade. The vast majority of migrants to British Columbia (about 80 per cent) were from the prairies. Given the much larger labour force in Ontario, the impact of prairie migrants on the total workforce was rather smaller. Ontario attracted a broader range of migrants, including most of the few who came from abroad, so that only some 40 per cent of the total were from the prairies.

By postwar standards, interprovincial movement by workers was not particularly high. In 1961, about 8 per cent of the labour force had lived in their current province for less than five years. Excluding immigrants may make the figures more comparable with those for the 1930s, since very few workers came to Canada during the Depression. About 4 per cent of Canadian workers moved across provincial boundaries between 1956 and 1961, suggesting that the rate for the decade 1951-61 was probably rather higher than that for 1931-41 (DBS, 1966, 1961 census, vol. 4, cat. no. 98-510, series J.1). Comparisons with US interstate migration will be somewhat affected by the smaller average size of American states. Again, however, the impression is that Canadian internal migration was no higher, and perhaps lower, than in the US. About 5 per cent of the US population had immigrated, or crossed state boundaries, between 1935 and 1940,[20] compared to 7 per cent in Canada from 1931 to 1941.

3.2   Government Action

When disaster struck in 1929 and it became evident that Canada was not experiencing a short sharp recession but rather a full-scale depression, Canadian governments adopted four policies to help alleviate hardship. Immigration was halted; minimum wage legislation (especially for women) was expanded; tariffs were increased sharply in 1930; and relief payments were initiated. Immigration almost certainly would have virtually dried up even without intervention as high unemployment rates among recent immigrants would have been a major disincentive.

By the late 1920s, most provinces had established minimum wages for women employed in manufacturing and some branches of trade and service (but not domestic service). Typically, minimum rates were set to take account both of differential living costs (rates were highest in the large cities) and experience (apprentices and learners had lower wages). The rates set in the late 1920s were almost always held constant throughout the 1930s, and there was some extension of the legislation's coverage. In the early 1930s, employers unsuccessfully fought to have the rates reduced at a time when most nominal wages as well as price levels were falling.

We noted in section 2 that minimum wage legislation had some effect in altering the composition of employment, since until the mid-1930s, it was generally legal to hire juvenile males at less than the female rate. The size of the impact of this legislation depends both on how many workers were paid minimum rates and on the difference between the regulated wage and the market clearing wage. How strictly minimum wages were enforced is an open question. For Toronto women, the highest minimum wages were $12.50 a week. Average weekly wages for all women workers aged 25 to 34 exceeded this level by 30 per cent in 1930-31, but by only 16 per cent in textiles. For women of 20 to 24, average wages were 14 per cent above, in textiles, only 4 per cent. However, younger women were more likely to be classed as learners, and were thus allowed to be paid a lower wage. Unfortunately, previous researchers have largely ignored the effects of minimum wages, although an increased use of sweated labour in the early 1930s is noted (Cassidy and Scott, 1935). Where wages could not be cut, a deterioration in working conditions might reduce labour costs. While Canadian provinces maintained or extended minimum wage coverage during the Depression, there were no sweeping attempts to raise wage levels, as in the US under the New Deal.

Partly in response to the Smoot-Hawley Tariff of 1930, partly to offset a potential balance of payments problem and partly to alleviate unemployment, the newly elected Bennett government raised Canadian tariff levels in September 1930 by close to 50 per cent on average, and also introduced a series of non-price trade barriers. The effect was immediate. Imports declined sharply both as a result of falling incomes and as a consequence of the new tariff schedule. Some of the principal industries affected were agricultural products, iron and steel, textiles and clothing, boots and shoes, and agricultural implements. With the exception of some clothing factories in Winnipeg, these new tariffs had one thing in common: the industries receiving increased protection were located in Ontario and Quebec.

Three consequences followed from increased protection. First, it worsened the terms of trade between the export-oriented provinces of the west and the manufacturing region in the central provinces, a point noted bitterly by western provincial premiers. The tariff exacerbated the income loss of western farmers as the price of manufactured products purchased from central Canada was artificially held up. Second, the policy stimulated growth in the protected industries. For example, the index of employment in the textile industry increased from 100 in 1929 to 118 by 1935 (Green, 1985, p.11). This provided some relief of unemployment, but at the cost of long-run resource misallocation. Third, the policy encouraged some US industries to set up branch plants in Canada, as more American firms found it necessary to produce in Canada if they were to retain a share of the market.

Throughout the Depression, relief remained a municipal responsibility. The higher levels of government contributed to relief expenditure, but administration was left almost entirely in the hands of each municipality. Thus it is difficult to make general statements about it, as the conditions under which relief was given, and the amounts paid out, varied widely. Before 1929, municipal relief was often publicly subsidised but administered by private charities, so that direct government involvement was kept to a minimum. By the early 1930s, most cities and towns had taken over responsibility for providing relief, although the scope (and need) for charitable activity remained very great. Up to 1933, the federal government took a much more active role in financing relief expenditures by the provinces and municipalities than did its counterpart in the US (Struthers, 1983, p.104). With the election of Roosevelt, and the introduction of the New Deal, however, the situation was reversed. While the New Deal increased the scale and variety of expenditure in the US, Canadian policies continued much as before. Although government initiatives (such as unemployment insurance) were much discussed, relief policies adopted in the early 1930s remained virtually unaltered throughout the decade.

While the federal government admitted that some form of financial assistance to ease the plight of the unemployed was needed, severe con-
stitutional problems hampered attempts at federal intervention, and the
federal government was extremely unwilling to take direct responsibility
for the provision of any form of social assistance. Beginning in 1930, the
dominion government introduced a series of annual relief bills. Most
dominion money was given to the provinces, to be spent on approved
forms of relief. Constitutionally, social welfare was a strictly provincial
responsibility, although the regulation of labour markets was held to be
at least partially a federal responsibility. Unless the provinces and the
dominion government could agree on a transfer of authority, and of tax-
ing capacity, innovations such as unemployment insurance were impossible. By the late 1930s, both a broadening of the role of government
and a reassignment of federal and provincial powers were seen as desirable, but changes occurred only after the outbreak of war. Despite the
lack of coherent policies, total expenditure on public welfare programmes
rose rapidly in the early 1930s, from less than 2 per cent of GNP in 1926,
to 6.6 per cent in 1933. In 1939, they accounted for 5.6 per cent of GNP.[21]

Early in the Depression, there was a strong emphasis on work relief.
Various public works were undertaken (especially road building) and
employable relief applicants were, whenever possible, given at least a
few days' work per month. In 1932, over half a million workers were
employed, on average for twenty-two days in the year (DBS, *Canada Year
Book, 1933*, p.774). These programmes proved to be extremely expensive, especially as public works were often organised in a haphazard
fashion, with the emphasis on employing as many men as possible rather
than on completing the projects. From 1932, federal government assistance for public works schemes was dropped as an economy measure, and
direct relief (the provision of assistance without any work requirement)
became even more important.[22] Single men, especially transients, were
typically excluded from receiving municipal relief, and the federal government came under strong pressure from the municipalities and provinces to provide help for this highly mobile and potentially dangerous
segment of the labour force. In response, work camps, mostly located in
remote areas, were set up.

Severe unrest in the camps in 1935 led to a scaling down of their activity, and there was more emphasis on placing single men on farms.
Throughout the decade, farmers were given subsidies to provide the un-
married with winter work and lodging. Up to half the total increase in
farm workers on the prairies between 1931 and 1936 could have been due
to this programme. However, since the census was taken in June, and
these were winter work programmes, it is impossible to state accurately

how many of these workers remained on the farm during the summer (Marsh, 1940, p.285).

From 1932 onwards, there are comprehensive records of the number of individuals on direct relief to which the dominion government contributed; the lack of figures before this is an indication of the *ad hoc* nature of the funding provided by the federal government. From 1932 to 1936, at least 700,000, and during the winters over 1,000,000 Canadians were on direct relief in urban areas each month.[23] In the early 1930s, most of those given work relief probably also received direct relief.

How close is the relationship between unemployment and relief? According to the 1936 census, and individual relief returns from London in the late 1930s,[24] not as close as one might expect. Very few relief families had any currently employed members, although in some cases an adult son or daughter was at work. However, the heads of some relief families had been employed (normally for less than thirty weeks) during the preceding year. Often, where recent employment was recorded, it was not in the applicant's usual occupation; more skilled workers were likely to report spells as labourers, farm hands and the like. Those who did pick up short-term jobs normally went off relief immediately and reapplied when they were again unemployed. In London, of those who were registered as relief recipients at any time from 1936 to 1940, almost all had been on relief for part of each year from 1933 to 1936. Virtually none were new to the London relief rolls in the late 1930s, and few had been off relief for as much as a year from 1933 on. The available evidence, coming as it does from the end of the decade, overstates the importance of long-term relief cases.[25] By 1936, labour market conditions had improved somewhat from the depths of 1933, so there is a presumption that most people on relief in the late 1930s were among the hard-core unemployed or were unemployable.

While almost everyone on relief was unemployed, a substantial proportion of the unemployed, even the long-term unemployed, were not on relief. In 1936 about 40 per cent of Winnipeg men who had been jobless for less than thirteen weeks before census day were on relief. This proportion rises to 70 per cent for men unemployed over two years. For unemployed women, rates are much lower at 11 to 40 per cent. Census takers were aware that respondents tended to interpret the question about when they last worked as when they last worked at their usual occupation, so some of the long-term unemployed had probably worked for short spells. Numbers on relief were always much higher in winter than in summer. It is therefore likely that some of the unemployed not on relief on 1 June 1936 had been on relief earlier in the year. Still, the question remains: how did the long-term unemployed survive without relief during the summer months? Living costs (especially for heating and clothing) were much lower in the summer, and dependants were more likely to pick up odd jobs over the summer and thus be able to contribute to the family budget. Why unemployed women were so much less likely to be on relief than men is unclear.[26] They may have found it easier to obtain charity, or to live with relatives, or it may have been harder for them to qualify for relief. The authorities were certainly most concerned with the plight of married men, and feared the social unrest caused by single men - the condition of unemployed women received scant attention.

The characteristics of London relief recipients confirm the impression that the very poorest among the unemployed were most commonly on relief.[27] A few building tradesmen, printers, and the occasional salesman were on the relief rolls, but the vast majority were unskilled workers. Immigrants were overrepresented among relief recipients, which is consistent with the census evidence on unemployment discussed above. The poverty of relief recipients is further illustrated by their extremely low levels of home ownership. While roughly half of all London householders were owner-occupiers in the 1930s, almost none of the relief families owned their home.

Clearly, relief was an important source of income for the unemployed, but a substantial proportion of the jobless were not on relief, or were on relief only for a few months each year. Sometimes temporary jobs permitted a family to get off relief for a short period, but most recipients in the late 1930s had received assistance for at least part of each of the preceding years. A further indication that relief was the last resort of the unemployed is the low proportion of recipients who had been on relief as early as 1931. About 20 per cent of those on relief in the late 1930s reported that they had first been relief cases in 1930 or 1931, and another 30 per cent in 1932. Many of those who reported their last regular work in 1929-31 only went on relief in 1933-34.

Sale of assets probably helped postpone the need to apply for relief. Throughout the country, the proportion of households owning their homes fell substantially between 1931 and 1941. Among relief families rent arrears were the norm, and the London evidence suggests fairly high mobility of relief cases - single men living in furnished rooms were especially prone to moving, and it seems highly probable that at least some of the moves were associated with the non-payment of rent. Given that most men on relief were unskilled workers, they were unlikely to have many assets to sell, so to survive without employment, and without relief, for two to four years must have entailed a considerable drop in already quite low living standards.

Relief, once it was obtained, was provided at a meagre level.[28] Much contemporary concern was expressed about the risk of encouraging unskilled labourers to quit work in order to qualify for relief, and the low levels of relief payment were justified both by lack of funds and by the low alternative income most relief families could expect to earn even if fully employed. It is true that in many cities a large family, on relief for the full year and in receipt of the maximum possible assistance, could indeed have an income not much lower than that earned by an unskilled labourer at work for nine or ten months of the year. However, as noted above, there was typically a substantial gap between the time a worker lost his job and when he went on relief. In addition, relief payments, especially allowances for rent and clothing, were discretionary, and average payments were often far below the maximum amount allowable.

Maximum relief payments for a family of five ranged from less than a third (in Saint John and Halifax) to about two-thirds (in Winnipeg) the wage of a fully employed building labourer. The relationship between actual relief payments and the maximum allowable is often tenuous. For example, in September 1936, Toronto had the highest allowable maximum among Ontario cities, but in terms of payments was close to the average. Generally, both maximum allowances and actual payments were lowest in the Maritimes and highest in the Prairie provinces.

Variation in relief scales was much more pronounced in Canada than Australia, where states, not municipalities, set levels of sustenance payments. However, in some cities the hypothetical family of five might do somewhat better on relief in Canada than on sustenance in Australia. An Australian family on relief received about 40 per cent of the building labourer's wage, if the father was not given relief work. If he was on relief work, they received about half the building labourer's wage. Both Canadians and Australians were typically at some disadvantage relative to the unemployed family in Britain, where benefits were roughly two-thirds of a building labourer's wage.[29]

Unemployment was the main cause of destitution in the cities. In rural areas, especially on the prairies, farm incomes fell dramatically, as a combination of drought, grasshoppers and wheat rust destroyed a high proportion of the wheat crop each year from 1929 on. Prices of farm products were low everywhere, but only the prairies were hit by severe declines in output. Typically, the living standards of farm families are thought of as being somewhat insulated from the effects of the trade cycle. Despite declining revenue, production for home consumption would at least permit an adequate food supply. For drought-stricken prairie farmers, however, this characterisation is very wide of the mark; crops and vegetable gardens failed, and little animal feed could be grown.

Thus the plight of wheat farmers is in some senses similar to that of unemployed wage earners; their only source of income disappeared, and subsistence production for home consumption was largely impossible. It is interesting to contrast the way in which relief was provided to prairie farmers and to unemployed workers. As with urban direct relief, direct relief to farm families was set at very low levels. More than half the expenditure on rural relief, however, was in the form of agricultural aid - seed, feed and fodder for animals, repairs to implements, and fuel and grease for tractors (Britnell, 1939, p.92). Rural relief was generally relief on loan, which was a significant difference from urban relief. In fact, as the agricultural crisis continued throughout the decade, the loans were written off. The rationale for giving loan relief was that while farmers in the drought area had current incomes close to zero, they typically had substantial assets in the form of land, animals and implements. Since larger farmers had more land to seed and stock to maintain, they received a higher share of agricultural aid. Thus rural relief operated in a manner fundamentally different to urban relief. In the cities, as we have seen, relief recipients came mainly from the ranks of the unskilled. They were desperately impoverished in the 1930s, but most had been poor in the 1920s, and probably remained poor in later years as well. More skilled and educated workers were less likely to be unemployed for long periods, and if they did suffer unemployment, were more likely to stay off relief by selling their assets. By contrast, there was a definite attempt to maintain farmers' assets, and in the drought areas of Saskatchewan in the early 1930s, farmers on relief were virtually indistinguishable from the average farmer.[30]

Since agriculture was the main industry of the Prairie provinces, the desire to keep its productive capacity intact is understandable. If farmers had been forced to sell most of their stock and implements, then recovery in agriculture, which was vital for the recovery of the national economy, would have been delayed after weather conditions improved. The contrast with the theory and practice of urban relief, however, is striking. Direct relief in both city and country was designed to maintain the destitute at subsistence levels, but in urban areas relief payments were rarely used to maintain productive assets. Very little effort was expended in attempts to maintain the skills of the unemployed, nor were loans advanced (for example) to shopkeepers whose operating expenses exceeded revenues.[31]

Unemployment was often attributed to the rapid urbanisation experienced in the 1920s, and some relief policies hinged on encouraging people to return to the countryside. It is therefore consistent that agricultural aid would be designed to let most farmers stay on their land, and be in a position to resume full production as soon as possible. The dominion government also helped to pay for land resettlement; over 9,000 families (almost 50,000 individuals) were moved to pioneer farming regions, or to abandoned farms.[32] Nearly half the total families moved were from Quebec, the province with the greatest faith in the superiority of rural life, and among the lowest urban relief payments in the country. Settlers generally had previous farm experience, and it was felt that it would be no more expensive to move them out of the cities and help them set up subsistence farms than to keep them on urban direct relief for an indefinite period. Other provinces followed the same policy, but not to such an extent. On the prairies, some farmers in the worst of the dried-out region were assisted to move further north. In the short term many settlers did become self-supporting. However, much of the land settled in the 1930s was, at best, marginal. Taking a longer-term view therefore, land resettlement, especially to northern Quebec and Ontario, simply created long-term poverty.

Rural relief, because it was used to maintain assets, was more generous than urban relief, and wealthier farmers received more help than poorer farmers. There is also some evidence that change in income, not level of income, was most important in determining whether an applicant would be granted relief, which reinforces the view that wealthier farmers gained most from agricultural aid. The high degree of local autonomy in the administration of relief makes it hard to confirm this impression, but in some areas we have studied, the farmers who were refused relief were among the poorest applicants. They were much closer to being subsistence farmers, and were judged able to get along without relief.

4   Conclusions

Unemployment in Canada during the Depression was very heavy for two reasons. As the United States was its major trading partner, the decline in American income was bound to have a severe impact in Canada. In addition, the prairie drought reduced the output of one of the country's major exports. In the smaller, more narrowly based Canadian economy, the drought had a relatively greater effect than in the US. Because the economy was quite highly integrated by the 1930s, the effects of the Depression were spread fairly evenly across the country. The demand for labour was quite insensitive to changes in wages; the main determinant of the pattern of unemployment throughout the decade was the differential decline in the demand for goods and services. Unemployment rates by occupation and therefore sex, and, later in the Depression, by age group, were highly unequal, and a high proportion of those who lost a job were unemployed for a protracted period.

The capacity and willingness of Canadian governments to protect the population from the effects of the Depression was relatively limited. In common with many other countries, Canada raised tariffs early in the Depression, which stimulated manufacturing output but tended to worsen the terms of trade between primary production and manufacturing. In the early 1930s, relief programmes were better organised, and on a larger scale, than in the US. However, Canadian governments did not subs-

equently introduce innovations in the way the Americans did. Local control of relief implied a much greater variation in payments than in Australia or the UK, but it appears that relief allowances in Canada were roughly
similar to those in Australia, although below British unemployment insurance benefit levels. On the basis of international comparisons, Canadian
governments were thus not exceptionally parsimonious, but government
action did little to reduce the income inequality among the wage earning
population caused by the highly uneven incidence of unemployment.

NOTES

* This research was supported by grants from Labour Canada, the SSHRCC and
the Advisory Research Committee of Queen's University. We thank Bina Rossi
and Les Reinhorn for excellent research assistance.

1 This macroeconomic model estimates separate equations for consumption, exports, imports and investment. There is provision for estimating money demand
and supply equations plus foreign exchange reserves (Green and Sparks, 1987).

2 Appendix 4: National Income, Report of *Royal Commission on Dominion-Provincial Relations* (1939), pp. 53-4 and *Population 1921-1971* (Statistics Canada,
1973), cat. no.91-512, pp. 17 and 20. During the period 1928 to 1931 the GNE deflator fell by 7 per cent while the CPI declined by 9 per cent and the WPI (excluding gold) by 25 per cent. The sharpest fall in export prices occurred between 1928
and 1931 (Leacy, Urquhart and Buckley, 1983, series K172, K8 and K33).

3 The terms "workers" and "the labour force" refer in this chapter to the gainfully
occupied, except when measures of employment and unemployment are discussed,
as these are only recorded for wage earners.

4 For Canada in 1930-31, the elimination of double counting reduces the total
number of wage earners losing time by about 6 per cent.

5 The Maritimes are the provinces of Prince Edward Island, Nova Scotia and New
Brunswick. The Prairie provinces are Manitoba, Saskatchewan and Alberta.

6 Beveridge (1944, p. 61) gives unemployment rates by region for 1929-37. See
Thomas, chapter 3, this volume, Table 3.10 for regional unemployment rates in
Great Britain in 1937.

7 The "no job" category excludes those on temporary lay-off, while the difference
between 52 and "weeks worked" includes all reasons for not being at work. Na-
tionally, only 6.6 per cent of male and 11.4 per cent of female weeks lost were due
to causes other than no job or temporary lay-off.

8 If union wage rates are reported, but many workers were not unionised, and employed at rates below the union level, the extent of short-time working is exaggerated.

9 We ignore in kind payments, which at least for agricultural labourers were usually a substantial share of total wages, and were unlikely to fall as much as cash wages.

10 This point will be discussed more fully in section 3.

11 For all occupations, for Canada as a whole, a plot of average weeks lost per worker losing time against the percentage of workers losing time for all occupations shows a weak positive correlation between the two. Especially for occupations with a low percentage of wage earners losing time, there is a high variance around the mean. Foremen stand out as the workers both least likely to lose any time, and if so, to lose very short spells. By contrast, although managers were also unlikely to lose time, those who did were very likely to be out for most of the year. MacLean *et al.* (1942, p.261.)

12 We concentrate on Manitoba's experience as recorded in the 1936 Prairie census because it was the most urbanised and least drought-affected of the three Prairie provinces. Therefore, it should be the best proxy for average Canadian conditions.

13 This statement may appear to contradict Table 10.4, which shows for each age group a similar proportion of men and women jobless for more than two years. It is a result of the very different age composition of the male and female workforce. Female employment rates fall rapidly with age. In 1931, close to 40 per cent of women aged 18-24 were wage earners, but only 9 per cent of women aged 35-44.

14 In 1940-41, for all wage earners, women worked slightly less than men. This is consistent with age-specific rates which show women working more weeks because a much higher proportion of women workers are under 25, and weeks worked by young employees of both sexes are much lower in 1940-41 than in previous years.

15 In 1921, a little over 2 per cent of married women were gainfully occupied. By 1931, this had risen to over 3 per cent, and in 1941, to nearly 4 per cent. About 17 per cent of single women were gainfully occupied in 1921, 19 per cent in 1931, and 23 per cent in 1941.

16 On census day in 1941, for the country as a whole, only 7 per cent of male and 6 per cent of female wage earners were not at work. The improvement in economic conditions was very rapid in early 1941.

17 See Thomas, chapter 3, this volume, Table 3.6 for British unemployment rates by age and sex.

18 Not all of the increase in the number of workers in prairie agriculture between 1931 and 1936 can be due to lower migration from the farm to the city. The 1936 census takers noted workers who listed their current occupation as being different from their usual occupation. While the proportion of workers listed in a temporary occupation was fairly small (usually less than 5 per cent), farm labour and general labour almost always were two of the main current occupations.

19 The information on the geographic mobility of the gainfully occupied was collected for all those over 14, so some of the younger members of the labour force would have moved with their families before employment considerations were relevant to them (DBS, 1946, 1941 census, vol. 7, Table 14, pp. 468-85).

20 US Department of Commerce (1946), *Population: Internal Migration 1935 to 1940, Age of Migrants*, Table 1, p.5.

21 These figures include expenditure on all programmes relating to health and social security, including old age pensions, mothers' allowances, hospitals, etc. In 1933, relief expenditure, by all levels of government, was about 40 per cent of the total (Guest, 1980, pp. 86 and 102).

22 In 1934, and again in 1938-40, the federal government provided some funds to help pay for public works, but direct relief continued to be the principal source of aid. Some cities required work from employable relief recipients throughout the decade.

23 Struthers (1983, Appendix II). The total for all types of relief reached a maximum of 1.4 million recipients, 12 per cent of the total population, in spring 1935.

24 London relief records are held in the Regional Collection of the D.B. Weldon Library, University of Western Ontario.

25 For the country as a whole, the proportion of heads of families continuously on relief for more than four years rose from 16 to 30 per cent between September 1936 and September 1937 (National Employment Commission, 1938, p. 62).

26 Few married women were in the labour force, so the difference between the proportions of unemployed men and women on relief cannot be explained by assuming that many unemployed women had wage earning husbands.

27 Marsh (1940, chapter 15) discusses several other surveys of relief recipients, which are broadly similar to results for London. He notes a higher proportion of professional and managerial workers were on relief in the western provinces.

28 In many areas, recipients were given groceries; in others, they received vouchers which could be spent only on approved items. Cash relief was the exception.

29 In Canada, payments per recipient were usually at least 10 per cent higher in the winter than in September, reflecting the need for extra fuel and clothing. Struthers (1983, Appendix IV, p. 221) reports maximum relief allowances for September 1936; 1936 wages are from DBS, *Canada Year Book, 1936*, p. 782. Data on relief payments per recipient come from the Public Archives of Canada, RG 27, Direct Relief Reports. Australian wages and sustenance rates for 1936 are from CBCS, *Labour Report, 1936*. Unemployment benefit rates in the UK for 1936 are from Burns (1941), p. 368. London building labourers' wages are from CBCS, *Labour Report, 1936*, p. 177. Since London wages were typically somewhat higher than in smaller cities, the implication is that benefits as a proportion of low skilled wages were somewhat higher outside London.

30 The proportion of the population on relief in southern Saskatchewan (about 50 per cent) during this period was far higher than in urban areas, so one would expect the characteristics of the recipients to be closer to those of the population as a whole. These conclusions are based on a sample of relief applications held by the Saskatchewan Archives Board.

31 Having sold his shop, the owner might be poor enough to go on relief. Relief supply contracts were often let to the friends of the town councillors, but they could be given to businesses which would otherwise be likely to fail, and in this sense urban relief might be used to maintain existing patterns of asset ownership.

32 From 1932 to 1940: DBS, *Canada Year Book 1940*, p. 767.

REFERENCES

Baily, M. N. (1983), "The Labor Market in the 1930's", in James Tobin (ed.), *Macroeconomics, Prices and Quantities*, Washington, DC: Brookings Institution.

Beveridge, William H. (1944), *Full Employment in a Free Society*, London: Allen & Unwin.

Blain, L., Paterson, D.G. and Rae, J.D. (1974), "The Regional Impact of Economic Fluctuations During the Inter-War Period: The Case of British Columbia", *Canadian Journal of Economics* 7, pp. 381-401.

Britnell, G.E. (1939), *The Wheat Economy*, Toronto: University of Toronto Press.

Burns, Eveline M. (1941), *British Unemployment Programs 1920-38*, Washington, DC: Social Science Research Council.

Butlin, N.G. (1984), *Select Comparative Economic Statistics 1900-40: Australia and Britain, Canada, Japan, New Zealand and USA*, Canberra: Australian National University, Source Papers in Economic History, no.4.

Cassidy, H.M. and Scott, F.R. (1935), *Labour Conditions in the Men's Clothing Industry*, Toronto: Institute of Pacific Relations.

Chandler, Lester V. (1970), *America's Greatest Depression, 1929-1941*, New York: Harper & Row.

Commonwealth Bureau of Census and Statistics (annual), *Labour Report*, Melbourne: H.J. Green.

Department of Labour (annual), *Labour Gazette*, Ottawa: King's Printer.

Dominion Bureau of Statistics (annual), *Canada Year Book*, Ottawa: King's Printer.

Dominion Bureau of Statistics (1934-1942), *Seventh Census of Canada, 1931*, Ottawa: King's Printer.

Dominion Bureau of Statistics (1938), *Census of the Prairie Provinces, 1936*, Ottawa: King's Printer.

Dominion Bureau of Statistics (1946-1950), *Eighth Census of Canada, 1941*, Ottawa: King's Printer.

Dominion Bureau of Statistics (1953), *Ninth Census of Canada, 1951*, vol. 5, Ottawa: Queen's Printer.

Dominion Bureau of Statistics (1966), *1961 Census of Canada*, vol. 4, cat. no.98-510, Ottawa: Queen's Printer.

Green, A.G. (1971), *Regional Aspects of Canada's Economic Growth*, Toronto: University of Toronto Press.

Green, A.G. (1985), *Policy Options in a Small Open Economy: Canada During the Great Depression*, Canberra: Australian National University, Working Papers in Economic History, no. 60.

Green, A.G. and Sparks, G.R. (1987), "A Macro Interpretation of Economic Recovery from the Great Depression: Australia - US - Canada", Queen's Discussion Paper, no. 615.

Green, A.G. and Urquhart, M.C. (1988), "New Estimates of Output Growth in Canada: Measurement and Interpretation", in D. McCalla (ed.), *Perspectives on Canadian History*.

Guest, Dennis (1980), *The Emergence of Social Security in Canada*, Vancouver: University of British Columbia Press.

Horn, Michiel (1984), *The Great Depression of the 1930s in Canada*, Ottawa: Canadian Historical Association.

Leacy, F.H., Urquhart, M.C. and Buckley, K.A.H. (1983), *Historical Statistics of Canada*, Ottawa: Statistics Canada.

Mackintosh, W.A. (1939, 1964 edn), *The Economic Background of Dominion-Provincial Relations*, Toronto: McClelland & Stewart.

MacLean, M.C., LeNeveu, A.H., Tedford, W.C. and Keyfitz, N. (1942), "Unemployment", in Dominion Bureau of Statistics, *Seventh Census of Canada, 1931*, vol. 13, Ottawa: DBS.

Marsh, Leonard C. (1940), *Canadians In and Out of Work: A Survey of Economic Classes and their Relation to the Labour Market*, Toronto: Oxford University Press.

National Employment Commission (1938), *Final Report*, Ottawa: King's Printer.

Palmer, Brian D. (1983), *Working Class Experience: The Rise and Reconstitution of Canadian Labour, 1800- 1980*, Toronto: Butterworth.

Pilgrim Trust (1938), *Men Without Work,* Cambridge: Cambridge University Press.

Report of the Royal Commission on Dominion-Provincial Relations (1939), Appendix 4: National Income, Ottawa.

Safarian, A.E. (1959), *The Canadian Economy in the Great Depression,* Toronto: University of Toronto Press.

Statistics Canada (1973), *Population 1921- 1971*, 91-512, Ottawa: Statistics Canada.

Statistics Canada (1984), *1981 Census of Canada*, vol. 1, National Series, 92-915, Ottawa: Statistics Canada.

Struthers, James (1983), *No Fault of Their Own: Unemployment and the Canadian Welfare State, 1914-1941*, Toronto: University of Toronto Press.

United States Department of Commerce, Bureau of the Census (1946), *Population: Internal Migration 1935 to 1940, Age of Migrants,* Washington, DC: US Government Printing Office.

Chapter 11

The Australian and US Labour Markets in the 1930s

R G Gregory, V Ho, L McDermott
and J Hagan*

1 Introduction

Over most of this century the Australian labour market has possessed two key institutional features: a high degree of craft trade unionism and a system of federal and state tribunals, which provide a centralised system of wage setting and dispute resolution. It is widely believed that these institutions exercise a considerable impact on the Australian labour market and impart a large degree of regulation and perhaps inflexibility.

The tribunals, for example, set minimum wages for each occupation so that the pay of university professors is fixed along with that of bus drivers, labourers, fitters and turners and so on. These rates of pay are called awards and are legally enforced minimums. Where the awards are set by the federal tribunal they are set on a nationwide basis. For example, all electricians, irrespective of the state or industry in which they work, will be covered by the same award rate of pay. The opportunity exists for over-award payments but most workers receive the award rate of pay for the job.[1]

The tribunals also arbitrate on conditions of work. These conditions include the standard hours to be worked each week, the number of paid holidays and the amount of sick pay, manning requirements and a whole host of other factors including the description of the job to be done by each worker and an allocation of that job to a particular union. The usual situation is to have a number of unions represented within the one enterprise, and many industrial disputes take place between unions fighting

B. Eichengreen and T. J. Hatton (eds.), Interwar Unemployment in International Perspective, 397–430.
© *1988 by Kluwer Academic Publishers.*

over which jobs belong to which unions. Thus, on a large building site, carpenters are not allowed to operate lifts, drive trucks, pick up tools which have been dropped from one floor to another, or do other jobs that belong to other unions. These conditions are written into awards and are also legally enforceable. This structure of tribunals, and an award system which tightly describes conditions of work, are encouraged and supported by the trade union movement although it is not necessary to be a trade union member to be covered by an award.

These labour market institutions were also important in the 1930s when, excluding the self-employed, trade union membership covered about 50 per cent of the labour force and the federal tribunal successfully pursued an incomes policy which fully adjusted wages each quarter for past price changes. This indexation policy had been in place since 1922.[2] Australia therefore has a long history of centralised wage fixing, incomes policies and a heavily regulated labour market.

In this chapter, we discuss the impact of the Depression on the regulated Australian labour market to provide a basis for speculation as to the effects of these institutional features. To facilitate the analysis we compare some of the Australian outcomes with those of the US labour market. In the US there was no centralised wage setting system and trade unions were not as extensive or as powerful. During the early years of the Depression, trade union membership in the US covered only 9.5 per cent of the non-farm labour force. This essay can be seen as a part of the recent literature which compares the relative performance, in the face of a large shock, of unregulated labour markets, in this instance the US, with those, such as Australia, which are dominated by consensus, incomes policies and centralised wage fixing (see Bruno and Sachs, 1984; McCallum, 1986).

In section 2 we compare the performance of the labour markets in the US and Australia. There are three major conclusions. First, the macro wage outcomes for each country were much the same during the 1930s, despite the different institutional frameworks. Both countries showed considerable flexibility in nominal wages but virtually no flexibility in real wages. Between 1929 and 1932 nominal wages fell by about 20 to 25 per cent in each country but, despite unemployment rates of 19 per cent or higher, real wages were either constant or marginally increased. Since the Depression was more severe in the US it might be said that the Australian labour market was more efficient. A high degree of trade unionism, combined with an incomes policy based largely on real wage maintenance, produced marginally greater flexibility in nominal wages than in the US and much the same real wage outcome.

Second, job sharing within firms was very different in each country. In Australia, almost all of the labour market adjustment to the reduced level of labour demand seems to have fallen on the unemployed. For each 1 percentage point reduction in output 1 percentage point of the workforce was laid off. For the employed workforce average hours of work per week did not appear to be significantly affected by the Depression and, as far as we can tell, labour productivity per hour did not fall. Job sharing within Australian firms appears to have been negligible. In the US, however, there was a strong degree of labour hoarding and job sharing. A 1 percentage point reduction in output was associated with less than half a percentage point reduction in employment.

Third, in both countries unemployment duration during the Depression was typically quite long and, once unemployed, workers found it very difficult to obtain a new regular job. In Australia, 50 per cent of the unemployed in 1930 had not found a regular job by 1933 and 65 per cent of those unemployed in 1933 had been without work for at least a year. Duration data are more difficult to find for the US, but those which are available present a similar picture. In the cities of Buffalo (New York), Lincoln (Nebraska) and Philadelphia (Pennsylvania), at least 60 per cent of the unemployed in 1933 had also been without work for a year.

In section 3 we provide more detail as to the effects of unemployment in Australia. We focus on the geographic dispersion of unemployment in cities and the extent of income loss experienced by the unemployed. It is quite clear that in Australia unemployment was primarily visited upon the lower socioeconomic groups who clustered together in particular parts of the cities. In some areas of Australian cities, in June 1933, over 40 per cent of the male labour force was unemployed. In other areas the male unemployment rate was less than 8 per cent. We have not been able to match these data with unemployment in US cities but it is likely that there was a similar outcome there.

If we put all these points together, a picture emerges of a regulated labour market in Australia which produced real and nominal wage flexibility to a degree similar to, or marginally better than, the less regulated US labour market. In addition, the duration of unemployment seems similar in both countries. Consequently, on the basis of these most commonly accepted criteria, the regulated Australian labour market performed as well as, or better than, the relatively free labour market of the US. The major difference between the two labour markets appears to lie in the inability of the Australian system to adjust hours of work and labour productivity per hour to the same degree as occurred in the US. The Australian system therefore appears to have been less equitable. Despite the emphasis of public discussion in Australia which focused on equality of sacrifice and sharing the burden there appears to have been very little sharing of jobs, especially within firms. The Australian system seemed to divide the labour force into two fairly distinct groups: the employed who maintained real wages and hours per week and tended to keep their jobs, and the unemployed who tended to remain without work for long periods of time.

2 The Australian-US Comparisons

2.1 Real and Nominal Wages

The Depression was largely imported into Australia by a considerable decrease in foreign currency earnings brought about by reduced export prices for agricultural commodities and a drying up of foreign capital inflows. Between 1929 and 1931 the Australian terms of trade fell 40 per cent and foreign capital inflows, which had been very important during the 1920s, had fallen away to virtually nothing by 1931. Although there were some adverse domestic factors at work, the Depression was primarily a response to the balance of payments crisis, which led to tariff increases, an exchange rate devaluation and a large fall in national income. The prevailing view for the US is that the Depression was initiated by domestic factors.

Indices for the GDP of each country, measured in real terms, are presented in Figure 11.1 where it is clear that the Depression was more severe in the US. Between 1929 and the trough of 1932, real GDP in Australia fell by 9 per cent and by 1934 the recovery was well under way as GDP had begun to exceed pre-Depression levels. In the US, real GDP fell 28.5 per cent between 1929 and the trough of 1933 and did not reach its previous peak until 1937. Between the trough of the Depression and the previous peak, real GDP fell an extra 20 per cent in the US.[3] In these terms the Depression can be thought of as being about three times worse than in Australia. In terms of income loss the Depression was much the same in both countries, perhaps marginally worse in the US. In Australia, there was a large shift of expenditure from imports to domestic goods, and as international trade was relatively more important, the fall in the terms of trade was more serious and exerted a larger impact to reduce national income relative to output. In Australia during the 1920s exports averaged about 22 per cent of GDP. In the US the ratio was much lower, around 6 per cent.

Aggregate prices and nominal wages in Australia appear to have been very flexible (see Figure 11.2). During the downswing prices and wages fell together by about 20 per cent. During the recovery phase prices and nominal wages increased together. At this time most occupations were already subject to award rates of pay laid down by Commonwealth or state arbitration tribunals. Wage tribunals set nominal wages but they were pri-

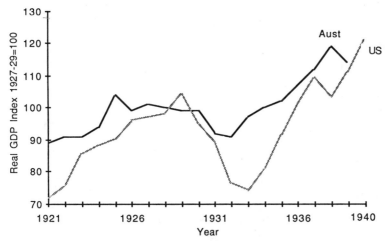

Figure 11.1   Real Gross Domestic Product in Australia and the United States, 1921-40

Sources: Australia: N.G. Butlin (1962), pp.460-461. USA: Kendrick (1961), Table A-III, Col.5, p.298.

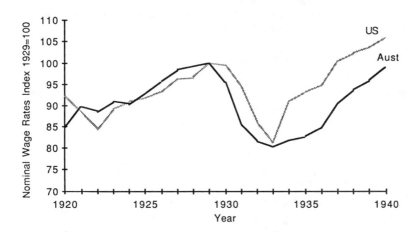

Figure 11.2   Nominal Wage Rates in Australia and the United States, 1920-40

Note: Australia: All industry wage-weighted average nominal weekly wage rate payable to adult male workers for a full week's work, divided by male standard hours worked per week at 31 December each year. USA: Average earnings per hour for all employees (full-time equivalent). Calendar year.

Sources: Australia: Labour Report (various issues, e.g. for 1929 see Report no.20), M.W.Butlin (1977), pp.90-92. USA: Baily (1983).

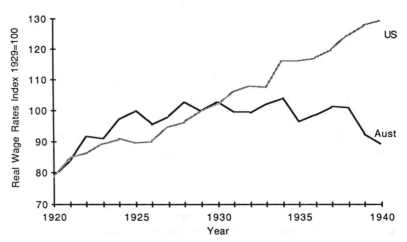

Figure 11.3   Real Wage Rates in Australia and the United States, 1920-40

Note: Australia: Nominal wage as in Figure 11.2 divided by private consumption deflator. USA: Nominal wage as in Figure 11.2 divided by consumer price index. *Sources:*   Australia: N.G.Butlin (1984), Table Aa3, Col.(a), and Figure 11.2 source. USA: N.G. Butlin (1984), Table U23, and Figure 11.2 source.

marily concerned with the maintenance of real wages, and during the crucial years before and after 1931 the Commonwealth basic wage[4] was indexed quarterly for price changes. On 1 February 1931, in response to a public hearing, the Commonwealth Court of Conciliation and Arbitration agreed, on application of employers, to reduce the basic wage component of all awards covered by its jurisdiction by 10 per cent. This was to be a real wage reduction to be followed by quarterly indexation for price changes. It is evident from Figure 11.3 that on average real wages were not reduced and the Commonwealth Court, although successful in its attempts to achieve full wage indexation for past price changes, failed in its attempt to cut real wages (see Gregory, McDermott and Ho, 1985). Apart from random year-to-year variations, Australian real wages measured in terms of consumer prices essentially remained constant between 1924 and 1934, after which there appears to have been a slow drift downwards.

In Figures 11.2 and 11.3 we also plot indices of the nominal and real wage for the US. The similarity of nominal wage outcomes of the "free market" in the US and the Australian centralised wage system operating a full wage indexation policy is very close. Only in one year, 1934, is there a large difference between the two countries and during this year nominal wage increases are much less in Australia. After 1934, nominal wage increases are much the same in both countries, and if account is taken of the depressed output levels, which are much greater in the US, then the Australian economy seems to have produced greater flexibility of nominal wages. In Australia, a nominal wage reduction of 20 per cent was not only associated with one-third of the output fall that occurred in the US but also occurred in the face of an exchange rate devaluation of 20 per cent. The centralised system based on full wage indexation for past price changes appears to have been very effective at reducing nominal wages and ensuring that the nominal exchange rate devaluation translated into an even larger real exchange rate fall. This point is worth noting because so often in simple models it is demonstrated that a real exchange rate devaluation requires a real wage reduction. In Australia the real exchange rate devaluation was achieved without a real wage reduction.

In both countries between 1929 and 1935, there are also minor differences in the path of real wages, relative to trend, but there is no evidence of a real wage increase in advance of the recession or a real wage fall in advance of the recovery. Real wages in both countries at the macro level appear to have an independent and fairly stable life of their own and seem to have played no part as an initiating force in the origins of the Depression or in the economic recovery. During the 1930s, the Australian institutional framework for centralised wage setting was regarded as a distinct advantage and the arbitration court was widely regarded as an institution which could facilitate wage flexibility (Copland, 1934; Reddaway, 1938). Reddaway comments on the Australian system as follows:

> Is there any advantage in having machinery for fixing the general level of wages, instead of leaving it to emerge from a large number of sectional decisions? The experience of this period surely shows that such a system is very valuable. The employment market in a country such as Australia does not, and never will, bear much resemblance to the text book version with its perfect competition, equality of opportunity, automatic adjustments and so on. *Without some general system of regulation it is doubtful whether money wages could ever have been reduced sufficiently to preserve the exporter and encourage new manufactures*; it is quite certain that the cuts would have fallen most unequally on different sections of the community....To secure the general fall in costs that was vitally necessary, *a general system of regulation was almost indispensable.* (Reddaway, 1938, p.335)

Reddaway probably had in mind a comparison with the UK labour market, where trade union membership was also high but there was no centralised wage setting. It is quite clear, from a macro perspective, that the wage outcomes in Australia were far better than in the UK where nominal wages did not fall significantly and there was a large increase in real wages.[5] But it is important to note that the Australian institutions probably gave a greater degree of macro nominal wage flexibility than the "free labour market" of the US. With regard to real wages the outcomes seem much the same. It appears that in Australia the combination of trade unions and centralised wage fixing can do as well, if not better, than a free market and certainly better than a market with a high degree of unionism but no incomes policy. This experience supports to some extent the recent work on wage setting and unemployment which discusses the merits of neocorporatism (see Bruno and Sachs, 1984; McCallum, 1986).

2. 2   Employment

Figure 11.4 presents the unemployment rates for each country. Once again it is evident that the Depression is more severe in the US. If we compare unemployment in 1929 with the peak unemployment of 1933, there is an increase of 22 percentage points in the US and 9 percentage points in Australia. This difference of 13 percentage points is approximately two-thirds of the 20 percentage point difference in the output loss between the two countries. The Australian unemployment record therefore seems relatively worse than might be expected from the output loss experience. This behaviour originates from the employment-output relationship and not from different participation rate relationships.[6] The employment paths of each country are presented in Figure 11.5.

During the period since the Second World War the usual response to an output fall in most developed countries is to undertake a high degree of job sharing within the firm. Hall (1980) suggests that in the US about two-thirds of the adjustment to an output fall during the 1960s and 1970s takes the form of reduced employment and one-third of the adjustment is in the form of job sharing through reduced hours of work and lower labour productivity. Similar relationships are evident in Australian postwar data and it is the conventional view in Australia that job sharing was important, especially during the early years of the Depression. This view is based largely on anecdotal evidence, media reports of the time and studies of individual firms.[7] However, the macro significance of job sharing has never been assessed. There are no data available on actual hours worked in Australia nor is there an annual series on the number engaged in part-time work. There are hours of work data for a full week's work that are written into awards and these "official" hours per week increased marginally during the Depression. The tribunals, therefore, did *not* attempt to facilitate job sharing within firms by altering the length of the working week that is written into awards.

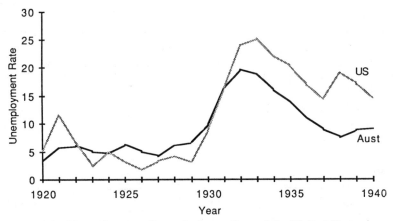

**Figure 11.4   Unemployment Rates in Australia and the United States,
1920-40**

Note: Australia: Average number of persons unemployed per year as a proportion
of the labour force (all persons employed, including defence forces serving over-
seas, all persons unemployed, absentees and some part-timers). Year ending 30
June (i.e. 1920 = 1919/20). USA: Unemployed as percentage of civilian labour
force. Average for calendar year.
Sources: Australia: N.G.Butlin (1984), Table U22, Col. (i). USA: N.G. Butlin
(1984), Table Aa33, Col. (f).

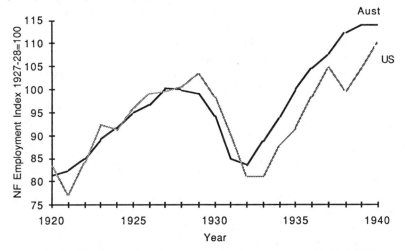

**Figure 11.5   Non-Farm Employment in Australia and the United States,
1920-40**

Sources: Australia: N.G. Butlin (1984), Table Aa34, Col.(n)-Col.(j)-Col.(a).
USA: N.G. Butlin (1984), Table U22, Col.(g).

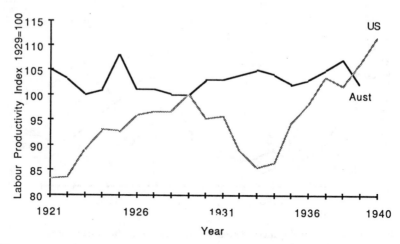

Figure 11.6 Labour Productivity in Australia and the United States, 1921-40

Note: Australia: Real gross domestic product divided by civilian employment. USA: Real gross domestic product divided by persons engaged.

Sources: Australia: M.W. Butlin (1977), pp.90-92, and Figure 11.1 sources. USA: Kendrick (1961), Table A- XIX, p.328, Col.2, and Figure 11.1 sources.

We will draw inferences on the extent of job sharing primarily from the behaviour of labour productivity, measured on a per capita basis and not adjusted for hours worked or for short-time working. If labour hoarding and job sharing through reduced hours worked per week are important, then labour productivity on a per capita basis should fall significantly as output falls and increase significantly as output increases.[8] For example, if output were to fall by 10 per cent and all the labour input adjustment took the form of reduced hours per week, then employment would remain unchanged and per capita labour productivity would fall by 10 per cent.

An overview of Australian labour productivity fluctuations during the interwar period is presented in Figure 11.6. It is apparent that labour productivity tended to increase marginally during the Depression period and that there is no pro-cyclical variation that might be expected on the basis of post-Second World War data. With the 1930s data, and at this level of aggregation, all the adjustment to the recession and recovery appears to have taken place by varying the degree of idle labour resources *outside* the firm. On average firms did not significantly hoard labour or share reduced work hours among employees. Because employment varied proportionately with output, most of the adjustment was forced upon the unemployed.[9]

The Australian experience is very different from that of the US where labour productivity measured on a per capita basis, and not adjusted for hours worked, drops by 15 per cent between 1929 and 1933 and then increases rapidly as output increases after 1934 (Figure 11.6). Indeed, between 1929 and 1933, about one half of the output fall in the US is translated into a labour productivity adjustment and one half into a reduction of employment. Labour hoarding seems more important during the interwar period than Hall suggested for the postwar period.

This difference in labour productivity behaviour between the two countries is very important. Any judgment as to the relative depth of the Depression will depend on whether output or labour market outcomes such as employment or unemployment are used as the measuring rod. On the basis of the output experience the Depression is far more serious in the US but with respect to measured unemployment the Depression appears to be only marginally worse.

The difference between the product and labour market outcomes can be illustrated by the following calculations derived from data in Table 11.1. If, for the given output paths, labour productivity in Australia had behaved in the same way as in the US, then, *ceteris paribus*, the increase in measured unemployment in Australia could have been significantly less, perhaps increasing to around 12 per cent of the labour force rather than 19 per cent in 1932. Or, putting the point the other way, if per capita labour productivity in the US had behaved in the same way as the Australian series, then, *ceteris paribus*, unemployment in the US would have been 39 per cent in 1933 instead of 25 per cent. Of course, since these calculations assume a given output path, they are very rough, but they do provide some indication of the quantitative importance of the different labour productivity behaviour.

We don't really know why the extent of job sharing in Australia appears to be so different from that of the US. However, it is worth spending a little time considering a number of conjectures. To begin, we divide the Australian Depression years into two segments: (a) 1929 to 1931, which is the period between the previous peak and the output trough, and (b) 1931 to 1935, which are the first four years of the recovery period. A similar division is undertaken for the US: (a) 1929 to 1931, to coincide with the Australian downswing, (b) 1929 to 1933, which is the period between the previous peak and the output trough, and (c) 1933 to 1937, which are the first four years of the recovery. The basic data for these subperiods are presented in Table 11.1 where the data for each row are defined as follows:

Row 1: the percentage output change for each period. In subsequent rows we partition the relationship between output and employment variations into the following components.

Table 11.1   Labour Hoarding: Australia and the United States

| | Australia | | USA | | |
	1929-31	1931-5	1929-31	1929-33	1933-7
Changes in:					
1. GDP	-8.1	14.3	-14.3	-28.9	47.4
2. Expected employment	-8.1	14.3	-15.7	-31.1	42.9
3. Actual employment	-8.9	13.4	-10.6	-16.9	21.7
4. Employment absorption	-0.8	-0.9	5.1	14.2	-21.2
Accounted for by changes in:					
5. Hours worked	n.a	n.a	3.1	5.6	1.1
6. Productivity per hour	n.a	n.a	2.0	8.6	-22.3
7. Total emp't absorption	-0.8	-0.9	5.1	14.2	-21.2

Sources: Australia: N.G. Butlin (1984), Tables Aa 2, Aa 34. USA: GDP: Kendrick (1961), Table A-III, p.299. Actual civilian employment: Kendrick (1961), Table A-VI, p.306. Man hours: Kendrick (1961), Table A-X, p.312.
Calculations: Trend labour productivity: 1.8 percentage points p.a., calculated as the average from 1919-28. Hours worked: calculated using 1929 as a base. Source: Kendrick (1961), Tables A-VI and A-X. Productivity per hour calculated as a residual.

Row 2: expected employment change. This is the employment change that would have occurred, given the change in output, and calculated on the assumption that labour productivity per capita remained on trend.

Row 3: actual employment change.

Row 4: total employment absorption. This is calculated by subtracting the actual employment change from the expected employment change. Employment absorption represents the adjustment in employment that did not occur because labour productivity per hour (Row 6) and average hours worked per week (Row 5) adjusted to the large change in output.

Row 5: hours worked. This is the change in employment that did not occur because average hours worked per week responded to the output variations.

Row 6: productivity per hour. This is the change in employment that did not occur because hourly labour productivity deviated from trend in response to the output variation.

This classification system can help us to analyse the different experiences of the two countries. Consider first the 1929-31 period. It is obvious that in Australia most of the labour market adjustment falls upon employment. The combined effect of adjusting hours worked per week and productivity per hour is not only quite small but in the wrong direction, reducing employment by 0.8 per cent.[10] This is in stark contrast with the US experience where, in response to the output fall, these two factors

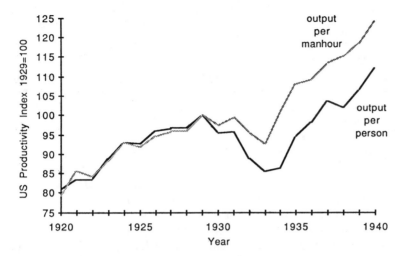

Figure 11.7   Productivity Measures for the United States, 1920-40

Note: Output per person - gross domestic product (constant prices) divided by civilian persons engaged (National economy). Output per manhour - gross domestic product (constant prices) divided by civilian manhours (National economy).
Source: Kendrick (1961), Table A-III, p.298, A-VI, p.306 and A-X, p.312.

cushion almost a third of the employment adjustment. Without these factors employment would have fallen another 5.1 percentage points in the US and, in the absence of a labour supply response, unemployment in 1931 would have been 21.3 per cent of civilian employment instead of 16.3 per cent.

These differences between the two economies are even more noticeable if we compare the full downswing in both countries. Over the 1929-33 period the adjustments to labour hoarding and weekly hours worked in the US account for 45 per cent of the labour market response. Without these adjustments, *ceteris paribus*, employment in the US would have fallen a further 14.2 per cent and, in the absence of a labour supply response, unemployment in 1933 would have been 39.4 per cent of the civilian labour force instead of 25.2 per cent. This is a massive change in unemployment.

Finally, we look at the recovery phase where most of the employment absorption responses of the downswing are reversed. In the US, the employment increases of the recovery phase are moderated, as hourly labour productivity rapidly converges back to its trend level. Average weekly hours worked, however, does not return to the 1933 level and consequently, for given output levels, the lower level of average weekly hours worked still continues to add to employment demand (Figure 11.7). Over the whole period, however, it seems to be variations in hourly productiv-ity which is the more important. In Australia, as expected from the experience of the downswing, the output increase translates fully into employment increases.

Most of the current discussion of labour market flexibility in Australia focuses upon wage outcomes of different labour markets with different institutional structures. During the 1930s, and at least with regard to the comparison between Australia and the US, there does not appear to be a great deal of difference in wage flexibility of the two countries, or, if anything, the Australian system seems to produce greater flexibility. It is the responsiveness of work conditions over the cycle, as measured by variability in hours worked per week and variations in hourly labour productivity, that seems to be far more important, and it is here that the differences between the labour markets seem to lie.

Perhaps one reason for the different labour productivity responses may be found in the institutional structure of each labour market. In Australia, the average number of standard hours worked per week is written into awards and the combination of strong craft unions and a centralised arbitration system ensures not only a high degree of uniformity of working hours but also quite clearly places conflict over the length of the working week near the top of the bargaining agenda. By 1929 most Australian workers had already fought for and gained a forty-four-hour standard working week, and both unions and the arbitration tribunals were traditionally opposed to part-time work and shorter hours to ration labour demand. In Figure 11.8 we plot an estimate of the average hours worked in the US and the standard working week written into Australian awards. It is evident that there is a very slow downward trend in standard hours worked in Australia as the forty-four-hour week spreads throughout the award structure. There are no sudden changes in response to the Depression. In Australia, anything more than a very temporary reduction in hours would require a fundamental change in award agreements. As a reduction in hours worked, without a significant increase in hourly pay, would involve a reduction in the average real income of the employed labour force,[11] the same forces that led unions to oppose real wage reductions also ensured that they opposed the systematic introduction of work sharing.

During this period the tribunals did not seriously discuss job sharing and the emphasis of discussions within the ambit of the federal tribunal was to reduce real wages if possible. On 1 February 1931, the federal tribunal attempted to reduce the Australian real wage by 10 per cent. This was to be achieved first by inviting participating employers within the federal system to apply for a 10 per cent real wage reduction, and then, as more employers availed themselves of the wage reduction, it was anticipated that the real wage reduction would flow into the decisions of the

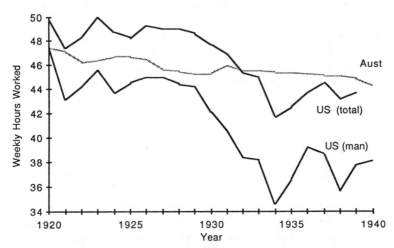

Figure 11.8 **Weekly Hours Worked in Australia and the United States, 1920-40**

Note: Australia: Male standard hours worked per week, all industries. USA: (Man.) Average hours worked per week for production workers, manufacturing. USA: (Total) Average hours worked per week, total economy.

Sources: Australia: M.W. Butlin (1977), Table IV.4, p.87. USA: (Man.) Baily (1983) Table 1. (Total) Kendrick, op. cit. (1961).

state tribunals. In the event, the initiative failed, presumably because trade unions were unwilling to have their real wage for a full-time working week eroded and, on average, employers were prepared to accept that outcome and not avail themselves of the opportunity offered by the Commission.

This unwillingness to accept real wage reductions was naturally associated with opposition to reductions in the number of hours worked. This attitude is clearly seen in a *Report to the Legislative Assembly of the State of New South Wales* (1933) where it was stated that hours reductions "are to be regarded as a normal feature of economic progress, but as being of little value as a method of bringing general recovery ..." (p.3). Furthermore, with regard to reducing unemployment it seemed pointless to ask employees "to accept lower weekly earnings to make possible the employment of 'outsiders'. The chances, therefore, of organising a shorter week or fuller rationing on a scale sufficient to contribute to a rapid absorption of our own unemployed appear to be slight" (p.3).

It is noticeable in the case of the US that the reduction of hours worked was not just a short-run response to the Depression. The number of average hours worked per week fell as output fell, but then did not recover back to its original level as employment increased. The hours reduction seems to have had a long-term, almost a permanent component. Between 1932 and 1937, for example, employment had increased by 22.7 per cent but average hours worked per week remained at about 16 per cent, less than the norm of the late 1920s. On the basis of these data the trend appears to be part of a move towards a forty-four-hour week and not only a response to the effects of the National Industry Recovery Act during the 1932-34 period (Darby, 1976). The Depression perhaps accelerated the introduction of a shorter working week but this longer-run influence was not the only factor. Average hours worked fell far below that which might be expected from a movement to a forty-four-hour working week.

To help support judgments as to the importance of different labour market institutions, it may be worthwhile to look at the UK economy where the degree of unionisation is similar to that of Australia, but where there is no centralised arbitration system. In the UK the extent of job sharing also appears to be relatively unimportant. Feinstein (1972) provides direct but partial estimates of the number of man years lost each year in short-time and part-time working. He suggests that 2.6 per cent of the total number of man years of employment takes the form of short-time working, but, more importantly, this fraction does not seem to vary over the Depression.[12] The UK experience, therefore, seems to be similar to that of Australia. It appears as though trade unions oppose job sharing, although it must be said that the evidence offered here as to the cause of the different behaviour patterns across countries needs to be augmented quite considerably. There is some evidence, for the post-Second World War labour market in the US, that is consistent with our story. It appears that the unionised sectors hoard labour to a greater degree during downswings than the non-unionised sectors (Medoff, 1979).

There are other conjectures that should be mentioned as possible explanations for the different degrees of job sharing. The Depression was more severe and a longer drawn out process in the US, and it seems possible that the allocation of labour demand between hours and employment may depend in part upon the depth of the depression. The greater the output reduction the more likely it is that the firm will be faced with making inroads into skilled staff, perhaps with firm-specific training, and, as a result, the greater the pressure for job sharing. For smaller output reductions perhaps most of the adjustment can be placed on unskilled workers and the skilled labour force can be hoarded for the time when output begins to increase.

Although this may be part of the answer it does not explain the fact that the recovery process in the US led to significant employment growth but not to significant growth in average hours worked per week. Furthermore, in the initial years of the Depression, when the output fall was much the same in both countries, and expectations as to the future were probably similar, a different response was already detectable.[13] Finally, perhaps the macro data are wrong for one or both of these countries. However, to assess the quality of the estimated output, employment and hours data for the economy as a whole is a massive task (see N.G. Butlin, 1966 and Keating, 1973 for Australia and Kendrick, 1961 and Lebergott, 1964 for the US). We do, however, look at some of the relevant data questions in Appendix 11.1.

2.3 Unemployment Duration

Some indication of the ease of finding another regular job, once unemployed in Australia, can be found in the 1933 census which included the following question: "If out of work at the time of the Census state the number of days or weeks or months since last regularly employed."

From row 1 of Table 11.2 we can see that the average length of time since unemployed males last had a regular job in Australia was 109 weeks or just over two years.[14] For females, the average length of time since last regularly employed was seventy-two weeks or just over one year. These are very long spells indeed. Furthermore, these are interrupted unemployed spells, and most of those unemployed in June 1933 would have remained without a regular job for a longer period.[15]

The turnover of the unemployment pool was so low during the early 1930s that the history of the Depression is evident in the distribution of unemployment duration. For example, in June 1933 more males had been unemployed for three to four years than for one to two years and more males had been unemployed for two to three years than for one to two years. None of the post-Second World War recessions has been severe enough to produce this pattern. In the post-Second World War data there are always fewer males unemployed for three to four years than for two to three years and fewer males unemployed for two to three years than for one to two years, and so on.

Another indication of the low turnover of the unemployment pool is given in Table 11.3 where the unemployment duration data from the census has been combined with M.W. Butlin's (1977) estimates of employment and unemployment for the years 1929 to 1933. These data enable us to calculate an estimate of the probability of getting a job once unemployed during the 1930s. Column 1 of Table 11.3 lists the change in employment in each year. It provides an indication of the course of the Depression. The worst year for employment loss was 1930-31, when 7 per cent of jobs were lost. By June 1933 the employment recovery was well under way. Column 2 lists the change in the labour force, and it is apparent that there was a strong discouraged worker effect operating.

Table 11.2   Unemployment Duration, 1933, 1935, 1939

	Average Duration of Uncompleted Spell (weeks)	Percentage whose uncompleted spells were of duration:							
		under 4 weeks	4-13 weeks	13-26 weeks	26-52 weeks	52-104 weeks	104 -156 weeks	over 156 weeks	over 1 year
MALES									
1933									
Australia	109	.04	.08	.09	.14	.14	.19	.33	.65
Buffalo	n.a.	.08	.12	.07	.06	n.a.	n.a.	n.a.	.68
Lincoln	100	.07	.06	.09	.14	.19	.24	.22	.64
Philadelphia	80	.05	.07	.06	.22	.34	.18	.08	.60
1935									
Philadelphia	114	.03	.06	.06	.15	.18	.16	.35	.69
1939									
Australia	42	.11	.23	.21	.19	.12	.04	.10	.25
United States	65	.03	.17	.25	.21	.15	.07	.11	.33
FEMALES									
1933									
Australia	72	.11	.15	.14	.17	.16	.14	.13	.43
Lincoln	80	.08	.05	.11	.25	.19	.16	.16	.51
Philadelphia	57	.09	.13	.08	.28	.26	.11	.05	.42
1935									
Philadelphia	85	.04	.09	.10	.20	.22	.15	.20	.57
1939									
Australia	n.a.	n.a.	n.a.	n.a.	n.a.	n.a.	n.a.	n.a.	n.a.
1940									
United States	47	.04	.19	.24	.21	.17	.07	.08	.22

Sources: Australia: 1933 census; National Register (1939), unpublished Report of the Australian Bureau of Statistics. USA: 1940 census; Woytinsky (1942).

Table 11.3   Unemployment, the Change in Employment and the Labour Force, and the Duration of Unemployment (all persons)

Year	Change in employment[1] (1,000s) (1)	Change in labour force[1] (1,000s) (2)	Unemp'd June 1933 classified by year of last regular job[2] (1,000s) (3)	Number unemployed (1,000s) (4)	Unemp'd each year with no regular job by June 1933 (%) (5)
Pre 1929-30			43		
1929-30	-88	-11	82	250	50
1930-31	-170	-1	89	419	51
1931-32	-47	49	60	514	53
1932-33	+122	124	168	516	

Source: 1: M.W. Butlin (1977), pp.90-92. 2: 1933 census (excludes those who did not state duration of unemployment; census total unemployment is 481,000).

During the years of the greatest job loss the labour force contracted and during the upswing of 1932-33 all the employment growth was matched by an increase in the labour force. Consequently, measured unemployment and its duration only tell part of the story of unutilised labour resources outside the firm.

Column 3 lists the unemployed of June 1933 by the year in which they were last regularly employed, and column 4 is the estimated number of unemployed each year. These two columns are combined in column 5 to provide an estimate of the percentage of the stock of unemployed each year that was still jobless in June 1933 and had not had a regular job in the interim. Thus, in 1929-30 there were 250,000 unemployed of which 125,000 (43,000 + 82,000), or 50 per cent, had not found a regular job by June 1933, three years later. Similarly, 51 per cent (214,000 out of 419,000) of the unemployment stock of 1930-31 had not found a regular job by June 1933, and so on. These ratios indicate a very low turnover of unemployment.

Although nationwide data are unavailable, it appears that the US experience is not much different. Woytinsky (1942) provides data for three cities, Buffalo (New York), Lincoln (Nebraska) and Philadelphia (Pennsylvania). For each of these cities there are data for 1933 and for Philadelphia we also list data for 1935 (Table 11.2). It is striking that the distribution of unemployment duration seems so similar across the countries. In each instance, the proportion of unemployed males who had been without a job for more than a year is between 60 and 68 per cent and for females the proportion is between 43 and 51 per cent. The profiles of unemployment for males in Lincoln in 1933 and Philadelphia in 1935 are almost identical with the Australian data. To the extent that these cities are typical of the US they suggest that the pattern of unemployment was not that different between the two countries. Unemployment was particularly concentrated on the long-term unemployed and once a job was lost it was not easy to get back into regular employment.[16]

By the end of the decade unemployment had fallen but the experience of the two countries was not the same. By 1939 unemployment in Australia had returned to the 1930 level of around 9 per cent but in the US the improvement was much slower and the unemployment rate was nearer 15 per cent (see Figure 11.4). This different rate of recovery is also evident in the duration data. In 1939 the Australian government instituted a national register of males in anticipation of the manpower planning requirements of the Second World War effort. This register included a measure of unemployment duration which can be compared with the duration measure as collected by the US census of 1940, and analysed by Robert Margo in chapter 9 of this volume (Table 11.2). In Australia, the average duration of an uncompleted spell of unemployment had fallen to about

40 per cent of the 1933 level. The reduction in the duration, however, was not evenly spread. There is still evidence of many long-term unemployed who lost their jobs at the beginning of the decade. For the US, and on the assumption that the three cities are typical, the reduction in the average duration was much less, falling to about 60 to 80 per cent of the 1933 levels. Once again there is evidence of a considerable group of long-term unemployed. In both countries, therefore, the unemployment pool seems to behave in much the same manner. Once long-term unemployment is created it takes a long time for it to be reduced. In modern terminology, hysteresis is evident in the data (Blanchard and Summers, 1986).

This evidence of an unemployment pool with low turnover is inconsistent with a number of labour supply theories of unemployment during the Depression. It is not easy to reconcile the long unemployment duration that is evident in Australia and the US with the following view of Lucas and Rapping (1969, p.748), who argue with respect to the US:

> Much of the unemployment during the 1930s is voluntary in the sense that measured unemployment ....[consists] of persons who regard the wage rate at which they could currently be employed as temporarily low and who therefore choose to wait or search for improved conditions rather than to invest in moving or occupational change.

As indicated in section 2.1, the real wage did not fall in either country and the unemployment duration was far too long for this sort of explanation to be appropriate (see Darby, 1976 and Kesselman and Savin, 1978 for further comments).

In chapter 3, Thomas analyses unemployment duration data from the UK register of unemployment benefit recipients. On the surface these data present a very different picture. There seem to be many more short spells of unemployment. These short spells led Benjamin and Kochin (1979, p.474) to write,

> The late twenties and thirties were characterised by high and rising real income, and the high unemployment of those times was the consequence almost solely of the dole. The army of the unemployed standing watch in Britain at the publication of the General Theory was largely a volunteer army.

In the absence of the dole, "unemployment would have been at normal levels through much of the period" (p.444).

Benjamin and Kochin's supply-side analysis seems to have little applicability to Australia and the US. The dole was very low in Australia and not generally available in the early years of the Depression. It certainly did not pay enough to lead workers to prefer it to a job. And, as indicated earlier, there was little part-time work that could be combined with the dole. The long duration of unemployment suggests that there was considerable hardship. There was no dole in the US and it appears that unemployment was typically of long duration there. A demand-side theory of unemployment seems more appropriate for both countries.

The question that is naturally posed, however, is whether it is possible to reconcile the data from the UK, on the one hand, with those from Australia and the US, on the other. This would be a major task, but one possible reconciliation is that unemployment is of much longer duration in the UK than is indicated. This would come about by the unemployed in the UK experiencing multiple spells of unemployment broken by jobs of short duration. The dole recording system would ensure that these breaks were measured but perhaps in Australia and the US the unemployed did not regard these short jobs as breaks in their unemployment duration and did not report them.[17]

3   Further Observations on Unemployment in Australia

3.1   Geographic Dispersion of Unemployment Within Cities

The Australian census has always published unemployment data classified by local government areas (LGAs). In this section we look at the dispersion of unemployment across the LGAs of Sydney and Melbourne, the two largest cities. In 1933 the Sydney metropolitan area accounted for 24.4 per cent of the Australian labour force, and had an unemployment rate of 24.7 per cent, and the Melbourne metropolitan area accounted for 19.5 per cent of the labour force, with an unemployment rate of 18.2 per cent. In 1933 the population size of an LGA within these cities varied between 2,364 and 92,112 people.

Some of our analysis will involve the matching of LGAs between 1921 and 1933 so that we can discuss the impact of the Depression on the spatial distribution of unemployment and incomes. Over this period there were some changes in boundaries so it was necessary to reduce the number of 1933 LGAs in our sample from 75 to 70. To facilitate the analysis the LGAs are grouped in deciles after ranking them by the rate of male unemployment, measured as a percentage of the labour force (Table 11.4).

It has always been believed in Australia, because job opportunities and wages are more evenly dispersed there, that the labour market produces more egalitarian outcomes than in the US. Even so there is quite a wide dispersion in unemployment across LGAs. This can be seen from the data

Table 11.4   Labour Force Characteristics of Local Government Areas Grouped into Deciles, Sydney and Melbourne, 1921 and 1933

	1	2	3	4	5	6	7	8	9	10
MALES										
1 Unemployment rate 1921	5.4	6.1	7.5	7.6	7.9	8.9	8.9	10.0	11.1	13.3
2 Unemployment rate 1933	13.1	16.5	20.2	21.7	23.3	25.4	27.9	31.5	37.2	42.6
3 Employment rate 1921	81.9	83.9	83.1	86.3	85.3	85.5	84.2	84.0	83.6	77.4
4 Employment rate 1933	73.5	71.1	69.5	69.0	66.9	66.6	62.8	59.4	55.4	48.9
5 Employment loss 1921-33	8.4	12.8	14.7	17.3	18.4	18.9	21.4	24.6	28.2	28.5
6 Proportion of the employment loss that translates into an unemployment increase	77.4	77.9	80.1	70.3	70.6	75.7	74.8	73.5	79.4	84.9
7 Part-time emp't 1933	3.3	4.2	4.7	5.5	5.2	6.3	6.5	6.8	6.8	6.6
8 Employed on own account 1933	8.4	8.5	7.5	6.7	9.3	6.9	7.3	7.0	6.7	6.7
9 Employer 1933	7.7	6.6	4.1	3.8	4.2	3.0	2.9	2.4	1.8	1.5
FEMALES										
1 Unemployment rate 1921	4.0	4.2	4.9	5.8	5.6	5.6	6.0	6.7	6.5	6.6
2 Unemployment rate 1933	8.2	9.6	12.3	14.0	13.9	17.3	16.6	19.0	23.7	24.0
3 Employment rate 1921	24.8	26.7	24.5	23.5	25.2	23.7	26.0	26.6	23.6	29.9
4 Employment rate 1933	26.7	27.3	24.0	23.1	25.2	23.7	25.1	24.2	20.2	24.4
5 Employment loss 1921-33	1.9	0.6	-0.5	-0.4	0.0	0.0	-0.9	-2.2	-3.4	-5.5
6 Proportion of the employment loss that translates into an unemployment increase	n.a.	n.a.	n.a.	n.a.	n.a.	n.a.	n.a.	n.a.	n.a.	n.a.
7 Part-time emp't 1933	1.1	1.3	1.3	1.5	1.4	1.6	1.8	2.2	2.1	2.2
8 Employed on own account 1933	2.0	2.4	1.7	1.8	2.1	1.6	2.3	1.8	1.3	3.2
9 Employer 1933	0.3	0.3	0.2	0.4	0.3	0.2	0.2	0.2	0.4	0.5

Source: 1921 and 1933 census.

for 1921, a year of 5.8 per cent unemployment which was just above average for the 1920s. In the LGA decile with the lowest unemployment rate, male unemployment was 5.4 per cent of the labour force. In the highest unemployment areas the unemployment rate was 13.3 per cent.

The same pattern of unemployment is observed in the female labour market, where unemployment, after grouping by the male unemployment rate, ranges from 4 to 6.6 per cent. This dispersion of unemployment is not a random effect, nor is it primarily the result of job shortages in particular geographic areas. The geographic spread of Sydney and Melbourne was not that large and the transport system was quite good so that workers could generally move within the cities if jobs were available. The dispersion is primarily a reflection of the fact that socioeconomic groups tend to cluster together and live in particular LGAs.

The onset of the Depression had little effect on the relative dispersion of unemployment. Those areas of relatively high unemployment in 1921 also experienced relatively high unemployment in 1933. A regression of the log of the 1933 unemployment rate of an LGA against the log of the 1921 unemployment rate produces an R^2 of 0.73 for the male equation and 0.67 for the female equation. Unemployment increases in all LGAs during the Depression, increasing about two and a half times in the low unemployment areas and tripling in the high unemployment areas. By 1933 unemployment had reached 42.6 per cent of the male labour force living in high unemployment areas and 13.1 per cent for low unemployment areas. One way of looking at the Depression is to say that the areas of the lowest unemployment in 1933 now experienced unemployment rates similar to the areas of highest unemployment during normal years.

Of course unemployment increases are not the only way labour markets adjust to depressed economic conditions. Where unemployment is highest we might expect reductions in the male participation rates, a greater degree of part-time working and so on. To facilitate calculation of a rough guide to these phenomena, each of the remaining variables in Table 11.4 is expressed as a percentage of the population aged 15 years and over. Row 3 is the employment rate in 1921, row 4 is the employment rate in 1933, and row 5 gives the job loss between the two census dates which ranges from 8.4 percentage points in areas of lowest unemployment to 28.5 percentage points in areas of highest unemployment. It is evident from row 6, which compares this job loss to the unemployment increase, that between 77.4 and 84.9 per cent of the male job loss was translated into unemployment increases and that hidden unemployment was not significantly higher, in proportionate terms, in those areas where the employment reduction was greatest. On the basis of this crude calculation, hidden unemployment seems to have been around 20-25 per cent of the job loss and fairly evenly spread across geographic regions within cities.

Data on part-time employment by LGA were not collected in the 1921 census. It is evident from the 1933 census, however, that although the overall extent of part-time employment is not large it is correlated with the level of unemployment; the areas of highest unemployment had the highest rate of part-time working. If hidden unemployment and part-time workers are added to unemployment as a measure of the true underutilisation of labour, then the unemployment rate in the worst affected areas may well have been over 50 per cent.

Similar calculations for the female labour force are also shown in Table 11.4 and once again areas are ranked by the male unemployment rate. It is noticeable that female unemployment levels are positively correlated with male unemployment, especially in 1933 when female unemployment ranges from 8.2 per cent to 24.0 per cent. With regard to the extent of job loss the story is different and complicated by the fact that the overall participation and employment rates increased in the interim between 1921 and 1933. Still, on the basis of a 1921 and 1933 comparison, it appears that during the Depression the job loss among the female labour force was heavily concentrated in areas of high male unemployment. For example, in the two deciles of highest male unemployment females lost between 15 and 20 per cent of their jobs. This is, however, a much lower rate of job loss than that experienced by the male labour force. In the areas of low male unemployment the employment rate of females increased between the census dates by between 2 and 7 per cent. To a small extent therefore the behaviour of the female participation rate between the census dates widened the dispersion of the income losses of the Depression by offsetting some of the job loss of males in low unemployment areas.

3.2 Income Maintenance

With such high rates and long duration of unemployment the extent of poverty must have been considerable. How did people survive? In Australia, there was an extensive system of government income maintenance but the level of individual and family support was low. When the Depression began sustenance or food rations were particularly important. To qualify it was necessary to have been unemployed for a significant period and not to possess any property which could be realised (except a house). The rations usually extended to milk, meat, bread and groceries and the family was taken as the basis of relief (see Bland, 1934). As the Depression continued the ration system tended to be phased out and relief work, which was allocated according to family circumstances, became more important. Job sharing in the public sector - either a fixed number of days per week or a fixed number of weeks on and off - also increased as full-time workers employed on public works were partially replaced by part-time workers (Snooks, 1986).[18]

Some quantitative estimate of the reduced income flows experienced by people can be found in the census for 1933, a year in which the male minimum wage for those under Commonwealth awards was £158. Table 11.5 presents the data for different income and population categories. For males in the labour force, 65.8 per cent replied that their income was less than the basic wage, 32.7 per cent received less than a third of the basic wage, and 12.5 per cent replied that they received no income at all for

Table 11.5   Annual Income of Individuals in 1933

Category	No income (%)	Proportion with income		
		Less than one-third basic wage (%)	Less than basic wage (%)	Greater than basic wage (%)
MALES				
Breadwinners	12.5	32.7	65.8	34.2
Married with dependent children	5.4	18.9	48.0	52.0
Wage and salary earners				
Full-time	n.a.	18.1	47.8	52.2
Part-time	n.a.	42.1	91.1	8.9
Unemployed	44.1	81.1	97.5	2.5
Total	11.3	36.3	64.4	35.6
FEMALES				
Breadwinners	7.8	42.3	88.8	11.2
Married with dependent children	5.6	49.7	89.1	10.9
Wage and salary earners				
Full-time	n.a.	36.1	88.7	11.3
Part-time	n.a.	65.4	99.5	0.5
Unemployed	50.8	38.1	99.6	0.4
Total	7.5	45.5	90.7	9.3

Source: 1933 census.

that year. For women, 88.8 per cent of the workforce received less than the male basic wage, 42.3 per cent earned less than a third, and 7.8 per cent reported receiving no income.

These income figures are very low, and there is no doubt that there was widespread poverty, but it is widely believed that there was considerable understatement of income in the census. The income data are not really consistent with the estimates of national income (N.G. Butlin, 1966), the labour productivity data of Figure 11.6, or the unemployment duration data, all of which suggest a much lower rate of job turnover and, by implication, a lower proportion of people reporting low incomes. A systematic reconciliation of these data with other indicators of national income remains to be done.

Ideally, we would like income data classified by family units but this grouping is not available from the census. It is possible, however, to provide a very rough guide to alternative possible sources of income available for the family.

First, it is apparent from Table 11.5 that married men with dependent children tended to report higher income than other men, but again there are large numbers with low income. For married men with dependent children, 48 per cent reported income of less than the basic wage, 18.9 per cent reported income of less than one-third of the basic wage and 5.4 per cent reported no income at all for the year.

Second, it was unusual for married women to be in the labour force during the 1930s so married women made very little contribution to family cash income. If the income of the 10 per cent of married women who received income is allocated evenly across married men, then married women would have contributed on average £8.5 per annum which is equivalent to about three weeks' work paid at the rate of the male basic wage, or about 5 per cent of the average male income reported for 1933.

Third, it is likely that single children living at home were more important than wives as providers of supplementary income. If we were to assume that all single men and women under 29 years of age lived at home, and that all their income was spread evenly across families, then single men would add about £38 per annum to the family income, which is about twelve weeks' work paid at the basic wage rate. Single women would add about £16, or about five weeks' work. It should be stressed that these calculations are hypothetical since not all single people live at home with their parents, we do not know what proportion of income would be given to the family, the incidence of work among single people is not likely to be evenly spread across families, and finally not every family had children living at home who were old enough to work. However, these rough calculations do provide some guidance in that they suggest that the income of children was probably more important than that of wives, and that even with the income of children and wives it is still difficult to imagine how families managed to survive.

4   Conclusion

This chapter is an initial attempt at a systematic comparison of the Australian and US labour markets and, as such, casts the performance of the Australian institutional structure in a new light. It suggests the need for a reappraisal of Australian labour market performance during the 1930s.

First, nominal and real wage flexibility for a full-time worker appear to be much the same in both countries, or, if account is taken of the greater output loss in the US, then it would appear that Australian institutions produced greater flexibility. On the basis of these criteria Australia's institutional structure performed as well as or better than the comparatively free labour market of the US. Nominal wages rapidly followed the price of primary commodities downwards and real wage changes in both countries remained very much on trend, playing no apparent role in the creation of the Depression or the recovery.

Today, there is considerable discussion as to the relationship between labour market institutions and the extent to which economies can adjust to large shocks (see Bruno and Sachs, 1984; McCallum, 1986). Similar discussions are taking place in Australia where it has become increasingly common to suggest that trade union power be reduced and the system of wage tribunals modified so that the unions exert less influence. The evidence from the 1930s suggests that with respect to wage outcomes the combination of wage tribunals and trade unions worked as well or better than the comparatively free labour market of the US. Of course, if the tribunals had not existed but trade union strength and membership had been much the same then the Australian institutional structure would have been more like that of the UK where there seemed to be less nominal and real wage flexibility. It may have been necessary, therefore, given the strength of unions in Australia, that a tribunal system should also be in place to produce these outcomes.

Second, with respect to the distribution of unemployment, the data seem to suggest that the two labour markets produced similar outcomes. Once unemployed, workers in both countries found it very difficult to get back into employment. Both economies produced a wide gulf between those with jobs and those without.

Third, the key difference between the two countries seems to relate to job sharing within the firm. The available evidence suggests that private sector job sharing was very important in the US and relatively unimportant in Australia. As a result, for a given path of output loss, the Australian economy produced much more unemployment. Instead of encouraging the widespread working of shorter hours within the firm the Australian system tended to throw people out of work, and once they were unemployed, the period without a new job tended to be very long.

Australian institutions have always placed a great deal of emphasis on egalitarian outcomes. And yet in respect of the labour market during the 1930s, and when measured against this criterion, it appears that these institutions were not especially successful, at least when compared with the US labour market. Changes in real wages per worker employed full-time and changes in unemployment duration were not that different in each country, but job sharing was. In the US the force of law was used to reinforce the market tendency towards shorter hours of work. In Australia the tribunals, reflecting the views of the union movement and the community generally, refused to go down this path and thus reinforced the tendency not to share jobs.

Finally, the question of job sharing and hours of work during the Depression has not been a well-researched topic in Australia. As indicated earlier, there have been studies of individual firms and government agencies, but the extent and significance of job rationing at the macro level has not been examined. We have brought to bear on this topic the implications of the existing national income (Butlin, 1966) and employment (Keating, 1973) figures for Australia. It may well be, in the light of our finding, that the data may be reworked and revised but the extent of revisions required to produce outcomes similar to the US would be quite significant. For example, if all the adjustment were to be made to only one of the Australian series then we would be looking for a downward output revision of about 7 to 10 per cent between 1929 and 1932, or an upward employment revision of a similar magnitude. We would conjecture that such a revision is unlikely and that the conclusion that job sharing was not as important here as in the US should be a robust one.

To conclude, it is not clear what effect this difference in flexibility had on the efficiency of the economy, or on its ability to recover from the Depression. Does flexibility of hours worked and flexibility of labour productivity per hour make for a more resilient economy that can recover more quickly from shocks and grow faster? We will not know until the reasons for this different job sharing behaviour are fully understood.

APPENDIX 11.1
Job Sharing in the Manufacturing Sector

Haig (1974-75) has provided a production index series for Australian manufacturing, based on production indices of 100 manufacturing subclasses, which can be compared to the Butlin (1966) estimates of the gross domestic product in manufacturing.[19] The Butlin manufacturing series is similar to his non-farm series in that labour productivity does not change in a pro-cyclical way during the Depression.[20] Over the four years 1929 to 1933, when manufacturing output falls by 24 per cent, labour productivity in manufacturing first increases and then returns to the 1929 level. Once manufacturing output expands labour productivity begins to fall. This behaviour is the opposite to labour hoarding and job sharing. There are other puzzles too. At the end of the decade, despite manufacturing output being 16 per cent greater than the previous peak of 1929, labour productivity is still 6 percentage points less.

The Haig series, shown in Figure 11.9, indicates the expected job sharing story, but the propensity to hoard labour, or to work short hours, is very mild and not as marked as in the US. According to the Haig estimates, between 1928-29 and 1931-32, manufacturing output fell by 29 per cent and was accompanied by a 5 per cent reduction in labour productivity per person. In the US, manufacturing output fell by 46.2 per cent over the same period and productivity per person fell by 16 per cent. Consequently

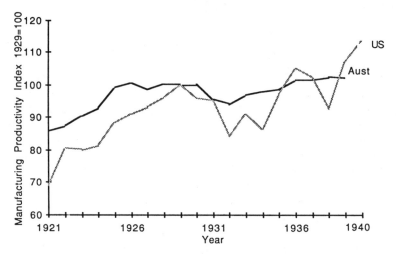

Figure 11.9 Manufacturing Productivity in Australia and the United States, 1921-40

Note: Australia: Value of production per head in manufacturing. USA: Output per person in manufacturing.

Sources: Australia: Haig (1974-75), Table 3, p.150. USA: Kendrick (1961), Table D-II, col. 3, p.465.

even if we preferred Haig's estimates of manufacturing output to the Butlin estimates, it would still be the case that job sharing in this sector is relatively unimportant and certainly much less important than in the US.

There is other macro evidence of very little job sharing among the employed labour force which does not depend upon labour productivity comparisons. If the average weekly wage bill for manufacturing, measured in real terms, is divided by the employed labour force, an average weekly earnings series is produced that reflects variations in hours worked. This series varies in a similar way to the average award real wage series for a *full-time unchanging standard work week*, and this is despite a 40 per cent reduction in manufacturing employment (see Figure 11.10). The behaviour of these two series suggests that in the Australian manufacturing sector part-time employment per week, and reduced average hours of work per week, were not important responses to the Depression. If they were then average earnings per week would fall relative to the average wage for a full week's work. However, we find the opposite result on the downswing. Award wages fall faster than the series for factory earnings. As the factory earnings series is calculated on an annual basis and the award wage series are calculated at quarterly intervals, this suggests that the data are dominated by leads and lags associated with the indexation of award wages for past price changes and that the effect of variations in hours worked per week on average earnings is trivial. This

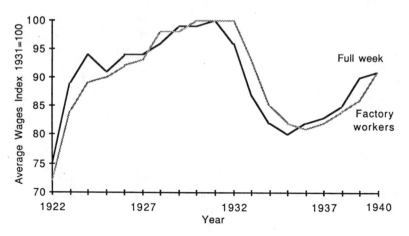

Figure 11.10 Average Wages for Australia, 1922-40

Note: Full week: Average wage for a full week's work - all industries. Factory workers: Average weekly earnings of factory workers.
Sources: Full week: *Labour Report* (various issues, e.g. for 1929 see no. 20, p.66); factory workers: *Production Bulletin* (various issues, eg. for 1929 see no.25, p.91).

view is supported by the results after 1935 when the relationship between the series changes and the average wage earned in manufacturing begins to increase more than the award wage for the standard work week. Before 1935 prices were falling and after 1935 prices were increasing.

This brief analysis suggests that the results for the manufacturing sector are much the same as for the economy as a whole. The different behaviour of the labour market in each country seems to be a real phenomenon and not an artefact of the data.

NOTES

* R.G. Gregory and J. Hagan, Department of Economics, Research School of Social Sciences, Australian National University. V. Ho is a graduate student at Stanford University. Most of the early work on unemployment duration was undertaken by L. McDermott in her honours thesis at Harvard University. The authors are grateful to Tim Hatton for constructive comments. Invaluable research assistance was provided by Eva Klug and Roslyn Anstie.

1 In May 1983, 83.6 per cent of the male labour force and 89.7 per cent of the female labour force were covered by awards. It is not known exactly what proportion of wage and salary earners was covered by awards during the 1930s but the proportion of the industrial workforce covered by 1923 has been estimated at 98 per cent (Macarthy, 1967).

2 There are tribunals at the state and federal level and the indexation policy often differed from one tribunal to another. Some states indexed the awards under their control less frequently than the federal tribunal. A detailed history of each wage setting system can be found in the Labour Reports of the Commonwealth Bureau of Census and Statistics.

3 Farm output did not fall significantly in either country so in proportionate terms the loss of non-farm output was even greater than the loss of real GDP. The farm sector share of GDP is about the same in each country, so the non-farm output loss is also about 20 per cent greater in the US.

4 The basic wage was the minimum of all awards that could be paid for a full week's work and was an identifiable part of each award. Consequently, those who were paid awards in excess of the basic wage did not receive full wage indexation. As a result there may have been significant changes in wage relativities during periods when the price level changed significantly.

5 In the UK nominal wages fell by only 5 per cent between 1929 and 1934 and real wages increased by 11.3 per cent (N.G. Butlin, 1984, Table B16).

6 Participation rates fell in Australia as unemployment increased between 1929 and 1931. The US labour force estimates (Lebergott, 1964) did not respond to the Depression. This is not an important difference, however, in terms of the different unemployment behaviour.

7 There is some evidence of job sharing among miners (*New South Wales Official Year Book, 1934-35*, p.752), and in the railways (see Pincus, 1985). These instances, however, do not seem to affect the aggregate economy data in a significant way. Forster (1987) recently suggested that job sharing may have reduced the unemployment rate by 3 percentage points for the year 1931-32. After that date, he believes, it rapidly decreased in importance.

8 Of course this is a very indirect measure of job sharing and labour productivity may be affected by a range of other factors including the nature of the production function within the firm (whether there are increasing or decreasing returns to scale), the market structure in which the firm operates (whether marginal cost is increasing or decreasing in equilibrium) and the changing distribution of output over industries and firms with different levels of labour productivity. Nevertheless, as a first approximation labour productivity on a per capita basis should be a useful indicator of the variations of average hours worked per week.

9 In terms of post-Second World War experience it seems odd that labour productivity did not change for two decades. Between 1959 and 1979, for example, labour productivity for the non-farm sector measured on the same per capita basis increased by 54 per cent. It is natural, therefore, to question the quality of the data in the interwar period. The lack of productivity growth, however, is consistent with the real wage series. Real wages are calculated from wage and price series that are independent of the employment and GDP estimates.

10 See Appendix 11.1 and Figure 11.9 for evidence of an insignificant adjustment to average hours worked in manufacturing.

11 It is difficult to explain why the hours outcome was so different across the countries, *given* that the real wage outcome was so similar.

12 At this stage we have not yet reconciled this view of the UK labour market with that suggested by Benjamin and Kochin (1979). They suggest that a large fraction of the unemployed workforce were working short-time and choosing to combine this with the dole in preference to working full-time.

13 It is also possible that the larger size of firms in the US and more capital-intensive production technologies played a part. It would be possible to pursue this conjecture further with the available data (see Bernanke, 1986; Haig, 1974-75). It would also be possible to look at the effects of the different industry mix in each country, although at the broad industry classification level the two economies seem almost identical. In 1929 the proportions of employment in various industries are as follows. Australia: manufacturing 21 per cent, construction 10 per cent, farm 22 per cent. USA: manufacturing 22 per cent, construction 5 per cent, farm 20 per cent.

14 Note that those unemployed who have never had a regular job are excluded from the estimates of unemployment duration. Also, and perhaps more importantly, the duration of unemployment calculated from responses of the unemployed may include spells of non-regular jobs.

15 Long unemployment duration was probably not the rule before the Depression. In 1921, average unemployment duration, as reported by the census, was nine weeks for both males and females and about 70 per cent of the unemployed had been jobless for less than twelve weeks. The question asked in the 1921 census was slightly different from that asked in 1933, but that should not significantly affect this comparison. The question was, "If out of work on 2nd April, state number of working days since last employed."

16 For a more detailed discussion of unemployment duration in the US see Baily (1983).

17 This possible reconciliation, however, would raise doubts as to the Feinstein estimate of little short-time working in the UK. If large numbers of the unemployed are to be combining the dole with part-time work then there should be greater evidence of job sharing.

18 See Kesselman and Savin (1978) for a description of the US work relief schemes.

19 The Haig output series are constructed from physical production measures and the construction is completely independent of the employment series and the price deflators.

20 The Butlin national income series (M.W. Butlin, 1977), which we have used throughout the text, are the standard data source for Australia.

REFERENCES

Baily, M.N. (1983), "The Labour Market in the 1930's", in J. Tobin (ed.), *Macroeconomic Prices, and Quantities: Essays in Memory of Arthur M. Okun*, Washington, DC: Brookings Institution.

Benjamin, D. and Kochin, L. (1979), "Searching for an Explanation of Unemployment in Interwar Britain", *Journal of Political Economy* 3, June, pp.441-78.

Bernanke, B.S. (1986), "Employment, Hours and Earnings in the Depression: An Analysis of Eight Manufacturing Industries", *American Economic Review* 76, no. 1, March 1986, pp.82-109.

Blanchard, O.J. and Summers. L. (1986), "Hysteresis and the European Unemployment Problem", *NBER Macroeconomics Annual*, Cambridge, Mass.: MIT Press, pp.15-77.

Bland, F.A. (1934), "Unemployment Relief in Australia", *International Labour Review* 30, pp.23-57.

Bruno, M. and Sachs, J. (1984), *The Economics of Worldwide Stagflation*, Cambridge: Cambridge University Press.

Butlin, M.W. (1977), "A Preliminary Annual Data Base 1900-01 to 1973-74", Reserve Bank of Australia, Research Discussion Paper no. 7701.

Butlin, N.G. (1966), *Australian Domestic Product, Investment and Foreign Borrowing, 1861-1938/39*, Cambridge: Cambridge University Press.

Butlin, N.G. (1984), "Selected Comparative Economic Statistics 1900-1940", Source Paper no.4, *Source Papers in Economic History*, Canberra: Australian National University.

Copland, D. (1934), *Australia in the World Crisis, 1929-1933*, Cambridge: Cambridge University Press.

Darby, M.R. (1976), "Three and a Half Million US Employees Have Been Mislaid: Or, an Explanation of Unemployment, 1934-1941", *Journal of Political Economy* 84, February, pp.1-16.

Feinstein, C.H. (1972), *National Income, Expenditure and Output of the United Kingdom, 1855-1965*, Cambridge: Cambridge University Press.

Forster, C. (1987), "Unemployment and the Australian Economic Recovery of the 1930's", mimeo, Canberra: Australian National University.

Gregory, R., McDermott, L. and Ho, V. (1985), "Sharing the Burden: The Australian Labour Market During the 1930's", *Working Papers in Economic History*, no. 47, August, Canberra: Australian National University.

Haig, B.D. (1974-75), "Manufacturing Output and Productivity, 1910-1948/49", *Australian Economic History Review* 14-15, pp.136-161.

Hall, R. (1980), "Employment Fluctuations and Wage Rigidity.", *Brookings Papers on Economic Activity*, no. 1, pp.91-123.

Keating, M. (1973), *The Australian Workforce: 1910/11 to 1960/61*, Department of Economic History, Research School of Social Sciences, Canberra: Australian National University.

Kendrick, J. (1961), *Productivity Trends in the United States*, New York: National Bureau of Economic Research.

Kesselman, J.R. and Savin, N.E. (1978), "Three and a Half Million Workers Never were Lost", *Economic Inquiry* 16, April, pp.205-225.

Lebergott, S. (1964), *Manpower in Economic Growth: The American Record Since 1800*, New York: McGraw-Hill.

Lucas, R.E. and Rapping, L. (1969), "Real Wages, Employment and Inflation", *Journal of Political Economy* 77, pp.721-754.

Lucas, R.E. and Rapping, L. (1972), "Unemployment in the Great Depression: Is There a Full Explanation?", *Journal of Political Economy* 80, pp.186-191.

Macarthy, P.G. (1967), "The Harvester Judgement - An Historical Assessment", Canberra: doctoral thesis, Australian National University.

McCallum, J. (1986), "Unemployment in OECD Countries in the 1980s", *Economic Journal* 96, December, pp.942-960.

Medoff, J.L. (1979), "Layoffs and Alternatives under Trade Unions in US Manufacturing", *American Economic Review* 69, no.3. June, pp.380-395.

National Register (1939), Unpublished Report of the Australian Commonwealth Bureau of Census and Statistics.

Pincus, J.J. (1985), "Aspects of Australian Public Finances and Public Enterprises, 1920 to 1939.", *Working Papers in Economic History*, no. 53, August, Canberra: Australian National University, August.

Reddaway, W.B. (1938), "Australian Wage Policy 1929-1937", *International Labour Review*, pp.314-38.

Report to the Legislative Assembly of the State of New South Wales, 1933.

Schedvin, C.B. (1970), *Australia and the Great Depression*, Sydney: Sydney University Press.

Snooks, G.D. (1986), " Government Unemployment Relief in the 1930s: An Expected Outcome", mimeo, Canberra: Australian National University.

Woytinsky, M.W.S. (1942), "Three Aspects of Labour Dynamics", Report prepared for the Committee on Social Security (Washington, DC, Social Science Research Council).

Index